What to Name Your Baby

MAXWELL NURNBERG
and MORRIS ROSENBLUM

WHAT TO NAME
YOUR BABY

From Adam to Zoe

COLLIER BOOKS

Macmillan Publishing Company

NEW YORK

COLLIER MACMILLAN PUBLISHERS

LONDON

Macmillan Publishing Company
866 Third Avenue, New York, N.Y. 10022
Collier Macmillan Canada, Inc.

FIRST COLLIER BOOKS EDITION 1962
REVISED 1984

ISBN 0-02-081010-5

10 9 8 7 6 5

This Collier Books edition is published by arrangement with the authors.

Printed in the United States of America

Permissions to quote from the following copyright material is gratefully acknowledged to:

MAXWELL ANDERSON: *Winterset.* Excerpt reprinted by permission of Anderson House. Copyright, 1935, by Anderson House, recopyrighted, 1959, by Maxwell Anderson.

CARL JOHN BOSTELMANN: "The Talisman of Names." 1951. By permission of the author and the *New York Times.*

ABBIE FARWELL BROWN: "Names" from *A Pocketful of Posies,* 1902. By permission of Houghton Mifflin Company, Boston.

WILLIAM CANTON: "Through the Ages" from *A Lost Epic.* 1873. By permission of Wm. Blackwood & Sons Ltd., Edinburgh and London.

THOMAS JOHN CARLISLE: "A Name," March 23, 1962. By permission of the author and the New York *Herald Tribune.* © 1962, New York Herald Tribune Inc.

GILBERT KEITH CHESTERTON: "Wine and Water" and "Lepanto." Reprinted by permission of Dodd, Mead & Company from *The Collected Poems of G. K. Chesterton.* Copyright 1932 by Dodd, Mead & Company, Inc. Also by permission of Miss D. E. Collins, Methuen & Co., Ltd., London, and A. P. Watt & Son, London.

ARTHUR COLTON: "Concerning Tabitha's Dancing of the Minuet" from *Harp Hung up in Babyland.* 1907. By permission of Holt, Rinehart and Winston, Inc.

HART CRANE: "To Walt Whitman" from *The Collected Poems of Hart Crane.* 1933. By permission of Liveright Publishing Corporation, New York.

EMILY DICKINSON: "Hope Is the Thing with Feathers" from *Poems.* 1890-1896. Little, Brown and Company, Boston.

Acknowledgments

We are grateful to the following persons who took time out of their busy lives to answer our questions about their own names or names used by members of their families:

Mr. Wyllys P. Ames, Mrs. Cricket H. Auld, Mr. Ariel Bankhead, General Omar N. Bradley, Mr. Yul Brynner, Congressman Omar Burleson, Miss Ilka Chase, Miss Deanie Clancy, Mrs. Perian Conerly, Mr. Chon Day, Miss Lani Despres, Miss Rhonda Fleming, Miss Greer Garson, Miss Rumer Godden, Mr. Quartus P. Graves, Miss Tammy Grimes, Mr. and Mrs. Ewart Guinier, Miss Uta Hagen, Mrs. Elizabeth Hayward, Miss Dody Heath, Mr. Elric Hooper, Mrs. Zada Hunter, Jillana, Miss Elana Joselit, Senator Estes Kefauver, Mr. Omar B. Ketchum, Mrs. Nedra Newkirk Lamar, Miss Neva Patterson, Mr. Williamson Pell Jr., Mrs. Eva K. Silberman, Mr. Datus C. Smith Jr., Mr. Torin Thatcher, Mr. Robert W. Wales, Mrs. Lael Tucker Wertenbaker, Mrs. Ella Rhome Woody, et al, including Mrs. David H. Byerly, Mr. Edsel Ford, Mrs. Cavada Humphrey Kilty, Mrs. Kelsie B. Harder, Miss Sarnia Hayes, and Mr. Vian Smith.

We wish to express our thanks to the staffs of the Genealogy, Slavonic, Hebrew, and Oriental Languages Rooms of the New York Public Library, where we spent many pleasant hours tracking down the meanings of names in their original languages.

We are also appreciative of the help given by the Embassies, Consulates, Information Offices, and Delegates to the United Nations of the following countries: Czechoslovakia, Denmark, Finland, France, Greece, Hungary, Israel, Italy, The Netherlands, Norway, Poland, Portugal, Sweden, and Yugoslavia. They evinced deep interest in the lists contained in the chapter "Names in Other Lands"; any errors therein are our own responsibility and are in no way to be attributed to the services, agencies, or individuals listed above.

We thank the following for their valuable suggestions and assistance: Mrs. Ellen N. Cole, Miss Ruth M. Goldstein, Dr. Morris Leider, and Mr. Jason Wingreen.

Thanks are due also to Miss A. G. Smith, Deputy City Clerk, Sarnia, Ontario, Canada.

Finally, we should feel ungrateful if we did not express our obligation to the editors of the many dictionaries and encyclopedias in English and other languages, especially to *The Reader's Encyclopedia* edited by

William Rose Benét, and to those predecessors in the field of onomatology whose works we have consulted, notably the following: Albert Dauzat, *Dictionnaire étymologique des noms de famille et prénoms de France;* Trefor Rendall Davies, *A Book of Welsh Names;* Eilert Ekwall, *The Concise Oxford Dictionary of English Place-Names;* Martin Noth, *Die israelitischen Personennamen;* Percy Hide Reaney, *A Dictionary of British Surnames;* Elsdon C. Smith, *The Story of Our Names;* George R. Stewart, *Names on the Land;* Ernest Weekley, *Jack and Jill,* *The Romance of Names, Surnames;* Elizabeth G. Withycombe, *The Oxford Dictionary of English Christian Names;* and finally, the pioneer in this type of intellectual investigation, Charlotte M. Yonge, *A History of Christian Names* (1863).

*Methinks their very names
 shine still and bright;
Apart—like glow-worms on
 a summer's night;
Or lonely tapers when far
 they fling
A guiding ray.*
    WILLIAM WORDSWORTH,
    Walton's Book of Lives

Contents

What to Name Your Baby

How to Use This Book

The young man waited impatiently for the lady to finish with the drugstore telephone directory. After she had turned page after page he said, "Madam, can I help you find the number you want?"

"Oh, I don't want a number," she replied. "I'm looking for a pretty name for my baby."

BELL TELEPHONE NEWS

If you are looking for a pretty name for your baby you ought to find it more easily in this book than in a telephone directory. After all, our alphabetical lists are shorter and much more to the point. The sections on "Names for Boys" and "Names for Girls" contain more than 2,000 names in each category, including their meanings and interesting information about them.

In addition, there are many other names scattered throughout the book. You may perhaps prefer the first or last name of a poet whose work is quoted, or you may hit upon some lovely saint's name no longer used but worthy of revival. Or you may find an attractive foreign name like *Casilda* or *Mafalda*. There are names everywhere in the book and if you're looking for the unusual you may find just what you want.

FORMAL—INFORMAL NAMES

In our lists we have labeled many as pet names, diminutives, or short forms. You don't have to pay too much attention to that. Since in our country informality is a way of life, it is not surprising to find that practically every pet name, short form, or diminutive is now used as an independent name. Dick, Ned, Bob, Bill, Jerry, Tom, Vicki, Fran, Toni, Mimi, etc. have become names of official and legal record.

WHAT'S IN A NAME

Philologists who c h a s e
A panting syllable through
*   time and space,*
Start it at home, and hunt
*   it in the dark,*
To Gaul, to Greece, and
*   into Noah's ark!*
WILLIAM COOPER, *Retirement*

In reading this book you may want to find more than merely a name for a baby. You may want to know the meaning of your own name or that of a friend. The tracking down of the meaning of some names is frankly a safari into an etymological jungle. For example, we heard of a young lady whose name is *Ilya*. We might have gone on to compare it with Russian names and write a learned account of its origin if we hadn't discovered in time that her mother had given her the name from the first letters of "I'll Love You Always."

Or there's the girl who spells her name *Ireene*. Etymology will not explain that extra "e." You see, Irene consulted a numerologist who told her that six letters would be luckier for her than five.

Then there's the name *Versa*. Is it Latin? Is it a facetious play on the phrase *vice versa?* Is it a geographical name honoring her birthplace, Versailles? No, Versa was so named because she was born on her parents' anniversary! One friend very understandably asked, "Anniversary, eh? Then why not just *Anni?*"

The first name of the novelist Anya Seton, author of *The Winthrop Woman, Dragonwyck,* and *Devil Water,* looks like a Slavic form or a variant of *Anna*. However, according to a story in the *New Yorker* (May 12, 1962), it was given to her by a Sioux chief, Little Bison. Her father, the late Ernest Thompson Seton, author and naturalist, asked Little Bison, who was visiting him at the time, to give an Indian name to his "little darling," who had been christened Ann and who was then about five years old. The chief suggested *Anutika,* which means "cloud-gray eyes." Miss Seton was never called Ann again, nor was she called Anutika for long, since the name was soon shortened to Anya. Incidentally, Miss Seton's eyes are hazel.

The final item of this kind concerns a student of names, Mrs. Kelsie B. Harder, Executive Secretary-Treasurer of the American Name Society. On the surface her first name looks like a family name or a feminization of a family name. Actually, *Kelsie* is merely *Elsie* with a *K* in front of it. Mrs. Harder has a sister named Elsie, not a twin. Their mother apparently liked the name *Elsie* so much that she bestowed a disguised form of it upon another daughter. However, even a student of names directly concerned cannot always learn the reason for the formation of a new name, for as Mrs. Harder wrote to us:

"Don't ask me why my mother gave me the name, for I have asked her, and I got a vague answer that it sounded good to her."

We have investigated the history of the use and meanings of names, we have corresponded with bearers of unusual names, and we have tracked down the meanings of names in the language of origin. In the interest of accuracy we have avoided guess work and refrained from making assumptions because of fancied or fanciful resemblances. Where we have definite clues, we label our derivation as "possible" or "probable."

We have also included a great many names of illustrious, interesting, and unusual personalities and characters—from real life and literature—who have made the name notable or have given it vogue at some time.

In addition, we have listed names of books, works of art, and musical compositions which have given luster and renown to the name. Our list of men and women active in many and varied fields is unusual in this respect: An encyclopedia would list them by their last names. Of course it has been impossible to enter all the outstanding bearers of a certain name, but you can play a sort of parlor game by trying to think of other distinguished bearers of that name.

Therefore, we hope you may want to read this book for pleasure and for odd bits of information. That's the way we designed it, for in it you will find stories, anecdotes, as well as excerpts from English and Biblical poetry and prose, all of them dealing with the subject at hand, names—and all of them selected for your entertainment and edification.

What Are the Names?

MIRIAMNE. Tell me your name.
MIO. *Mio. What's yours?*
MIRIAMNE. *Miriamne.*
MIO. *There's no such name.*
MIRIAMNE. *But there's no such name as Mio!*
M.I.O. It's no name.
MIO. *It's for Bartolomeo.*
MIRIAMNE. *My mother's name was Miriam, so*
they called me Miriamne.
MIO. *Meaning little Miriam?*
MIRIAMNE. *Yes.*

MAXWELL ANDERSON, *Winterset*

No one compiling a book of names today for use in this country would dare to say. "There's no such name!" Not if he reads his daily newspapers carefully; not if he gets around in this wide and free country of ours, to which names have been carried from all parts of the world. No such name? But there it is— spoken or printed or signed. It exists; therefore it is. And the number of new names keeps on growing daily.

So far as first names go, anything goes. In the United States we have no legal or traditional restrictions—such as can be found in some other countries— on the use of first names.

In Brazil there is actually a law which gives the recording clerk the right to refuse to register "a name which may expose its bearer to ridicule."

In France there exists a similar control over names, as evidenced in the following Reuter's despatch from Paris, October 16, 1961:

A father wanted to register the name of his daughter at the local town hall as Daisy.

"Sorry. *Daisy* is not a French name. I can't accept it," the clerk said after peering down a long list.

Recently, in another Paris town hall. the name *Laita* was rejected, even though it is the name of a river in Brittany. A compromise of *Marie-Laita* was accepted.

The choice of acceptable first names is laid down by an ancient French law. . . .

"Exceptions are admitted only in special circumstances," said a Paris lawyer.

Such restrictions do not seem to exist in the Soviet Union. For example, the name of one of the leading Ukrainian dancers is Rio Rita Dubitskaya. When her company was on tour in the U. S. A. recently, a *New York Times* reporter asked her how she had come by her non-Russian given names. She replied, "My father had the record of the America song 'Rio Rita' and he liked it so much he named me Rio Rita." (*New York Times,* May 4, 1962)

THE PERENNIAL SEARCH FOR THE UNUSUAL

Parents have always tried to find unusual names for their unusual children. The *Oxford Classical Dictionary* points out that in Greece as far back as the second century B.C. parents were strongly motivated by "the ever-present tendency to find novel names" for their children. With the passing centuries, this desire to get away from the hackneyed has become intensified, resulting in an ever-growing list of names to choose from.

To keep pace with new names and new tendencies, we have for the past years carefully read the society pages of the *New York Times.* We also scanned such sources as magazines and newspapers for interesting "new" names.

In our page-turning we've come upon hundreds of names we had never seen or heard before—some lovely ones, some surprising ones. Many of these we have been able to accommodate either among our categories or in our lists of girls' and boys' names. We added *Eglantine* to our category of flower names; we found a place for *Mirette* as a diminutive variation of *Mira;* we grouped *Celine* with the *Celia* variations; we even tried to absorb the innumerable respellings that are current.

But there were still many others for which we could find no place in the body of this book. Some were mosaics made up of parts of several names; some were revivals of names of literary characters or historical figures; and some were whims—often lovely ones—of romantic parents.

For example, the announcement of the engagement of a girl named Tria in the *New York Times* intrigued us. Here was a new name, we thought. Her father, Williamson Pell Jr., informed us that Tria had been born "during the War when you had to register the name promptly. She was our third daughter and since my wife and I have always loved Greece, *Tria,* from the Greek word for *three,* seemed to us like a very attractive name."

It is indeed an attractive name, and to us it is a three-fold Greek name, for it can also be considered, if one so pleases, the terminal short form of *Demetria* (see DEMETRIA), which has a classical background, or it can be taken from the initial syllables of *Triantaphylla*, or *Triantafil(l)ia*, the modern Greek word for "rose."

So for the seeker after the unusual, we have a selected list of such names in the section called "A Galaxy of the Unusual."

EVERY TOM, DICK, AND HARRY

Despite this increasing search for the novel and unusual, most of the names still entered on birth certificates are the "good old names." Recent studies of the frequency of names show that such names are still the most popular, though not in the exclusive way they used to be. In the past, certain names had a practical monopoly. Early English registers of male names show that *John, William, Thomas, Richard,* and *Robert* accounted for 80% of the names. So few names accounted for so large a part of the population that James I referred scornfully to popular opposition with the expression, "Then Jack, and Tom, and Will, and Dick shall meet and censure me and my council." With the use of four names he included the greater number of Englishmen.

From 1550 to 1800, according to Elizabeth G. Withycombe, author of the excellent *Oxford Dictionary of Christian Names,* the names *William, John,* and *Thomas* were given to more than 50% of all boys born in England, and in the years 1650-1699 these three names accounted for 62.5% of the male population.

AND GIRLS' NAMES, TOO

The frequency of girls' names, according to the same source, shows that *Mary, Elizabeth,* and *Anne* represented more than 50% of all girls' names in the seventeenth century. In the eighteenth century, these three names accounted for more than 55% of all girls' names.

NAME TRIVIA GAME TO JOG YOUR MEMORY

Can you give the last names of these film and TV celebrities? The answers are on pp. 350-351.

Agnes (M), Al (P), Albert (F), Alec (G), Alexis (S), Ali (Mc), Angela (L), Angie (D), Anouk (A), Anthony (Q), Audrey (H), Ava (G).

Barbra (S), Beau (B), Bernadette (P), Bette (D, M), Brenda (V), Brigitte (B), Brooke (S), Bruce (D), Burl (I), Burt (L, R).

Candice (B), Cary (G), Charlton (H), Chevy (C), Chill (W), Chita (R), Christopher (P), Cicely (T), Claudette (C), Claudia (C, Mc), Cleavon (L), Clint (E), Colleen (D), Cyd (C).

Deborah (K), Debra (W), Diahann (C), Diana (R), Diane (K), Dina (M), Dinah (S), Dionne (W), Dolly (P), Dom (De), Dudley (M), Dustin (H), Dyan (C).

Eartha (K), Edie (A), Efrem (Z), Elaine (S), Elizabeth (A, M, T), Elke (S), Elliott (G), Elsa (L), Esther (R, W), Eva (G), Eva Marie (S), Eve (A).

Farrah (F), Fay (B), Faye (D), Fernando (L), Franco (N), Frank (S).

Gary (C), Gena (R), Gene (H, K), Glenda (J), Glenn (C), Glynis (J).

Hedy (La), Hermione (B, G), Herschel (B), Hope (L).

Imogene (C), Ingrid (B), Irene (D).

Jacqueline (B), Jane (F, W), Janet (G), Jason (R), Jeanette (Mac), Jennifer (J), Jill (St.), Joanne (W), Jodie (F), Johnny (C), José (F), Judy (G), Julie (A, C).

Karen (B), Karl (M), Katharine (H, R), Keir (D), Kevin (H, Mc), Kim (H, N, S), Kirk (D), Kris (K), Kristy (Mc).

Larry (H), Lauren (B), Laurence (H, O), Lena (H), Leslie (C, H), Lili (P), Lily (T), Linda (C, R), Liv (U), Loni (A), Loretta (S), Lynn (R).

Maggie (S), Marcello (M), Mariel (H), Mariette (H), Marlene (D), Marlon (B), Marsha (M), Matt (D), Maurice (C), Max (Von), Maximilian (S), Mel (B, F), Melvyn (D), Meryl (S), Mia (F), Michael (C, L), Milton (B), Myrna (L).

Nastassia (K), Natalie (W), Noël (C).

Olivia (De, NJ), Omar (S), Orson (B, W).

Pamela (R), Paul (H, M, N), Pearl (B), Peter (F, L, O'T, S), Petula (C), Phil (D), Piper (L).

Rex (H, I), Ricardo (M), Richard (B, D, P), Rip (T), Rita (M), Robby (B), Robert (De, R), Roberta (F, P), Rock (H), Rod (S, T), Rory (C), Ruby (D), Ryan (O'N).

Sal (M), Sally (F), Samantha (E), Sandy (D), Sean (C), Shelley (D, W), Shirley (J, Mac), Signe (H), Siobhan (Mc), Sissy (S), Slim (P), Sophia (L), Spencer (T), Susannah (Y), Suzanne (P), Sylvester (S).

Tatum (O'N), Teri (G), Trevor (H), Tuesday (W).

Uta (H).

Valerie (H, P), Vanessa (R), Vera (M), Vincent (G, P), Viveca (L), Vivien (L), Vladimir (S).

Warren (B), Wendy (H), Will (G), William (H), Woody (A).

Yul (B), Yvette (M).

Zero (M).

INITIAL THESE

Many famous writers seem to disdain their given names and are known in the world of books by their intials. If you were asked whether you had read any novels by Herbert Wells or David Lawrence, you would probably hesitate. But you would respond quickly to the question if asked about books by H. G. Wells or D. H. Lawrence.

At the time I was working on the introduction to this book I was also reading *The Life of Katherine Mansfield* by Anthony Alpers, and I came upon this sentence (p. 34, lines 2-6):

At this time—1904—the Countess had as tutor to her own three girls a Mr. Morgan Forster, a young Cambridge friend of her nephew Sidney Waterlow.

Who was Morgan Forster? I mused. Never heard of him. And then I read the next sentence:

He too had written a book—it was called Where Angels Fear to Tread.

A shock of recognition. I had read a book with that title by E. M. Forster. But who was this impostor Morgan Forster? E. M. Forster? Yes.

What's in a name? Sometimes it's just two identifiable initials.

See how many of the following you can recognize.

Attach the initials in Column A to the proper last name in Column B to find the names of famous writers.

	COLUMN A	COLUMN B
1)	A. A.	Auden
2)	A. E.	Barrie
3)	A. J.	Bentley
4)	C. P.	Chesterton
5)	C. S.	cummings
6)	D. H.	Cronin
7)	E. B.	Eliot
8)	E. C.	Forester
9)	e. e.	Forster
10)	E. M.	Gilbert
11)	G. B.	Housman
12)	G. K.	James
13)	H. G.	Lawrence
14)	H. L.	Mencken
15)	I. A.	Milne
16)	J. D.	Naipaul
17)	J. M.	Perelman
18)	J. R. R.	Richards
19)	P. D.	Salinger
20)	P. G.	Shaw
21)	S. J.	Snow
22)	S. S.	Tolkien
23)	T. S.	Van Dine
24)	V. S.	Wells
25)	W. H.	White
26)	W. S.	Wodehouse

ANSWERS

1) A. A. Milne 2) A. E. Housman 3) A. J. Cronin 4) C. P. Snow 5) C. S. Forester 6) D. H. Lawrence 7) E. B. White 8) E. C. Bentley 9) e. e. cummings 10) E. M.

Forster 11) G. B. Shaw 12) G. K. Chesterton 13) H. G. Wells 14) H. L. Mencken 15) I. A. Richards 16) J. D. Salinger 17) J. M. Barrie 18) J. R. R. Tolkien 19) P. D. James 20) P. G. Wodehouse 21) S. J. Perelman 22) S. S. Van Dine 23) T. S. Eliot 24) V. S. Naipaul 25) W. H. Auden 26) W. S. Gilbert

Let me add that writers are not the only people who are known exclusively by their initials instead of by their given names. Here is a sampling: P. T. Barnum, E. I. Dupont, W. C. Fields, D. W. Griffith, E. F. Hutton, R. H. Macy, J. P. Morgan, J. C. Penney, O. J. Simpson, H. B. Warner.

A 1957 Report

According to a study made by George Gallup of names given to boys in the United States between 1946 and 1956, the name *John* still maintained its place at the top of the list but *Charles, George, Henry,* and *Edward* were no longer among the first ten. Mr. Gallup's first ten were *John, Michael, James, Robert, William, David, Thomas, Stephen, Richard,* and *Joseph.*

There were even greater changes in the popularity of girls' names. Only *Mary, Barbara,* and *Margaret* remained among the top ten, and *Mary,* which had headed the list from 1906 to 1946, dropped to second place, giving way to *Linda.* Some old favorites like *Nancy, Elizabeth,* and *Ann(e)* still ranked high, but newcomers like *Sharon, Judith, Carolyn,* and *Janice* were near the top. Mr. Gallup's first ten were *Linda, Mary, Deborah, Susan, Carol, Patricia, Catherine, Margaret, Barbara,* and *Karen.*

LOCAL STUDIES

Three lists of the ten most frequently used names in three successive generations, taken from New York City Department of Health records show changes in the relative popularity of first names in New York City.

BOYS

1898	1928	1983
John	John	Michael
William	William	Christopher
Charles	Joseph	Jason
George	James	David
Joseph	Richard	Daniel
Edward	Edward	Anthony
James	Robert	Joseph
Louis	Thomas	John
Francis	George	Robert
Samuel	Louis	Jonathan

GIRLS

1898	1928	1983
Mary	Mary	Jennifer
Catherine	Marie	Jessica

GIRLS

1898	1928	1983
Margaret	Ann(i)e	Melissa
Annie	Margaret	Nicole
Rose	Catherine	Stephanie
Marie	Gloria	Christina
Esther	Helen	Tiffany
Sarah	Teresa	Michelle
Frances	Jean	Elizabeth
Ida	Barbara	Lauren

NAMES IN ENGLAND

Simeon Potter, author of *Our Language*, made a count of all names announced in birth notices printed in *The Times* of London in 1948. He found the ten most frequent names for boys to be *John, David, Michael, Peter, Richard, Chistopher, Charles, Anthony, Robert,* and *James.* The ten leading girls' names were *Ann(e), Mary, Elizabeth, Jane, Susan, Margaret, Penelope, Caroline, Frances,* and *Sarah.*

A later study (1959) in the same paper showed *John* and *Jane* leading the list. *David, James,* and *Charles* followed *John,* while *Mary, Ann, Elizabeth,* and *Sarah* followed *Jane.*

Where Our Names Come From

The old blood thrills in answer,
As centuries go by,
To names that meant a challenge,
A signal or a sigh.

ABBIE FARWELL BROWN, *Names*

There are so many names to choose from because our names, like the language we speak, come to us from many languages. Every invasion of England brought new names with it. Until the twelfth century the majority of the names used by the English came from the Teutonic, or Germanic, languages, for England was occupied by invading Anglo-Saxons, Norsemen, and Danes. The Norman invaders brought with them more Germanic names. At about this time the names of saints came to be widely used. These were mainly of Greek, Latin, and Hebrew origin. With the revival of classical learning after the Middle Ages, more names from Latin and Greek became popular. And from Scotland, Ireland, and Wales, where languages derived from Gaelic and Celtic were spoken, came still more names.

In our own country the early Dutch, French, and Spanish settlers left their influence on our names. Then the great national immigrations of the nineteenth and early twentieth centuries—from almost every country in the world—added hundreds upon hundreds of names. (See section "Names in Other Lands.")

HOLLYWOOD

Who hath not own'd, with
rapture smitten frame,
The power of grace, the
magic of a name?
THOMAS CAMPBELL,
Pleasures of Hope

More recently some foreign names have come to us through the invasion of Hollwood by individual continental European and British stars, who from theater marquees have flashed their names to parents all over the nation, such names as *Chita, Greta, Sophia, Marlene, Liv, Marcello, Ludmilla, Jean-Pierre, Ricardo, Boris, Mischa, Simone, Samantha, Nastassia, André, Galina, Werner, Jerzy, Maxi-*

23

milian, Yves, Yvette, José, Cesar, Xavier, Trevor, Ingrid, Fernando, Hedy, Helmut.

Hollywood, of course, has always been a tremendous influence in introducing trends and vogues in names. Directly traceable to the movie gods and goddesses is the popularity at different times of such names—can you identify them all?—as Barbra, Brooke, Kevin, Myrna, Mariel, Beau, Bo, Meryl, Shelley, Jeff, Shirley, Cary, Rip, Lin, Glenda, Michael, Glenn, Angie, Kirk, Karen, Jennifer, Liza, Vanessa, Colleen, Debra, Sean, Paul, Marlo, Mia, Valerie, Clint, Audrey, Marlon, Jessica, Charlton, Kris, Julie, Sylvester, Maureen, Woody, Rod, Dudley, Bette, Angela, Wayne, Gregory, Farrah.

But Hollywood creates not only stars but names. A baby is born Roy Sherer Jr. When he grows up, thinking of an acting career, he adopts his maternal grandfather's name and becomes Roy Fitzgerald. But for Hollywood even this name doesn't give off the right emanations. So in September 1947, a new name is born. You take the Rock from the Rock of Gibraltar and Hudson from the Hudson River and what do you get? A very handsome young fellow named Rock Hudson!

And then there was a girl named Janet Cole. But David O. Selznick one day told her,

"Janet Cole could be anyone, but Kim Hunter has individuality and will go far as an actress." A prophet as well as a name-giver!

There was also a girl named Phyllis Isley. Good name for the movies, you'd think. But again Mr. Selznick stepped in and changed her name to Jennifer Jones. "He thought it more glamorous," she told Sidney Skolsky, syndicated columnist of Hollywood Is My Beat, in an interview. Nevertheless, Mr. Selznick changed her name again when he married her!

This practice seems to be largely a thing of the past. Today's actors evidently take some pride in their own names and prefer not to have them glamorized by some agent or Hollywood mogul. A star is a star. . . . No matter what the name, it excites its own glamor. A few examples? Jack Lemmon, Sissy Spacek, Jeff Goldblum, Swoozie Kurtz, John Travolta, Madeline Kahn, Loretta Swit, Lou Gossett, Jack Maclovich, Steve Guttenberg.

ROMAN NAMES

There would have been little need for a book of this kind among the ancient Romans, because the number of first names was limited. About twenty first names were all that were used for naming boys. The most common was *Caius,* or *Gaius.* So common was this name that it was used as the symbol of the Roman male. No matter what the names of the couple were, the marriage formula included a declaration by the bride, *"Ubi tu Gaius, ego Gaia,"* meaning, "Where you are Gaius, I shall be Gaia," a pledge corresponding to our "till death do us part."

Of the Roman first names only *Lucius, Marcus, Quintus,* and *Titus* are used today as English names.

Gens Names

A Roman regularly had three names. The first was his given name, or *praenomen,* the second his *gens* name, or *nomen,* and the third his family name, or *cognomen.* From these last two names have come many of the names used in English. So, Gaius Julius Caesar belonged to the *gens Julia* or the Julian *gens. Gaius* was his given name and *Caesar* the name of his immediate family, which was a branch of the *gens.* A *gens,* or clan, consisted of a number of families whose members traced their descent to a common ancestor. They were united by their common "gentile" name and by certain religious rites.

Girls' Names Among the Romans

Among the Romans there was no problem in choosing a name for a girl. She was generally given the *gens* name in the feminine form, ending in the letter "a." So, Caesar's daughter was named Julia. You might like to know what names would have been used if, like Mr. Dionne or Eddie Cantor, he'd had five daughters. No problem at all! The first would have been called *Julia maior* or *senior,* the second *Julia minor* or *junior,* the third *Julia tertia,* the fourth *Julia quarta,* and the fifth *Julia quinta.*

English Names from Roman Gens Names

These *gens* names have given us many of our personal names. *Claude* and *Claudia* come from *Claudius,* the name of the Claudian *gens, Fabius, Fabia,* and *Fabiola* from *Fabius,* the name of the Fabian *gens, Cecil* and *Cecilia* from *Caecilius,* the name of the *Caecilian* gens, *Lelia* and *Loelia* from *Laelius,* the name of the *Laelian* gens, and *Portia* from *Porcius,* the name of the *Porcian* gens, etc.

Originally these names may have had some significance but the story of their origins is often traditional and unsubstantiated. *Claudius* may have meant "lame," *Fabius,* "a bean grower," *Caecilius,* "blind," *Ovidius,* "a shepherd," and *Porcius* may have meant a farmer who raised pigs, such names indicating characteristics or occupations of the distant ancestor of the particular *gens.*

We find something of the sort in Tennessee Williams' play *The Rose Tattoo,* when the young truckdriver complains about the origin of his name *Mangiacavallo*, meaning "eat a horse," saying sorrowfully that he is saddled with it because one of his ancestors had once been very hungry.

Some English names derived from *gens* names end in *ian*, such as *Fabian* and *Julian*. The story behind such names is interesting. When a Roman was adopted into a family with a different *gens* name, he took the name of the new *gens* and kept his own with a change from *ius* to *anus*. So, Gaius Octavius became Gaius Julius Caesar Octavianus after his adoption by his great-uncle Gaius Julius Caesar. That is why he is sometimes called Octavius and at other times Octavian.

Roman Family Names

The Roman family name was often a nickname. The last name of the greatest of Roman orators, Marcus Tullius Cicero, means "a small pea." According to Plutarch, the first man to bear the name *Cicero* had a dent at the tip of his nose called in Latin *cicer*, "a small pea or chick-pea." (The word *chick* in "chick-pea" comes from *cicer*.) When Cicero began to rise in the Roman world he was advised to drop this name because it was ridiculed by his opponents but, like so many others who have names of this type, he was proud of it and determined to make it famous. So fond had he become of his name that when he ordered some silver

dishes he asked the artist to engrave on them the names *Marcus* and *Tullius*, and instead of the third name to add the design of a small pea.

HEBREW NAMES

The names used by English-speaking peoples are indicative of the main elements in our civilization: Anglo-Saxon, Latin, Greek, and Judaean. The religious heritage of the Holy Land affected the giving of names based on personages in the Old and New Testaments. The Bible is, of course, one of the principal sources of names used in Europe and the Americas, and therefore many of our names are Hebrew in origin.

A number of names in the Old Testament refer to circumstances at birth. A good example occurs in Exodus 2:22 where the birth of the son of Moses and Zipporah is thus related: "And she bare him a son, and called his name *Gershom:* for he said, I have been a stranger in a strange land." This name is written *Gershon* or *Gerson* today, and is often Americanized as *Garson*.

SAINTS' NAMES

Beginning with the Middle Ages the nomenclature of all European countries was influenced by religion. The names of saints were given to children, and in many countries laws were passed limiting the type of name a child could be given. The names of saints came from Hebrew, Aramaic, Greek, Latin, Germanic, Celtic, and occasionally from some of the Oriental languages. Their influence has persisted not only among those groups obligated to use them but among others. See the section "A Calendar of Saints" for further information.

In some European countries and in the Latin-American countries, unusual saints' names are used more extensively than in the United States. For example, there was once a Cuban ball player who was called "Sandy." His first name was actually Sandalio, probably from St. Sandalus of Cordova, Spain. The first name of another Cuban ball player was Procopio. Procopius was a famous sixth-century writer, but it is more likely here that *Procopio* commemorates St. Procopius of Alexandria or of Caesarea.

PURITAN NAMES

After the Reformation, the use of Biblical names increased. The Protestants turned mainly to the Old Testament in their desire to avoid the use of saints' names not mentioned in the Scriptures. Finally, the Puritans, wishing to set themselves apart from the other sects, chose unusual and obscure names from the Bible or abstract names, and even words or phrases that had some moral or religious connotation.

The *less* extravagant names given were *Repentance, Comfort, Increase, Preserved, Sindeny,* and *Fear-not!* Of this type the five most often met today are *Faith, Hope, Charity, Mercy,* and *Prudence.*

We thought we had found another such name when the *Times* and the *Herald Tribune* on January 7, 1962, announced the engagement of a young girl with the lovely first name of *Solace,* a synonym for *Comfort!* However, her father, Robert W. Wales, writes us, "My wife, daughter, and granddaughter are all named Solace. It is derived from the surname of the Sollace family of Philadelphia, Mrs. Wales' paternal grandmother being Frances Sollace." Doing a little further research, however, we discovered in Ernest Weekley's *Surnames* an entry on "quality" surnames that equates the family names *Cumfort* and *Sollas.* (Spelling was once a do-it-yourself fun-thing especially with names, as indeed it is today.) Therefore, it may well be that—after all—the family name *Sollace* is a "quality" name going far back into history.

GERMANIC ELEMENTS

As used in this book, Germanic (also known as Teutonic) means the language which gave rise to Old English, modern German, Dutch, the Scandinavian language, and part of the Frankish language spoken by the Normans. Where the name discussed is common in one form or another to many languages, we have labeled it Germanic, but where it developed chiefly in one language, we have attributed it to that language.

The old Germanic names were usually composed of two parts joined together without any grammatical relationship. These names or elements generally referred to qualities, virtues, symbols or emblems of war, and animals. Nothing unflattering is intended when the name origin denotes an animal. Ancient peoples admired the strength, courage, and craftiness of animals, and used animal names as symbols of these qualities.

In the course of time these name elements were used without regard to their original meaning, and in many instances that meaning is unknown or doubtful. Some of the more important Germanic elements found in our names are these:

aelf, alf, elf	elf
beald, bald	bold
aethel, ethel	noble
al	bold, noble; elf
beorht, bert	bright
beorn, born	bear; warrior
ead, ed	happiness, prosperity
frith, fred	peace
helm	helmet, protection
herd, heard, hurd	strong, hard
her, here	army, soldier
mund, mond	protection
os	a god, divinity
raed, rede, red	counsel, wisdom
ric, rick	rich; rule
vin, win, wine	friend
weald, wald	power, rule
weard, ward	guard, protection
wil, will	resolution, will

These elements could be combined in any order so that *Harold* and *Walter* are the same names with the parts placed in reverse order. *Harold* is *here* ("army") and *wald* ("rule"); *Walter*, or *Walther*, is *wald* ("rule") and *here* ("army").

CELTIC

Before the Roman conquest, Celtic, a branch of the Indo-European languages, was spoken widely in Gaul (ancient France), the British Isles, Spain, and as far east as Galatia in Asia Minor. Its modern surviving languages are Irish, Gaelic, Welsh, Breton, Cornish, and Scottish. As in the case of our use of the term *Germanic*, we call a name *Celtic* when it is not limited to one branch of the language, but we indicate the particular country when the name is more common there than elsewhere.

WHY WE HAVE SO MANY NAMES

With the growing tendency to use family names as first names, boys' names have gotten out of hand and the number of possible first names for boys has become unlimited. The number of girls' names has been steadily increasing, chiefly through variations achieved by processes of accretion, fission, and restyling —all of which will be explained to you as you read ahead.

HOW SURNAMES ORIGINATED

Because so few first names were used in early times, great confusion arose in identifying the inhabitants in any locality in England. Some descriptive distinguishing tag had to be added. Four principal methods of identification were used:

1. by a person's trade, as John the miller or Joseph the carpenter
2. by the location of his home, as Thomas at the brook or William at the well
3. by a nickname, as Richard the strong, or James the stout
4. by a parent's name, as Harry son of John or Margaret.

From these descriptive phrases have developed most of our last names, or surnames. *Sur* in the word *surname* stands for *super*, which here means "in addition to." A surname is therefore a family name added to the given, baptismal, or Christian name.

English people did not begin using surnames until after the Norman Conquest, and for centuries they could take one or not as they wished. In 1465 Edward IV had a law passed compelling certain of his subjects to adopt family names. This law read in part:

"They shall take unto them a surname, either of some Towne or some Colour as Blacke or Brown, or some Arte or Science, as Smyth or Carpenter, or some office as Cooke or Butler."

Names from Trades

Among names from trades or occupations, many of which are treated in our lists of boys' names, are *Carter, Clark, Coleman, Faulkner, Foster, Fowler, Gardner, Naylor, Norris, Shepard, Sherman, Tyler, Ward,* and *Wright.* Other interesting last names of this type which are sometimes used as first names are *Baxter*, "a female baker," *Brewster*, "a female brewer," *Webster*, "a female weaver," *Latimer*, "one who spoke Latin" (i.e., a Latiner), *Palmer*, "a pilgrim," and *Ryder* or *Rider*, "a mounted forester."

Names from Places

The town in which a person was living or had lived was an important mark of identification. If he moved to another town, he would probably be known by the name of the town he had left. So, John who moved from London to Liverpool might be called John of London and eventually his surname might become *London*.

If a person always lived in the same town, he would be likely to receive a surname that showed the location of his home—at the bridge or well, at the ash tree, at the ford in the river. *At the* was written *atte*, or *atten* before a vowel. So, George who lived near the clump of ash trees might be known as George atten ash, which eventually became *Nash*.

When the greater part of the population couldn't read they often depended on pictures such as those drawn on signposts and tavern signs. The sign of a thorn on a tavern notice might give rise to the name Thorn or Thorne, which is sometimes used as a first name today. A *croft* meant "a small enclosed field," and combining these two elements Arthur Conan Doyle fashioned the picturesque name *Thorneycroft* as the first name of a schoolteacher called Thorneycroft Huxtable. With *croft* he also invented *Mycroft*, the name of Sherlock Holmes' omniscient brother.

In this book, unless otherwise noted, all place names refer to places in England and are of Anglo-Saxon origin.

Here are some common place-name elements that may help you figure out the meaning of many last names:

ay, ey	island; marshy meadow
by	farm, hamlet, town
croft	fenced-in field
den, dene	valley, pasture
don, dun	hill, slope
garth	homestead, enclosure
gear	castle
hale, hall	corner; also house
ham	farm, homestead
holt	wood
holm	island
law, low	small hill
lay, lee, ley	clearing, meadow
mor, more, moor	marshy, barren land
shaw	small wood
stan, staun	stone
stow	place
thorpe	settlement
ton, ton	village, town; hill
wal	foreigner; wall
wald, weald	forest land
wick, wich, wyck	farm, especially dairy farm
worth, worthy	enclosure; homestead

Nicknames

The word *nickname* comes from *an ekename*, a name added to the original name or substituted for it. Nicknames, describing personal characteristics, peculiarities, actions, and dress, were used as means of identifying persons before surnames were used. So, Thomas the rugged became Thomas Hardy. Later bearers of that name might not have the same characteristics, but the name was kept, often in a changed spelling, as Ralph Reid for Ralph the Red. Even when the nickname was unflattering it was still kept, as we saw in the case of Cicero; such is the attachment of persons to their names.

Patronymics

A *patronymic* is a name formed from the name of the father or other male ancestor. The ancient Greeks identified male members of the population by putting after the given name the name of the father in the form meaning "of" and the name of the township. So, legally, Socrates was "Socrates, son of Sophroniscus, of the deme or township of Alopece."

One of the ways of identifying an Englishman before he began to use a surname was to connect him with his father. Walter, the son of John, became Walter Johnson, patronymics being formed by adding a syllable like *son* or the letter *s* after the name of the father. *Watson* is therefore "son of *Wat* or *Walter*" and *Tennyson* is "son of *Dennis*." In other parts of the British Isles, a syllable like *Mac* or a letter like *O'* was placed in front of the father's name.

In Wales the syllable *ap* in front of the father's name formed a patronymic. This syllable was shortened to *b* or *p*. Hence come such names as *Bowen* from *ap Owen*, *Bevan* from *ap Evan*, and *Powell* from *ap Howell*.

Wamba, the clown in Scott's *Ivanhoe*, satirizes this use of *ap* by Welshmen to show their pedigree. He sings of a Welsh gentleman who comes to woo a widow:

Sir David ap Morgan ap Griffith ap Hugh
  Ap Tudor ap Rhice, quoth his roundelay;
She said that one widow for so many was too few,
  And she bade the Welshman wend his way.

Mac (also shortened to *Mc*) is Gaelic for *son*, a sure sign of a Scottish or Irish name. *O'* is Irish and *Fitz* is a variation of *Fils* (pronounced *feece*), the French word for *son*. Names with *Fitz* were introduced by the Normans into England and became very popular in Ireland

The Russian use of patronymics is so interesting that it calls for special treatment.

The full name of a Russian consists of three parts: the given first name, the patronymic, and the family name. So, in Turgenev's novel *Fathers and Sons*, Eugene Vassilich Bazarov is Eugene Bazarov, son of Vassil. Great importance is attached to the patronymic. For example, when Bazarov is introduced by his host to a young woman, this exchange takes place:

"What is her name?"

"Fenishka . . . Fedosya."

"And her patronymic? That too I must know."

"Nicolaevna."

Bazarov himself had been asked by his host's father:

"What is your name and patronymic?"

The reply was:

"Eugene Vassilich."

In this novel, friends and members of the family address each other by their first names, others use the first two names, but not the last name, which seems reserved for the author's use.

SOME REPRESENTATIVE PATRONYMICS

Arabic	*ibn–*
Aramaic	*–bar, Bar*
Armenian	*–ian*
Chinese	*–tse*
Danish	*–sen*
Dutch	*–zon, –sen*
English	*–son, –s, –kin*
Finnish	*–nen*
French	*de*
German	*–sohn, –zohn*
Greek	*–idas, –ides* (ancient); *–p(o)ulos, –oula* (modern)
Hebrew	*ben, Ben*
Irish	*O', Mac, Mc, Fitz*
Italian	*–i*
Latin	*–idius, –ilius*
Norman	*–Fitz*
Norwegian	*–sen, –datter*
Polish	*–ski, –czyk, –wiak, –wicz*
Rumanian	*–esco, –escu, –vici*
Russian	*–i(t)ch, –vich, –ef, –ev –off; –vna* (fem.)
Saxon	*–ing*
Scottish	*Mac*
Spanish	*–ez*
Swedish	*–son*
Welsh	*Ap, Up, –s*

Matronymics

A name formed from the mother's name is called a matronymic or metronymic. Occasionally, when the mother came from a family of great influence, the son might take his surname from her name. Among surnames which are matronymics are *Margaretson, Margotson, Beeson,* and *Beatson* or *Beaton* (son of *Beatrice*), and *Betts,* (son of *Elizabeth*).

FISSION

If a name has more than one syllable it can probably be broken up into at least two names, each of which may "grow up" into a fully independent name. *Abigail,* by the process of fission, breaks up into *Abby (Abbe, Abbey)* and *(Gail, Gayle, Gael),* and *Abby* and *Gail* are no longer merely pet forms or abbreviations used for *Abigail;* they are names in their own right and are often given without any thought of their once having been abbreviations of *Abigail.*

Through the centuries one of the most popular of all

girls' names has been *Elizabeth*. Through fission we can get—if we count respellings and foreign variants occasionally used in this country—about forty names that are used independently. We snip off the first letter and we get *Lisabeth* and such variants as *Lizabetta, Lisabet, Lisabette,* and *Lisbeth*. If we concentrate on the first part of *Elizabeth* we get *Eliza, Liza, Liz, Lizzie, Lizzy, Lizette, Lisa, Lise, Lisette, Else, Elsie, Elise,* and *Ilse*. The middle section gives us *Isabel, Isabella, Isbel, Ishbel, Isobel,* and *Ysbel*. The last syllable yields *Beth, Bess, Bessie, Betsie, Betsy, Betta, Bette, Bettie, Betty, Bettina,* and *Bettine*. By a telescoping of the entire name we get *Lillibet, Libby, Elsbeth, Elspeth,* and *Elspet*. Two-score names from one!

The name of *Margaret* is only slightly less prolific, producing (reading from first to last syllable) the following: *Meg, Peg, Peggy, Maggie, Maggi, Maggy, Megan, Maisie, Meta, Margy, Margie, Madge, Marjorie, Marjery, Margo, Margot, Margalo, Greta, Gretchen, Grete, Gretta, Rita,* and finally *Marguerite,* which (translated back from the French) gives us *Daisy!*

PET NAMES

Yes, call me by my pet name!
Let me hear
The name I used to run at when
a child . . .
ELIZABETH BARRETT BROWNING,
Sonnet XXXIII

Parents of every nationality, in their desire to show their great love for their children, have always tried to improve on their names by shortening them or altering them or even lengthening them—all in the cause of making them more endearing and affectionate.

A friend of ours whose first name is Garibaldi, and whose friends call him Gari, was never called Garibaldi by his parents. "My father," he told us, "used to call me *Garibaldino*. My mother wanted to show she loved me even better, so she called me *Garibaldinetto*. My grandmother, not to be outdone by *her* children called me *Garibaldinettuccio*. When I grew older, and they wanted me in a hurry—though they didn't love me any less—they called me *Dino*."

Dino, a popular modern Italian name (sometimes Americanized as *Dean*) is merely the short pet form of such names as *Bernardino, Gerardino,* and *Garibaldino*. The well known young Italian painter, Giuseppe Gambino, is known to his friends as *Pino* ("Peeno"), cut back from the lengthened pet name *Giuseppino*.

This European tendency to use the last part of a name as a diminutive or pet name is not confined to the Continent. No Englishman named *Albert* or *Alfred* would be called *Al* by his close friends; they would be more likely to greet him as "*Bert* (or *Bertie*) old thing" or "*Fred* (or *Freddy*) old boy."

In English, we have many more diminutive suffixes than there are in Italian or French or German or Spanish, simply because we use not only our own but many from those languages as well.

DIMINUTIVE FORMS

In the United States, if boys' names are shortened, they are usually cut down to one syllable (the first) with the suffix *y* or *ie* added, as *Thomas* to *Tom* to *Tommy* or *Edward* to *Ed* or *Eddie*. On the other hand the diminutive suffix is usually added to the full names of girls.

Below are listed the more popular feminine suffixes—most of them originally contained the idea of "small" but some are now merely decorative endings.

AS IN

alie	*Rosalie*
an, ana	*Marian, Gloriana*
een, ene	*Pegeen, Marlene*
ella	*Cinderella*
elle	*Sarelle*
et, ette	*Janet, Annette*
etta	*Marietta*
ice, is	*Clarice, Janis*
ie, ey, y	*Bessie, Jenny*
illa	*Marilla*
ille	*Lucille*
ina	*Bettina*
ine, inne, yn	*Maxine, Corinne, Carolyn*
ita	*Anita*
lyn	*Marilyn*
inda	*Clarinda*

If we take a name like *Rose* or *Dora* as a base we can see how many different names can be made by adding the diminutives of the various languages:

ROSE: *Rosalie, Rosanna, Rosella, Roselle, Roseen, Rosetta, Rosette, Rosina, Rosine, Rosita, Roslyn.*

DORA: *Doreen* (also an independent Irish name), *Dorella, Dorielle, Doretta, Dorette, Dodie, Dody, Dorina, Dorine, Dorita, Dorinda, Dorie.*

Some of these diminutives have themselves become independent names (with or without the final consonant sound of the name to which they are attached): *Etta, Yetta, Ina, Mina, Tina, Lyn, Lita, Nita, Rita, Zita.* Sometimes a name can go full cycle—be cut down and then built up again—thus: *Geraldine* to *Geri* to *Jeri* to *Jerilyn.*

BABY PET FORMS

A child that is loved has many names.
HUNGARIAN PROVERB

The forms favored by children are obviously the shorter ones, those they can pronounce more easily. There's hardly a name that can't in some way be shortened. *Robert* becomes *Rob* and, by rhyming, *Bob.* In the same way *Margaret* becomes *Meg* and then *Peg,* and finally *Peggy.* *Richard* becomes *Rick* and then *Dick* and *Dicky, Gwendolyn* becomes *Wendy* and *Mary* changes to *Polly* via *Molly* (from *Mally*).

Because babies sometimes find their names difficult to pronounce, and mispronounce them most delightfully, the mispronunciation becomes the name, usually within the family, but often within the circle of friends and even in the outside world. So it was with the young hero of Dickens' novel *Great Expectations*. The young man himself tells us in the first paragraph of the first chapter:

My father's family name being Pirrip, and my Christian name Philip, my infant tongue could make of both names nothing longer or more explicit than Pip. So I called myself Pip, and came to be called Pip.

If later the child becomes famous enough to have attention called to the name, another name has been added to the galaxy. *Ouida* was the original owner's baby version of *Louisa*. *Mala*, according to releases from Hollywood, where names as well as stars are "made," is the best that Mala Powers, the Roxane of *Cyrano*, could do as a baby with her name, Mary Ellen. The many duplicative names such as *Dede, Dody, Lulu, Mimi, Fifi, Jojo,* and *Bebe* were probably the results of what baby did when she tackled her name for the first time (like *mamma, daddy, choo-choo,* and so forth).

A letter to us from actress Dody Heath, confirms what we have written here:

"Dody" seems to be a nickname for Dora, Dorothy, *or* Dolores. *But when I was very young, I couldn't pronounce* Dolores, *and "Dody" is what came out instead. It was many years later that my parents and I learned that* Dody *was the legitimate nickname for* Dolores. *Up to that time, my parents were amusingly proud of my having named myself!*

FLOWERS AND PLANTS

Flowers and plants offer another source of names, especially for girls. Although used only infrequently before, such names as *Hazel, Ivy, Myrtle, Heather,* and *Rosemary* suddenly burst into full bloom toward the end of the nineteenth century and still retain a certain popularity. Since then many flower and plant names have been added. We have noted *Blossom, Brier, Clover, Dahlia, Eglantine, Fern, Holly, Laurel, Linden, Lotus, Magnolia, Marigold, Pansy, Peony, Poppy,* and *Yasmine.*

FROM GEOGRAPHY

Any point on a map that has an interesting name and some romantic association for parents may become a child's name. Thus Florence Nightingale owes her first name to her being born in Florence, Italy, and to her parents' love of that city.

Other names that come right off the map are *Asia, China,*

Denver, Florida, Geneva, India, Indiana, Kenya, Kerry, Louisiana, Maryland, Odessa, Nevada, Ohio, Oregon, Persia, Portland, Roma, Savannah, Shannon, Tallulah, Tennessee, Troy, Volga, and *Myrna,* which according to Myrna Loy's account was taken from a station sign her father saw while traveling on a cattle train from Montana to Chicago.

In this country the names *Carolina, Virginia,* and *Georgia* may also be geographical. We have even heard of a girl named *Ossining;* so there must be many others. At any rate, the possibilities for adding more names are unlimited, for only recently we came across Claddagh (in Ireland) and Sarnia (in Ontario) used as first names.

FROM HISTORY

Some parents, carried away by the excitement of a great moment in history or by enthusiasm for a great personality of the day, may commemorate the event or the hero through a name given to a child born on that very day. So, Century Milstead, famous football star of an earlier era, relates that his father had the unusual first name all ready for him when he was born on the first day of the twentieth century. Moreover, a number of girls born on December 7, 1941 were named Pearl Harbor. Finally, the names *Orbit* and *Orbita* were bestowed upon children born on February 20, 1962,

in honor of Colonel Glenn's orbital flight.

There are dangers attending the giving of such names. The bearer, when grown-up, may not care to have the date of birth reevaled so obviously. He (or she) may not wish to bear the burden of an illustrious name or to become conspicuous because of the name, like the boy whose parents named him General Douglas MacArthur. His first name is not *Douglas,* it is *General!*

FROM LITERATURE

Writers are like parents, only they have a great many more children to name. They too think their unusual characters are deserving of names that are different, and occasionally they create names as well as characters. When such names are lovely and their associations pleasant, they may step out of the library and come into the drawing-room. Among the names that have sprung full-grown from the brains of authors or have been popularized by them are *Evangeline, Imogene, Lorna, Lucasta, Malvina, Miranda, Orville, Pamela, Rima,* and *Vanessa.*

But writers have had an even greater influence in reviving or giving vogue to already established names. Popular novels have been followed by a spate of "hero" and "heroine" names given to children born under their romantic influence. Many a child owes its name to the fact that a mother was enchanted by some character in a novel, play, poem, or opera, and decided while still under its spell that her next child would bear that name. For this reason we have, in our entries of names, cited novels, poems, and plays or operas that were probably influential in the naming of children.

Reading somewhere that *Nila* was an abbreviated form of *Cornelia,* but being somewhat skeptical, we telephoned to Miss Nila Mack, CBS creator, director, and writer of the then favorite children's radio program *Let's Pretend,* and were told, "My name has nothing to do with *Cornelia,* but everything to do with my mother, who was a very romantic person. When she was seventeen, she read a poem that was dedicated to *Nila,* the goddess of the Nile, and there and then she decided that if she ever had a daughter, that would be her name. And that's how I got *Nila.* My mother also gave me a second name, *Arah,* which I don't know the meaning of at all. I do remember, though, that she called me *Arah* only when I was being spanked."

Nila Mack has made her name famous and has been happy with it. Not so a boy we know who is named *Garth.* "Before I was born," he told us, "my parents went to see a play in which one of the characters was named Garth (*Winterset* by Maxwell Anderson). My parents liked it and so they named me Garth. Personally, I'd rather be named something else."

FROM FAMILY TRADITION

And at thy birth the cricket chirp'd.

SAMUEL ROGERS, *Italy*

Finally, there are those names which arise from some story or incident forming part of a family tradition. They are handed down as a heritage, and although they may invite inquiry and comment, they form conversation pieces in which the bearers engage with pride, for they are sentimentally attached to their unusual names.

A striking example is the first name of Mrs. Cricket H. Auld, librarian of Midland Park, New Jersey, who wrote us in a delightful letter:

As to Cricket . . . it all started 180 years ago, in England. Seems that the family could not decide upon a name for the baby girl. Grandparents of both sides argued for several months until one evening the father called a "meeting" of the families. While they sat about the fire, pondering, a cricket chirped! "THAT'S IT! Listen to the child's happy chirping. And, if she should have a daughter, the child will be called CHIRP!"

My own daughter is named CHIRP, for that reason. However, the girls always have other names following. Mine is Crick-

et-*Helen Louise. My daughter is Chirp-Judy Carter Auld. Strange, but true! I do not mind your asking about it, not in the least. It has sometimes been rough to explain because banks and colleges invariably will drop the First Real Name!*

As they sit about their fireside, Charles Dickens' *Cricket on the Hearth* (a title taken from John Milton's *Il Penseroso*) will always have pleasant associations, not only at Christmas, as will lines like these from an early sonnet by John Keats, *On the Grasshopper and Cricket:*

The poetry of earth is ceasing never:
  On a lone winter evening when the frost
Has wrought a silence, from the stove there shrills
The Cricket's song, in warmth increasing ever.

Fashions in Names

> Our names are written equal
> In Fame's wide-trophied hall; 'tis ours to gild
> The letters, and to make them shine with gold
> That never tarnishes.

WILLIAM BLAKE, *King Edward the Third*

MODERN TENDENCIES IN BOYS' NAMES

Double Names

Statistics for the United States and England show that about 80% of all the people bear two first names, with the names of newly born children showing an even higher percentage.

There are several advantages in giving a child two first names. When a last name is not an unusual name, the middle name often serves as further identification in school, on a social security check, or on a personal check.

Think of how important Paul is in the name John Paul Jones. John Jones could be anyone of perhaps thousands, but the Paul in John Paul Jones says, "I have not yet begun to fight!"

The giving of two names if the family name is a common one in the United States (Smith, Jones, Miller, Johnson, Williams) is a must, as is the giving of a middle initial. The middle initial also gives the bearer the opportunity to choose a name built on the initial when the bearer grows up.

Ellen Goodman, in an article in the *Boston Globe* in which she discusses Gary Hart's name change, writes: "Legally, we can and often do call ourselves anything we like. It's considered a right. Gerald Ford, you may recall, was Leslie King, Jr., before he was adopted by his stepfather."

Where the family name is common, the given name should not be one of the often repeated given names. The Mr. Smith who often appears on "Washington Week in Review" was given an unusual name by his parents. Hedrick Smith is a distinctive name.

Although his mother never called him anything but Tom, Thomas Lanier Williams changed his given name to the unique Tennessee. And by so doing he honored his family's contributions to that state.

Thousands of famous writers, composers, artists, and statesmen are known today *only* by their middle names. How many of you know the actual first names of two famous Augustes—Rodin and Renoir? (We'll tell you: François Auguste Rodin and Pierre Auguste Renoir.)

But let's make it easier; let's come closer to home. How many of you know the given names of three of our Presidents — Grover Cleveland, Woodrow Wilson, and Calvin Coolidge? (You'll have to look those up yourself.)

Therefore, in this book you will find our famous men and women under the names they made famous. For instance, you will find the French composer Berlioz under *Hector*, not *Louis;* the English actor Gielgud under *John*, not *Arthur;* the American novelist Lewis under *Sinclair*, not *Harry*.

Family Names as First Names

Authorities on the history of names point out that it was not until the late sixteenth century that the practice arose in England of using surnames as first names. The classic example is that of Lord Guildford Dudley, the husband of Lady Jane Grey, who took his first name from the name of his mother's family.

In the United States this practice is now fairly common. Many last names (*Seymour,* *Sidney, Lester, Howard, Russell, Douglas, Sheldon*) have become so popular as first names that they are treated as such and no thought of a continuing family name is involved when a child is named.

However, we have found hundreds of names used as first names that are associated with particular families and are given to perpetuate the family name of an ancestor. Obviously, caution should regulate the use of such names outside the family. A sampling of such names includes *Beaufort, Berwick, Biddle, Bixby, Blashford, Boles, Breading, Brownrigg, Budge, Busch, Cadwallader, Chessman, Cotton, Colwell, Delancey, Devereaux, Fiske, Foxhall, Franchot, Fremont, Goodhue, Grafton, Heyliger, Huyler, Kaighn, Le Grand, Ligon, Lightner, Lyster, MacNeill, Masefield, Messmore, Minot, Nesbitt, Ordway, Peyton, Peverell, Sabin, Sayre, Statler, Whitelaw, Wray.*

On the other hand, such family names as *Carlyle, Clifford, Clifton, Clinton, Clyde, Granville, Lloyd, Melville, Stewart, Stuart,* and *Wayne* are now clearly public property.

CURRENT FASHIONS IN GIRLS' NAMES

Fashions in girls' names like fashions in women's clothes change with the times and sometimes, to paraphrase the French saying, *The more they change, the more they remain the same*. What seems like a new tendency may merely be a revival of something that used to be fashionable. In one's search for the unhackneyed, one may reach back to something so old that it seems new again.

SPELLING: The Ubiquitous Y

One of the ways of giving a name a new look is to play around with the spelling. Right now—as in the fourteenth, fifteenth, and sixteenth centuries —y is the magic letter. It can take the place of any vowel, but especially of *i* and *e*. So strong is this tendency that *Kathryn, Caryl*, and *Carolyn* are seen more often than the standard spellings, but any name is susceptible and amenable to this change. We have come across *Adelyne, Alys* (a fifteenth-century variant), *Ellyn* (also fifteenth-century variant), *Gayle, Lynda, Myna, Robyn, Ynes*, and the boys' names *Myrwyn* and *Wyllys*—one particular Wyllys naming his daughter *Phyllys*. Fair enough! One day soon we expect to find *Yvylyn* and then we predict a reverse trend will set in.

SPELLING: Ye Olde E

What happens when a name already has a y in it? That's easy.

You change the *y* back to *i* or *e* or drop it altogether, and again you get a chic and novel effect.

Abbe, Audre, Bette, Cathi, Evonne, Kathe, Maggi, Mari, Nelle, Rubi, and *Sali* have the same pronunciation as of old but they undoubtedly have a new look.

Or you can go back to the days of "Ye Olde Shoppe" and add an *e* to a name ending in *y* (*Faye, Gaye, Sadye*) or indeed to any name. We have seen *Ferne, Ruthe, Gayle*, and *Faythe*—the last two combining two tendencies—the omnipresent *y* and the quaint, antique final *e*.

SPELLING: Phonetic, Simplified, and Unpredictable

No one likes to have his name mispronounced. One of the current tendencies is to spell a name phonetically—to spell it in such a way as to leave no doubt about its pronunciation. *Helayne* or *Helaine* is replacing *Helene*. *Ileen* is becoming a popular variant of *Aileen* and *Eileen*, and *Letisha* and *Marsha* are met with frequently for the standard spellings *Letitia* and *Marcia*.

A further simplication is taking place with names that have a very weak syllable, so that we find *Debra* replacing *Deborah, Madlin* used occasionally for *Madeleine*, and *Margrit* for *Margaret*.

Sometimes a change in pronunciation of a name will result in a change of spelling. As the name *Candace* became more popular the pronunciation changed from CAN' da see to CAN' diss with a resulting re-spelling of the name as *Candis* or *Candice*. For the same reason *Marleen* is gradually replacing *Marlene*.

Finally there is a kind of game to see how many different ways you can spell a name and still get back the right pronunciation —Shakespeare is said to have spelled his name in at least twenty different ways. An example of this kind of respelling is *Patrece* for *Patrice*. This we regard as mere caprice, or should we write *caprece*?

Nevertheless, we are ready to defend the right of anyone to spell his (or her) name in any way that pleases him and pronounce it in any way he likes. It's his (or hers) and he (or she) can use it as the spirit moves.

The Masculine Influence

Almost any boys' name can become a girls' name by the simple addition of a feminine ending like *a, ina, ine, etta,* or *ette* (*Roberta, Georgina, Maxine, Henrietta, Bobette*). In pet names the final *y* of a boy's pet name is generally changed to *i* or *ie. Toni, Jeri, Freddie, Eddie, Bobbie, Jamie, Billie, Tomi, Frankie* are all girls' names.

We have also come across the following "girls' " names: *Alix, Aubrey, Christian, Daryl, Dean, Duncan, Dwight, Eliot, Evan, Glenn, Jeremy, Keith, Kevyn, Kirke, Kyle, Llewellyn, Lloyd, Michael, Merwin, Neal, Paule, Percy, Sidney, Timothy,* and *Tristram,* and even *Ivor.*

But any name is possible, as witness this AP dispatch:

JAMES WANTS HER NAME BACK

Seattle, Feb. 7 (AP)— "That's right," said Attorney Robert Royce, when questioned about filing of a divorce suit. The filing read:

"James M. Martin vs. James M. Martin." "The complaint is correct," the attorney said. "The lady's name is James M. Martin. So is her husband's."

Mrs. Martin asks restoration of her maiden name, James M. Peace.

The Paternal Influence

In many families it is the tradition to name the first boy after the father. What happens if it's a daughter? Even then the father's vanity may have to be appeased and names are coined, using the father's name as a base. Walteen's father's name is Walter; Arenette's, Aaron; Cyra's, Cyrus; Shermaine's, Sherman; Darrylin's, Darryl; Alana's, Alan.

Family Influence

A fairly recent trend is to give family names as first names to girls—where such family names are a matter of pride or a reminder of past glories. Our research indicates that, whereas practically any family name is used for a boy, the family name must somehow suit or be made to suit a girl. Family names ending in an *ay* or *ee* sound or even silent *e* seem appropriate without change. We have come across the following family names for girls: *Ainsley, Ansley, Ashley, Atlee, Bourke, Brooke, Carney, Chelsey, Courtenay, Crosby, Dagny, Darcy, Hayley, Kelly, Kirby, Lacey, Lasalle, Lindley, Lindsay, Milne, Murray, Riley, Selby, Shelby,* and *Whitney.*

Sometimes the family name is made to fit by the simple process of substituting or adding an *a* or an *ie*, as in *Reida* from *Reid.*

Three such names aroused our interest and we inquired about them. Rhoma's mother wrote us:

My maiden name was Ella Rhome. When after my marriage my first child was born I named her Rhoma. Had she been a boy I would have called him Rhome, but for a girl I decided to change the e to a. Rhome is an old Dutch name.

The father of Hyla wrote us:

We derived the name Hyla from my mother's family name of Huyler, *retaining practically the same pronunciation but making it look like a girl's name. The name very naturally adjusted itself to the nickname* Heidi *which my daughter is usually called. Over the years, we have learned of two families which use the first name* Hyla.

Deanie herself wrote us about her name:

My mother's family is English, and there has been a Theresa Deane (the Deane *being the surname) in the family for generations. Somewhere along the line, it was converted to* Deanie, *and I use that, as you have seen, even for business purposes.*

Girls' names we have come across that do not end in an *ay* or *ee* sound or an artificial *a* or *ie* substitution are: *Aiken, Alden, Altmore, Aubin, Canning, Carter, Carson, Carvel, Craig, Deming, Drew, Fairfax, Harper, Hopeton, Leland, Lordes, Manton, Newell, Ordell, Randall, Schuyler, Selden, Taylor, Temple, Thayer, Trencherd, Townsend, Wingate,* and *Winslow.*

Some of these names go far back and show that giving family names to girls when those names were suitable and a matter of pride is merely a continuing rather than a new fashion. About the name *Aubin*, Mrs. Louise Z. Redfield wrote us:

I have heard my grand-mother say that it was origi-nally a surname. The first mention of it in some records of hers occurs when my grandfather John Odlin Hutchins married Aubin Markham of Virginia in 1820. They had four daugh-ters and each daughter named one of her daughters Aubin, and the name has been car-ried down in several branches of the family since.

The Alden we know about is a direct descendant of John and Priscilla Alden and is the daugh-ter of Ned (Edgar) Calmer, au-thor and CBS newscaster and commentator.

On the subject of using fam-ily names as first names for girls, the distinguished British novel-ist, author of *Black Narcissus, The River, Greengage Summer,* and a delightful children's story *The Mousewife,* strikes this cau-tionary note in her letter to us:

Rumer is a family name and I don't think any baby should be saddled with it. You have to answer questions about it all the time.
    Yours with best wishes,
    RUMER GODDEN

Two Names

The society pages of the *New York Times* and *Herald Tribune* reveal that about 75% of all girls mentioned there have two given names—in one form or another. A study of the birth announce-ments indicates that nine out of ten newly-born children have more than one given name.

Two-Name Combinations

We have found six different ways of giving girls two names.
1. Where the two names are separate entities, the child being known only by the first name, with the second merely an added or reserve name.
2. Where the two names are treated as one and always used together: *Betty Lou, Betty Jane, Mary Margaret, Barbara Ann, Mary Ann, Barbara Sue, Sarah Ann, Virginia May, Margaret Sue, Julie Mae,* etc.
3. Where to insure the insep-arability of the two names a hyphen is used to couple them: *Ruth-Ann, Adah-Grace, Marie-Josephine, Vera-Ellen.*
4. Where the two names merge smoothly to form one name: *Roseanne, Saralinda, Claribelle, Bethana, Vidabeth, Lauranne, Ermelinda, Michael-ann.*
5. Where the two names are telescoped producing a new name: *Marimar: Mary* plus *Margaret; Ruthelma: Ruth* plus *Thelma; Fancille: Frances* plus *Lucille; Enith: Enid* plus *Edith; Willaret: William* plus *Margaret.*
6. Where the second name, a family name, is coupled with the

first name by a hyphen: *Mary-Lloyd, Nancy-Ross*.

Combined Influences

The given names borne by Mrs. Lael Tucker Wertenbaker, author of *Death of a Man* (dramatized as *A Gift of Time*), and her daughter, Timberlake, show a number of tendencies and influences.

Mrs. Wertenbaker's first name is actually a Biblical masc. name (NUMBERS 3:24). In answer to our inquiry, she wrote us a charming letter of explanation, from which we quote in part:

My father, an Episcopal clergyman, spotted Lael in a list of Biblical names. He and my mother loved its shape and sound (so do I) and christened their eldest daughter so. I consider it a gift from them.

In turn, Mrs. Wertenbaker bestowed the gift upon her daughter, Lael Louisiana Timberlake Wertenbaker, who was also named after her great-great-grandmother, Louisiana Timberlake. Thus, there are at least four combined influences in the daughter's name: the use of a masc. name, the use of a family name, the use of a name from geography, and the use of more than one given name.

The girl is generally called Timberlake. Mrs. Wertenbaker writes that children love the sound of *Timberlake*. In France, where the family lived for some years, children transformed the name into the euphonious *Télélé*.

ANDROGYNOUS NAMES

A woman we know told us that if she gave birth to a girl she would name the child Samantha so that she could call her daughter Sam or Sammy. Indeed, there is a growing tendency to give a child a name that makes no gender distinction.

Here is a list of such names:

Alex, Ashley, Beryl, Brett, Claire, Dale, Dallas, Dana, Daryl, Duncan, Eliot, Evan, Evelyn, Gene, Gerry, Glenn, Hilary, Jamie, Jay, Jerry, Jody, Joyce, Kelly, Kelsey, Kerry, Kevin, Kim, Kyle, Lane, Lauren, Lee, Leslie, Lindsay, Marion, Morgan, Mead(e), Meredith, Michael, Page, Perry, Robin, Sandy, Shelley, Shirley, Stacy, Sydney, Toby, Tracy, Tristram, Vivian.

When you give a girl a name such as Alex, Sydney, etc., it doesn't cause any problems. In fact, it's considered rather chic. But if you are naming a male child, be on your guard in choosing any of these androgynous names. If you saddle a male child with a name that leans heavily on the feminine (Claire, Evelyn, Robin, Shirley, etc.), he is likely to suffer from peer harassment. Youngsters are merciless with each other. If there's a way of making fun of a name, they will find it.

Another development in the same direction is seen in names that sound the same as boys' names but are differentiated by spelling the endings with an *ie* or an *i* instead of a *y*—Bobbie or Bobbi (for Roberta or Barbara), Freddie or Freddi (for Frieda), Teddie, Toni, Charlie, Billie, Marti, Frankie, etc.

CURRENT TRENDS

At this writing, biblical names are "in" again. In California, a tabulation of the names for birth announcements published by a local Jewish Federation branch shows that in 1983 Sarah was the most popular name, followed by Rebecca, for girls; Daniel and Joshua tied for first place, followed by David and Nathan, for boys.

Other popular biblical names are Deborah, Judith, Rachel, and Hannah for girls; Joseph, Jesse, and Matthew for boys.

The traditional way of naming a child is still observed among Jews. Newborn infants are named in memory of a grandmother, grandfather, or some other beloved relative. The name so honored need not be taken over whole. Often only the same initial letter is used, thus affording the parents a wide choice. For example, Boris, the name to be memorialized, may become Bruce, as it did for one of America's leading scientists.

Another trend in names is the use by famous black athletes and writers of African or Moslem names. The very talented basketball superstar who won the NBA's Most Valuable Player award in 1971 was Lew Alcindor. In 1972 he won the award again as Kareem Abdul-Jabbar. And nearly everyone knows that Muhammad Ali's name, when he became heavyweight champion in 1964, was Cassius Clay.

American playwright and poet LeRoi Jones changed his name to Imamu Amiri Baraka. The successful author of the play *For Colored Girls Who Have Considered Suicide/When the Rainbow Is Enuf*, is named Ntozake Shange. The naming of some babies Kinte (from Alex Haley's *Roots*) gives further evidence of this surge toward African and Moslem names.

PLURAL TENDENCIES

Parents of twins, triplets, and quads sometimes not only dress them alike but try to give them names that sound alike. They accomplish this by the use of the same initial or by rhyme.

Triplets—all girls—born recently were named *Judy Mae, Julia Fae,* and *Jodie Lee.* One set of quadruplets—all girls—born a few years ago were called *Jane, Jean, Joan,* and *June.* Quadruplets, two girls and two boys, whose father's name was *Kenneth* and mother's name *Ann,* were named *Krystal, Kristine, Kenneth,* and *Keith.* Vanity, thy name is father!

How to Choose a Name

Giving a name, indeed, is a poetic art;
all poetry . . . is but a giving of names.

THOMAS CARLYLE, *Journal*, May 18, 1832

FIRST NAMES FIRST

Not since the days before people acquired family names have first names been so universally used as they are today. It is a sign of our times; it represents a desire to show our friendliness. In high school, more and more teachers are dropping the formality of last names (preceded by Miss for girls) and address their pupils by their first names. The MC on any radio or TV program, with few exceptions, calls his guests by their first names and they usually return the courtesy.

Whereas, not too long ago, asking a girl whether you might call her by her first name was tantamount to a proposal of marriage, today young people (and older people, too) are actually introduced by their first names. We are living in an age of *Jack* and *Bill, Peggy* and *Sue.*

We live in a country where adults begin calling each other by their first names at the tip of a hat, where first names are almost used as a kind of punctuation.

It is not so in many other countries. Old World formality has been only slightly touched by our all-out informality. There is the amusing true story of the German refugee scientist—let's call him Dr. Hans Berger—who went to Idlewild Airport with several American scientists to meet a former colleague of his —let's call her Dr. Hilda Feuer —who was arriving here from England.

As she walked down the ramp, Dr. Berger came forward and greeted her warmly with, "I am very happy to see you, Hilda. How are you?" A little while later when the American welcoming group had dispersed he took her aside and said apologetically, "There is something I shall have to explain to you. When we are among other Americans, I shall call you Hilda and you will call me Hans. But when we are alone—then I shall call you Dr. Feuer and you will call me Dr. Berger. Yes?"

A great deal of care and thought should, therefore, be given to the selection of the name by which your child is going to be known for the rest of his life. The possible variations on the theme that is his name must also be taken into consideration. That is why we have listed the short and pet forms of all names so you can measure the hazards before you make your choice.

THE "EAR" TEST

Though your child will most often be called by his first name, it is important in choosing it to see how well it combines in sound with your family name.

The National Baby Institute's consultants in psychology and pediatrics suggest this simple "ear test": "Say each name you are considering aloud with your own family name. The sounds should be harmonious and the rhythm pleasing. Hard-sounding family names like 'Becker' or 'Pratt' sound best with soft names like 'Arthur' or 'Ellen.' It is advisable to use two- or three-syllable first names with short family names. Long last names should have one- or two-syllable first names."

To this we might add our own advice that where the surname is a rather usual one (like Jones or Brown or Smith) an interesting first name often makes a happy and distinctive combination. Hollywood has offered us Jennifer Jones, Vanessa Brown, Alexis Smith (her actual name), and, on the day we wrote this, morning newspapers announced the engagement of Damaris Smith and the publication of

Pride of the Moor by Vian Smith. In his letter to us, after explaining that the name *Vian* has been in his family for generations — probably a Devonshire variant of *Ian*—Mr. Smith concludes with this interesting observation:

When I went to school I hated the name. People were always asking me to spell it. But when I began to write professionally I realized that the combination of an unusual Christian name and common surname could be a readily remembered asset.

FOLLOWING THE BEAT

English poetic rhythms are based on the regular alternation of *one* accented syllable with *one* or *two* unaccented syllables. From the various combinations thus made possible, we get our four basic rhythmic patterns.

1. One unaccented syllable followed by an accented syllable (called an iamb):

an INfant CRYing. IN the NIGHT

an INfant CRYing FOR the LIGHT

and WITH no LANGuage BUT a CRY.

2. An accented syllable followed by one unaccented syllable (called a trochee):

I the HEIR of ALL the Ages IN the FOREmost FILES of TIME.

(The proud boast that every new-born baby can make.)

3. An accented syllable followed by two unaccented syllables (called a dactyl):

TALK not of WAsted afFECtion! afFECtion NEVer was WAsted.

4. Two unaccented syllables followed by an accented syllable (called an anapest).

and the SHEEN of their SPEARS was like STARS on the SEA.

A combination of names that follows any of these patterns is sure to be pleasantly rhythmic. Here are some well-known examples:

EDna saint VINcent milLAY
DEborah KERR
ANNabelle LEE
EVelyn HOPE
eLISSa LANdi
vaNESSa BROWN
seLEna ROYLE
GREGory PECK
GARy COOper
JOHN van DRUten.

The names given above also illustrate one of the other principles advocated by the National Baby Institute: the use of a two- or three-syllable first name with a short family name or the use of a one- or two-syllable first name with a long family name.

If you are choosing two first names it is also important to use the "ear" test. Let's try a few.

Barbara Joan or Joan Barbara?

Virginia May or May Virginia?

Roberta Sue or Sue Roberta?

Elizabeth Mary or Mary Elizabeth?

If you read these over aloud to yourself, we think you will agree that, in the first three, the rhythm is better when the short name comes second. In the fourth case, however, the effect is better when *Mary* comes first, since MARy eLIZabeth consists of two successive dactyls forming a smooth rhythmic pattern, whereas eLIZabeth MARy forms an irregular rhythmic pattern.

EXCEPTIONS

However it is best not to stick too strictly to the rules or to let the rules exercise a veto over the choice of a name you like. Somehow frequent repetition of names in combination or an association you may have with them will frequently override any fixed rules of rhythm. How else account for our preference for the sound of *Walt Whitman* over *Walter Whitman*, while we prefer the sound of *Walter Lippman* to *Walt Lippmann*? What we get used to, what we feel at home with will usually produce a pleasing effect.

CAUTIONS

However, there are other considerations that are perhaps more important than rhythm but, unfortunately, they can be stated only in negative terms—

warnings about what to avoid rather than suggestions about what to choose—a list of *don'ts* rather than a list of *do's*.

DON'T BE DIFFICULT

Don't give names that are too difficult or too long. One of our correspondents, Deanie Clancy, writes:

> I have a cousin who says that when she names her children (she has seven) she always keeps in mind how hard it is going to be for them to write their names in the first grade. As a result, my young relatives may not be the most literate in the primary class, but they're much happier than kids named *Gwendolyn* or *Bartholomew*.

We know a little six-year-old boy named Frederick Goldsmith who one day came home from school with this loud and bitter complaint: "By the time I write my name on my paper, the other kids are finished with their work."

How much sadder the lot of the girl in the following UP despatch of June 4, 1955:

> Pellston, Mich., June 4 (UP)
> Aleatha Beverly Carol Diana Eva Felice Greta Harline Io Joanne Karen Laquita Maurine Naomi Orpha Patricia Queenie Rebecca Shirley Teresa Una Valeeta Wanda Xelia Yolanda Zoe Karkofen was graduated from Pellston High School last night.

That's the way her name—which has every letter in the alphabet—appeared on her diploma too. But youth will find a way. The despatch continues by telling us that she has shortened her name somewhat. "Just call me Pat," she said.

DON'T BE FANCIFUL

Try to avoid names that will be a burden of glamour or romance. What may be a pleasant memory to a parent may become a painful experience to a child. Mrs. Elizabeth Hayward, distinguished genealogist and author of many books, sends us these wise words of advice:

"Please remind parents that in naming a child, they're not just naming a baby. What's appropriate and cunning for an infant may look pretty silly on a social security card, on a veteran's application, on a diploma, or on a check. And more's the pity, for most of us exist as adults a lot longer than we do as toddlers." (See "From History" in the chapter "Where Our Names Come from.")

DON'T BE FUNNY

If you have a sense of humor, forget it. Earl Wilson, in his syndicated column *It Happened Last Night* tells about Spencer

Hare, a Broadway publicist, who named his first child Hedda! When asked what he would name a second daughter, he facetiously replied, "Oh, Lotta, of course." "And a son?" "Oh, in that case," he quipped, "I'd name him Noah.' Such goings on may make good copy but they may not always be good for the child. One young lady, whose family name is Barr, has a father who exercised that kind of humor and named her Candy. Fortunately, she thinks it very sweet!

Ilka Chase, however, in her autobiography, *Free Admission*, has recorded her gratitude to her mother for not choosing the name *Meribah* and thus leading her a Merry Chase through life. In general it is wise to avoid first names that form dubious combinations with surnames or that may easily be changed to an unflattering sequence.

BEWARE OF ACRONYMS

Watch the initials to make sure that when put alongside one another they do not form an unflattering word. Sally Ann Peterson would either have to drop her middle name or have her things stamped with the initials S. A. P.

Felicia Ardsley Townsend, said like that, is a lovely name but the initials add up to FAT. By the way, an acronym is a name or word forming the initials of the words for which it is used as an abbreviation—such words as WAVES (*W*omen *A*ppointed for *V*oluntary *E*mergency *S*ervice) and CARE (*C*o-operative for *A*merican *R*elief *E*verywhere). Major General James Ewell Brown Stuart, one of the most famous of the Southern generals, was known as Jeb Stuart.

ONE FINAL DON'T

Don't pay too much attention to the advice given here or anywhere else. If you like a name, if your heart is set on it, if after you say it aloud at intervals it still pleases you, if it has the feeling you want to convey, and if it sounds like music to your ears, you've probably made a wise choice.

At any rate, one of the best birthday gifts you can bestow on a child is a name that he will be able to put on with ease and wear with pride.

MEANING OF TERMS

abbrev.	abbreviation.
dim.	diminutive, sometimes a pet form, may often be longer than the original name.
fem. and (f)	feminine.
masc. and (m)	masculine
gens name	Roman name of a group of families united by common name and ancestry.

patronymic name formed from father's name, usually containing the idea of "son of" or "descended from."

pet form familiar, affectionate form of the original name.

surname family or last name, frequently used as first name for boys, occasionally for girls.

terminal name ending used as dim. or pet form or independent name.

NAMES IN SMALL CAPS are names or variants of names that are explained or entered in their proper alphabetical place in the sections "Names for Boys," "Names for Girls," and "A Galaxy of the Unusual."

NAMES FOR BOYS

A Name

*A name is required. To whom are we indebted
and who to us? A name. A name. But what
does a name mean? Derivation uncertain, always uncertain. Someone fathered the last
name and mothered the middle and christened
the first. I am proud of the name I was given
—given to give a son or a book or a star and
at last to a cross or a stone. A name. A name
is required. No number describes me as well.
I can fill out a name, give it muscles and heart,
temper, humor, specifics. I can give it a face,
unique mind-prints as whorled as my singular
fingers. It compasses me and I it. I shall know
when they call me. A name is required.*

THOMAS JOHN CARLISLE
(New York *Herald Tribune*, March 23, 1962)

Names for Boys

Some talk of ALEXANDER, *and some of Hercules;*
Of Hector and Lysander, and such great names
as these.

OLD BALLAD, *The British Grenadiers*

Aaron Hebrew, possibly Egyptian, "light" or "mountain." ARON. Biblical: First high priest of Israel, brother of Moses. The Arabic equivalent of *Aaron* is found in *Haroun-al-Raschid*, the name of the Caliph of Bagdad in *The Arabian Nights' Entertainments.*

And thou shalt put upon Aaron the holy garments, and anoint him, and sanctify him; that he may minister unto me in the priest's office.

EXODUS, 40:13

Abbot(t) Aramaic, "father." ABBA, ABBE(Y). Related to ABRAHAM, *Abba* was a title of respect in Aramaic, a language group spoken in Palestine and other parts of Asia Minor; Jesus and the Apostles spoke a form of Aramaic.

Abel Hebrew, "breath." Biblical: Second son of Adam and Eve, killed by his brother Cain in the first recorded murder.

And Abel was a keeper of sheep, but Cain was a tiller of the ground.

And the LORD *said unto Cain, Where is Abel thy brother? And he said, I know not: Am I my brother's keeper?*

GENESIS 4:4, 9

Literature: The hero of W. H. Hudson's novel *Green Mansions,* whose full name is Abel Guevez de Argensola but who "wished to be known simply as 'Mr. Abel.'" Journalism: Abel Green, editor of *Variety.*

Abner Hebrew, "of light." AB, AVNER. Biblical: Commander of King Saul's army. Literature: *Uncle Abner, Master of Mysteries* (1911-1918) by Melville Davisson Post, stories of detection written in an almost Biblical style about a wise and patriarchal American in the early days of our country.

. . . and the name of the captain of his host was Abner, the son of Ner, Saul's uncle.

I SAMUEL 14:50

Abraham Hebrew, "father of a multitude." ABE, BRAHAM, BRAM. Biblical: The first Hebrew patriarch, who migrated from Ur in Chaldea and settled in the land of Canaan.

"In Abraham's bosom" refers to Paradise.

In the Civil War song *We Are Coming, Father Abraham,* the reference is, of course, to President Abraham Lincoln.

As for me, behold my covenant is with thee, and thou shalt be a father of many nations. Neither shall thy name any more be called Abram, but thy name shall be Abraham; for a father of many nations have I made thee.

GENESIS, 17:4, 5

Abram Hebrew, "exalted father." AVRAM, AVROM, BRAM. Abram was the original name of Abraham. The middle name of President James A. Garfield was Abram.

Adalbert (ADD' ell bert *or* a DELL' bert) Germanic, "noble-bright." DALBERT, DELBERT. See also ALBERT.

Adam Hebrew, "man" or "red earth."

And the LORD GOD formed man of the dust of the ground.

And out of the ground the LORD GOD formed every beast of the field, and every fowl of the air; and brought them unto Adam to see what he would call them: and whatsoever Adam called every living creature, that was the name thereof.

GENESIS, 2:7, 19

Adam Smith (1723-1790), author of *The Wealth of Nations,* founded the science of political economy. Literature: *Adam Bede,* a novel by George Eliot.

When Eve upon the first of Men The apple press'd with specious cant,
Oh! what a thousand pities then That Adam was not adamant!
THOMAS HOOD, *A Reflection*

Adlai (ADD'lay) Hebrew, "justice of Jehovah." Politics: Adlai E. Stevenson, popular political figure, U. S. ambassador to the UN in the Kennedy Administration.

Adolf (AY' dolf *or* ADD' olf *or* a DOLF'). Germanic, "noble wolf" or "hero." AD, ADOLPH, ADOLPHE, ADOLPHUS, DOLF, DOLPH. This was once a favorite name of German nobility and royalty.

Adrian Latin place name, *(H)adria,* "black earth." ADRIEN, HADRIAN. Fem., ADRIENNE. The Roman emperor Hadrian was born in Adria, now called Atri, the scene of Longfellow's *Bell of Atri.* Nicholas Brakespeare (1100-1159), the only Englishman to become a Pope, took the name Adrian IV. Music: Sir Adrian Boult, conductor.

I know you well, sir, and you know me; your name, I think, is Adrian.

WILLIAM SHAKESPEARE, *Coriolanus*

Alan Celtic, "handsome" or "harmony." ALAIN (AL' in), ALAYNE, ALLAN, ALLEN, ALLEYN, ALLYN. Fem., ALAIN, ALA(Y)NE, ALANA. Literature: Allen-a-Dale (or Alan-a-Dale), the celebrated minstrel of old English legends; character in Scott's *Ivanhoe*.

"What is thy name?" then said
    Robin Hood,
    "Come tell me without any
      fail."
"By the faith of my body," then
    said the young man.
    "My name it is Allen-a-Dale."
      OLD BALLAD, *Robin Hood*
        and Allen-a-Dale

TV: Alan Alda ("M*A*S*H"). Aeronautics: Alan B. Shepard Jr., first American astronaut (May 5, 1961). Theater: Alan Jay Lerner, lyricist and librettist of the Lerner-Loewe team (*My Fair Lady, Camelot,* etc.). Literature: Alan Paton, author of *Cry, the Beloved Country*.

Alastair (AL' a ster *or* AL is TAIR') ALASTER, ALISTER, ALISTIR, ALLISTER. Scottish forms of ALEXANDER. Screen: Alastair Sim. Journalism and TV: Alistair Cooke, host of the Masterpiece Theatre series on P.B.S.

Alban Latin, "white." ALBEN, ALBIN, ALVA. St. Alban (about 300) was the first British martyr. The Latin word *albus,* "white," has given us the words *albino, album,* and *albumen,* as well as the place names *Albania, Albany, Albion*. Politics: Alben W.

Barkley (1877-1956), who, as Vice President under Truman, popularized the use of the term "Veep."

Albert G e r m a n i c, "noble-bright." AL, ALBRECHT, BERT, BERTIE. Fem., ALBERTA. This name became extremely popular in England after the marriage of Queen Victoria and Prince Albert in 1840.

Dear to thy land and ours, a
    Prince indeed,
Beyond all titles, and a house-
    hold name,
Hereafter, thro' all times, Albert
    the Good.
    ALFRED, LORD TENNYSON,
    Idylls of the King: Dedication

Art: Albrecht Dürer (1471-1528), famous for his paintings, engravings, and woodcuts. The greatest Alberts of our time are the scientist Albert Einstein and the humanitarian Albert Schweitzer. Another Albert who came into prominence is the Zulu chief Albert John Luthuli, winner of the Nobel Prize for Peace in 1961. The French author Albert Camus won the Nobel Prize for Literature in 1957.

Albin See ALBAN.

Aldo Germanic, "rich" or "old" or "wise." ALD(O)US (AWL' dus *or* AL' dus). This name, once popular in Italy and still used there today as the terminal short form of names like *Bonaldo, Rinaldo* (see REYNOLD) and *Edgaldo* (see EDGAR), was Latinized as *Aldus*. The Aldine editions of Greek and Latin authors, beautiful examples of early printing, are named after Aldus Manutius (Aldo Manuzzi), Venetian printer (1450-1515), inventor of *italic* type.

Aldous See ALDO. Literature: Aldous Huxley, brilliant contemporary writer, author of *Brave New World, Point Counterpoint*, etc.

Aldrich Germanic, "wise ruler." ALDRIDGE. See also ELDRIDGE.

Alexander Greek, either "warding off men" or "protecting men." This name goes back to Homer, for in the *Iliad* Paris is also known as *Alexandros*. AL, ALASTAIR (Gaelic), ALEC, ALEX-(IS), ALICK, ALISANDER, ALISTAIR, ALISTER, SA(U)NDER, SANDY, ALEXANDRE (French), ALESSANDRO (Italian), SANDRO, SASCHA (Russian dim.). Fem., ALEXANDRA, ALEXIS, ALIX.

Like Caesar and Napoleon, Alexander the Great symbolizes the conqueror:

Like Alexander I will reign,
And I will reign alone.
My thoughts shall evermore disdain
A rival on my throne.

JAMES GRAHAM, *Montrose to His Mistress*

In an anonymous poem found in one of the old McGuffey readers, an inquiring child asks: *How big was Alexander, Pa, That people called him great?* Alexander was great in war, but there have been other "big" Alexanders, great in the arts of peace.

Music: Alessandro Scarlatti (1659-1725), considered the founder of modern opera. Art: Sandro Botticelli (1444-1510), famous painter (*The Birth of Venus, Spring*, etc.). Literature: The poet Alexander Pope (1688-1744), noted for his quotable epigrammatic lines, such as:

To err is human, to forgive divine,
and
For fools rush in where angels fear to tread.

Three other literary Alexanders: Pushkin (1799-1837), poet, dramatist, short-story writer; Alexandre Dumas *père* (*The Three Musketeers, The Count of Monte Cristo*) and Alexandre Dumas *fils* (*La Dame aux Camélias*, or *Camille*). Science: Alexander Graham Bell (1847-1922), inventor of the telephone; Sir Alexander Fleming (1881-1955), sharer of a Nobel Prize (1955) for the discovery of penicillin. Screen and Stage: Sir Alec Guinness, winner of an Oscar in 1957 (*The Bridge on the River Kwai*).

With the publication of the papers of Alexander Hamilton (begun by the Columbia University Press in 1961), the name

Alexander is receiving fresh prominence.

Alfonso Germanic, "noble-ready" or "eager for battle." AL, ALONSO, ALONZO, ALPHONSE, ALPHONSO. This name was popularized by the early kings of Spain after its introduction by the invading Visigoths in the fifth century.

Alfred Anglo-Saxon, "elf-counsel." ALF, AVERY, FRED, FREDDIE, FREDDY. Fem., ALFREDA. Alfred the Great (849-901) was the wise and scholarly king who united the English people and drove back the Danish invaders.

Truth-teller was our England's Alfred named.
ALFRED, LORD TENNYSON, *Ode on the Death of the Duke of Wellington*

Literature: Alfred Edward Housman, generally referred to as A. E. Housman, author of *A Shropshire Lad* (1896). Science and Industry: Alfred Bernhard Nobel (1833-1896), the Swedish inventor of dynamite, who left the funds for the famous prizes. Politics: "Al" (Alfred Emanuel) Smith (1873-1944). Stage: Alfred Drake, star of the musicals *Oklahoma!, Kiss Me, Kate,* etc.; the incomporable Alfred Lunt.

Alger Anglo-Saxon, "elf-spear." ALGAR, ELGAR. See also ALGERNON.

Algernon (AL' jer non) Old French, "with whiskers." AL, ALGY, ALGER. This name was originally a nickname. Most of the Norman invaders of England were clean-shaven but not William de Percy, who was called *aux gernons*, "bewhiskered." Like PERCY and REGINALD, the name *Algernon* came to us from warriors.

Literature: Algernon C. Swinburne (1837-1909), poet renowned for the musical effects of his verses; Algernon Blackwood (1869-1951), an early writer of stories of the supernatural (*The Man Whom the Trees Loved*).

Alistair See ALASTAIR.

Allan See ALAN. ALLEN.

Alonso See ALFONSO. ALONZO, LON. Football: Alonzo Stagg, famous coach.

They gazed on each other with tender delight,
Alonzo the Brave was the name of the knight—
The maiden's was the Fair Imogene [Imogine].

MATTHEW G. LEWIS, *Alonzo the Brave*

Alphonse French form; see ALFONSO. Literature: Alphonse Daudet (1840-1897), beloved French writer, author of *Tartarin de Tarascon, Lettres de Mon Moulin,* and other charming stories of life in Paris and *La Belle Provence*.

Alton (AWL' *ton*) Place name, "old or high town."

Alva(h) See ALBAN.

Alvin Germanic, "noble friend" or "loved by all." AL, ALVAN, ALWIN, ALWYN. See also ELWIN. Fem., ALVINA. Alvin C. York is the famous Sergeant York, the American hero of World War I whose exploits have been celebrated in books and movies.

Ambrose Greek, "immortal." This name comes from the same Greek root from which we get *ambrosia*, the food of the gods that brought immortality. St. Ambrose, bishop of Milan in the fourth century, is noted for his learning and writings. Appropriately enough, on December 7, 1961, Pope John XXIII designated Saint Ambrose the patron saint of educational radio and television, because St. Ambrose "knew well the art of moving the spirit and conscience of men by his word and pen."

*Never, surely, was holier man
Than Ambrose, since the world
  began.*

　　JAMES RUSSELL LOWELL,
　　　　　　　　Ambrose

Literature: Ambrose Bierce (1842-1914), American journalist and short-story writer (*An Occurrence at Owl Creek Bridge*).

Amory (AYM' o ree) Germanic, "work-ruler" or "ever rich." AMERY, EMERY, EMMERY. Also fem. name. The old Germanic names *Amalric, Amelric,* and *Emmerich* were Latinized into *Almericus* and *Americus;* so this name is perpetuated in *America,* named after the Italian navigator Americus (Amerigo) Vespucci (1451-1512).

Literature: Amory Blaine, hero of F. Scott Fitzgerald's *This Side of Paradise*.

Amos (AY' mos) Hebrew, "burden" or "bearer of a burden. Biblical: A prophet.

Then answered Amos, and said to Amaziah, I was no prophet, neither was I a prophet's son; but I was an herdsman, and a gatherer of sycamore fruits.

And the LORD *took me as I followed the flock, and the* LORD *said unto me, Go, Prophesy unto my people Israel.*

　　　　　　　　AMOS 7:14, 15

Anatol(e) Greek, "of the East." Literature: Anatole France (1844-1924), winner of a Nobel Prize in 1921; *Anatol* ("The Affairs of Anatol"), a play (1893) by Arthur Schnitzler, from which movies and a musical have been made.

Andrew Greek, "manly." ANDRÉ, ANDRES, ANDREA(S), ANDERS, ANDY. Fem., ANDREA. St. Andrew the Apostle is the patron saint of Scotland and of Russia. Two of our Presidents, Jackson and Johnson, have had this first name. Literature: André Maurois author of romanticized biographies; André Malraux, author of *Man's Fate* (*La Condition Humaine*); André Gide, winner of the Nobel Prize in 1947. Music: Andres Segovia, virtuoso of the guitar. Photography: Andreas Feininger, one of the outstanding photographers and writers on the medium. Art: Andrea del Sarto (1486-1531), "The Faultless Painter" of Florence, about whom Robert Browning wrote a poem which contains the oft-quoted lines:

Ah, but a man's reach should exceed his grasp.
Or what's a Heaven for?

Aneurin (a NYE' rin) Welsh, "very golden"; or Latin, "honorable," from the Roman name *Honorius*. ANEIRIN, NYE. Aneurin was an early Welsh bard who composed a song of victory called *Gododin:*

Prince of bards was old Aneurin:
He the grand Gododin *sang;*
All his numbers threw such fire in,
Struck his harp so wild a twang.
GEORGE MEREDITH, *Aneurin's Harp*

Politics: Aneurin Bevan (1897-1961), British labo(u)r leader.

Angel(l) Greek, "messenger:" ANGE. Fem., ANGELA, ANGELINA. Literature: Angel Clare, hero of Thomas Hardy's novel *Tess of the D'Urbervilles.*

Angus Gaelic, "unique choice." A popular Scottish name, often used to translate the name of the Trojan hero Aeneas. Angus Óg is a god or spirit of laughter and love, wisdom and understanding in Irish folklore; he is a prominent character in *The Crock of Gold* by James Stephens. Angus Wilson is an important modern British author (*Anglo-Saxon Attitudes*).

Angus, . . .
I well may say of you,
That never king did subject hold,
In speech more free, in war more bold,
More tender and more true.
SIR WALTER SCOTT, *Marmion*

Anselm Germanic, "divine helmet." ANSELMA, SELMA. Originally a Lombard name, Anselm was made known to the English by St. Anselm (1033-1109), a Lombard, Archbishop of Canterbury.

Anson Germanic, "son of John." HANSON.

Ant(h)ony Latin, name of a *gens*. The Latin forebear, *Antonius,* had no *h*, which is a much later addition. ANTON, ANTOINE, ANTONE, TONY. Fem., ANTONIA, ANTOINETTE, TONI. St.

Anthony is the patron saint of Italy. Marcus Antonius, better known as Marc, or Mark, Antony, was the friend of Caesar, who delivered the "Friends, Romans, countrymen" speech in Shakespeare's *Julius Caesar*. He appears also in Shakespeare's *Antony and Cleopatra* as the foe of "young Octavius" Caesar (Octavian) and as the immortal lover of Cleopatra.

And when my own Mark Antony
Against young Caesar strove,
And Rome's whole world was set in arms,
The cause was,—all for love.
ROBERT SOUTHEY,
All for Love

Art: *The Temptation of St. Anthony* by Hieronymus (Jerome) Bosch. Music: Anton Dvořák, composer of a beautiful cello concerto and *The New World Symphony*. Literature: Anton Chekhov, short-story writer, and one of the world's great dramatists, author of *The Cherry Orchard, Three Sisters*, etc.; Anthony Trollope (1815-1882), novelist of English life in the days of Queen Victoria (*Barchester Towers*, etc.); Anthony Powell, modern English novelist compared with Proust (*A Dance to the Music of Our Time*). Stage and Screen: Anthony Quinn.

Archer Latin via Germanic, "bowman." Also dim. form; see ARCHIBALD.

Archibald Germanic, "nobly or genuinely bold." ARCH, ARCHIE, ARCH(I)BOLD.

I am called "Archibald the All-Right," for I am infallible.
WILLIAM S. GILBERT, *Patience*

Literature: Archibald MacLeish, lecturer, dramatist, poet, winner of three Pulitzer prizes (last one in 1959, for the play *J. B.*).

Ariel (AIR' i el) Hebrew, "lion-(ess) of God." Biblical: A chief who followed Ezra; also a name applied to Jerusalem by Isaiah, with the probable meaning of "God's altar." *Ariel* is used not only as a masc. name, especially among the Mormons, but also as a fem. name. In medieval folklore Ariel was a light and graceful spirit of the air. Because of the similarity of sound *Ariel* is often associated with *aerial*. Hence, the name given by Shakespeare in *The Tempest* to the airy sprite who is Prospero's messenger of all work is most appropriate.

Literature: *Ariel* (1925), a biography of Shelley by André Maurois. Shelley often referred to himself as Ariel:

Your guardian spirit, Ariel, who,
From life to life, must still pursue
Your happiness;—for thus alone
Can Ariel ever find his own.
PERCY BYSSHE SHELLEY,
With a Guitar, to Jane

Armand (ARM' AND *or* ARE MON') Germanic via French, variant form; see HERMAN. AR-MANT.

Armin Variant form; see HER-MAN.

Arnold Germanic, "eagle-power," "strong as an eagle." ARN(I)E. Literature: Arnold Bennett, author of *The Old Wives' Tale* (1908), a classic novel of this century. History: Arnold von Winkelried, national hero of Switzerland, whose heroic action at the battle of Sempach (1386) beat the Austrians.

Behold him—Arnold Winkelried!
There sounds not to the trump of fame
The echo of a nobler name.
　　JAMES MONTGOMERY, *The Patriot's Password* ("Make Way for Liberty.")

Artemas Greek, "safe and sound"; associated by some authorities with Artemis, or Diana, to mean "gift of Artemis." ARTE-MUS. Fem., ARTEMIA, ARTEMISIA. Biblical: Artemas appears in the New Testament (TITUS 3:12). Literature: Artemus Ward, pen name of the humorist Charles Farrar Browne (1834-1867), whose shrewd observations and folk humor made him the Will Rogers of his day.

Arthur Celtic, "noble"; Welsh, "bear-hero"; Norse, "Thor's eagle." ARTHER, ART, ARTY, ATRIE, ARTUR. Italian, ARTURO. Literature and Legend: The ancient British king who led the nights of the Round Table:

Arthur, my lord, Arthur the faultless king.
That passionate perfection, my good Lord . . .
　　ALFRED, LORD TENNYSON, The *Idylls of the King: Guinevere*

Literature: *Morte d'Arthur* by Sir Thomas Malory (1394-1471); *The Idylls of the King* by Alfred, Lord Tennyson; *A Connecticut Yankee in King Arthur's Court* by Mark Twain; Sir Arthur Conan Doyle (1859-1930), who gave life to Sherlock Holmes and Brigadier Gerard and who wrote the stirring historical novel *The White Company*. Theater: Arthur Miller, author of *Death of a Salesman* (Pulitzer Prize, 1948). Music: Arturo Toscanini (1867-1957), the conductor who made musical history; Artur Rubinstein, world-renowned pianist; Sir Arthur Sullivan, words by Gilbert. Journalism: Arthur Daley, sports columnist of distinction and urbanity (*Times at Bat, Sports of* The Times).

Arvin Germanic, "people's friend."

Asa (AY' sa) Hebrew, "physician."

Asher Hebrew, "fortunate."

Ashley Place name, "ash-tree meadow."

Aubrey (AW' bree) Germanic via French, "elf rule." AVERY. *Oberon,* (variant, AUBERON, name of the "elf king" in Shakespeare's *Midsummer Night's Dream,* is *Aubrey* in a changed dim. form.) Art: Aubrey Beardsley, artist of the English Esthetic Movement of the 1890's. Literature: Aubrey Menen, modern author (*The Prevalence of Witches, Rome for Ourselves,* etc.).

August, Augustus (aw GUS' tus) Latin, "majestic, worthy of reverence." AUGIE, AUGUSTE (French), GUS. Fem., AUGUSTA. Gaius Julius Caesar Octavianus, grand-nephew of Julius Caesar, was the first Roman emperor. From the Senate he received the title Augustus, which formerly had religious significance. Later Roman emperors, with one exception, were also called *Augustus,* a title "hedged with majesty." The name of the eighth month is a constant reminder of the first Augustus:

The Emperor Octavian, called the August,
  I being his favorite, bestowed his name
Upon me, and I hold it still in trust,
  In memory of him and of his name.
HENRY WADSWORTH LONGFELLOW, *The Poet's Calendar*

Art: The sculptors (François) Auguste Rodin (1840-1917) and Augustus Saint-Gaudens (1848-1907); the painters (Pierre) Auguste Renoir (1841-1919) and Augustus John (1878-1961).

Augustine (AW' gus teen *or* aw GUS' tin) See AUGUST. AUGUSTIN (aw GUS' tin). AUSTIN. Fem., AUGUSTINA. St. Augustine (354-430), one of the four great Fathers of the Church, author of *The Confessions* and of *The City of God,* has exercised a tremendous influence on Christian philosophy through his voluminous writings.

Saint Augustine! Well hast thou said,
That of our vices we can frame
A ladder if we will but tread
Beneath our feet each deed of shame.
HENRY WADSWORTH
LONGFELLOW,
The Ladder of St. Augustine

Augustus See AUGUST.
Augustus was a chubby lad:
Fat ruddy cheeks Augustus had:
And everybody saw with joy
The plump and hearty healthy boy.
HEINRICH HOFFMAN, *Augustus*

Austin. Short form; see AUGUSTINE. Literature: (Henry) Austine Dobson (1840-1921), author of biographies, sketches, and light verse.

Averil(l) (AY' ve rill) Anglo-Saxon, "boar-favor." AVERELL.

Avery (AY've ree) See ALFRED and AUBREY.

Avram (AY' vrim *or* AVV' rim) See ABRAM. AVRIM, AVROM.

Aylmer (AIL' mer) Germanic, "noble fame." AYMER, AYLMAR. See also ELMER. Literature: Aylmer Maude, noted translator of Russia authors.

B

Father calls me William, sister calls me Will
Mother calls me Willie, but all the fellers call
me BILL!

EUGENE FIELD, *Jest 'Fore Christmas*

Bainbridge Place name, "fair bridge" or "direct bridge."

Baldwin Germanic, "bold friend."

Bancroft Place name, "pasture between terraces."

Barclay (BARK' lee *or* BARK' lay) Place name, "birch meadow." BERKELEY.

Bard Celtic, "poet." The Scottish variant BAIRD may also be related to "beard(ed)."

Olympian bards who sung
Divine ideas below,
Which always find us young,
And always keep us so.
RALPH WALDO EMERSON,
The Poet

Barnabas, Barnaby Aramaic-Hebrew, "son of prophecy or exhortation" (*bar* = "son of" in Aramaic). Biblical: A close associate of Paul.

A lovable and imaginative lad named Barnaby is the subject of a syndicated comic strip by Crockett Johnson.

This day the sunne is
in his chiefest hight
With Barnaby the bright.
EDMUND SPENSER, *Epithalamion*

Barnard See BERNARD.

Barnet(t) See BERNARD.

Barney See BERNARD.
As I was on the high-road
That leads to Miller's Run,
I met my lover Barney
Riding in the sun.
AMORY HARE, *Wet or Fine*

Barret(t) Germanic, "bear-rule"; or place name, "ancient hill."

Barry Irish "spear"; or Welsh, "son of Harry." Some authorities believe that this name is a place name, *Berri* in France, from which Mme. DuBarry got her name. No matter how *Barry* originated there is little doubt that in modern usage it is often a popular substitute for and diminutive of names like BERNARD, BARNEY, BARUCH.

Bartholomew (bar THOLL' o myou) Aramaic-Hebrew, "son of *Talmai* (abounding in furrows)." BART, BARTLETT(T), BARTLEY. Biblical: One of the Twelve Apostles.

Bartholomew is very sweet
From sandy hair to rosy feet.
NORMAN GALE, *Bartholomew*

66

It was in St. Bartholomew's Hospital, London, whose medical college is familiarly referred to as Bart's, where Holmes and Watson were introduced and where Holmes uttered the deathless words, "You have been in Afghanistan, I perceive." A plaque was set up in 1953 at the supposed site to commemorate this historic meeting on New Year's Day, 1881. The plaque was erected by The Amateur Mendicant Society of Detroit and the Baker Street Irregulars of New York.

Baruch (BARR' ook *or* ba ROOK') Hebrew, "blessed." Philosophy: Baruch Spinoza (1632-1677).

Basil (BAZZ' il *or* BASS' il) Greek, "kingly." See also ROYAL. St. Basil (329-379) was one of the learned men (called "doctors") of the early church. Stage and Screen: Basil Rathbone, noted impersonator of Sherlock Holmes. Literature: Father of Evangeline:

Basil the blacksmith,
Who was a mighty man in the
village,
and honored of all men.
    HENRY WADSWORTH LONG-
    FELLOW, *Evangeline*

Bayard (BYE' erd *or* BAY' erd) French, name of a renowned hero. Pierre du Terrail (1475-1524), better known as the *Chevalier de Bayard,* a formidable warrior for King Francis I and a national hero of France, is the symbol of the peerless knight. He is called *le chevalier sans peur et sans reproche* ("the knight without fear and without reproach").

Oh for a knight like Bayard,
    Without reproach or fear;
My light glove on his casque of
    steel,
    My love-knot on his spear!
    JOHN GREENLEAF WHITTIER,
        The Hero

Benedict Latin *benedictus,* "spoken well of, blessed." BEN, BENSON, BENNET(T), BENEDICK (old variant), found in Shakespeare). Fem., BENEDICTA, BENETTA, BENITA. St. Benedict established the Benedictine Order and founded the monastery at Monte Cassino. A *benedict* is a newly married man, especially one who has been a confirmed bachelor but has changed his mind in the manner of one of Shakespeare's heroes:

Here you may see Benedick the
    married man.
    Much Ado About Nothing

Benjamin Hebrew, "son of the right hand." BEN, BENN, BENNO, BENNIE, BENNY, BENJY, BENSON. Biblical: Youngest and pet son of Jacob. One President, Benjamin Harrison, has had this first name. Our great Ben is, of course, Benjamin Franklin. "Rare Ben Johnson" is the epithet of the great poet, contemporary of Shakespeare.

And Marlowe, Webster, Fletcher, Ben,
Whose fire-hearts sowed our furrows when
The world was worthy of such men.
ELIZABETH BARRETT BROWNING,
Lady Geraldine's Courtship

Some other Benjamins, past and present, distinguished in various fields: Rush, noted physician, signer of the Declaration of Independence; Disraeli, British statesman and novelist; Cardozo, a Justice of the U. S. Supreme Court; Ben Hecht, co-author of *The Front Page* and *20th Century;* Benny Goodman of clarinet fame; the British composer, Britten; and Dr. Spock, mother's indispensable helper.

Bennet(t) See BENEDICT.

Benson Originally a surname; see BENEDICT. This name and the previous one are often used in place of BENJAMIN.

Berkeley. See BARCLAY.

Bernard Germanic. "stern bear." BARNARD, BARNET, BARNEY, BERNARR, BERNHARD, BERNIE. Fem., BERNARDA, BERNADETTE, BERNARDINE. St. Bernard of Menthon, patron saint of mountain climbers, founded the hospices of the Great and Little Saint Bernard in the tenth century. Literature: G.B.S., (George) Bernard Shaw. Politics; Bernard Mannes Baruch,

also known as Barney Baruch, businessman noted for his sage reflections, adviser to Presidents Wilson and Roosevelt.

Blithe was Bernard of Ventadorn
As is the spirit of spring
When April quickens everything
From root of reed to tip of trees.
CLINTON SCOLLARD,
Bernard of Ventadorn

Bernarr See BERNARD.

Bert Short form; see ALBERT. BERTRAM, BURTON, BERTIE. Literature: The comical zany, Bertie Wooster of the Pelham Grenville Wodehouse novels of the British upper classes. Stage, Screen, and TV: Comedian Bert Lahr, the "inimitable."

Bert(h)old Germanic, "bright-power." Literature: Bertold Brecht (1898–1956), essayist, poet, satirist, dramatist (*Mother Courage, The Threepenny Opera*, etc.).

Berton See BURTON.

Bertram Germanic, "bright raven" or "illustrious." BERT, BERTIE, BERTRAND. Philosophy, Bertrand Russell, Nobel Prize winner for literature, 1950.
The dark shall be light,
And the wrong made right,
When Bertram's right and Bertram's might
Shall meet on Ellangowan's height.
SIR WALTER SCOTT,
Guy Mannering

Bill See WILLIAM. BILLY. Fem., BILLIE.

Oh, where have you been Billy boy, Billy boy?
Oh, where have you been, charming Billy?

OLD SONG

Literature: *Billy Budd* by Herman Melville. Folklore and Show Business: Buffalo Bill (William Frederick Cody); Billy Rose. Screen: Director and writer Billy Wilder, winner of two Oscars (*The Lost Weekend* in 1945, and *The Apartment* in 1960). Cartoons: Bill (William Henry) Mauldin, one of the leading political cartoonists of today, famed for his cartoons of soldiers of World War II (*Up Front*, etc.).

Blair Gaelic, "field" or "battle."

Bob See ROBERT. BOBBY. English policemen are called Bobbies after Sir Robert Peel, Home Secretary when the London Metropolitan Police Act was passed in 1828.

The finest thing in London is the Bobby;
Benignant information is his hobby.

ARTHUR GUITERMAN,
The Lyric Baedeker: London

Some men are better known by the short or pet form *Bob* than by the more formal name. Robert Burns is often referred to as Bobby Burns. In other fields there are: Bob Fitzsimmons, who was both heavy- and middleweight champion before the turn of this century (real name Robert Prometheus Fitzsimmons); Bobby Jones, a "grand-slam" winner of the British and U. S. Open and Amateur titles in 1930; Bob Feller, amazing speedball pitcher elected to the National Baseball Hall of Fame in 1962; Bob Cousy, wizard of the basketball court; comedians Bob Newhart and Bob Hope.

Boris (BAW′ riss) Russian, "warrior" or "fight." Boris Godunov, czar of Russia in the sixteenth century, is the subject of a powerful opera by Moussorgsky. Literature: Boris Pasternak, winner of the Nobel Prize in 1958. Screen and TV: Boris Karloff.

Boyce French place name, "living near the woods (*bois*)." Literature and Folklore: Boyce House (1897-1961), conductor of column "I Give You Texas," prodigious author of best sellers on Texan folklore.

Bradley Place name, "broad meadow."

Bram Sometimes used as a short form of ABRAM and ABRAHAM, but as a name by itself it is related to Old English *bream*, "fierce" or "famous," *bramah*, or *braham*, "dweller by the broom plants," or to Gaelic *bran*, "dark," hence, "raven." BRAN. See also BRAMWELL, BRANDON, and BRENDAN. From *bran* come the fem. BRANWEN and BRANGWAIN. BRAM is also Dutch for ABRAHAM.

Mythology: Bran the Blessed was a god of enormous size and strength, as well as a poet and skilled harpist.

Literature: *Dracula* (1897), the book by Bram Stoker on which the movie thriller of the same name was based.

Bramwell Place name, "at Bram's well" or "the well where the broom plant grows." See BRAM. BRANWELL. Stage: Bramwell Fletcher. Literature: (Patrick) Branwell, brother of three sisters named Brontë.

Brandon Anglo-Saxon, "sword" or place name, "flaming hill."

Brendan Celtic, "sword." Name of an Irish saint. Literature: The colorful and talented Brendan Behan, author of the play *The Hostage*.

Brian (BREYE' an) Celtic, possibly "strong." BRION, BRYAN, BRYANT. Brian Boru (926-1014), a heroic king of Ireland, defeated the Danish invaders. Stage and Screen: Brian Aherne, Brian Donlevy.

Bret(t) French, "native of Brittany." Literature: Bret (Francis Brett) Harte (1836-1902), poet and short-story writer noted for his stories of the West (*The Luck of Roaring Camp, Outcasts of Poker Flat*, etc.).

Broderick Germanic via Welsh, "son of Roderick," BROD. Screen: Broderick Crawford, winner of 1949 Oscar (*All the King's Men*).

Brooks English place name, Anglo-Saxon, "living near the brook." BROOK, BROOKE. Journalism: Brooks Atkinson, essayist, former dramatic critic of the *New York Times*.

Bruce French place name, *Bruis* or *Bruys*, a castle near Cherbourg, "brushwood thicket." Robert de Bruis, a Norman, was the ancestor of Robert Bruce, the national hero of Scotland.

Avenger of thy country's shame,
Bless'd in thy sceptre and thy sword,
Restorer of her injured fame,
De Bruce, fair Scotland's rightful Lord.

SIR WALTER SCOTT,
The Lord of the Isles

The use of this surname as a first name is increasing in popularity together with the use of SCOTT and STUART. Literature: Bruce Catton, an outstanding modern writer on the Civil War.

Bruno Germanic via Italian, "brown." Fem., BRUNETTA. Music: Conductor Bruno Walter.

Bryan See BRIAN. BRYANT.

Budd Anglo-Saxon, "messenger" or "commander"; Gaelic, "victorious."

Burgess (BUR' jess) Germanic, "townsman." Stage: Burgess Meredith.

Burl This name is known today chiefly because of Burl Ives, singer of folk songs turned actor (winner of an Oscar in 1958 for a supporting role in *The Big Country*). He was christened Burl Icle Ivanhoe Ives. When asked about his unusual first name, he replied that he did not know why it had been given to him, and continued, "Webster's says it's a knot in a stick of wood. That suits me fine." Apparently he agrees with one of the *Anglo-Latin Proverbs* (1639) of John Clarke:

Names and natures do often agree.

Further agreement can be found in the possible origin of BURL from *burly* or from the surname Burrell, "homespun." The form BURLIE is also found. BURL may be a short form of a surname like Burleigh, "town (in a) field."

Burris Anglo-Saxon, "of the town."

Burton English place name, "hill or borough town"; or Germanic "bright." BERT, BERTON, BURT. Hollywood: Burt Lancaster, winner of an Oscar in 1960 (*Elmer Gantry*).

Byron Anglo-Saxon, "bear"; English place name, Byrom; French place name, Biron. Whatever may be the source of this name, it is undoubtedly used as a first name because of the fame of the poet Lord Byron.

Byron Raymond ("Whizzer") White was appointed an Associate Justice of the U. S. Supreme Court in 1962.

C

What CAESAR did, yea, and what CICERO said,
Why grass is green, or why our blood is red,
Are mysteries which none have reached into.

JOHN DONNE, *On the Progress of the Soul*

Caesar Latin, "hairy" or "cut down." Actually, the origin of this name is doubtful; the second has been suggested because Caesar is said to have been delivered at birth by the operation commonly known as a Caesarean section. However, *Caesar* was a Roman family name that existed before Julius Caesar was born. The greatest Roman of them all (not according to Shakespeare) was Gaius (Caius) Julius Caesar, from whose family name come *kaiser* and *czar*, meaning "ruler." French, CÉSAR (say ZAR'); Italian, CESARE (CHAY' za reh).

A wonderful man was this Caesar!
You are a writer, and I am a fighter, but here is a fellow
Who could both write and fight, and in both was equally skilful!
HENRY WADSWORTH LONG-
FELLOW, *The Courtship of Miles Standish*

History: Caesar Rodney; for story see under RODNEY. Music: César Auguste Franck (1822-1890), composer, organist, teacher, who had a great influence on other composers; Cesare Siepi of the Metropolitan Opera.

Caleb (KAY' leb) Hebrew; "impetuous, bold" or "faithful."

Calvin Latin, "bald." CAL. Originally a last name arising from a Roman nickname, *Calvin* became a first name in honor of John Calvin, the Protestant reformer of the sixteenth century. Many American boys born during the presidency (1923-1928) of (John) Calvin Coolidge were named Calvin.

Cameron Scottish clan name from nickname, "wry-nose."

Camillus (ka MILL' us) Latin, "noble youth aiding in religious services." French, CAMILLE. Fem., CAMILLA, CAMILLE. Music: Camille Saint-Saëns (1835-1921), composer of the opera *Samson et Dalila*, etc.

Canute See KNUT.

Car(e)y English place name, Carew, "fort." Also Welsh, "stony island." Screen: Cary Grant.

Carl See CHARLES. KARL. Fem., CARLA. Literature: Carl Sandburg, poet, biographer of Lincoln.

Carl(e)ton Place name, "at Charles' town or homestead."

Carlisle, Carlyle Celtic, "city" and name like *Lewelgild;* also taken to mean "wall of god Lungus." Better known as surname distinguished by the author Thomas Carlyle.

Carlo, Carlos Italian and Spanish forms, respectively, of CHARLES. Literature: *Don Carlos,* tragedy by Schiller. Music: Verdi's opera of the same name based on Schiller's play.

Carrol(l) From Latin form *Carolus;* see CHARLES, CAROL, CARYL., Fem., CAROL(E).

Carson Welsh, "son of Caer (castle)."

Carter Occupational name, Old Norse and Anglo-Saxon, "driver or maker of carts"; or Anglo-Saxon, "wool carder"; Irish, possibly short form of *MacArthur,* "son of Arthur." Literature: Carter Dickson, pseudonym of John Dickson Carr, well-known name in detective-mystery writing.

Caspar See JASPER. CASPER, KASPAR.

Cassius (KASH′ us *or* KASH′ i us *or* KAS i us). Latin, name of a distinguished *gens.* This name is sometimes given today because of the association of Cassius

with Marcus Junius Brutus as a liberator. See under JUNIUS.

> *Cassius from bondage will deliver Cassius:*
> *Therein, ye gods, you make the weak most strong.*
> WILLIAM SHAKESPEARE,
> *Julius Caesar*

Science: Cassius Jackson Keyser (1862-1947), eminent authority on the foundations and philosophy of mathematics (*Mathematics and the Dance of Life.,* etc.). History: Cassius Marcellus Clay (1810-1903), politician, diplomat, famed Abolitionist leader; the modern boxer bearing the identical name was named after him.

Cecil (SEE′ sil *or* SESS′ il) Latin, *Caecilius,* "blind," name of a *gens.* Fem., CECILIA, CECILY. Hollywood: Cecil Blount de Mille, "showman extraordinary," producer and director of super-colossal pictures, especially on Biblical themes. Photography and Stage Design: Cecil Beaton.

Cedric (SEDD′ rik *or* SEED′ rik) From literature; name invented by Sir Walter Scott for the guardian of Rowena in *Ivanhoe. Cedric* may be a variant of *Cerdic,* the name of a Saxon king, as in the novel *The Right Line of Cerdic* (1961) by Alfred Duggan, or of *Cedrych,* a Welsh name meaning "bounty-spectacle." For a time the name was in vogue because of the novel *Little Lord Fauntleroy* (1886) by Frances Hodgson Burnett, in which the boy hero was named Cedric. Stage, Screen, and TV: Sir Cedric Hardwicke.

Chad Dim. of *Chadwick, Chadbourne,* and similar place names referring to a castle; also Celtic, "defender."

Chandler Occupational name, from Latin, "candle"; originally a candle-seller, later a merchant providing wares to ships.

Channing Anglo-Saxon, "king" or "knowing."

Charles Germanic, "man" or "strong." CARL, KARL, CARROLL, CARYL, CHARLOT, CHARLEY, CHARLIE, CHIC(K), CHUCK. Italian, CARLO; Spanish CARLOS. Fem., CHARLOTTE. Emperor Charles the Great, better known as Charlemagne (742–814), made his name popular in France and Germany; later it became a favorite with the kings and princes of the Stuart family. Today it may receive new popularity in England from the name of the first son of Queen Elizabeth II and Prince Philip—Prince Charles Philip Arthur George.

An' Charlie, he's my darling,
  My darling, my darling,
Charlie, he's my darling,
  The young Chevalier!
    ROBERT BURNS,
    Charlie, He's My Darling

Six famous bearers of this name: Lamb, Baudelaire, Dickens, Darwin, Lindbergh, De Gaulle. *Charlot.* (French for Charlie) was the name by which Charles (Charlie) Chaplin was once known throughout the world. Games: Charles Goren, "Mr. Bridge" himself. Science: Charles Proteus Steinmetz (1865–1923), prodigious inventor. Stage and Screen: Charles Boyer; Charles Laughton, winner of an Oscar in 1933 (*The Private Life of Henry VIII*).

Charlton Place name, "from Charles' town." Hollywood: Charlton Heston, winner of an Oscar in 1959 (*Ben Hur*).

Chauncey French place name, village near Amiens; possibly also from French word for "chancellor." CHON, nickname of cartoonist Chauncey A. Day.

Chester English place name, from Latin, "camp." CHET. Chester Alan Arthur was the twenty-first President of the United States. TV: Chet Huntley, co-winner with David Brinkley, of news-analyst award.

Christian Greek, "follower of Christ, the anointed." CHRIS, KRIS. Fem., CHRISTINE, CHRISTINA. Kriss Kringle is another name for Santa Claus, derived from the German word for Christ-child. Literature: Hero of John Bunyan's *Pilgrim's Prog-*

ress; Christian de Neuvillette, lover of Roxane in *Cyrano de Bergerac* by Edmond Rostand. Fashions: Christian Dior, world-famous *couturier*.

Christopher Greek, "bearing the Christ." CHRIS, CHRISTY, KIT. St. Christopher, who is said to have carried the Christ-child across a river, is the patron saint of travelers, especially of motorists.

Some renowned Christophers: Marlowe and Morley in literature; Christy "Bix Six" Matthewson in baseball; Kit Carson, Western trapper and guide; and of course, Columbus.

A. A. Milne wrote about his son Christopher Robin in books popular with children; the name appears in its French form in Romain Rolland's masterpiece *Jean Christophe*. Music: the composer Christoph Willibald Gluck (1714-1787).

Clare See CLARENCE. CLAIR(E). Fem., CLARA, CLAIRE, CLARICE, CLARISSA.

From Chepstow's towers, ere dawn of morn
Was heard afar the bugle-horn;
And forth, in banded pomp and pride,
Stout Clare and fiery Neville ride.

SIR WALTER SCOTT,
The Norman Horse-Shoe

Clarence Latin, "bright, famous." CLARE, CLAIR(E).

Clarence, my boy-friend, hale and strong!
O he is as jolly as he is young.

JAMES W. RILEY,
The Boy-Friend

Clark Latin via Anglo-Saxon, "learned." CLARKE, CLERK. Centuries ago, men of learning in England were usually members of the clerical order or clergy (*clerici*). The word *clerk* (still pronounced "clark" in England) meant a priest or a scholar in those days. Clerics were exempt from punishment by the civil courts ("by benefit of clergy") if they could pass a fixed reading test.

Clerk Saunders and may [maiden] *Margaret*
Walked owre yon garden green;
And deep and heavy was the love
That fell thir twa between.

OLD BALLAD, *Clerk Saunders*

Literature: The Clerk of Oxenford (Oxford) in Chaucer's *Canterbury Tales,* a noble example of a scholar who prefers books to finery, learning to riches. ("Gladly would he learn, and gladly teach"). Screen: The long and illustrious career of Clark Gable, from his early success in *It Happened One Night* (Oscar winner, 1934), to the final *Misfits* in 1960 made millions aware of this name. (Incidentally, it was his middle name, his first being William.)

Claud(e) Latin, *Claudius,* "lame," the name of a *gens.* CLAUDIUS. Fem., CLAUDIA, CLAUDETTE. Literature: Hamlet's uncle; *I, Claudius* and *Claudius the God* by Robert Graves, brilliant novels about the early Roman emperor.

Oh, Caesar, great were thou!
And Claudius was thy name!
EDNA ST. VINCENT MILLAY,
The King's Henchman

Music: (Achille) Claude Debussy (1862-1918), French composer (*Pelléas et Mélisande, L'Après-midi d'un faune,* etc.). Art: Claude Monet (1940-1926), a leading Impressionist painter. Screen and Stage: Claude Dauphin, Claude Rains.

Claudian Latin, "of Claudius." See CLAUDIUS. Literature: Claudius Claudianus (fourth century), usually called Claudian-(us), last of the great classical poets, a Greek who wrote in Latin.

Clayton English place name, "town on clay site."

Clement Latin, "merciful." CLEM. Fem., CLEMENCE, CLEMENTINE. The name of a disciple of St. Paul has been used by a number of Popes. Literature: Clement C. Moore, author of *A Visit from St. Nicholas,* (" 'Twas the night before Christmas"), a favorite since 1822.

Cleon (KLEE' on) Greek, "famous." KLEON. Fem., CLEONA, CLEONE. History: A leader of the Athenian people during the Peloponnesian War. Stage: Cleon Throckmorton, designer.

Cleon the poet (from the sprinkled isles,
Lily on lily, that o'erlace the sea,
And laugh their pride when the light wave lisps "Greece")—
To Protos in his tyranny: much health!
ROBERT BROWNING, *Cleon*

Cletus (KLEE' tus) Greek, "called, summoned." CLETE, CLETIS. Baseball: Cletis Boyer.

Cleveland Place name, "cliff land." Literature: Cleveland Amory (*The Last Resorts, Who Killed Society?*)

Clifford English place name, "crossing at the cliff." CLIFF. Theater: Clifford Odets, playwright (*Waiting for Lefty, Golden Boy,* etc.).

Clifton English place name, "town at the cliff." Radio, TV, and Criticism: Clifton Fadiman.

Clinton Germanic, "hill town." CLINT. Screen: Clint Eastwood ("Make my day!").

Clive Anglo-Saxon, "cliff." Originally a last name, *Clive* became popular as a first name because of the fame of Robert Clive, British conqueror of India.

Clyde Scottish place name, Clyde River; Celtic, "heard from far away."

The roaring that was in Clyde's water
Wad flayed [frightened] five hundred men.
OLD BALLAD, *Clyde Water*

Animal Training: Clyde Beatty, whose motto is "Don't be afraid to live."

Cole Dim. of COLEMAN and COLIN; also from Welsh *coel*, trust." "Old King Cole" refers to an early Welsh ruler. Theater: Cole Porter, composer and lyricist (*Night and Day, Begin the Béguine, Kiss, Me, Kate*, etc.).

Col(e)man Occupational name, "charcoal vendor"; or derived from *Columba*, "dove." See COLE, MALCOLM, and COLIN.

Colin (KOLL′ in *or* KOE′ lin) French dim. form; see NICHOLAS; or Latin via Scottish, from *Columba*, "dove"; see MALCOLM. COLE, COLVIN, CULLEN, CULVER. Fem., COLETTE. *Colin Clout* was the name assumed by the poet Edmund Spenser in *The Shepherd's Calendar* (1579) and in *Colin Clout's Come Home Again* (1595). *Colin* has been a favorite name for shepherds in English poetry. It received new fame in World War II because of the heroism of the American flyer Colin Kelly.

And I to thee will be as kind,
As Colin was to Rosalind,
Of courtesy the flower.
MICHAEL DRAYTON,
The Ballad of Dowsabel

Conrad Germanic, "able in counsel." CON, CONNIE, CONNY, KONRAD, KURT. Literature: *Conrad in Quest of His Youth* (1903), a charming novel by Leonard Merrick; Conrad Aiken, winner of the Pulitzer Poetry Prize in 1930, author also of the famous short story *Mr. Arcularis*.

Constantine Latin, "firm." CON, CONNIE, KONSTANTIN. Fem., CONSTANCE. Constantine the Great was the first Christian emperor of the Roman world (306–337).

Conway Welsh place name, "head river." Screen and Stage: Conway Tearle, former matinee idol. Literature: "Glory" Conway, the hero of James Hilton's *Lost Horizon*, the novel which gave us the term *Shangri-La* to denote a land of eternal youth.

Cor(e)y Scottish place name, "ravine, mountain glen."

Cormac Irish, "charioteer," or translation of CHARLES.

Cornelius (kor NEEL′ yus) Latin, possibly "pertaining to a horn or to the cornel tree," the name of a *gens*. CONNIE, CONNY, CORNEL, CORNELL, NEEL, NEELY.

Fem., CORNELIA. Among t h e members of the distinguished Roman Cornelian *gens* were Cornelia, mother of the Gracchi, and Publius Cornelius Scipio Africanus, conqueror of Hannibal (202 B.C.). In modern times the best known bearer of this name was Cornelius McGillicuddy, affectionately known as Connie Mack, manager of the Philadelphia Athletics for more than fifty years until his retirement in 1950. Screen: Cornel Wilde.

Corydon (KOR′ i don) Greek, "lark," a name first used in pastoral poetry by the Greek poet Theocritus and by the Roman Vergil, later by English poets to denote a young shepherd or swain. CORIDON.

PHYLLIDA: *I will gather flowers, my Corydon,*
  To set in thy cap.
CORYDON: *I will gather pears, my lovely one,*
  To put in thy lap.
ANON., *Phyllida's Love-Call*

This name has come back into use—Dr. Corydon N. Wassell was an outstanding hero of the Pacific fighting in World War II.

Cosmo (KOZZ′ moe) Greek via Italian, "world" or "orderly arrangement." COSIMO (KOZZ′ i moe). Fem., COSIMA.

Courtney (KORT′ nee) French place name; legendary meaning, "short nose." COURT, COURTENAY.

Craig Celtic, "stony hill." Literature: Craig Kennedy, first scientific detective, created by Arthur B. Reeve (1880-1936).

Crosby Place name, "near the cross or crossroad."

Curt Short form of CURTIS or variant spelling of KURT.

Curtis Old French, "courteous, courtier." CURT, CURTICE.

Cuthbert Anglo-Saxon, "famous-bright."

Cyril (SIRR′il) Greek, "lord." Fem., CYRILLA. St. Cyril, apostle to the Slavs in the ninth century, invented the Cyrillic alphabet, based on Greek and now used in Russia and parts of the Balkans.
  Stage: The versatile Cyril Ritchard, who has not only acted in the theater but has directed and appeared in opera (*La Périchole*).

Cyrus (SYE′ rus) Persian via Greek, "throne" or "sun." CY. Fem., CYRA.

O Man! whosoever thou art, and whencesoever thou comest, for come I know thou wilt, I am Cyrus, founder of the Persian empire.
  PLUTARCH, *Life of Alexander*

Cyrus W. Field, considered a visionary in his time, promoted the laying of the first trans-Atlantic cable (1854-1866).

But Cyrus was a valiant man,
  A fellow of decision;
And heeded not their mocking words,
  Their laughter and derision.
                    JOHN G. SAXE,
          How Cyrus Laid the Cable

Baseball: The immortal "Cy" (Denton T.) Young, a pitcher of the early days of base-ball, who holds the record for lifetime number of victories—511. In his honor the Cy Young Award is given to "The Major League Pitcher of the Year." Inventions: Cyrus Hall McCormick (1809-1884), inventor of the reaper.

D

The ballad-singers and the Troubadours,
  The street-musicians of the heavenly city,
The birds, who make sweet music for us all
In our dark hours, as DAVID did for Saul.

HENRY WADSWORTH LONGFELLOW,
  The Birds of Killingworth

Dalbert Short form; see ADAL-
BERT.

Dale Germanic, "valley." Fem.,
DALE. *Thal*, the original form of
this name, appears in the last
names Lilienthal, Rosenthal, and
Thaler. The word *dollar*, originally *thaler*, comes from the
name given to coins first minted
(1519) in Joachims*thal*, St.
Joachim's Valley in Bohemia.

Dallas Celtic, "wise"; originally a Scottish place name and
later a surname. "Few Americans can even identify George
Mifflin Dallas," writes George
R. Stewart, but his name is preserved in everyday speech because, although "an unremem-
bered vice-president [under
Polk], he is honored by a larger
city than is any other president
except Washington" (from
Names on the Land).

Dalton English place name,
"valley town." See DALE. Hollywood: Dalton Trumbo, novelist (*Johnny Got His Gun*) and
award-winning scenario writer
(*Thirty Seconds over Tokyo*,
etc.).

Damon (DAY' m'n), Greek,
probably "tamer," or subduer."
The friendship and devotion of
Damon and Pythias of Syracuse
in Sicily (fourth century B.C.) is
proverbial. Because a shepherd
in one of Vergil's pastoral poems
is called Damon, the name was
used by later poets to denote a
swain, a young lover (like CORY-
DON and STREPHON):

My Damon was the first to wake
  The gentle flame that cannot
  die;
My Damon is the last to take
  The faithful bosom's softest
  sigh.

  GEORGE CRABBE, *Meeting*
Literature: (Alfred) Damon
Runyon (1884-1946), chronicler
of Broadway, whose stories of
"Guys and Dolls" gave a phrase
to the language and material for
a successful musical and movie.

Dan Hebrew, "judge." Sometimes used as short form of
DANIEL. Biblical: Son of Jacob;
name of one of the twelve tribes
of Israel. The expression *from
Dan to Beersheba* means "from
one end to the other," since Dan
and Beersheba were the northern

and southern limits of ancient Palestine.

> *Dan shall judge his people, as one of the tribes of Israel.*
> GENESIS, 49:16

Dana (DAY′ na) Scandinavian, "a Dane"; or Celtic mythology, "mother of all the gods." DANE. Fem., DANA. Stage and Screen: Dane Clark, Dana Andrews.

Daniel Hebrew, "God is my judge." DAN, DANNIE, DANNY. Fem., DANIEL(L)E. Daniel was the prophet who interpreted Nebuchadnezzar's dreams and the writing on the wall at Belshazzar's feast, and who was delivered from the lions' den into which he was thrown for refusing to obey a decree of King Darius of Persia. "A Daniel come to judgment" (from Shakespeare's *Merchant of Venice*) means a wise pleader in court.

> *Didn′ my Lord delive(r) Daniel,*
> *delive(r) delive(r) Daniel?*
> *He deliver'd Daniel from de lion's den,*
> *Jonah from de belly ob de whale,*
> *And de Hebrew chillun from de fiery furnace,*
> *And why not every man?*
> SPIRITUAL

Literature: Daniel Defoe (1659-1731), author of *Robinson Crusoe*. History: Daniel Boone (1734-1820), the Kentucky pioneer and backwoodsman whose exploits have become part of American folklore; Daniel Webster (1782-1852), politician and magnificent orator ("Liberty and Union, now and forever, one and inseparable"), whose eloquence is commemorated in *The Devil and Daniel Webster* by Stephen Vincent Benét. Stage, Screen, and TV: The inimitable Danny Kaye.

Dante (DAN′ tee *or* DAHN′ tay, Italian) Italian, short form of *Durante*, "lasting." Fem., DANTIA. Literature: Dante Alighieri (1265-1321), one of the great poets of the world (*Divina Commedia*, etc.). See also under BEATRICE. In modern times the name was borne by Dante Gabriel Rossetti (1828-1882), Pre-Raphaelite painter (*Dante Drawing the Angel, Dante's Dream*, etc.) and poet (*The Blessed Damozel, Dante and His Circle, Ballads and Sonnets*, etc.).

> *King that hast reigned six hundred years and grown*
> *In power, and ever growest, since thine own*
> *Fair Florence honoring thy nativity . . .*
> *Hath sought the tribute of a verse from me,*
> *I, wearing but the garland of a day,*
> *Cast at thy feet one flower that fades away.*
> ALFRED, LORD TENNYSON,
> *To Dante*

(Written in 1865 at the request of the Florentines for the festival honoring the six-hundredth anniversary of the birth of Dante)

Darius (da RYE' us) Persian, "wealthy." DARIO. Fem., DARIA. Name of a number of ancient Persian rulers, one of whom invaded Greece and was defeated at Marathon (490 B.C.).

In *Darius Green and His Flying Machine* by J. T. Trowbridge, an early poem on aviation, Darius Green asks this famous question:

The Birds can fly, an' why can't I?

Music: Darius Milhaud, modern French composer.

Darryl, Darrell French place name, *D'Orrell;* English place name, "region of wild animals." Sometimes also connected with "dear" and "darling." Hollywood: Darryl F. Zanuck, producer and director.

David Hebrew, "beloved." DAVE, DAVIS, DEWEY. Fem., DAVIDA, VIDA. Biblical: The "sweet psalmist of Israel," second King of Israel, who as a boy killed the giant Goliath with a slingshot.

There David stands with harp in hand
As Master of the Quire:
Ten thousand times that man were blessed
That might his music hear.
ANON.,
Jerusalem, My Happy Home

Literature: *David Copperfield* by Charles Dickens; *David Harum* (1898), a novel of humorous folk philosophy by E. N. Westcott; D. H. (David Herbert) Lawrence, author of *Lady Chatterley's Lover.* History: Admiral David Glasgow Farragut of Mobile Bay fame in the Civil War, a member of the Hall of Fame; David Ben-Gurion, Israeli statesman.

Screen: David Lewelyn Wark Griffith (1875-1948), one of the pioneer producers and directors, still considered one of the greatest (*The Birth of a Nation, Intolerance,* etc.); David Niven, Oscar winner in 1958 (*Separate Tables*). Theater: David Garrick (1717-1779), celebrated Shakespearean actor associated with the Drury Lane Theatre, London, The almost legendary David Belasco (1854-1931), producer, director, dramatist (*The Girl of the Golden West, Madam Butterfly,* etc.).

Davy Pet form; see DAVID. DAVEY. This pet name is known to millions because of Davy Crockett, one of the heroes of the Alamo.

Dean Anglo-Saxon, "valley"; Latin, "leader of ten." DEANE. *Den* or *Dene* appears in some place names that are now last names, like Ashen*dene,* Cam*den,* and Hamp*den.* DEAN is also related to the Latin word *decanus,* meaning at first "a leader of ten" and later "an officer of the church." DEAN is often used to Americanize names like *Dino* and CONSTANTINE. Fem., DEAN-(I)E.

Delbert Short form; see ADALBERT and EDELBERT. DEL. Movies: Delbert Mann, director, Oscar winner in 1955 (*Marty*).

Delmar Place name; "near a pool." DEL, DELMER.

Delmore Place name, "at a marsh." Literature: Delmore Schwartz, poet.

Demetrius (de MEET' ree us) Greek "of Demeter the earth mother." DMITRI. Fem., DEMETRIA, DEMETRIS. Biblical: Silversmith of Ephesus (ACTS 19:24-41). Music: Composer Dmitri Shostakovich.

Den(n)is Greek and Latin via French, *Dionysius*, "of Dionysos (or Dionysus)," god of vegetation and wine. Actually, the use of the name DENNIS is connected with an Athenian converted by Paul (ACTS 17:34) and several saints named Dionysius. St. Denis, or Denys, is the patron saint of France. DENNY, DENYS, DION, SIDNEY. Fem., DENISE. Tennyson is one of several last names derived from DENNIS.

Dennis was hearty when Dennis was young,
High was the step in the jig that he sprung.

                    MOIRA O'NEILL,
                    The Grand Match

Derek (DERR' ick) Stage and Screen: Derek Jacobi (*I, Claudius; Richard II*).

Dermot English form of Irish *Diarmaidh*, "a free man," a name which is often replaced by JEREMIAH in Ireland. DIARM(A)ID.

Desmond Irish place name, "from South Munster." Literature: Desmond Young, adventurer, journalist, biographer (*Rommel the Desert Fox, All the Best Years*).

Dewey Welsh variant of pet form; see DAVID.

DeWitt, Dewitt (de WITT') Dutch, "white." Renowned family name used as a first name. Under Governor DeWitt Clinton of New York the Erie Canal was opened in 1825.

Dexter Latin, "on the right, fortunate."

Dick See RICHARD. This pet-name form of RICHARD is forever associated with the story of Dick Whittington, the orphan boy who become Lord Mayor of London,

Beneath this stone lies Whittington,
Sir Richard rightly named,
Who three times Lord Mayor served in London,
In which he ne'er was blamed.

                    ANON., *Epitaph*

Diego Spanish form; see JAMES. Art: Diego Rivera (1886-1957), Mexican painter, famous for murals.

Dion See DENNIS. Theater: Dion Boucicault, originally Dionysius Lardner Boursiquot (1820-1890), actor and playwright of melodramas (*The Octoroon*, etc.).

Dir(c)k Variant forms; see DEREK. Screen: Actor Dirk Bogarde. Science: Dirk J. Struik, mathematician.

I sprang to the stirrup,
and Joris, and he;
I galloped, Dirck galloped,
we galloped all three.
ROBERT BROWNING,
How They Brought the Good
News from Ghent to Aix

Dolph See ADOLPH and RUDOLPH. DOLF.

Dominic (DOMM' in ik) Latin, "belonging to the Lord." DOM, DOMINICK. Fem., DOMINICA, DOMINIQUE. The Italian, French, and Spanish words for *Sunday* come from *dies dominicus*, "the Lord's day." At first the name *Dominic* may have been given to boys born on a Sunday.

Donald Gaelic, "world ruler." DON, DONNY, DONAL. Fem., DONALDA. The MacDonald (son of DONALD) clan is one of the most ancient of all Scottish clans; in Ireland the name *O'Donnell*, meaning the same as *MacDonald*, dates back 1,000 years.

Donald Caird's come again!
Donald Caird's come again!
Tell the news in brugh [borough]
and glen,
Donald Caird's come again!
SIR WALTER SCOTT,
Donald Caird

Literature: Don Marquis, whose full name was Donald Robert Perry Marquis (1878-1937), conductor of the famous column *The Sun Dial*, author of *archy and mehitabel*, poet, humorist, dramatist (*The Old Soak*.)

Dorian (DAW' ri an) English adjective and noun from Greek *Dorios*, Latin *Dorius*, "an inhabitant of, or pertaining to, the region called *Doris* or *Doria*." The Spartans belonged to the division of the Greeks known as the Dorians. Fem., DORIA. See also DORIS (f). The masc. name became well known through Oscar Wilde's famous novel *The Picture of Dorian Gray* (1891).

Douglas(s) Scottish, "dark water." DOUG. The ancestors of the Scottish Douglas clan settled near a river noted for its dark waters; the river, town, estate, and family were all named after the color of the water. The Douglas name is mighty in Scottish history, legends, songs, and poetry. Screen: Douglas Fairbanks, Sr. and Jr. Army: General Douglas MacArthur.

> O Douglas, O Douglas!
> Tendir and trewe.
> RICHARD HOLLAND,
> The Howlat (1450)

Drew Germanic via French, "trusty."

Duane Place name, "on the downs"; Celtic, "song." DWAYNE.

Duke Latin, "leader." Music: Duke Ellington, bandleader.

Duncan Celtic, "brown warrior." Duncan Phyfe is a household name applied to a type of furniture because of the work of a Scottish-born designer of furniture who set up shop in New York about 1783. Literature: The King of Scotland in Shakespeare's *Macbeth*.

> Duncan was a lad o'grace,
> Ha, ho, the wooing o't!
> ROBERT BURNS, Duncan Gray

Dunstan Place name, "stone hill" or "brown stone."

Dustin G e r m a n i c , "brave fighter." Screen: Dustin Hoffman, Oscar 1979 (*Kramer vs. Kramer*).

Dwight Old English, *thwaite*, "a cutting or clearing." This word element became a surname by itself or was attached to another name or word to form a place name or surname such as *Braithwaite*. Another possibility is that it is derived from the dim. *Diot*, which comes from the same Latin Word, *Dionysius*, fem., *Dionysia*, from which DENNIS is derived. As a surname DWIGHT was given prominence by two former presidents of Yale University, Timothy B. Dwight (from 1795 to 1817) and Timothy Dwight (from 1886 to 1899). More recently one thinks, of course, of this name in connection with our former President, General Dwight David Eisenhower.

Dylan (DILL' in) Welsh, "influential" or "son of the wave." Literature: Dylan Thomas (1914-1953), known chiefly for his poetry but also author of the prose piece *A Child's Christmas in Wales*, which promises to become a Christmas classic.

E

*But with the breath which fills
Their mountain pipe, so fill the mountaineers
With the fierce native daring which instils
The stirring memory of a thousand years,
And EVAN's—Donald's—fame rings in each
clansman's ears!*

GEORGE GORDON BYRON,
Childe Harold's Pilgrimage

Earl Anglo-Saxon, "nobleman." EARLE, EARLY, ERLE, ERROL. Fem., EARLENE, EARLINE. Government: Earl Warren, Chief Justice of the U.S. Supreme Court. Literature: Erle Stanley Gardner, prolific writer of mysteries and detective stories, creator of Perry Mason.

Eben (EBB' en) Abbrev. of EBENEZER.

Ebenezer (ebb en EE' zer) Hebrew, "stone of help."

Then Samuel took a stone, and set it between Mizpeh and Shen, and called the name of it Ebenezer, saying Hitherto hath the LORD helped us.

I SAMUEL 7:12

Eberhard, Eberhart Germanic, "boar-strong." EVERARD, EVERETT, EVRARD, EWARD.

Ed Short form of names like EDGAR, EDWARD, EDWIN, etc. EDD, EDDIE, EDDY. TV: Ed Sullivan of the long-running Sunday night programs; Ed Wynn, the old favorite of films, radio, and stage.

Edelbert (AID' el bert *or* EDD' il bert) Variant; see ADALBERT.

Edgar Anglo-Saxon, "happy warrior" or "rich-spear." ED, NED. Literature: Edgar Allan Poe (1809-1849), America's genius among poets and short-story writers, inventor of the dective story, in whose honor the Mystery Writers of America annually award an "Edgar"; Edgar Lee Masters (1869-1950), poet of the Middle West famous for his *Spoon River Anthology.*

Edmund Anglo-Saxon, "happy protection." ED, EDMOND, NED, and the Irish form EAMON (AY' mon). Politics: Eamon de Valera, former president of Ireland, born in New York City. Literature: Edmund Spenser (1552-1599), author of *The Faërie Queene;* Edmund Burke (1729-1797), noted orator; Edmond Rostand, author of *Cyrano de Bergerac* (1897); Edmund Wilson, distinguished modern critic.

*O, Brignall banks are fresh and
  fair,
  And Greta woods are green;
I'd rather rove with Edmund
  there
  Than reign our English queen.*
SIR WALTER SCOTT, *Rokeby*

Edward Anglo-Saxon, "happy
protector" or "keeper of prosper-
ity." ED, EDDIE, EDDY, EDOUARD,
EDUARDO, EWARD, NED, TED. Literature: *Edward, Edward*, one
of the best known ballads. History: The name of many Saxon
kings and of eight English kings.
Edward III and his son, the famous Black Prince, Edward,
Prince of Wales, are referred to
in the following lines:

*I am the last of noble Edward's
  sons,
Of whom thy father, Prince of
  Wales was first
In war was never lion rag'd more
  fierce
In peace was never gentle lamb
  more mild,
Than was that young and
  princely gentleman.*
WILLIAM SHAKESPEARE,
Richard II

Literature: *Edward II* by
Christopher Marlowe; Edward
Gibbon (1737-1794), author of
*The Decline and Fall of the
Roman Empire;* Edward Fitz-
Gerald (1809-1883), whose
translation of the *Rubáiyát* of
Omar Khayyám is a beautiful
poem in its own right; Edward
Lear (1812-1888), painter and
poet, master of whimsey, famous
for his limericks, author of *The
Owl and the Pussy-Cat.* Photography: The grand old master Edward Steichen. Stage and Screen:
Edward G. Robinson. Ballet:
Edward Villella of the phenom-
enal leaps. Public Information:
Edward R. Murrow of TV and
the U.S. Office of Information,
described by Carl Sandburg as
"reporter, historian, inquirer,
actor, ponderer, seeker."

Edwin Anglo-Saxon, "rich
friend." ED, NED. Fem., EDWINA.
Literature; *Edwin Drood*, an unfinished mystery by Charles
Dickens; Edwin Arlington Robinson (1869-1935), three times a
winner of the Pulitzer Poetry
Prize. Stage: The great Shakespearean actor Edwin Thomas
Booth (1833-1893), a member
of the Hall of Fame.

Egbert Anglo-Saxon, "sword-
bright."

Egon (AY' gon) Germanic,
"powerful."

Einar (EYE' nar) Germanic,
"chief."

Elbert See ALBERT.

Eldon, Elton, Elden Place
name, "alder valley or hill"; or
Germanic, "older." ELDO.

Eldred Anglo-Saxon, "old in
counsel."

Eldridge Place name, "ancient hill"; Germanic, "wise ruler." See also ALDRIDGE and ALDRICH.

Eleazar (ell ee AY' zer) Hebrew, "God has helped." ELIE-ZER.

And Eleazar the son of Aaron the priest shall be chief over the Levites, and have the oversight of them that keep the charge of the sanctuary.

NUMBERS, 3:32

Eli (EE' lye) Hebrew, "height." ELY (EEL' ee). Biblical: High priest who trained the prophet Samuel. "Old Eli" is the nickname of Yale University, named after Elihu Yale, an early benefactor. Eli Whitney invented the cotton gin in 1793; he is now a member of the Hall of Fame. Stage, TV, and Screen: Eli Wallach.

Elias (ee LYE' as) Greek form: see ELIJAH. ELIA. Elias Howe (1819-1867) invented the sewing machine; he is now a member of the Hall of Fame.

Elihu (ELL' i hyou *or* ee LYE' hyou) Variant form; see ELIJAH.

Elijah (ee LYE' ja) Hebrew, "Jehovah is my God" ELIA, ELI-AS, ELLIOTT, ELLIS. Biblical: Prophet during the reign of the wicked Ahab. Music: Subject of Mendelssohn's oratorio *Eljah*.

Where, or where, is the good Elijah,

Where, or where, is the good Elijah,
Who went up in a chariot of fire?
  Safe now in the Promised Land.

ANON., *Where Are the Hebrew Children?*

Eliot(t) See ELIJAH. ELLIOT(T). Screen: Elliott Gould.

Elisha (ee EYE' sha) Hebrew, "The Lord is salvation." Biblical: The successor of Elijah.

The spirit of Elijah doth rest upon Elisha.

II KINGS 2:15

Ellery Anglo-Saxon, place name, "on the island where the alders grow." This name has become well known because of the made-up name *Ellery Queen* assumed by the team of detective writers, Frederic Dannay and Manfred Lee.

Ellis See ELIJAH.

El(l)sworth Place name, "at Ell's farm." ELLSWERTH.

Elmer Anglo-Saxon, "noble and famous." This variant of the old English name AYLMER seems to be used almost exclusively in the United States. Literature: *Elmer Gantry* by Sinclair Lewis; *Elmer the Great* by Ring Lardner; Elmer Rice, author of *Street Scene* (Pulitzer Prize, 1929).

Elmo Possibly the Italian version of ANSELM or ERASMUS. St. Elmo's fire refers to luminous effects about ships during storms or great darkness. See ERASMUS.

Elroy Latin via French, "royal." ELROY. See also LEROY.

Elton Variant form; see ALTON.

Elwin Anglo-Saxon, "friend of the elves." ELVIS, ELVYN, ELWYN. See also ALVIN.

Emanuel Hebrew, "God with us." EMMANUEL, IMMANUEL, MANUEL, MANNIE, MANNY. Fem., MANUELA. Philosophy: Immanuel Kant (1724–1804), author of *Critique of Pure Reason.*

Emerson "Son of EMERY." See AMORY.

Emery See AMORY.

Emil (EE' mil *or* AY' mil) Germanic, "work"; or Latin *Aemilius,* name of a *gens,* "striving." ÉMILE. Fem., AMELIA, EMILY. The English word *emulate,* "strive to equal," is derived from the same Latin root. Jean-Jacques Rousseau wrote an educational classic, *Émile,* on the bringing-up of children according to nature's laws. Literature: Émile Zola (1840-1902), famous not only for his novels but also for his ringing cry *J'accuse* in the Alfred Dreyfus case. Screen: Emil Jannings, a great stage actor under Max Reinhardt and in silent films (*The Last Laugh* and *The Blue Angel* with Marlene Dietrich), winner of the 1928 Oscar (*The Way of All Flesh, The Last Command*).

Emlyn Welsh, from a place name. The root may mean "cling to" or "border." *Emlyn* is often assumed to be the Welsh form of EMIL from the Latin *gens* name *Aemilius.* EMLEN, EMELEN. Stage and Screen: Emlyn Williams, actor, director, playwright (*Night Must Fall* and *The Corn Is Green*). He calls his autobiography *George,* his actual first name which he does not often use.

Emmet(t) Surname formed from EMMA. Used as a first name in honor of Robert Emmett (1778–1803), Irish patriot who led the Dublin uprising in 1803 against the English.

The name may also have originated as a nickname from *emmet,* "ant."

Emory Variant spelling; see AMORY.

Enoch (EE' nok) Hebrew, "teacher" or "dedicated." Biblical: Father of the long-lived Methusaleh. Literature: Hero of poem by Tennyson.

A luckier or a bolder fisherman,
A carefuller in peril, did not breathe
For leagues along that breaker-beaten coast
Than Enoch.

ALFRED, LORD TENNYSON,
Enoch Arden

Enos (EE' nos) Hebrew, "man."

Enrico Italian form; see HEN-RY. The golden voice of Enrico Caruso (1873–1921) brought honor to this name; and in 1938 Enrico Fermi won the Nobel Prize for physics.

Ephraim (EEF' ray im *or* EEF' ri um) Hebrew, "very fruitful." EFREM. Biblical: Second son of Joseph; founder of the tribe of Ephraim, which occupied central Palestine. Music: Efrem Zimbalist, distingushed violinist.

Erasmus Greek, "beloved" or "lovable." St. Erasmus (fourth century), also known as Elmo, is the patron of sailors. See ELMO. However, the name is better known as the assumed name of the Dutch scholar Gerhard Gerhards (1466-1536), who translated his given names into Desiderius Erasmus, both of these Latinized names having the connotation "desirable."

Erastus (e RAST' us) Greek, "beloved."

Erhard Germanic, "strong resolution." ERHART.

Eric Norse, "ruler." ERIK, German, ERICH. Fem., ERICA, ERIKA. *Eric* is sometimes used as a dim. of FREDERIC. Leif Ericson ("son of Eric"), a Norse navigator, is said to have reached America about five centuries before Columbus. Eric, Leif's father, had previously founded a colony in Greenland.

But when the Eric the Norseman leads,
Heroic deeds
Will be done today!
  HENRY WADSWORTH LONGFELLOW, *King Olaf's War Horns*

Literature: Eric Ambler, popular author of novels of intrigue and mystery; Erich Maria Remarque (the last name is Krämer spelled backwards), author of the classic novel of World War I, *All Quiet on the Western Front*. Screen: Eric von Stroheim, one of the great directors of movie history (*Greed*), also memorable as the monocled actor in many movies, especially the unforgettable *Grand Illusion*.

Ernest Germanic, "vigor" or "intent." ERNIE, ERNST. Fem., ERNA, ERNESTA, ERNESTINE. Oscar Wilde, whose last name lent itself to punning by other wits, punned on the name Ernest in *The Importance of Being Earnest*, one of the most witty and clever comedies ever written.

GWENDOLEN FAIRFAX: *My ideal has always been to love some one of the name of Ernest. There is something in that name that implies absolute confidence. . . . It is a divine name. It has music of its own. It produces vibrations.*

The first name of Hemingway was certainly appropriate to his vigorous style and active, adventuresome career. As a writer he was honored with the Nobel Prize in 1954, and with the Pulitzer Prize in 1953 for his symbolic story *The Old Man and the Sea.* Hollywood: Ernst Lubitsch, (1892–1947) famous director; Ernest Borgnine, Oscar winner in 1955 (*Marty*). Hollywood and TV: Ernie Kovacs (1919–1962), creative comedian, producer, a n d director honored posthumously in February 1962 as the best television director of 1961 (*Ernie Kovacs Special,* "a study in silence with no dialogue").

Errol See EARL. Screen: Errol Flynn.

Erwin See IRWIN. Fem., ERVA.

Esme (EZZ′ me) old English variation of *Aimé,* "beloved"; or from OSMOND. Also used as a fem. name.

Estes (ESS′ tiss) Latin and Greek, *Ateste,* Italian place name, modern Este. Politics: Estes Kefauver.

Ethan Hebrew, "firm." Ethan Allen, leader of the Green Mountain Boys, lived up to the meaning of his name that morning of May 10, 1775, when he is said to have thundered at the British commander of Fort Ticonderoga to surrender "In the name of the Great Jehovah and the Continental Congress!" Literature *Ethan Frome* (1911),

Edith Wharton's beautiful tragic novelette.

Ethelbert Germanic, "noble-bright." See also ADALBERT and EDELBERT. Fem., ETHELBERTA. Music: Ethelbert Nevins (1862–1901), composer of *The Rosary, Mighty Lak′ a Rose,* etc.

Eugene Greek via Latin, "well-born." EUGEN, GENE. Fem., EUGENIA, EUGENIE, EUGÉNIE. Four Popes were named Eugene, but the popularity of the name arose from the brilliant career of Prince Eugene of Savoy (1663–1736), conqueror of the Turks and associate of the Duke of Marlborough in the victories over Louis XIV.

"Great praise the Duke of Marlborough won
  And our good Prince Eugene."
"Why, 'twas a very wicked thing!"
  Said little Wilhelmine.
"Nay, nay, my little girl," quoth he,
"It was a famous victory."
        ROBERT SOUTHEY,
        The Battle of Blenheim

Literature: Eugene Field (1850–1895), American journalist and "poet of childhood"; Eugene O'Neill, winner of Nobel Literature Prize in 1936 and of three Pulitzer Prizes for the plays *Beyond the Horizon* (1920), *Strange Interlude* (1928), and *Long Day's Journey into Night* (1957, posthumously);

Eugene Ionesco, avant-garde playwright (*Rhinoceros,* etc.). Politics: Eugene V. Debs (1855–1926), organizer of the Social Democratic Party of America, leading figure in the labor movement. Music: Eugene Ormandy, conductor.

Eustace (YOU′ stis) Greek, "steadfast" or "rich in corn." EUSTIS, STAC(E)Y. Fem., EUSTACIA.

Evan See JOHN. EWEN. *Evan* is generally regarded as the Welsh equivalent of JOHN, or it may mean "youth." The surnames Bevin and Bevan mean "the son of Evan." Literature: Evan Hunter, author of *The Blackboard Jungle* and of the "Ed McBain" mysteries.

Evelyn (EEV′ lyn) Often used as boys' name in England; from a surname. See also EVELYN (f). Literature: Evelyn Waugh, contemporary British author.

Everard See EBERHARD. EWART.

Everet(t) See EBERHARD. EVERIT.

Ewan, Ewen See EVAN.

Ewart Variant of EBERHARD and EDWARD. A name sometimes given in honor of the British statesman William Ewart Gladstone. EWARD.

Ezekiel (ee ZEEK′ yel *or* ee ZEEK′ i el) Hebrew, "God strengthens." EZEKIAH, EZEKIAL, ZEKE. Biblical: A prophet-priest whose writings and sermons are contained in the book of Ezekiel in the Old Testament.

Ezekiel saw de wheel, de wheel,
Way up in de middle of de air.
                              SPIRITUAL.

Ezra Hebrew, "helper." With the permission of King Artaxerxes of Persia, Ezra led the Israelites back to Jerusalem to rebuild the temple.

This Ezra went up from Babylon; and he was a ready scribe in the law of Moses.
                              EZRA 7: 6

One of our great universities takes its name from its cofounder, Ezra Cornell, who was also the organizer of Western Union. Literature: Abraham ben Meir ben Ezra, called "The Admirable" for his great attainments in various fields of scholarship in twelfth-century Spain, is the supposed speaker in Robert Browning's celebrated poem *Rabbi ben Ezra,* which opens with these oft-quoted lines:

Grow old along with me
The best is yet to be,
   The last of life for which
      the first was made.

F

King FRANCIS *was a hearty king,
and loved a royal sport.*

LEIGH HUNT, *The Glove and the Lions*

Fabian (FAY′ bi an *or* FAYB′ yan) Latin, *Fabius,* the name of a *gens,* "bean grower." The strategy of Quintus Fabius Maximus, the Roman consul who tried to wear Hannibal down by the use of delaying tactics, gave rise to the expression *a Fabian policy,* referring to a slow and gradual method of attaining one's ends.

Fairfax Anglo-Saxon, "fair-haired."

Falkner, Faulkner Old English occupational name, "trainer of falcons" or "one who hunts with falcons." FALCONER. Better known as a last name. Literature: William Harrison Faulkner, winner of the 1949 Nobel Prize for literature.

Farley Irish, "strong leader" or "superior (in) war"; English place name, "fair meadow." Hollywood and TV: Farley Granger.

Felix (FEE′ liks) Latin, "fortunate, blessed." FELIKS. Fem., FELICIA. Four Popes and several saints have been named Felix. Music: Felix Mendelssohn (1809–1847), conductor, composer (*Songs Without Words, Italian Symphony, Wedding March,* etc.).

Feodor, Fyodor Russian forms; see THEODORE. Music: Feodor Chaliapin, great basso. Literature: Fyodor Dostoyevsky, author of *Crime and Punishment, The Brothers Karamazov,* etc.

Ferdinand Germanic, "bold peace" or "journey-risk." FERD(E), FERDIE, FERDAND. Fem., FERNANDA. Imported by the Goths into Spain, *Ferdinand* became popular there as *Fernando* and *Hernando.* Both of these names are linked to American history. Under the auspices of Ferdinand and Isabella, Columbus set sail for the New World; Hernando Cortes (Cortez) conquered Mexico.
   Literature: Ferdinand, lover of Miranda in Shakespeare's *Tempest.*
   A distinguished modern bearer of this name was Ferdinand de Lesseps (1805–1894), associated with the building of the Suez and Panama Canals.

Fergus Irish, "man-choice" or "strong man"; Gaelic, "chief choice"; Scottish. "fiery." Also used as Irish translation of FERDINAND.

Ferris French place name, indicating an industry of a certain

93

region, from Latin, "iron"; considered also as a Celtic variant of PIERCE. See PETER.

Fleming English, "coming from Flanders" or "Flemish."

Fletcher Anglo-Saxon, "arrow-maker."

Florian Latin, "blooming."

Floyd Welsh, "dark-complexioned." See LLOYD. This name is said to have come from the inability of the English to pronounce the Welsh name *ap-Lloyd*, "son of Lloyd." Boxing: Heavyweight champion Floyd Patterson.

Forbes Scottish clan name, "headstrong" or "cold-brow."

Forrest Latin, "woodsman." FORRESTER.

Foster Latin, "keeper of the woods"; abbreviation of FORRESTER.

Fowler Old English occupational name, "hunter of wild fowl." See also FAULKNER.

Francis Latin *Franciscus*, "Frenchman," from Germanic and Old French, *franc*, "free." FRANCOIS, FRANK, FRANZ. Fem., FRANCES, FRANCINE, FANCHON. This was originally a nickname referring to a person of French origin or proficient in speaking French. St. Francis of Assisi (1182–1226), christened *Giovanni* ("John"), is said to have received the name *Francesco* ("Francis") because he was fluent in French. Literature: Essayist Francis Bacon (1561–1626). History: Francis Drake, explorer (1545–1596). In this country FRANCIS will be remembered because of Francis Scott Key (1779–1843), author of the *Star-Spangled Banner*. The novelist F. Scott Fitzgerald was named after him, the full name being Francis Scott Key Fitzgerald. Hollywood: Francis X. Bushman, matinee idol of former days.

François French form; see FRANCIS. Fem., FRANCOISE, FANCHON. Literature: François Villon (15th century), romantic poet whose exploits are depicted in *The Vagabond King* and *If I Were King;* François Rabelais, (1494–1553), satirist, author of *Gargantua and Pantagruel*.

Frank Short form: see FRANCIS. FRANKIE, FRANK(E)Y. Hollywood, Stage and TV: Frank Sinatra. Hollywood: Frank Capra, director. Literature: Frank O'Connor (Michael O'Donovan), author of short stories.

Franklin Germanic, "freeman." FRANK. In the fourteenth and fifteenth centuries the title *Franklin* designated a landowner of free but not noble birth, a member of the middle class. A franklin was one of the Canterbury Pilgrims in the poem by Chaucer. Two of our Presidents have had this first name; Franklin Pierce (1804–1869) and FDR—Franklin D. Roosevelt (1882–1945). Literature: FPA —Franklin Pierce Adams (1881–1960), famous columnist and humorous poet whose column *The Conning Tower* encouraged and first printed many young writers.

Franz German form; see FRANCIS and FRANK. Literature: Franz Kafka (1883–1924), whose mystical, allegorical novels and short stories have had a great influence on many modern writers, author of *The Trial*. Music: Franz Schubert (1797–1828), known for his *lieder* and *Unfinished Symphony;* Franz Liszt (1811–1886), one of the great pianists of history, composer of the *Hungarian Rhapsodies,* etc.

Fraser, Frazer Scottish clan name, Germanic *frithu,* via French, "peace." See FREDERICK.

Frederic(k) Germanic, "peace-rule." FRED, FREDRIC, FREDDY, FRIEDRICH, FRITZ. See also ERIC. Fem., FREDERICA. Frederic is the hero of a Gilbert and Sullivan opera whose nurse apprenticed him to pirates instead of pilots:

*When Frederic was a little lad he
  proved so brave and daring,
His father thought he'd 'prentice*

him to some career seafaring.
WILLIAM SCHWENCK GILBERT,
The Pirates of Penzance

History: Frederick II of Prussia (1712–1786), known as Frederick the Great and *der alte Fritz,* a patron of the arts. Art: Frederic Remington (1861–1909), noted for his paintings, drawings, and sculpture of the West. Music: Frédéric François Chopin (1810–1849), famed composer and pianist. Stage, Screen, and TV: Fredric March, winner of an Oscar in 1946 (*The Best Years of Our Lives*); Fred Astaire, dancer, actor, director; Frederick Loewe, composer of *Brigadoon, My Fair Lady, Camelot,* etc.).

Friedrich German form; see FREDERIC. Literature: (Johann Christoph) Friedrich von Schiller (1759–1805), poet and dramatist, author of the play *Wilhelm Tell* and of beautiful lyrics that have been set to music. His *Ode to Joy* is part of Beethoven's *Ninth Symphony.* Friedrich Duerrenmatt, Swiss novelist (*The Pledge,* etc.) and dramatist (*The Visit, Romulus,* etc.)

Fritz German dim. form; see FREDERIC. Fem., FRITZI. Music: The beloved Fritz Kreisler (1875-1962), composer (*Caprice Viennois*) as well as performer, known as the greatest violinist of his time, who "had an inherent, uncanny ability to stir the hearts and the imagination" of his listeners. Politics: Fritz Mondale.

Fulton Place name, "field town"; Scottish, "leafy town." Religion: Bishop Fulton J. Sheen, known for his books and appearances on TV.

G

Gabriel (GAY' bree el) Hebrew, "man of God" or "God is mighty." Fem., GABRIEL(L)A, GABRIELLE. Gabriel the Archangel was present at the burial of Moses, helped destroy the army of Sennacherib, explained visions to Daniel, and brought the tidings to Mary in the Annunciation.

Betwixt the rocky pillars Gabriel sat,
Chief of the angelic guards.
    JOHN MILTON, *Paradise Lost*

Gale Irish, "stranger"; or Scandinavian place name, "ravine." Also Norse, "to sing." GAIL. Variant GAEL, "an inhabitant of Ireland." Fem., GAIL, GAYLE.

Galen (GAY' len) Greek, "calm"; name of a distinguished second-century Greek physician long considered a supreme authority.

Gamaliel (ga MAY' li el) Hebrew, "The Lord is vengeance or recompense." Since Gamaliel was the teacher of Saul of Tarsus (St. Paul; see ACTS 22 : 3), the term *Gamaliel* is sometimes applied to a teacher. The middle name of President Warren G. Harding is Gamaliel.

Gardner Anglo-Saxon; occupational name. GARDENER, GARDINER. Cartoonist: Gardner Rea.

Garret(t) Anglo-Saxon, "powerful with the spear." This is a modern variation of *Gareth* (Welsh, "gentle"), the name of one of King Arthur's knights, who appears in Malory's *Morte d'Arthur* and in Tennyson's *Gareth and Lynette*:

To whom Sir Gareth drew
(And there were none but few goodlier than he)
Shining in arms, "Damsel, the quest is mine.
Lead and I follow."

Garson Old English, "son of Gar (warrior or spear)"; see also GARRETT, GERALD, and GERARD. Sometimes used for *Gershon.* Theater: Garson Kanin, director and playwright (*Born Yesterday, A Gift of Time,* etc.).

Garth A short form of GARETH; see GARRET. It may also be an Anglo-Saxon occupational name, "keeper of a yard or enclosure." or "herdsman" or "gardener." Literature: A character in Maxwell Anderson's *Winterset* (1935).

Gary Germanic, "spear carrier." GARRY. Sometimes used as a diminutive of GERALD, *Gary* is also used to Americanize names like *Garibaldi*. Hollywood: Gary Cooper, who did so much to popularize this name, winner of two Oscars, in 1941 (*Sergeant York*), and in 1952 (*High Noon*).

Gaspar See JASPER. CASPAR.

Three kings came riding from
far away,
  Melchior and Gaspar and Bal-
thasar;
Three Wise Men out of the East
were they,
And they traveled by night and
they slept by day,
  For their guide was a beauti-
ful, wonderful star.
    HENRY WADSWORTH LONG-
    FELLOW, *The Three Kings*

Gavin (GAVV' in) Scottish form of Gawain, presumed to mean "white hawk"; also Scottish occupational name, "smith." Gawain was one of King Arthur's knights. Literature: Gavin Maxwell, an entertaining British writer on nature, author of *People of the Reeds* and *Ring of Bright Water*.

Gay(e)lord Either simply "gay" and "lord" or occupational name, "jailer," (the English spell "jail" "g-a-o-l").

Gene Short form; see EUGENE. Boxing: Gene Tunney (James J. Tunney), former heavyweight champion and Shakespeare enthusiast. Screen and Dance: Gene Hackman, Oscar 1971 (*The French Connection*); Gene Kelly.

Geoffrey (JEFF' ree) Germanic "God's peace" or "land-peace." See also GODFREY. GEOFF, JEFFREY, JEFFRY. Literature: Geoffrey Chaucer, author of *The Canterbury Tales* (1388). Lord Jeffry Amherst's name is perpetuated in the name of Amherst College, which is nicknamed "Old Jeff." Some last names coming from *Jeffrey* are Jefferson, Jeffries, and Jepson.

George Greek, "farmer." GEORDIE, GEORGIE. Fem., GEORGIA, GEORGETTE, GEORGIANA. St. George, a Roman military tribune who became a martyr, is associated with the killing of a dragon. St. George became the patron saint of England after Edward III dedicated the Order of the Garter (founded in 1349) to him as his favorite saint. Four kings named George ruled England in succession for 116 years; the name *George* received additional honor in this country through our first President.

Saint George of Merry England,
  the sign of victory.
    EDMUND SPENSER,
    The Faërie Queene

Literature: Lord George Noel Gordon Byron; GBS, or George Bernard Shaw; George Orwell, author of *Animal Farm* and *1984;* Georges Simenon, prolific author of psychological novels, creator of Inspector Maigret; George Jean Nathan (1882–1958), dynamic critic, often devastating, associated with Henry L. Mencken. George Alfred Henty (1832–1902), from whose many historical novels boys learned more about history than from texts. Philosophy: George Santayana (1863–1952), also an eminent critic. Stage: George M. Cohan (1878–1942), actor, playwright, lyricist, composer (*Yankee Doodle Dandy, Over There,* etc.). George Arliss, noted for his interpretation of Disraeli on stage and screen, winner of an Oscar in 1930 (*Disraeli*).

Ballet: The renowned choreographer and manager, George Balanchine. Baseball: The one and only "Babe," or "Bambino," George Herman Ruth (1895–1948) whose total output of 714 home runs is still the record. Science: George Washington Carver (1864–1943), noted for his research on the uses of peanuts. Music: Georg(e) Friederich Handel (1685–1759), prolific composer of chamber music, opera, oratorios (*The Messiah,* etc.); George Gershwin (1898–1937), composer of *Rhapsody in Blue, Porgy and Bess,* and *Of Thee I Sing,* which was awarded the Pulitzer Prize for Drama in 1932, the first time this award was given to a musical.

Gerald Germanic, "spear-rule." GERRY, JERALD, JERRY. Fem., GERALDINE.

Gerard Germanic, "spear-hard." GERRY, GERHARD. Literature: Love story of Gerard, father of the scholar Erasmus, in Charles Reade's famous historical novel, *The Cloister and the Hearth;* Brigadier Gerard, swashbuckling hero of the Napoleonic Wars in the stories by Sir Arthur Conan Doyle.

Giacomo (JA' ko moe) Italian form; see JAMES. Music: Giacomo Puccini (1858–1924), composer of *La Bohème, Tosca, Madam Butterfly,* etc.

Gideon (GIDD' ee un) Hebrew, "great warrior," or "hewer." Biblical: A judge who, with a devoted army of only 300, delivered his people from the Midianites. The Gideon Bible placed in hotel rooms owes its name to Gideon's exploit as a symbol of a great work done by a devoted few.

If you belong to Gideon's band, Oh, here's my heart and here's my hand.

OLD SONG

Gilbert Germanic via French, "bright pledge." WILBERT, WILBURT, WILBUR. *Gilbert* and WILBERT are the same names; the letter *w* of Germanic words often changed to *g* through French; so, *ward* and *guard* show the same change.

Art: Gilbert Stuart (1755–1828), portrait painter known especially for the Washington portraits. Literature: Gilbert K. Chesterton (1874–1936), essayist, poet, and creator of Father Brown, a philosophic detective. Classics: Gilbert Murray, famous professor of Greek at Oxford, translator, and author of numerous works (*The Rise of the Greek Epic, The Classical Tradition in Poetry*, etc.); Gilbert Highet, one of his students, later one of his colleagues, Anthon Professor of Latin at Columbia, critic, editor, lecturer, author (*The Classical Tradition, People, Places, and Books*, etc.).

Giles (JILEZ) Greek via Latin, "shield-bearer" or "kid." St. Aegidius came from Athens to France in the sixth century; his name was changed to the French forms *Gilles* and *Gide*, which became very popular names because of the marvelous adventures and cures of St. Giles. The expression, *under the aegis of*, meaning "under the protection or auspices of," comes from the Greek word for *shield* found in St. Giles' original name.

Gino Italian; terminal form of *Ambrogino*, pet form of *Ambrogio*, or terminal of *Luigino*, pet form of *Luigi*. See AMBROSE and LOUIS. Fem., GINA.

Gino is also derived from GIOVANNI.

Gioacchino (JOE' ak key noe) Italian form; see JOAQUIN. Music: Gioacchino Antonin Rossini (1792–1868), composer of *The Barber of Seville*, etc.

Giovanni (jo VAH' nee) Italian form; see JOHN. Art: Giovanni Bellini (1430–1516), renowned for Madonnas and altar-pieces. Literature: Giovanni Boccaccio (1313–1375), author of the *Decameron*. Fem., GIOVANNA. Short forms: GIAN, GIANNI. Music: Gian Carlo Menotti, composer (*Amahl and the Night Visitors, The Medium, The Consul*, etc.).

Giuseppe (joo SEP' peh) Italian form; see JOSEPH. Three eminent bearers of this name: Mazzini (1805–1872), fighter for the liberation and unification of Italy; Garibaldi (1807–1882), active in the same cause under the slogan *Roma o Morte* ("Rome or Death"); Verdi (1807–1882), the "Shakespeare of Italian opera" (*Rigoletto, Aida, La Traviata, Otello*, etc.).

Glenn(n) Celtic, "valley." GLYN(N). Fem., GLYNIS; see also GLENDA and GLENNA. Music: Glenn Gould, brilliant Canadian pianist.

Godfrey Germanic, "God's peace." See GEOFFREY. GOTTFRIED. Godfrey de Bouillon, the chief character in Tasso's epic, *Jerusalem Delivered*, was a leader of the First Crusade.

Go(o)dwin Anglo-Saxon, "good friend" or "God-friend."

Gordon Place name, Anglo-Saxon, "round hill." Originally the name of a Scottish clan, *Gordon* achieved popularity as a first name in honor of the heroic British general, Charles George "Chinese" Gordon (1833–1885).

Graham (GRAY' um) Anglo-Saxon, "warlike." Name of a distinguished Scottish clan. Graham crackers and Graham flour were named after an American, Dr. Sylvester Graham (1794-1851). Literature: Graham Greene, novelist and playwright (*The Power and the Glory*).

Grant French, variation of *grand*, "great." Art: Grant Wood, famous for "American Gothic."

Granville French place name, "large city."

Gregory Greek, "watchful." GREG, GREER. Sixteen Popes assumed the name Gregory; one of them, Gregory the Great, Established the Gregorian calendar (1582), which we now use. Screen: Gregory Peck.

And wha will build a bonny ship,
And set it on the sea?
For I will go to seek my love,
My ain love Gregory.

OLD BALLAD,
The Loss of Lochroyan

Grover Germanic, "gardener" or "living in a grove" or "engraver." (Stephen) Grover Cleveland was our twenty-second and twenty-fourth President, the only man to have been President for two non-successive terms. Baseball: The renowned pitcher Grover Cleveland Alexander, elected to the National Baseball Hall of Fame in 1938.

Guglielmo (goo LYEL' moe) Italian form; see WILLIAM. Science: Guglielmo Marconi (1874–1937), maker of first successful experiments with wireless telegraphy, co-winner of Nobel Prize for Physics (1909).

Guillaume (GHEE YOME') French form; see WILLIAM.

Gunther Anglo-Saxon, "a warrior." GUNTER, GUNNER.

Gus Short form; see AUGUSTUS and GUSTAVE.

Gustave Germanic, "staff." GUS, GUSTAF, GUSTAVUS. This name was once used mainly in Sweden but the fame of the Swedish king Gustaf Adolf, whose name was Latinized to *Gustavus Adolphus*, made *Gustave* a popular name in other parts of Europe. Gustavus Adolphus (1594-1632), "The Lion of the North," a leader in the Thirty Years' War, is generally considered one of the great military leaders of all time. Literature: Gustave Flaubert (1821-1880), great French novelist, author of *Madame Bovary* and *Salammbô*. Music: Gustav Mahler, composer of monumental symphonies.

Guthrie Anglo-Saxon, "war hero."

Guy French, "guide"; or Germanic, "woods," but meaning is not certain. A popular name in England for many centuries, *Guy* lost its favor for a time because of its association with Guy Fawkes and the Gunpowder Plot (1605). Two books helped restore it: *Guy Mannering* (1815), a novel by Walter Scott; and Charlotte M. Yonge's *Heir of Redclyffe* (1853), in which *Guy* is the name of the hero. Literature: Guy de Maupassant (1850-1893), one of the greatest of all short-story writers.

Sir Guy was a doughty crusader,
  A muscular knight,
  Ever ready to fight,
A very determined invader,
  And Dickey de Lion's delight.
  WILLIAM SCHWENCK GILBERT,
                Bab Ballads

H

*O when shall English men
With such acts fill a pen?
Or England breed again
Such a King HARRY?*

MICHAEL DRAYTON, *Agincourt*

Hadrian See ADRIAN. Literature: *The Memoirs of Hadrian* by Marguerite Yourcenar.

Hal See HAROLD and HARRY. Fem., HALLIE.

Hals(e)y Place name, "hazel-tree island."

Hamilton Place name, Hambleton, "fortified castle."

Hamish (HAY' mish) Gaelic form; see JAMES.

Hans See JOHN. Literature: *Hans Brinker or the Silver Skates* by Mary Mapes Dodge, a favorite children's book since its publication in 1865; Hans Christian Andersen (1805-1875), whose *Fairy Tales* are a favorite with young and old; *Hänsel and Gretel*, favorite fairy tale, also opera (1893) by Engelbert Humperdinck.

Harcourt (HAR' kort) French place name, Germanic, "soldiers' courtyard."

Harlan(d) Place name, "army-land." A distinguished bearer of this name was Harlan F. Stone, Chief Justice of the U.S. Supreme Court from 1941 to 1946.

Harley Place name, "long field" or "army-meadow." Harley Street in London is "Doctors' Row." Robert Harley (1661-1724) was a distinguished statesman and collector. Part of his collection (the Harleian manuscripts) is in the British Museum.

Harlow Place name, "army-hill" or "rough hill." Science: Harlow Shapley, astronomer.

Harold Anglo-Saxon, "army-power." HAL, HARALD, HARRY. Harold was the last of the Saxon kings of England. His story has been told by Tennyson in the poem *Harold*, by Bulwer-Lytton in the novel *Harold, the Last of the Barons*, and by Hope Muntz in the highly praised novel *The Golden Warrior*. Berlioz composed a dramatic symphony *Harold in Italy* based on Byron's poem *Childe Harold*. The title *Childe* means a youth of noble birth; it was used as a first name by the American artist Childe Hassam (1859-1935).

103

The bickering lightning, nor the rock
Of turret to the earthquake's shock,
  Could Harold's courage quell.
    SIR WALTER SCOTT,
    Harold the Dauntless

Hollywood: Harold Lloyd, the comedian whose antics delighted millions. Science: Harold C. Urey, discoverer of heavy hydrogen, winner of a Nobel Prize in 1934.

Harper Germanic, "harp player."

Harry See HAROLD and HENRY. HARRIS. Fem., HARRIET. Despite its spelling, *Henry* was once pronounced "Harry." Harry S Truman: only President with that first name. Sir Harry Lauder (1870-1950), singer and composer, brought joy to his listeners with such songs as *I Love a Lassie, a Bonnie, Bonnie Lassie.* Another singer appealing to huge audiences: Harry Belafonte. Still another singing and acting Harry is better known as Bing Crosby.

The game's afoot:
Follow your spirit; and upon this charge
Cry "God for Harry! England and Saint George!"
    WILLIAM SHAKESPEARE,
    Henry V

Hart Anglo-Saxon, "hard" or short form of HARTLEY. Originally both were surnames. Litera-

ture: Hart Crane (1899-1932), an influential mystic poet.

Hartley Place name, "deer meadow" or "stony meadow."

Harvey Germanic, "army-battle"; or from *Hervé*, French saint-name. HERVEY. This is also a famous last name. William Harvey discovered the circulation of the blood (1628). Harvey Cushing (1869-1939) was one of the greatest American surgeons and brain specialists. Literature: Robert Browning's poem, *Hervé Riel*, which recalls the French form of the name; *Harvey*, Pulitzer Prize play (1945) by Mary C. Chase, later made into a movie; Harvey Cheyne, hero of Kipling's *Captains Courageous.*

Hector Greek, "support, prop." Fem., HECTORINA. *Hector* was a fitting name for the warrior "of the shining helmet," the Trojan hero of the *Iliad*, who was the "stay" of his people.

Protect my son!
Grant him, like me, to purchase just renown,
To guard the Trojans, to defend the crown,
Against his country's foes the war to wage
And rise the Hector of the future age!
    HOMER, *Iliad*
(translated by Alexander Pope)

Music: (Louis) Hector Berlioz (1803-1869), renowned French composer and author of a delightful book of memoirs. Literature: Hector Hugh Munro (1870-1916), better known as Saki, author of humorous stories and novels (*Reginald*, *The Chronicles of Clovis*, etc.).

Heinrich German form; see HENRY.

Henry Germanic, "home-rule." HAL, HARRY, HANK. Ever popular as a name, first or last, borne by kings, scientists, writers, and by "every Tom, Dick, and Harry." Fem., HENRIETTA, HENRIE(TTE).
Literature: *John Henry* ballads; Thackeray's *History of Henry Esmond;* George Gissing's *Private Papers of Henry Ryecroft;* Henry Wadsworth Longfellow (1807-1882); Henry James (1843-1916), whose novels and short stories are enjoying present popularity not only as books but as the subject of movies, TV adaptations, plays, and operas; Henry David Thoreau (1817-1862), author of *Walden;* Henry Brooks Adams (1838-1918), author of *Mont-Saint-Michel* and *The Education of Henry Adams,* which won a Pulitzer Prize (for autobiography) in 1919; the redoubtable Henry L. Mencken (1880-1956), editor, essayist, satirist, who exercised a tremendous influence on American intellectual life, authority on the American language.
History: Henry Hudson, the navigator after whom a river, bay, and strait were named. Stage and Screen: Henry Fonda.

In other lands many famous men have borne forms of the name *Henry.* HENRI, French: Henri Quatre (Henry IV), *le bon roi Henri,* also called Henry of Navarre, "the greatest but above all the most essentially French of all the kings of France." He antedated President Hoover in his wish that every peasant might have a chicken in the pot on Sundays.

Oh! was there ever such a knight,
in friendship or in war,
As our Sovereign Lord, King
Henry of Navarre?
THOMAS BABINGTON MACAULAY,
Ivry

HEINRICH, German: Heinrich Heine (1797-1856), especially famous for *lieder,* among which is the well-known *Lorelei;* Heinrich Schliemann (1822-1890), who, inspired by his boyhood reading of Homer, excavated Troy and Mycenae. HENRIK; Norwegian: Henrik Ibsen, (1828-1906), author of *A Doll's House, An Enemy of the People,* etc., one of the greatest of modern dramatists. HENRYK, Polish: Henryk Sienkiewicz (1846-1916), author of *Quo Vadis,* winner of a Nobel Prize in 1905. See also ENRICO.

Herbert Germanic, "bright army." HERB, HERBIE. Famous men: Herbert Spencer (1820-1903), English philosopher; Sir

Herbert Beerbohm Tree (1853-1917), English actor and director; our thirty-first President, Herbert C. Hoover. It is not generally known that the initials H. G. stand for Herbert George in the name H. G. Wells.

Herman Germanic, "army-man." ARMIN, HARMAN, HARMON, HERMON, HERMANN. Fem., ARMINA. This name goes all the way back to Roman times, when it was Latinized as *Arminius*. In 9 A.D., a German chief by that name revolted against the Romans and cut three legions to pieces. Literature: Herman Melville (1819-1891), author of *Moby Dick;* Herman Hesse, who fled from Germany to Switzerland, author of the powerful novel *Steppenwolf,* winner of a Nobel Prize in 1946.

Hervey See HARVEY. Literature: Hervey Allen, author of *Israfel,* a biography of Poe (1926), and the novel *Anthony Adverse* (1933).

Heywood Anglo-Saxon, "forest enclosure." HAYWOOD, WOODY. The beloved newspaper columnist and humanitarian Heywood Broun (1888-1939) made this name better known.

Hilary (HILL' a ree) Latin, "cheerful." HILAIRE. Fem., HI(L)-LARY. Literature: Hilaire Belloc, prolific writer of poetry and essays.

Hillel Hebrew, "greatly praised." Religion: Famous Rabbi Hillel, reputed originator of the *Talmud.*

Hiram (HYE' ram) Hebrew, "exalted." HY. Biblical: Also called Huram; helped Solomon build the temple.

And Solomon sent to Huram the king of Tyre, saying, As thou didst deal with David my father, and didst send him cedars to build him an house to dwell therein, even so deal with me.
                II CHRONICLES 2:3

Hobart (HOE' bart *or* HOE' burt) See HUBERT. HOBE, HOBIE, HOBEY.

Holbrook Place name, "valley brook."

Homer Greek, "pledge." The *Iliad* and *Odyssey* of Homer are the two earliest epics of European literature and still the greatest.

The song is divine, but divine Homer wrote it down.
                GREEK ANTHOLOGY, IX, 455

The saying, "Sometimes even the good Homer nods," by the Roman poet Horace, implies that even men of genius may make a mistake but:

Those oft are stratagems which errors seem,
Nor is it Homer nods, but we that dream.
                ALEXANDER POPE,
                An Essay on Criticism

The translation of Homer by George Chapman inspired John Keats to write one of his most beautiful sonnets:

Round many western islands have I been
Which bards in fealty to Apollo hold.
Oft of one wide expanse had I been told
That deep brow'd Homer ruled as his demesne.

Horace, Horatio Latin *Horatius,* the name of a *gens.* Fem., HORATIA. The Roman poet Quintus Horatius Flaccus is usually referred to as Horace. A number of legendary Roman heroes were named Horatius, of whom Horatius at the Bridge is the best known:

With weeping and with laughter,
Still is the story told,
How well Horatius kept the bridge
In the brave days of old.
         THOMAS B. MACAULAY,
         The Lays of Ancient Rome

The form HORATIO was used by Shakespeare as the name of Hamlet's friend to whom Hamlet said:

There are more things in heaven and earth, Horatio,
Than are dreamt of in your philosophy.

Horatio Nelson is the great naval hero of the British; and on this side all Americans know about Horatio Alger and his stories that spell success. The *Captain Horatio Hornblower* stories by C. S. Forester have called attention to the name in recent times.

Some famous Horaces: Walpole (1717-1797), author of letters, novels, and essays; Mann (1796-1859), member of the Hall of Fame, innovator of teaching methods; Greeley (1811-1872), political leader and journalist, often credited with the command, "Go West, young man"; Gregory, winner of the 1961 Academy of Poets Award.

Hosea (ho ZEE' a *or* ho ZAY' a) Hebrew, "salvation."

Houston (HYOU' ston *or* HOW' ston) Place name, "hill town" or "Hugh's town."

Howard Germanic, "strong mind" or "watchman." HOWIE.

Howard, than whom knight
Was never dubb'd more brave in fight;
Nor, when from war and armor free,
More fam'd for stately courtesy.
         SIR WALTER SCOTT,
         Lay of the Last Minstrel

Music: Conductor Howard Barlow. Theater: Howard Lindsay, actor and playwright, co-author of *Life with Father* and of *State of the Union* (Pulitzer Prize, 1946).

Hubert (HYOU' bert) Germanic, "bright mind." HOBART. St. Hubert is the patron of hunters. From *Hubert* comes the last name immortalized in *Old Mother Hubbard.*

Approbation from Sir Hubert Stanley is praise indeed.
THOMAS MORTON,
A Cure for the Heartache

Sir (George) Hubert Wilkins (1888-1958) was a renowned polar explorer. Fashions: Hubert (James Taffin) de Givenchy, couturier.

Hugh (HYOU) Germanic, "mind." HUEY, HUGO. The fame of St. Hugh, Bishop of Lincoln (1135-1200), gave this name a vogue in England.

Cold's the wind, and wet's the rain,
Saint Hugh be our good speed.
Ill is the weather that bringeth no gain,
Nor helps any good hearts in need.
THOMAS DEKKER,
Shoemaker's Holiday

Literature: *Hugh Wynne, Free Quaker* (1897), a novel of the American Revolution by Dr. S. Weir Mitchell.

Hugo Latinized form of HUGH, popular as a German name but best known as the last name of Victor Hugo. Music: Hugo Wolf (1860-1903), Austrian composer, considered one of the greatest composers of songs (*lieder*).

Humbert Germanic, "giant-bright." Literature: Humbert Wolfe (1885-1940), English poet.

Hume (HYOOM) Place name, "home" or "river island." Stage: Hume Cronyn.

Humphrey Germanic, "giant-peace." HUMPHRY, HUMFREY. Literature: *Humphry Clinker,* novel by Tobias Smollett (1771). Sir Humphry Davis (1778-1820) invented the miner's safety lamp. In modern times Humphrey Bogart gave a he-man luster to the name.

Hunter Occupational name.

Hurd Anglo-Saxon, "hard, strong." Stage and Screen: Hurd Hatfield.

Hyman, Hymen Hebrew, "life"; masculine of EVE. HY, HYMIE. Two famous bearers of this name (CHAIM and HAYYIM are the Hebrew forms): Chaim Solomon, for his help in the American Revolution, and Chaim Weizman, for his part in establishing the state of Israel. In the United States, the views of Admiral Hyman G. Rickover, author of *Education and Freedom* have provoked discussion. Journalism: Syndicated columnist Hy Gardner. Literature: The *Education of* H*Y*M*A*N K*A*P*L*A*N. by Leonard Q. Ross (Leo Calvin Rosten).

I

*In Heaven a spirit doth dwell
"Whose heart-strings are a lute";
None sing so wildly well
As the angel ISRAFEL,
And the giddy stars (so legends tell)
Ceasing their hymns, attend the spell
Of his voice, all mute.*

EDGAR ALLAN POE, *Israfel*

Iago (ee AH' go) Spanish and Welsh form; see JAMES. Literature: The villain in Shakespeare's *Othello. Santiago* is the Spanish version of *St. James.*

Ian (EE'an *or* EE' ahn *or* EYE' an) Gaelic; see JOHN. IAIN. Literature: Ian MacLaren, pseudonym of John Watson, author of the delightful book about Scottish life, *Beside the Bonnie Brier Bush* (1894).

Ichabod Hebrew, "inglorious." Literature: The schoolmaster in Washington Irving's *Legend of Sleepy Hollow.*

Ignace (EEN' yas) French form; see IGNATIUS. Music: Ignace Paderewski, (1860-1941), pianist and statesman, first Premier of Poland after World War I, considered by many the greatest of modern pianists.

Ignatius (igg NAY' shi us *or* igg NAY'shus) Greek, a name whose meaning is not known. St. Ignatius of Loyola.

Ignatz German form; see IGNATIUS.

Ignazio Italian form; see IGNATIUS. Literature: Ignazio Silone, author of *Fontamara* and *Bread and Wine.*

Igor (EE' gor) Scandinavian via Russian, from *Ingvarr,* a hero name. See also INGRID. IGOR is often used as a translation of GEORGE. Music: Igor Stravinsky, composer; Igor Oistrakh, violinist; *Prince Igor,* an unfinished opera by Borodin.

Immanuel See EMANUEL.

Ingram Germanic, "angel-raven." Also connected with *Ingvi,* a hero name. See also IGOR and INGRID. INGRAHAM.

Inigo (INN' igg o) Spanish and Welsh form; see IGNATIUS. Architecture: Inigo Jones (1573-1672), reconstructor of St. Paul's in London.

Ira (EYE' ra) Hebrew, "watcher." Biblical: Name of a priest and a captain at the time of King David.

Irvin(g) Scottish place name, Gaelic, "beautiful." ERWIN, IRV, IRVING, IRVINE, IRWIN. Once used mainly as a last name, *Irving* achieved prominence through Washington Irving the author and Sir Henry Irving the actor (1838–1905), born John Henry Brodribb. Science: Irving Langmuir, winner of Nobel Prize for chemistry (1932). Music: Irving Berlin, composer and song writer (*Alexander's Ragtime Band, White Christmas, God Bless America,* etc.); Irving Caesar, song writer (*Tea for Two, Is It True What They Say about Dixie?, Songs of Safety,* etc.).

Irwin Anglo-Saxon, "sea friend." See IRVIN. Fem., ERVA, IRVA. Education: Irwin Edman (1896–1954), beloved professor of philosophy at Columbia, poet and essayist.

Isaac Hebrew, "laughter." IKE, IZA(A)K.

And Abraham called the name of his son that was born unto him, whom Sarah bare to him, Isaac.

And Sarah said, God hath made me to laugh, so that all that hear will laugh with me.

GENESIS 21:3, 6

Famous men: Izaak Walton, author of the classic, *The Compleat Angler* (1653); Isaac Newton, discoverer of the laws of motion and gravity (1685). Music: Isaac Stern, violinist.

Isaiah (eye ZAY' a) Hebrew, "God is my helper" or "salvation of God." Isaiah was the great prophet of Israel whose most famous words set forth the dream of mankind:

And he shall judge among the nations, and shall rebuke many people: and they shall beat their swords into plowshares, and their spears into pruninghooks; nation shall not lift up sword against nation, neither shall they learn war any more.

ISAIAH 2 : 4

Isidor(e) Greek, "gift of ISIS." ISADORE. Fem., ISIDORA, ISADORA. Two Spanish saints bore this ancient Greek name, which was then adopted by the Spanish Jews. Sometimes shortened to DORE. Science: Isidor Isaac Rabi, winner of the Nobel Physics Prize for work on atoms (1944).

Israel (IZ' ree el *or* IZ' rah el) Hebrew, "ruling with the Lord" or "wrestling with the Lord." The new nation Israel receives its name from the name given to Jacob after his wrestling with the Lord, and through that name the modern land of Israel continues the heritage of Jacob and his descendants:

And God said unto him, Thy name is Jacob; thy name shall not be called any more Jacob,

*but Israel shall be thy name: and
he called his name Israel.*

*And the land which I gave
Abraham and Isaac, to thee I
will give it, and to thy seed after
thee will I give the land.*

GENESIS, 35 : 10, 12

History: Israel Putnam, a hero
of the American Revolution.

Ivan Russian form; see JOHN.
YVAN. Literature: Ivan Turgenev
(1818–1883), novelist (*Fathers
and Sons*). Art: Ivan Mestrovic
(1884–1962), one of the greatest
sculptors of modern times.

Ives Celtic name found in old
French romances. YVES. See IVOR.

Ivor (EYE' vor *or* EE' vor) Germanic, "bowman"; Anglo-Saxon,
"hero"; Scandinavian, "youth";
also Anglicized form of Welsh
IFOR, "lord." IVAR, YVES, YVON,
Fem., YVETTE, YVONNE.

The Old French forms of
this name, IVO and IVES, or
YVES, may also mean "Knight of
the Lion." St. Ives, a town in
Cornwall associated with the
nursery rhyme, "As I was going
to St. Ives," received its name
from St. Ives in Brittany. Literature: Ivor Brown, a modern
English essayist and writer on
words; Ivor Novello, composer
of the song *Keep the Home Fires
Burning*.

J

Feather beds are soft,
And painted rooms are bonny,
But I would leave them all
For my handsome, winsome JOHNNY.

OLD IRISH SONG, *I Know Where I'm Goin'*

Jabez (JAY' bezz) Hebrew, "He will bring sorrow."

Jack, Jackie Pet forms of JOHN. JOCK, JOCKO. Boxing: Jack Johnson and William Harrison Dempsey, better known as Jack Dempsey, former heavyweight champions. Baseball: Jackie Robinson, an all-around great player as well as the first Negro in the Big Leagues, elected to the National Baseball Hall of Fame in 1962. Hollywood: Jackie Cooper; Jackie Coogan, "The Kid" in the Chaplin classic film by that name. TV: The unpredictable Jack Paar. Stage and TV: Jackie Gleason.

But if love's the best of all,
That can a man befall
Why Jack's the king of all,
For they all love Jack!

OLD SONG, *They All Love Jack*

Jacob Hebrew, "supplanter." JACK, JAKE; Latin, JACOBUS; French, JACQUES; see also JAMES. Biblical: *Jacob* means also "following after," since Jacob was younger than his twin brother Esau:

And after that came his brother out, and his hand took hold
on Esau's heel; and his name was called Jacob.

GENESIS 25 : 26

Jacques (ZHAK) French form; see JACOB and JAMES. Fem., JACQUELINE. J a q u e s (pronounced JAY' kwees) is the philosopher in Shakespeare's *As You Like It*, who makes the famous "Seven Ages of Man" speech, which begins with "All the world's a stage." One of the earliest foreign-language songs most pupils learn is *Frère Jacques.*

History: Jacques Cartier, navigator, discoverer of the St. Lawrence River (1536). Music: Jacques Offenbach (1819–1880), composer of light operas (*Tales of Hoffman, La Périchole, La Belle Hélène,* etc.).

James From *Jacobus,* Latinized form of JACOB. JAMESY, JIM, JIMMIE, JIMMY. French, JACQUES; Gaelic, HAMISH (HAY' mish); Spanish, JAIME (HIGH' may); Irish, SEUMAS, SHAMUS, Italian, GIACOMO. Fem., JAMIE, JAMESINA. St. James the Great, one of the Twelve Apostles, is the patron saint of Spain under the name San Diego, or Santiago. Five Presidents were named James: Madison, Monroe, Polk, Buchanan, and Garfield.

And Normans call me James Fitz-James.
Thus watch I o'er insulted laws,
Thus learn to right the injured cause.

SIR WALTER SCOTT,
The Lady of the Lake

We have listed JAMIE as a girl's name because it is used as such today, but in Scotland especially it is a pet form of *James* (m). *Jamie* occurs in many of the poems of Robert Burns, as in his *Epistle to James Smith:*

Then, Jamie, I shall sae nae mair,
But quat [give up] my sang.
Content wi' you to make a pair.
Whare'er I gang.

Literature: Three remarkable Jameses: Boswell, Joyce, and Thurber. Also notable: James Fenimore Cooper for his *Leatherstocking Tales;* James Russell Lowell, American poet (*The Vision of Sir Launfal*); James Stephens, Irish poet and novelist (*In the Land of Youth, Here Are Ladies*, see also under ANGUS).

(See also GIACOMO and JACQUES.)

Science: James Watt (1736–1819), inventor of the steam engine. Screen: James Stewart, winner of an Oscar in 1940 (*The*

Philadelphia Story); James Cagney, winner in 1942 (*Yankee Doodle Dandy*).

Jan Dutch form; see JOHN. Art: Jan Vermeer of Delft (1632–1675), the perfect painter of interiors and light and shade. Music: Jan Peerce of the Metropolitan Opera.

Jared (JA' rid *or* JA' red) Hebrew, "descending." See JORDAN. Literature: Jared Sparks (1789–1866), pioneer in the teaching and study of American history.

Jarvis Germanic via French, form of *Gervase*, "sharp spear" or "spear servant" or "war leader."

Jascha (YASH' a) Russian pet form of JACOB and JAMES. Music: Jascha Heifetz, modern virtuoso and grand master of the violin.

Jason Greek, "healer." JAY. Mythology: Leader of the Argonauts in their quest of the Golden Fleece. Biblical: Kinsman of St. Paul (ROMANS 16 : 21). The names Jesus and Joshua were often changed to Jason in ancient times:

As thou wast Joshua once and now art Jason,
And from a Hebrew hast become a Greek.

HENRY WADSWORTH LONGFELLOW, *Judas Maccabeus*

Stage and Screen: Jason Robards Jr.

Jasper Persian, "treasurer." See GASPAR. Jasper is the usual English form of CASPAR and GASPAR.

Jay Bird-name. Without reference to origin, *Jay* is commonly used as a short form of names like JACOB and JASON.

Literature: Jay Gatsby in F. Scott Fitzgerald's novel of the 20's, *The Great Gatsby*. Music: Jay Gorney, composer of *Meet the People* and of the great song of the Great Depression, "Brother, Can You Spare a Dime?"— words by E. Y. ("Yip") Harburg.

Jean French form; see JOHN; see also JEAN (f.). Literature: Jean Valjean, hero of Victor Hugo's *Les Misérables;* Jean Racine (1639-1699), greatest French writer of classic tragedy (*Phèdre, Athalie,* etc.); Jean-Baptiste Poquelin, better known as Molière, one of the greatest writers of comedy in any language; Jean-Jacques Rousseau (1712–1788), author of the classic autobiography *Confessions;* Jean-Paul Sartre, essayist, novelist, dramatist (*No Exit*), leading exponent of Existentialism.

Screen and Literature: Jean Cocteau, Surrealist poet, novelist, dramatist (*The Infernal Machine*), director and writer of surrealist motion pictures (*Blood of a Poet*). Three more modern playwrights named Jean: Anouilh; Genet; Giraudoux. Screen: Jean Gabin.

Jed Short form of *Jedidiah,* Hebrew, "God is my friend."

Jeffrey JEFF. Hollywood: Jeff Goldblum.

Jennings Anglo-Saxon, "descendants of John."

Jerald Variant spelling; see GERALD. JERROLD.

Jeremiah (JERR e MY' a) Hebrew, "God is high." JEREMY, JERRY, JERE. Biblical: One of the greatest of the Hebrew prophets, whose lamentations on the fate of Jerusalem and his people have given us the word *jeremiad.*

So it's Jeremiah, Jeremiah,
  What have you to say
When you meet the garland girls
  Tripping on their way?
        ALFRED NOYES,
        The Barrel-Organ

Jeremy (JER' e mee) Popular spelling of JEREMIAH. JERE (JER' ee). Philosophy: Jeremy Bentham (1748–1832). Screen: Jeremy Irons (*Brideshead Revisited, Betrayal.*)

Jermyn Latin, *Germanus,* "a German." Fem., GERMAINE.

Jerome Greek via Latin, *Hieronymus,* "sacred name." JERRY. St. Jerome (340–420) was a most learned scholar whose Latin translation of the Scriptures forms the basis of the Vulgate. *Geronimo* is the Italian form of *Jerome.*

Literature: Jerome K. Jerome (1859-1927), humorist, author of *Three Men in a Boat*. Music:

Jerome Kern (1885–1945), composer of *Roberta, Show Boat*, which contains *Ol' Man River*, etc.). Ballet, Theater, Hollywood: Jerome Robbins, director of plays and films, choreographer (*Ballets: U.S.A.*).

Jerrard Variant form; see GERARD.

Jerrold Variant form; see GERALD.

Jerry Pet and dim. form of GERALD, JEREMIAH, JEREMY, and JEROME.

You that are sneering at my profession,
  Haven't you juggled a vast amount?
There's the Prime Minister in one Session,
  Juggles more games than my sins'll count.
      GEORGE MEREDITH,
        Juggling Jerry

Jesse (JESS' ee) Hebrew, "God exists." JESS. Biblical: Father of David, ancestor of Jesus by New Testament genealogy.

From Jesse's r o o t behold a branch arise,
Whose sacred flower with fragrance fills the skies.
  ALEXANDER POPE, *Messiah*

Jethro (JETH' ro *or* JEETH' ro) Hebrew, "pre-eminence." Biblical: Father-in-law of Moses.

Jim Pet form; see JAMES. Literature: *Lord Jim*, a powerful novel by Joseph Conrad; Jim, the loyal Negro friend of Huckleberry Finn; Jim Bludso, the brave engineer of a Mississippi steamboat who sacrificed himself to save the passengers when the boat caught fire:

He weren't no saint,—but at jedgment
I'd run my chance with Jim,
'Longside some pious gentlemen
  That wouldn't shook hands with him.
      JOHN HAY, *Jim Bludso of the Prairie Belle*

Stage, Screen, and TV: The ever popular and durable Jimmy Durante.

Joachim (JOE' a kim) Hebrew, "The Lord will judge." Spanish, JOAQUIN (hwah KEEN'); Russian, AKIM. Literature: Joaquin Miller (1841–1931), flamboyant poet of the West, famous for *Columbus*, which contains the stirring line: *Sail on! Sail on! Sail on!*
(See also under GIOACCHINO.)

Job Hebrew, "the afflicted." Fem., JOBINA, JOBYNA. Biblical: The patriarch who was tested as recounted in the Book of Job. The expression "Job's comforter" refers to a person whose sympathy adds to one's sorrow by saying that the sufferer brought his suffering on himself.

Ye have heard of the patience of Job.
      JAMES 5 : 11

Jock Pet form of JOHN. JOCKO, JOCKEY. See also JACK.

When Jockey dances on the green,
He looks so neat
And smiles so sweet
There's none of blythe and bonny mien
Can dance as well as he.
He talks to me of this and that,
My little heart goes pit-a-pat,
Each lassie'll frown
And looking down,
Will envy happy me.
    S. ARNOLD JR., *Jockey*

Joe See JOSEPH. JOEY.

The lusty days of long ago,
When you were Bill and I was Joe.
    OLIVER WENDELL HOLMES,
    Bill and Joe

Two outstanding Joes of the sports world made this name prominent not so long ago: Joe DiMaggio, "The Yankee Clipper," and heavyweight champion Joe Louis (Barrow).

Joel (JOE' el) Hebrew, "Jehovah is the Lord." Biblical: A Hebrew prophet. Literature: Joel Chandler Harris (1848–1908), author of the *Uncle Remus* stories.

Joey Pet form; see JOSEPH.

Oh, Jenny's as pretty as doves in a ditty;
And Jenny, her eyes are black;

And Joey's a fellow as merry and mellow
As ever shouldered a sack.
    JAMES CARNEGIE,
    The Flitch of Dunmow

Johann(es) German form; see JOHN. Four celebrated bearers of this name: Johann Sebastian Bach (1685–1750), composer, a monumental name in music; Johannes Brahms (1833–1897), another great composer; Johann Wolfgang von Goethe (1749–1832), author of *Faust*, a titanic figure in world literature; Johann Strauss (1825–1899), "The Waltz King," (*The Blue Danube, Tales from the Vienna Woods,* opera *Die Fledermaus,* "The Bat.").

John Hebrew, "Jehovah has been gracious." JACK, JACKIE, JACKY, JON, JONI, JONNEL, JOHNNY, JOCK, JAN. Fem., JOHANNA, JOAN(NA), JANE, JEAN. Biblical: John the Baptist and John the Evangelist. This name of Hebrew origin has become the most popular first name for boys. Despite changing trends in the giving of first names, John ranks as Number 1, being the first name of about 6,000,000 males in the United States. It is equally the leader in other countries, with about 100 variations in different European languages, among them *Evan* in Welsh, *Jan* in Scottish, *Shawn, Sean* in Irish, *Juan* in Spanish, *Giovanni* in Italian, *Hans* and *Johann* in German, *Jan* in Dutch, *Jean* in

French, and *Ivan* (dim. *Vanya*) in Russian. Last names from John or its variations are Jones, Jackson, Jensen, Jansen, Jenks, Jenkins, and Hanson. Three Presidents named John: John Adams and his son John Quincy Adams, and John Fitzgerald Kennedy. (See also under CALVIN.)

John Anderson my jo [sweetheart], *John,*
When we were first acquent
Your locks were like the raven,
Your bonnie brow was brent [smooth].
ROBERT BURNS, *John Anderson*

A quartet of great authors of the past named John: Bunyan, Milton, Donne, and Keats. A quintet of later authors of note: John Greenleaf Whittier (1807–1892), "The Quaker Poet," author of *Snow-Bound, The Barefoot Boy, Maud Muller, Barbara Frietchie;* Ruskin, critic, reformer, essayist; Galsworthy, dramatist, short-story writer, novelist (*The Forsyte Saga*); Masefield, Poet Laureate since 1930 (*Sea Fever*); Steinbeck, winner of a Pulitzer Prize in 1940 for *Grapes of Wrath*, great novel of the Dust Bowl. Detective Literature: John H. Watson, M. D., who shared 221B Baker Street with Sherlock Holmes and was his chronicler and Boswell.

Philosophy: John Locke (1693–1704), author of *An Essay on Human Understanding;* John Dewey (1859–1952), who exercised a great influence on modern educational practices. Religion: John Wesley (see under WESLEY). History: John Paul Jones (1747–1792), American naval hero of the Revolution ("I have not yet begun to fight!"). Art and Nature Study: John Jacob Audubon (1785–1851), ornithologist and painter of birds (the classic *Birds of America*). Stage: John Barrymore (1882–1942), "The Profile"; Sir John Gielgud, noted for Shakespearean roles. Aeronautics: Astronaut John H. Glenn Jr., "the hale and hearty" astronaut made known to the entire world on February 20, 1962.

(See also under GIOVANNI, HANS, JAN, JEAN, and JOHANN.)

Johnny   Pet form; see JOHN.

Johnny had a golden head
  Like a golden mop in blow,
Right and left his curls would spread
  In a glory and a glow,
And they framed his honest face
Like stray sunbeams out of place
Like stray sunbeams out of place.
  CHRISTINA ROSSETTI, *Johnny*

Folklore: Johnny Appleseed, nickname of John Chapman, who went about the Ohio countryside planting apple seeds in the early days of the nineteenth century.

Remember Johnny Appleseed,
  All ye who love the apple;
He served his kind by Word and Deed,

In God's grand greenwood chapel.

WILLIAM HENRY VENABLE,
Johnny Appleseed, A. Ballad of the Old Northwest

TV: Johnny Carson, king of talk shows; quickest wit in the west.

Jonah (JOE' na) Hebrew, "dove." JONAS. Biblical: Jonah the Prophet, who was swallowed by a whale.

. . . Jonah prays
And sings his canticles and hymns,
Making the hollow vault resound
God's goodness and mysterious ways,
Till the great fish spouts music as he swims.

ALDOUS HUXLEY, *Jonah*

Medicine: Dr. Jonas Salk, discoverer of the polio vaccine.

Jonathan (JONN' a than) Hebrew, "Jehovah gave." JON. The friendship of David and Jonathan, son of King Saul, is as proverbial as that of Damon and Pythias.

And it came to pass, when he had made an end of speaking unto Saul, that the soul of Jonathan was knit with the soul of David, and Jonathan loved him as his own soul.

I SAMUEL, 18 : 1

Literature: Jonathan Swift (1667–1745), poet and satirist,

author of *Gulliver's Travels* and *Journal to Stella.*

Jordan Biblical, name of the famous river in Israel, Hebrew, "descending." Same as JARED.

Joseph Hebrew, "He shall add." JO, JOE, JOEY, JOSÉ. Fem., JOSEPHINE. Long a favorite name, not only because of Joseph who ruled in Egypt but also because of Joseph, husband of Mary.

And she called his name Joseph; and said, the LORD shall add to me another son.

GENESIS, 30 : 14

Literature: Joseph Addison (1672–1719), poet and essayist; Joseph Conrad (1857–1924), of Polish birth, original name Teodor Józef Konrad Korzeniowski, author of beautiful short stories and novels of the sea, character, and adventure. Music: Joseph Haydn (1732–1809), affectionately called "Papa Haydn," one of the great composers (*The Creation, The Seasons,* etc.). Medicine: Joseph Lister (1827–1912), English surgeon considered the founder of antiseptic surgery. Dance: José Greco. Stage and Screen: José Ferrer, winner of an Oscar in 1950 (*Cyrano de Bergerac*); José Quintero, director.

(See also under GIUSEPPE.)

Joshua Hebrew, "Jehovah saves." JOSH. Biblical: Joshua led the Israelites over the Jordan into the Promised Land after the death of Moses.

*Joshua fit de battle ob Jericho,
An' de walls come tumblin'
down.*

SPIRITUAL

Art: Sir Joshua Reynolds (1723–1792), renowned English portrait painter (*The Tragic Muse*, portrait of the actress Sarah Kemble Siddons). Stage: Joshua Logan, director and producer, sharer of the 1950 Pulitzer Prize (*South Pacific*).

Josiah (jo SIGH′ a) Hebrew, "Jehovah supports." JOSIAS. Biblical: An upright king of Judah. Josiah Wedgwood (1730–1795) founded the firm that raised pottery to a fine art in England.

Jotham (JOE′ tham) Hebrew, "Jehovah is perfect."

Joyce Germanic, "of the Gothic people." JOCELYN. See also JOYCE (f). Literature: Joyce Kilmer (1886–1918), poet (*Trees*); Joyce Cary, modern English novelist.

Judah Hebrew, "praise." JUDAS, JUDD, JUDE. Judah was the fourth son of Jacob by Leah:

*Now will I praise the LORD;
therefore she called his name
Judah.*

GENESIS 29 : 35

Judah was the name of the tribe of Judah's descendants, also of the kingdom of ten tribes formed after the death of Solomon.

*Bright the vision that delighted
Once the sight of Judah's seer.*
RICHARD MANT,
Bright the Vision

Judas Maccabeus led a revolt against the Syrians and Greeks in the second century B. C. Music: *Judas Maccabeus*, oratorio by Handel, which is often presented at the Festival of Lights, or Chanukah, commemorating the spirit of freedom symbolized by Judas Maccabeus. St. Jude was one of the Twelve Apostles; he is also known as Thaddeus.

Literature: *Jude the Obscure*, powerful tragic novel by Thomas Hardy. History: Judah B. Benjamin (1811–1884), member of Jefferson Davis' cabinet. Music: Yehudi Menuhin, virtuoso violinist (he uses a Hebrew form of the name).

Judd, Jud(d)son Patronymic, "son of JORDAN," but also used in place of JUDAH.

Jules French form; see JULIUS. Literature: Jules Verne (1828–1905), author of *Twenty Thousand Leagues under the Sea, Around the World in Eighty Days*, etc.). Music: Jules Massenet (1842–1912), composer of the operas *Thaïs* and *Manon*.

Julian (JOOL′ yan) Latin, "belonging or related to Julius." Fem., JULIANA. St. Julian the Hospitaler is the patron saint of travelers. Julian was a Roman emperor of the fourth century.

Dr. Julian Wolff, cartographer by avocation, is the editor of the *Baker Street Journal* and Commissionaire (head) of the Baker Street Irregulars (s e e under IRENE and SHERLOCK).

Julius Latin, *Julius,* possibly from Greek, "downy," the name of a *gens,* but *not* a Roman family or first name. JULE, JULES, JULEY, JULIAN. Spanish, JULIO: Italian, GIULIO. Fem., JULIA, JULIE. The full name of Julius Caesar is Gaius (or Caius) Julius Caesar. The month of July was named in his honor.

> *There may be many Caesars Ere such another Julius.*
> SHAKESPEARE, *Cymbeline*

Junius Latin, *Junius,* the name of a *gens.* The name may be related to the goddess Juno; the month of June, *Junius* in Latin, was named after the clan or the goddess. Brutus, one of the slayers of Julius Caesar, belonged to the Junian clan, his full name

being Marcus Junius Brutus. Even his foe Mark Antony admitted that Brutus acted as he did in "common good to all" and said of him:

> *This was the noblest Roman of them all.*
> WILLIAM SHAKESPEARE, *Julius Caesar*

Hence, to many, Brutus has become the symbol of freedom, the image of an unselfish worker for his country's good so that some parents name a son after him: Junius Brutus Booth, actor, father of the actor Edwin Thomas Booth.

Justin Latin, "just." JUSTINIAN, JUSTUS. Fem., JUSTINE. Justin the Martyr lived in the second century. Justinian I (483–565), Emperor of the Eastern Roman Empire, "The Lawgiver," codified Roman law.

Literature: Justin Huntly McCarthy, author of the popular novel *If I Were King* (1901), which was made into a musical.

K

In Xanadu did KUBLA KHAN
A stately pleasure-dome decree:
Where Alph, the sacred river, ran
Through caverns measureless to man
Down to a sunless sea.

SAMUEL TAYLOR COLERIDGE, *Kubla Khan*

Karl German form; see CHARLES. CARL. Karl Baedeker (1801–1859), originated the series of guides which have been so popular that the term *Baedeker* loosely signifies any guide book. The best-known bearer of the name is, however, Marx.

Kasper See GASPAR and JASPER. KASPAR.

Keith (KEETH) Scottish place name, "enclosed place." This was originally the name of a Scottish clan. It is an increasingly popular name together with KENNETH, SCOTT, and STUART.

Kenelm Anglo-Saxon, "brave-helmet" or "brave warrior."

Kenneth Celtic, "handsome." KEN, KENNY. The first king of Scotland was named Kenneth. Sir Kenneth appears in *The Talisman* by Scott. Kenneth Grahame (1859–1932), who considered children "the only really living people," wrote three delightful books about children, *The Wind in the Willows*, a masterpiece of charming fantasy, *The Golden Age*, and *Dream*

Days. Criticism: Kenneth Tynan, brilliant, incisive English dramatic critic (*Curtains*).

No sluggard's part is Kenneth's role,
But breathless presses toward the goal.

ANON., *Catalogue of Names in Rhyme*

Kent English place name of a county south of London; possibly Germanic, "corner."

Kent, in the Commentaries Caesar writ,
Is term'd the civil'st place of all this isle:
Sweet is the country, because full of riches;
The people liberal, valiant, active, wealthy.

WILLIAM SHAKESPEARE, *II Henry VI*

Kermit Celtic, probably "free."

Kevin (KEVV' in) Irish, "handsome." This is a name growing in popularity. See under KEITH. St. Kevin is the name of one of the patrons of Dublin. In Ireland the name of Kevin Barry, eighteen-year old hero in the struggle

(1920) against the English is cherished:

Early on a Sunday morning,
High upon a gallows tree,
Kevin Barry gave his young life
For the cause of liberty.
                ANON., *Kevin Barry*

Kim From Celtic *Cyn*, "chief," an element found in many Welsh names, and which Shakespeare probably used to coin the name *Cymbeline*. As used today, *Kim* is a short form of place names and surnames such as Kimberley and Kimball (Kemble). The latter is believed to mean "chief-war," and from it the first well-known use of *Kim* was derived —in the title of Kipling's novel (1901) of life in India. Its hero is an Irish boy named Kimball O'Hara, better known simply as Kim. This name is now used as a fem. first name; see KIM (f).

King Anglo-Saxon, "ruler" or "wise."

Kirby English place name, Anglo-Saxon, "church town."

Kirk Scottish, "church." Screen: Kirk Douglas.

Kit See CHRISTIAN and CHRISTOPHER.

Knut (KNOOT) Danish, "kind, race." CNUT, CANUTE. King Cnut, or Canute, a Danish invader, ruled over England from 1017 to 1035. Canute is the king who, in the famous story, commanded the waves to stand still as a test of his power.

Literature: Knut Hamsun, Norwegian novelist, author of *Growth of the Soil*, Nobel Prize winner in 1920. Football: Knute Kenneth Rockne (1888–1931), the football coach at Notre Dame whose career has become a legend.

Konrad See CONRAD.

Konstantin See CONSTANTINE. Theater: Konstantin Stanislavski (1863–1938), actor, co-founder and director of the Moscow Art Theater, a great influence on styles of acting because of his "method."

Kurt Short form; see CONRAD. Music: Kurt Weill (1900–1950), renowned composer of songs and music for the theater (*The Threepenny Opera, Lost in the Stars*, etc.).

Kyle Gaelic, "handsome," or Celtic place name, "living near the chapel."

L

*There is no name in all our country's story
So loved as his today:
No name which so unites the things of glory
With life's plain, common way.*

ROBERT WHITAKER, *Abraham Lincoln*

Lambert Germanic via French, "bright land."

Lance Germanic, "land." LANCELOT.

Lancelot (LANN' cell ot *or* LANCE' lot) Probably a name invented by early poets; but also considered a diminutive of LANCE. LAUNCELOT. Lancelot was the greatest of King Arthur's Knights.

*Then Arthur charged his warrior
    whom he loved
And honor'd most, Sir Lancelot,
    to ride forth
And bring the Queen . . . .*
    ALFRED, LORD TENNYSON,
        The Coming of Arthur

Science: Lancelot Hogben (*Mathematics for the Millions.*)

Lane Place name, "at the passage."

Langdon, Langston Place name, "long town, hill, or valley." Literature: Langston Hughes poet, novelist, and dramatist (*Shakespeare in Harlem, Black Nativity,* the *Simple series,* etc.).

Lanny A name from literature. Lanny Budd, full name Lanning Prescott Budd, is the hero of Upton Sinclair's series of novels dealing with Lanny's efforts to cope with the problems arising from World War I. LANNY is sometimes used as a variant of LENNIE; see LEONARD. Fem., LANNIE.

Lathrop (LAY' throp) Place name, "at the low village."

Laurence, Lawrence Latin place name, "of *Laurentum,*" possibly related to "bay tree" or "laurel." LARRY, LAURIE, LAURANCE, LAWRANCE, RANCE, LOREN, LORENZO. Fem., LAURA. St. Laurence was a third-century martyr. Literature: The kindly Friar Laurence, who marries the two lovers in *Romeo and Juliet;* Laurie Lee, author of *Cider with Rosie, A Rose for Winter;* Lawrence Durrell, British poet and novelist (*Alexandria Quartet,* etc.). Stage and Screen: Sir Laurence Olivier, one of the great actors of modern times, winner of an Oscar in 1948 (*Hamlet*); Laurence Harvey. History: Lorenzo de' Medici (1449-1492), "The Magnificent," ruler of

123

Florence, patron of literature and art, a poet of originality.

Laverne, LaVerne See VERNON.

Lawton Place name, "law-town" or "meadow-hill" or "hill town."

Lazarus (LAZZ' a rus) Hebrew via Greek, "God will help." See ELEAZAR. LAZAR. Biblical: The Beggar in the parable of Dives ("the Rich Man") and Lazarus; also name of the brother of Martha and Mary.

Leander (lee AND' er) Greek "lion-man," appropriate name of the mythological stalwart who swam the Hellespont to see his lady-love Hero.

And lo, with what clear omen in the east
On day's great threshold stands the eager dawn,
Like young Leander rosy from the sea
Glowing at Hero's lattice!
JAMES RUSSELL LOWELL,
Columbus

Lee Anglo-Saxon, "meadow." LEIGH. *Lee* is often used as a diminutive of LEO and LEONARD. It is also popular as a last name. Henry ("Light Horse Harry") Lee, a Revolutionary cavalry leader, is remembered for his tribute to George Washington, "First in war, first in peace, and first in the hearts of his countrymen." The Southern general Robert Edward Lee was his son. Screen: Lee J. Cobb, Lee Marvin, Oscar 1965 (*Cat Ballou*).

Leigh (LEE) See LEE. James Henry Leigh Hunt (1774–1859), better known as Leigh Hunt, a liberal journalist and poet, wrote *Abou Ben Adhem*.

Leland (LEE' land) Place name, "meadow land." Stage, Movies, TV: Producer and director Leland Hayward.

Lemuel (LEMM' you el) Hebrew, devoted to the Lord." Literature: Lemuel Gulliver, hero of Swift's satire *Gulliver's Travels*.

Leo Latin, "lion." LEON. Fem., LEONA, LEONE, LEONIA, LEONIE, LEONTYNE. Thirteen Popes have been called Leo. Literature: Count Leo Tolstoy (Lev Nikolaevich Tolstoy) one of the great writers of the last century (*War and Peace, Anna Karénina,* etc.). Music: Léo Delibes (1836–1891), composer of ballets (*Sylvia, Coppelia*) and operas (*Lakmé*). Science: Leo Szilard, world-renowned in nuclear physics and genetics. Instrumental in ushering in the atomic age, he considered the liberation of atomic energy as the liberator of mankind from poverty and war. Awarded the Albert Einstein Commemorative Award in 1962 for work in science; author of delightful and penetrating "fiction-essays," *The Voice of the Dolphins.*

Leonard (LENN' ard) Germanic, "bold lion." LEN, LENNY. Art: Leonardo da Vinci (1452-1519), painter of the *Mona Lisa* and *The Last Supper,* inventor, writer, a truly great genius, epitome of the versatility of the Renaissance Man. Music: Leonard Bernstein, pianist, conductor, composer, lecturer. Journalism: Leonard Lyons, widely syndicated columnist ("The Lyons Den").

Leonidas (lee ON' i das) Greek "like a lion." LEONIDE. History: Leader of the heroic 300 Spartans at the pass of Thermopylae against Xerxes and the Persians.

Every great crisis of human history is a pass of Thermopylae, and there is always a Leonidas and his three hundred to die in it, if they cannot conquer.
GEORGE W. CURTIS,
The Call of Freedom

Leopold Germanic, "bold people." Fem., LEOPOLDINE. A name once popular with European nobility and royalty. Music: Leopold Stokowski, conductor; Leopold Auer (1845-1930), violinist, teacher of three gifted pupils: Jascha Heifetz, Mischa Elman, and Efrem Zimbalist.

Leroy (LEE' roy *or* l'ROY') French, "the king." LEROY, LE- ROI, ROY. See also ELROY, REX, REGIS, ROYAL, KING.

Leslie Scottish place name, "low meadow." LES, LESLEY. Old Scottish clan name; a popular girls'. name also. Stage and Screen: The lovable Leslie Howard (1893-1943).

Lester English place name, "Leicester." LES. The Latin word *castra,* which appears in English place names as *caster, cester, ceister, chester,* means "camp."

Levi (LAY' vee *or* LEE' vye) Hebrew, "joined in harmony." Biblical: son of Jacob and Leah; name of the priestly tribe of Israel.

And she conceived again, and bore a son: and said, Now this time will my husband be joined unto me, because I have borne him three sons: therefore was his name called Levi.
GENESIS 29:34

Lewis See LOUIS and LLEWEL- LYN. LEW. General Lew Wallace wrote three best-sellers, one of which, *Ben Hur* (1880), is still popular, especially in Hollywood. Lewis Carroll is the pen name of Charles Lutwidge Dodgson, author of *Alice in Wonderland.*

Liam (LYE' um) Irish form; see WILLIAM. Literature and Screen: Liam O'Flaherty wrote the story that was turned into the great motion picture *The Informer* (1935).

Lincoln place name, *Lindocol-onia,* from Welsh, "lake," and Latin, "colony." The use of *Lincoln* as a first name arose, of course, from a deep feeling of reverence for President Abraham Lincoln. Journalism: (Joseph) Lincoln Steffens (1866-1936), leader of the Muckrakers (*The Shame of the Cities,* etc.); Lincoln Ellsworth (1880-1951), outstanding polar explorer.

Hail, Lincoln! As the swift years
*   lengthen*
*   Still more majestic grows thy*
*   fame;*
The ties that bind us to thee
*   strengthen;*
*   Star-like immortal shines thy*
*   name.*
            NATHAN HASKELL DOLE,
                Lincoln's Birthday

Lindsay, Lindsey (LINN′ zee) English place name, Anglo-Saxon, "linden-tree island or hedge." LINDESAY. Radio and TV: Lindsey Nelson, sports reporter.

Linus (LYE′ nus) Greek, "flax." Linus was the second Pope. Science: Linus Pauling, winner of the Nobel Prize for chemistry (1954).

Lionel French dim. form; see LEO.

The friend, the neighbor, Lionel,
*   the beloved,*
The loved, the lover, the happy
*   Lionel,*

The low-voiced, tender-spirited
*   Lionel.*
        ALFRED, LORD TENNYSON,
                The Lover's Tale

Hollywood, Stage, and TV: Lionel Barrymore (1878-1954), winner of an Oscar in 1931 (*A Free Soul*).

Llewel(l)yn (loo ELL′ in) a popular Welsh name probably meaning "lightning" or "lionlike" or "leader." LLYWELYN, LYN(N). LEWIS may also be derived from this name. Llewellyn I and Llewellyn II were princes of Wales in the thirteenth century when Wales was independent. Literature: Richard Llewellyn, pen name of Richard David Vivian Llewellyn Lloyd, author of *How Green Was My Valley.*

The spearmen heard the bugle
*   sound,*
*   And cheerily smiled the morn,*
And many a brach [hunting dog]
*   and many a hound*
*   Obeys Llewelyn's horn.*
            WILLIAM R. SPENCER,
                Beth-Gêlert

Lloyd Welsh, "gray" or "dark-complexioned." David Lloyd George (1863-1945), usually referred to as Lloyd George, was Prime Minister of England during World War I.

Logan Place name, Celtic, "hollow meadow." Medicine: Logan Clendening (1884-1945), author of the popular book *The Human Body.* Literature: Logan

Pearsall Smith (1865-1946), author of charming essays called *Trivia*.

Lon Dim. form; see ALONSO. LONNY. Screen: Lon Chaney (1883-1930), still remembered for his vivid interpretation of Quasimodo in *The Hunchback of Notre Dame*.

Loren, Lorin Short forms; see LAURENCE. Fem., LORENE. Music: Lorin Maazel, conductor, "a child prodigy who made good"; Lorin Hollander, pianist.

Louis (LOO' iss *or* LOO' ee) Germanic, "renowned warrior" or "warrior prince." LEW, LEWIS, LOU, LOUIE. ALOYSIUS, the name of a famous saint, is a Latinization, from which ALOIS is derived. German, LUDWIG; Italian, LUIGI; Spanish, LUIS. Fem., LOUISE, LOUISA, LOU, ALOUISE. *Chlodowig*, the name of the first Frankish king of France (466-511), became *Clovis* and *Ludovicus* via Latin, and eventually LOUIS via French. Eighteen kings of France bore this name, of whom Louis XIV (1638-1715), called the Great, *le Grand Monarque*, and *le Roi Soleil* ("The Sun King"), is the best known. Under him the arts flourished but he was the model of the true autocrat; to him is ascribed the saying *L'état, c'est moi* ("I am the state"). Science: The great Louis Pasteur (1822-1895); Baseball: Lou Gehrig (1903-1941), "The Pride of the Yankees," whose career was an inspiration to youth. Literature: Louis Untermeyer, poet, humorist, anthologist, poetry consultant to the Library of Congress. Music: Louis "Satchmo" Armstrong, trumpeter, bandleader, a great name in jazz.

Lowell Germanic and Latin, "little wolf." LOVEL. *Lowell* is also a last name of distinction. Among the famous Lowells are James Russell Lowell (1819-1891), poet, editor, diplomat, author of *The Vision of Sir Launfal*, Amy Lawrence Lowell, the poet (1874-1925), her brothers, Abbot Lawrence Lowell, president of Harvard (1909-1933), and Percival Lowell, the astronomer.

And this is good old Boston,
   The home of the bean and the cod,
Where the Lowells talk to the Cabots,
   And the Cabots talk only to God.

   JOHN C. BOSSIDY,
On the Aristocracy of Harvard

Lucian (LOO' shan) Greek name, meaning not known. *Lucianus*, the Latinization of *Loukianos*, the Greek original, has been confused with the name of the Latin poet Lucan and with LUCIUS and LUKE. LUCIEN. Fem., LUCIENNE. St. Lucian was a Syrian martyr of the third century. Literature: Lucian (born about about 120 A.D.), author of satires.

Lucius (LOO' shus) Latin, "bringing light." Fem., LUCIA, LUCY. This was a widely used Roman first name.

Boy! Lucius! fast asleep? It is no matter;
Enjoy the honey-heavy dew of slumber:
Thou hast no figures nor no fantasies
Which busy care draws in the brains of men;
Therefore thou sleepest so sound.
                    WILLIAM SHAKESPEARE,
                         Julius Caesar

Journalism: Lucius Morris Beebe, writer on railroads, society, Western folklore.

Ludwig German form; see LOUIS. Music: Ludwig van Beethoven (1770-1827), the titan of composers.

Luke Greek, from Latin place name, "a person from Lucania." LUCAS. *Lucanus* (the Latin form) is the surname of the author of the Latin poem on the civil war between Caesar and Pompey. St. Luke is the Evangelist, patron saint of doctors and painters, "the beloved physician" (COLOSSIANS 4:14).

Luther Germanic, "illustrious warrior." LOTHAR. Fem., LORRAINE. This old German name, to which the Italian *Lot(h)ario* is related, is often given in honor of Martin Luther, the religious reformer (1483-1546). Stage: Luther Adler.

Lyle French, "of the island." LISLE.

Lyman Place name, "from the valley."

Lynn Anglo-Saxon place name, "mountain torrent." LYN. See also LLEWELLYN.

M

Here we are! here we are!! here we are again!!!
There's Pat and MAC *and Tommy and Jack and*
Joe.

CHARLES KNIGHT, *Here We Are*

Mac Celtic, "son of." MACK. Used as a diminutive of any name beginning with *Mc* or *Mac;* or pet form of MAX.

Magnus Latin, "great."

Mahlon Hebrew, "sickness." Biblical: First husband of Ruth.

Malachi, Malachy (MAL' a kye) Hebrew, "my messenger" or "messenger of the Lord." Biblical: Name of the last book of the Old Testament. Literature: *Prophecies of St. Malachy* by St. Malachy, famous Irish saint of the twelfth century.

Let Erin remember the days of
*   old,*
* Ere her faithless sons betrayed*
*   her;*
When Malachi wore the collar of
*   gold*
* Which he won from the proud*
*   invader.*

THOMAS MOORE,
Let Erin Remember

Malcolm Celtic, "disciple of Columbia." See COLIN. Literature: Son of King Duncan in Shakespeare's *Macbeth;* Malcolm Cowley, critic and editor.

Manfred Germanic, "man of peace." FRED. Literature: Drama by Byron. Music: Composition by Berlioz. See also under EL-LERY.

Manuel See EMANUEL. Fem., MANUEL(L)A. Music: Manuel de Falla (1876-1946), Spanish composer (*La Vida Breve, The Three-Cornered Hat,* the cantata *Atlantida*).

Marc See MARK. Art: Marc Chagall, modern French artist; the exhibition (1961-1962) of stained glass windows made by him drew enormous crowds to the Museum of Modern Art, New York City. Music: Marc Blitzstein, composer and librettist; his adaptation of *The Three-penny Opera* ran for more than seven years.

Marcel French form; see MARCELLUS. Literature: Marcel Proust (1871-1922), one of the greatest novelists of our century, author of *Remembrance of Things Past;* Marcel Pagnol, author of the trilogy (*César, Marius, Fanny*) which has been made into movies, plays, and musicals. Stage: Marcel Marceau, French mime *par excellence.*

129

Marcello Italian form; see MARCELLUS. Screen: Marcello Mastroianni, star of *La Dolce Vita, La Notte,* etc.

Marcellus Latin dim. form; see MARCUS. Fem., MARCELLA.

Marcus See MARK. A name ennobled by the Roman emperor Marcus Aurelius (121-180), called "The Philosopher," whose Stoic reflections on life entitled *Meditations,* or *To Himself,* have been a comfort to many. *Marcus* was one of the most popular of Roman masc. first names; among those who bore it are Brutus and Antony.

Marion Originally the diminutive of MARY. See MARIAN. The spelling "Marion" is usually reserved for boys. As a last name it is known through the exploits of General Francis Marion, "The Swamp Fox," against the British in the American Revolution.

Well knows the fair and friendly moon
The band that Marion leads ...
WILLIAM CULLEN BRYANT,
Song of Marion's Men

Marius Latin, *gens* name. Italian, MARIO. History: Gaius Marius, great Roman general, seven times consul, uncle of Julius Caesar. Literature: *Marius the Epicurean,* the classic philosophic novel by Walter Pater. Stage and Screen: Marius Goring. Philology: Mario Pei, authority on names, words, and languages.

Mark Latin, possibly from *Mars,* the name of the god of war. MARC, MARCUS. Fem., MARCIA. St. Mark (Italian San Marco), one of the four Evangelists, is the patron saint of Venice. Mark Hopkins (1802-1887) was a renowned educator, president of Williams College, of whom President James A. Garfield is supposed to have said, "My idea of a college education is Mark Hopkins on one end of a log and a student on the other." The name *Mark* is not included in *Mark Twain,* the pen name adopted by Samuel L. Clemens. "Mark twain," a term used by Mississippi River pilots in making soundings, indicated that the depth of the water reached two ("twain") fathoms (twelve feet).
   Literature: Mark Van Doren, editor, critic, novelist, poet, winner of the Pulitzer Poetry Prize in 1940; *Marco Millions* (1928), play by Eugene O'Neill, and *Messer Marco Polo* (1921), a charming romance by Donn Byrne, both dealing with the fabulous explorer.

Marlin French popular form; see MERLIN. The unusual name *Marlon* has come into prominence because of Marlon Brando, vivid personality and actor who on stage created the unforgettable role of Stanley Kowalski in Tennessee Williams' *Streetcar Named Desire,* and won both the New York Film Critics' Award and an Oscar in 1954 (*On The Waterfront*). Marlon Brando's family is of French descent, the original surname being *Brandeau*. The names closest to *Marlon* used in France are *Marlot* and *Merlot*, which are related to MERLE and MARLIN.

Marshal(l) Germanic via French, "military commander." A last name made known through John Marshall (1755-1835), Chief Justice of the Supreme Court (1801-1835), whose decisions fixed principles of constitutional law, and through General George C. Marshall; associated as a first name with the Field family of merchants.

Martin Latin, "of Mars." MART, MARTEN, MARTYN, MARTY. Fem., MARTINA, MARTINE. St. Martin was a Roman military officer stationed at Amiens, France, in the fourth century. The favorite story about him is that he divided his cloak with a beggar, who later appeared before him as Christ. From this incident we get the word *chapel*, because *cappella*, the late Latin word meaning "cloak," was applied to the sanctuary where the cloak was kept as a sacred relic. Martin Luther further added to the popularity of this first name. Our eighth President was Martin Van Buren. Literature: *Martin Chuzzlewit*, a novel by Dickens; *Martin Eden* (1909), an autobiographical novel by Jack London.

Marvin Celtic, "beautiful sea"; or Anglo-Saxon, "sea friend" or "famous friend." MARV, MERVIN, MERWIN, MERWYN, MYRWYN, MURVYN, MYRVYN.

Mason French occupational name, "worker in stone."

Mat(t), Matty See MATTHEW.

Ah! Matt: old age has brought to me
Thy wisdom, less thy certainty:
The world's a jest, and joy's a trinket:
I knew that once: but now—I think it.

JAMES K. STEPHEN,
Senex to Matthew Prior

Matthew Hebrew, "gift of the Lord." MAT, MATTY, MATTHIAS. Biblical: One of the four Evangelists. The surnames Mayhew, Mayo, Mace, Macey, Macy, Machen, Madison, Mattheson, Mattison, and Massey come from *Matthew*. Literature: Matthew Arnold (1882-1888), critic, essayist, and poet; Matthew Josephson, critic and biographer, author of the classic economic study *The Robber Barons* (1934), *Life Among the Surrealists* (1962), etc. Photography: Mathew B. Brady (1823-1896), "Mr. Lincoln's Photographer," first important American photographer, whose pictures of the Civil War are not only museum pieces but also historical data.

Matthew, Mark, Luke, and John,
The bed be blest that I lye on.
                    THOMAS ADY,
        A Candle in the Dark (1656)

Maurice (MAW' riss *or* MORR'
iss *or* muh REES') French-Latin,
"Moorish, dark." MAURY, MOR-
RIS, MORRIE, MORSE, MOSS, MOR-
ITZ, MURRAY. St. Moritz, the
noted Swiss winter resort, is
named after St. Maurice, a
Greek legionary in the Roman
army, who suffered martyrdom
in the third century. *Maurice* is
used to translate the Irish name
Moriarty, "sea warrior," a name
familiar to all readers of the
Sherlock Holmes stories.

Childe Maurice sat in Silver
   Wood.
He whistled and he sang
"I think I see the woman coming
That I have loved so long."
    OLD BALLAD, *Childe Maurice*

Stage, Screen, and TV:
Maurice Chevalier; Maurice
Evans. Music: Maurice Ravel,
composer (*Bolero*, etc.).

Max See MAXIMILIAN and MAX-
WELL. MAC, MACK, MAXEY,
MAXIE. Fem., MAXINE, MAXITA.
Literature: Sir Max Beerbohm
(1872-1956), "The Incomparable
Max," wit, parodist, critic, aes-
thete (*Seven Men, Zuleika Dobson*). Science: Max Planck, winner of the Nobel Prize for
physics (1918). Stage and Screen:
Max Reinhardt (1873-1943), director and producer (*The Mira-
cle, Everyman*).

Maximilian Latin, *maximus,*
"greatest." MAX, MAXIE, MAXIM.
The origin of this name, said to
have been coined by Frederick
III of Germany in 1459, indicates how universal is and always has been the problem of
choosing a name.

A new name, first devised by
Frederic the third Emperor, who
doubting what name to give his
son and heire, composed this
name of two worthy Romans,
whom he most admired, Quintus
Fabius Maximus, and Scipio
Aemilianus, with hope that his
son would imitate their vertues.
          WILLIAM CAMDEN,
   Remaines Concerning Britaine
              (1615-1623)

Literature: Maxim Gorki
(1868-1936), short-story writer
and dramatist, author of *A
Night's Lodging*. Screen: Maximilian Schell, winner of 1962
Oscar (*Judgment at Nuremberg*).

Maxwell Anglo-Saxon and Scottish place name, "Maccus' or
Macca's well"; see MAGNUS for
the root of these names. MAC,
MAX. Maxwellton is a town in
southern Scotland, famed for the
reference to it in the line from
Annie Laurie, "Maxwellton's
braes are bonnie." Literature:
The dramatist Maxwell Anderson (1888-1959), winner of a
Pulitzer Prize in 1933 (*Both
Your Houses*).

Mayer See MEYER.

Maynard Anglo-Saxon, "intense strength."

Melville Place name, Anglo-Saxon, "hill," and French, "city."

Melvin Celtic, "chief." MALVIN, MELVIN, MEL, MAL. The poet James Macpherson (1736-1796) coined the feminine name MALVINA in his Ossianic poems; from this may have come the masculine *Malvin* and its variations. Screen and Stage: Melvyn Douglas. Radio and TV: Sports reporter Mel Allen.

Merle French, "blackbird"; originally a nickname applied to a person who loved to whistle or sing like a blackbird; as attested by these quotations:

Four and twenty blackbirds,
 Baked in a pie;
When the pie was opened,
 The birds began to sing.
  NURSERY RHYME,
   Sing a Song of Sixpence

That Latin was no more difficile
Than to a blackbird 'tis to
 whistle.
  SAMUEL BUTLER (1600-1680),
   Hudibras

MYRLE is a variant form. *Merle* is also used as a fem. name.

Merlin Celtic, "sea." MARLIN; see also MARWIN and MERVIN. The original Merlin was a Welsh bard whose story has been woven into the Arthurian cycle. He became the symbol of the enchanter; he appears in such varied forms of literature as the works of Geoffrey of Monmouth, Malory, Spenser, Tennyson, Edwin Arlington Robinson, Mark Twain, Rodgers and Hart, Lerner and Loewe.

She call'd him lord and liege,
Her seer, her bard, her silver star
 of eve,
Her God, her Merlin.
  ALFRED, LORD TENNYSON,
   Idylls of the King: Vivien

Merrill Celtic, "of Muriel." See MURIEL. MERYL. This name is widely known because of the firm Merrill Lynch, Pierce, Fenner & Smith ("We, the People," "The Thundering Herd"). Literature: Merrill Moore, psychiatrist and poet, who writes only in sonnet form (*M*, which contains 1000 sonnets).

Merton Anglo-Saxon place name, "town by the sea."

Mervyn See MARVIN. MERVIN, MURVYN. Related to MERLIN.

Merwin Anglo-Saxon, "famous friend"; or Germanic, "friend of the sea." See also MARVIN. Names that look and sound alike tend to merge, no matter what their origin may have been, so that MARVIN, MERWIN, MERVIN and their variations have all become as one.

Meyer Germanic, "farmer" or "overseer"; or possibly Latin, "greater." Also Hebrew, "bringer of light." MEIR, MEIER, MYER, MAYEER, MAYER, MAYOR.

Micah (MYE' ka) Hebrew, "Who is like Jehovah?" Biblical: Prophet and name of a book of the Old Testament.

. . . and what doth the LORD require of thee, but to do justly, and to love mercy, and to walk humbly with thy God?
MICAH 6:8

Literature: *Micah Clarke*, an exciting historical novel by Sir Arthur Conan Doyle.

Michael Hebrew, "Who is like the Lord?" MICHAIL, MIKE, MICK(E)Y, MITCH, MITCHELL. French, MICHEL; Spanish, MIGUEL; Italian, MICHELE. Fem., MICHEL(L)E, MIC(H)AELA. Biblical: An archangel. The full name of the master sculptor and painter Michelangelo Buonarrotti refers to this angel. Screen: Michelangelo Antonioni, director of *La Notte*, *L'Avventura*, etc.

In England the festival of St. Michael on September 29 is called Michaelmas.

Go, Michael, of celestial armies prince.
MILTON, *Paradise Lost*

Stage: Sir Michael Redgrave. Screen: Michael Caine.

Michel (mee SHEL') French form; see MICHAEL. Literature: Michel Eyquem de Montaigne (1533–1595), one of the greatest of all essay writers.

Mick, Mickey See MICHAEL. Stage and Screen: Mickey Rooney. Baseball: Mickey Mantle.

Miguel (mee GHEL') Spanish form; see MICHAEL. Literature: Miguel de Cervantes (Saavedra), author of *Don Quijote* (*Quixote*), one of the great books.

Miles Germanic, possibly "merciful." MYLES. Some authorities consider this name another form of MICHAEL through the French *Michel* and *Mihiel*. Literature: Name of the little boy in *The Turn of the Screw*, the masterly psychological story by Henry James.

Strode with a martial air, Miles Standish the Puritan captain.
HENRY WADSWORTH LONGFELLOW, *The Courtship of Miles Standish*

Millard (MILL' erd) Occupational name, "caretaker of the mill." Millard Fillmore, thirteenth President.

Milo (MY' loh) Germanic, source of the name MILES. This name is also Greek. Milo (or Milon), a mighty wrestler of the sixth century B.C., was a six-time Olympic winner. Occasionally an art lover has named a son Milo, after the Venus de Milo, which was found on the island of Melos.

Milton English place name, "by the mill town or farm." MILT. Literature: John Milton (1608–1674), considered second only to Shakespeare as a poet.

God-gifted organ voice of England,
Milton, a name to resound for ages.
ALFRED, LORD TENNYSON, *Milton*

TV: Milton Berle, affectionately known as "Uncle Milty" and "Mr. Television" during the early days of television. Music: Milton Cross, associated with the radio broadcasts of Metropolitan Opera, author of books on music.

Miner, Minor Occupational name, or Latin, "junior, younger."

Mischa Russian form: see MICHAEL. Music: Mischa Elman, esteemed violinist.

Mitchell See MICHAEL. MITCH.

Monroe (mun ROE') Place name, Celtic, "mouth of the Roe River." MUNRO. This was the last name of a prominent Irish family, of a Scottish clan, and of our fifth President, James Monroe.

Montague (MONT' a gyou) French place name, "sharp mountain." Drogo, a follower of William the Conqueror, gave the name of his home town, Mont Aigu, a place near Caën, to the land assigned to him in Somerset, England. Literature: In *Romeo and Juliet*, name given by Shakespeare to the family of Verona, Italy, to which Romeo belonged.

Monte Dim. form; see MONTAGUE and MONTGOMERY; or from Latin via French, Spanish, Italian, "mountain." MONTY.

Montgomery Place name, Norman-French, Mont Goumeril. Hollywood: Montgomery Clift.

Mordecai (MORE' de kye) Hebrew, probably from *Marduc*, Persian god. MORT, MORDY, MORTY. The wise counsels of Mordecai, cousin of Queen Esther, helped her save the Jews from destruction at the hands of Haman. See ESTHER.

For Mordecai the Jew was next unto King Ahasuerus, and great among the Jews.
ESTHER 10 : 3

Morgan Gaelic, "sea-white" or "sea-born"; Welsh, "great" or "bright."

Morley Place name, "moor meadow."

Morris See MAURICE. MORRIE, MORSE, MOSS. Fem., MAURA, MORISSA. Stage: Moss Hart

(1904–1961), producer, director, dramatist, author of a notable stage autobiography, *Act I*, co-author of *You Can't Take It With You* (Pulitzer Prize, 1937); Morris Carnovsky, actor.

Mortimer French place name, "still water"; or Celtic "sea warrior." MORT, MORTY.

Morton Anglo-Saxon p l a c e name, "village on the moor."

Moses Hebrew, "saved"; or possibly Egyptian, "child." MOE, MOEY, MOSS. Biblical: The great Hebrew leader who brought down the Ten Commandments from Mt. Sinai. Two renowned philosophers named Moses: Rabbi Moses ben Maimon (1135–1204), better known as Maimonides (*ides=ben*, "son of"), often referred to as Rambam; Moses Mendelssohn (1729–

1786), known as "the German Socrates," grandfather of the composer Felix Mendelssohn. Classics: Moses Hadas, Jay Professor of Greek at Columbia University, eminent teacher, scholar, editor and writer (*Hellenistic Culture, Humanism,* etc.).

> *Go down, Moses,*
> *Way down in Egyp' land,*
> *Tell ol' Pharaoh*
> *To let my people go.*
>
> SPIRITUAL

Murray English, "merry"; Scottish place name, "great water"; or Gaelic, "dark red." MURRY. Originally a last name; sometimes used instead of MORRIS.

Myron Greek name, possibly "fragrant." Art: Myron, a distinguished sculptor (fifth century B.C.), whose best-known work is *The Discus Thrower.*

N

The charm of scenes untried shall lure,
And NED, *a legend urge the flight—*
The Typee-truants under stars
Unknown to Shakespeare's Midsummer-Night.

HERMAN MELVILLE, *To Ned*

Nahum (NAY' hum) Hebrew, "compassion." Biblical: Prophet who predicted the fall of Nineveh.

Napoleon Greek, "lion of the woodland dell." This is the general interpretation of the meaning of the name, which more probably is related to *Napoleone,* Italian, "from the city of Naples." *Napoleon* was the name of a fourth-century saint of Alexandria, and was later used by prominent Italian families before Napoleon Bonaparte made it famous. Baseball: Napoleon Lajoie, "Nap the Nonpareil," one of the earliest entries into the National Baseball Hall of Fame (1937).

Nathan Hebrew, "gift." NAT, NATE. Biblical: The prophet who rebuked David for his treachery to Uriah. Literature: *Nathan the Wise* (1779), drama by Lessing. Music: Nathan Milstein, violinist.

And Nathan said to David, Thou art the man.
II SAMUEL 12 : 7

Nathaniel (na THAN' yell) Hebrew, "gift of God." NAT, NATE, NATHANAEL. Biblical: Also called Bartholomew; one of the twelve disciples of Jesus. Literature: Nathaniel Hawthorne, author of *The Scarlet Letter* and *The House of the Seven Gables;* Natty Bumppo, scout and pioneer, the Deerslayer, Leatherstocking and Hawkeye of James Fenimore Cooper's *Leatherstocking* novels; Nathanael West, author of *Miss Lonelyhearts.*

Neal See NEIL.

Nehemiah (NEE' e MY a *or* NEE' he MY a) Hebrew, "compassion of Jehovah." Biblical: A prophet who helped rebuild Jerusalem after the Babylonian captivity. Stage and Screen: Nehemiah Persoff.

Neil Irish, "chief" or Latin, "dark," via NIGEL, NIEL, NIALL. Stage and Screen: Neil Simon, playwright and screen writer (*The Odd Couple*).

Nelson Son of NEIL; see NEIL. The victories of Lord Nelson gave this name a vogue which has lasted to this day.

Of Nelson and the North
Sing the glorious day's renown,
When to battle fierce came
forth
All the might of Denmark's
crown.

THOMAS CAMPBELL,
The Battle of the Baltic

Stage, Screen, and Radio: Nelson Eddy, the singer who was so popular in the early days of radio, co-star with Jeannette MacDonald in many superb musical films.

Nestor Greek, "newly speaking." Mythology: The wise old king of Pylos, who joined the Greek expedition against Troy. His name has become a symbol for wisdom. See also SOLON.

Nevil, Nevil(l)e, French place name, "new city." Literature: Nevil Shute, author of *On the Beach.*

Nevin(s). Anglo-Saxon, "nephew."

Newbold Place name, "new building."

Nicholas Greek, "victory of the people." COLAS, COLIN, COLET, NICOLAS, NICK, NICKY, NICHOLS, NIXON. Fem., NICOLETTE, CO-LETTE. St. Nicholas (fourth century) is the patron saint of Russia, of schoolchildren, of sailors, scholars, and of pawnbrokers. The three balls of gold appearing above pawnbrokers' shops represent the three bags of gold said to have been given by St. Nicholas to the three daughters of a poor man. Santa Claus is Dutch for Saint Nicholas. Literature: *Nicholas Nickleby* by Charles Dickens. In 1890 a new dime novel called *Nick Carter, Detective,* appeared. Different authors, notably Frederick Van Renselaer Dey, and the Rev. Samuel Charles Spaulding, all using the pseudonym Nick Carter, turned out more than a thousand of these stories, which are now sought after by collectors.

Nigel (NYE' jel) Latin, "black." See NEIL. Literature: *The Fortunes of Nigel* by Scott; *Sir Nigel* by Arthur Conan Doyle. Stage, Screen, and Radio: Nigel Bruce, who played Dr. Watson to Basil Rathbone's Sherlock Holmes. Screen: Nigel Patrick.

Niles Danish, "son of Neil"; see NEIL and NELSON. NILS (dim. of NICHOLAS), NIELS. Science: Niels Bohr, Nobel Prize (1922) for work on atoms.

Noah (NOE' a) Hebrew, "wandering" or "rest." The two possible meanings of his name summarize the career of Noah who came to rest after his wanderings on the Ark. Noah Webster (1758–1843) wrote not only the original *Webster's* dictionary but also a series of spellers which were best sellers for decades.

*And Noah he often said to his
wife when he sat down to dine,
"I don't care where the water
goes if it doesn't get into the
wine."*
  GILBERT K. CHESTERTON,
   Wine and Water

Noble Latin, "well-born, of renowned family."

Noel, Noël (NOE' ell) French
from Latin, *dies natalis Christi*,
"birthday of Christ, "Christ-
mas." Once children born on
Christmas were given this name.
Fem., NOELLE, but see also NAT-
ALIE. Stage and Screen: Noel
Coward, playwright, actor, di-
rector, composer (*Cavalcade,
Private Lives, Sail Away*, etc.).

*Nowell, Nowell, Nowell, we
 sing.
Minstrels and maids, stand
 fourth on the floor.
From far away we come to
 you,
 To tell of great tidings
 strange and true.*
  WILLIAM MORRIS,
   From Far Away

Noll Pet form; see OLIVER. A
nickname often used for Oliver
Cromwell and Oliver Goldsmith.

Norbert Germanic, "sea-
bright" or "divinely bright."
Science: Norbert Wiener, prominent in the field of cybernetics,
or cybernation, which deals with
automatic data-processing ma-
chines.

Norman Anglo-Saxon, originally "Northman," or "Norse";
later applied to the invaders
from Normandy.

*Kind hearts are more than
 coronets,
 And simple faith than Norman
 blood.*
  ALFRED, LORD TENNYSON,
   Lady Clare Vere de Vere

Literature: Norman Douglas,
author of *South Wind* (1917);
Norman Mailer, author of *The
Naked and the Dead* (1948),
ranked among the great novels
of men in war. Politics: Norman
Thomas, "respectable rebel," six
times a Presidential candidate as
head of the U. S. Socialist Party.
Art: Norman Rockwell, famed
for magazine covers. Theater,
Architecture, and Design: Norman Bel Geddes. Journalism:
Norman Cousins, editor of the
Saturday Review.

Norris Place name, "from the
north"; or occupational name,
"nurse." Better known as a surname. Literature: Frank Norris
(1870–1902), author of *Mc-
Teague, The Pit,* and *The Octo-
pus.*

Norton Place name, "from the
northern village or town."

O

> My name is OZYMANDIAS, king of kings.
> Look on my works, ye Mighty, and despair!
>
> PERCY BYSSHE SHELLEY, *Ozymandias*

Obadiah (o ba DY' a) Hebrew, "servant of God." Short form, OBED, "servant."

> Young Obadias,
> David, Josias,
> All were pious.
> NEW ENGLAND PRIMER (1688)

Octavus (ok TAVV' us) Latin, "eighth." French, OCTAVE. Fem., OCTAVIA. From *Octavius*, name of a *gens*. The most celebrated member of this *gens* was Augustus, the first Roman emperor, formerly called Octavius and Octavianus. See under ANTONY, AUGUST, and QUINTUS.

> Come Antony, and young
> Octavius, come,
> Revenge yourselves alone
> on Cassius.
> WILLIAM SHAKESPEARE,
> *Julius Caesar*

Ogden English place name, Anglo-Saxon, "oak valley or hill." Literature: Ogden Nash, writer of light verse with ingenious rhymes.

Olaf (OH' laff) Norse, "ancestor." OLAV. St. Olaf was the first Christian king of Norway (about 1000).

> At Drontheim, Olaf the King
> Heard the bells of Yule-Tide
> ring,
> As he sat in his banquet-hall.
> HENRY WADSWORTH
> LONGFELLOW,
> *The Saga of King Olaf.*

Olin (OH' lin) Possibly derived from OLAF. Fem., OLA, OLINE. Music: Olin Downes, former critic.

Oliver French, from OLAF; or Latin, "olive tree"; or Germanic, "elf host." OLLIE, NOLL. Fem., OLIVE, OLIVIA. Oliver was one of Charlemagne's paladins or champions, a friend and rival of Roland. The expression *a Roland for an Oliver* means "blow for blow," "compliment for compliment," or "tit for tat," because the exploits of the two heroes were so alike that it was difficult to tell one from the other. Literature: Shakespeare brought the two names together in *As You Like It* by calling two brothers Oliver and Orlando (or ROLAND). Oliver Cromwell and Oliver Goldsmith are two distinguished bearers of this name. See NOLL.

England all Olivers and Rolands bred.

> WILLIAM SHAKESPEARE,
> *I Henry VI*

History: Oliver Hazard Perry, American officer at the battle of Lake Erie (1813), who sent the message: "We have met the enemy and they are ours."

Omar Hebrew, "eloquent"; Arabic, "builder" or "life." A grandson of Esau was named Omar (GENESIS 36:11), but the name is best known because of Omar Khayyám, "The Tentmaker," whose *Rubáiyát* (Quatrains) was freely translated (1859) by Edward FitzGerald:

These pearls of thought in Persian gulfs were bred,
Each softly lucent as a rounded moon;
The diver Omar plucked them from their bed,
Fitz-Gerald strung them on an English thread.

> JAMES RUSSELL LOWELL,
> *In a Copy of Omar Khayyám*

Often the name Omar or Omer, which is listed next, is given without reference to the poet. For example, according to information supplied to us, General Omar Nelson Bradley received his first name from that of an editor friend of the family.

Omer Germanic, *Audomar,* "rich-famous." This became Omer in French; there is a saint of that name after whom the city of St. Omer was named. *Omer* and *Omar* are often confused. See OMAR.

Oren (OH' ren), Or(r)in Hebrew, "pine." ORAN. Literature: Orin in Eugene O'Neill's *Mourning Becomes Electra,* so named to parallel the role of Orestes in Greek tragedy. See ORESTES.

Orestes (o RESS' teez) Greek, "mountain." ORESTE. Mythology and Drama: Son of Agamemnon and Clytemnestra, avenger with his sister Electra of his father's murder; appears in plays by Aeschylus, Sophocles, and Euripides.

Orlando Italian form; see ROLAND. Literature: The hero of Shakespeare's *As You Like It,* in love with Rosalind:

Run, run, Orlando, carve on every tree
The fair, the chaste, the unexpressive she.

Ormond From English place name, "bear or ravine mound." Also Germanic, "edge, front" and "protector."

Orson Latin, "bear-like." ORSINO. Stage and Screen: Orson Welles; Orson Bean.

Orton English place name, "ravine town" or "hill town" or "garden town." HORTON.

Orville French, "gold town." Name invented by Fanny Burney (1779) for hero of the novel *Evelina*. Orville Wright (1871-1948) and his brother Wilbur were pioneers in aviation (of *Kitty Hawk* fame).

Osbert Anglo-Saxon, "divinely bright." Osbert Sitwell is a member of the formidable Sitwell writing trio.

Osborn(e) Anglo-Saxon, "divine-bear" or "godly strength." OS-BOURN(E).

Oscar Anglo-Saxon, "divine spear." OSSIE, OZZIE, OSKAR. Literature: Son of the Gaelic chief Ossian in the poems by James MacPherson (1760-1763). *Oscar*, or *Oskar*, became a favorite Swedish name after Napoleon, an admirer of the Ossianic poems, bestowed that name on his godson, who later became King of Sweden. Another Ossianic admirer gave this name to his son, Oscar Wilde. Hollywood: The gold-covered statuette established as the award of the Academy of Motion Picture Arts and Sciences in 1927 had no name until 1931. In that year, when Mrs. Margaret Herrick, then librarian of the Academy, first saw the figure, she exclaimed, so the story runs, "He reminds me of my Uncle Oscar." The name stuck; the real Oscar is a Mr. Oscar Pierce, a merchant, actually Mrs. Herrick's second cousin.

Light Opera: Oskar Straus (1870-1954), whose comic opera *The Chocolate Soldier*, an adaptation of Shaw's *Arms and the Man*, anticipated another adaptation of a Shavian play, *My Fair Lady* from *Pygmalion*. Stage and Films: Oscar Hammerstein II, librettist for many of the Richard Rodgers musicals (*South Pacific*, Pulitzer Prize, 1950); Ossie Davis, actor and playwright.

Osgood Anglo-Saxon, "divinely good."

Osmond Germanic, "divine protection." OSMUND.

Oswald Anglo-Saxon, "divine power."

Otis Originally only a family name, most probably derived from *Oates* and *Otes*, "son of Odo, or Otto." See OTTO. Theater: Otis Skinner (1858-1942).

Otto Germanic, "rich." *Otto*, a favorite name of German and Austrian nobility, was formerly *Odo*. Other forms of the name are *Otho*, name of an early Roman emperor, and *Othello*. Screen: Producer and director Otto Preminger (*Exodus*, etc.).

Ovid (ov′ id) Latin, *Ovidius*, "shepherd," name of a *gens*. Literature: Ovid, Latin name Publius Ovidius Naso, polished and urbane poet, author of *Meta-morphoses,* etc.

Ovid, the soft philosopher of love.

JOHN DRYDEN,
Love Triumphant

Owen (O' en) Welsh, "youth" or "young warrior" or "lamb"; possibly connected with Latin and Greek, "well-born"; see EUGENE; also connected with JOHN and EVAN. EWEN.

Owen's praise demands my song, Owen swift, and Owen strong.

THOMAS GRAY,
The Triumphs of Owen

Literature: Owen Glendower in *I Henry IV* by Shakespeare. Literature, Hollywood, and TV: Owen Wister (1860-1938), Harvard alumnus, musician, banker, lawyer, friend of Theodore Roosevelt, creator of "horse opera." His novel *The Virginian,* which contains the deathless words "When you call me that, *smile!*" set up the romantic image of the cowboy as a modern Knight of Kings Arthur's Round Table. It has been a best seller since 1902, the subject of four motion pictures since 1914, and of a spectacular TV serial since 1962.

P

See there the olive-grove of Academe,
PLATO's *retirement, where the Attic bird*
Trills her thick-warbled notes the summer long.

JOHN MILTON, *Paradise Regained*

Pablo Spanish form; see PAUL. Music: Pablo Casals. Art: Pablo Picasso.

Paddy Pet form; see PATRICK.

O Paddy dear, an' did ye hear the news that's goin' 'round?
ANONYMOUS,
The Wearin' o' the Green

Padraic Irish form; see PATRICK. Literature: Padraic Colum, playwright, poet, author of books on myths and folklore.

Page Greek via French, occupational name of chivalry, "boy attendant." PAIGE.

Page and monarch, forth they went,
Forth they went together.
J. M. NEALE,
Good King Wenceslas

Palmer Medieval Latin via French, "pilgrim." A palmer wore two crossed palm leaves as a sign that he had visited holy places.

I'll give my jewels for a set of beads. . . .
My sceptre for a palmer's walking staff.
WILLIAM SHAKESPEARE,
King Richard II

Park(e), Parker Place and occupational name, "guardian of the *park* or preserve for game."

Parry Welsh, *ap-Harry*, "son of Harry." See PERRY, BARRY, and HARRY.

Patrick Latin, "of noble birth." PAT, PATRIC, PADDY, PATSY, RICKY, RICK. Fem., PATRICIA, PATRICE. St. Patrick, born in England and educated in France, landed in Ireland in 432 and became the patron saint and apostle of that country. According to legend he cleared Ireland of snakes.

So, success attend St. Patrick's fist,
For he's a saint so clever;
Oh! he gave the snakes and toads a twist,
And bothered them forever!
HENRY BENNETT, *St. Patrick*

Literature: *Sir Patrick Spens*, famous Scottish ballad. History: Patrick Henry ("Give me liberty or give me death!")

Paul Latin, "small." Fem., PAULA, PAULE, PAULINE. Biblical: St. Paul, originally named Saul, the great missionary and apostle of Christianity. Screen and Stage: Paul Newman. Stage:

Paul Scofield, one of the world's great actors. Art: Paul Cézanne (1839-1906). Literature: Paul Verlaine (1844-1896), French poet. Music: Paul Hindemith, modern composer.

History: Paul Revere.

*Through all our history to the
    last,
In the hour of darkness and peril
    and need,
The people will waken and listen
    to hear
The hurrying hoof-beats of that
    steed,
And the midnight message of
    Paul Revere.*

HENRY WADSWORTH
LONGFELLOW,
Paul Revere's Ride

Payne, Paine Latin, *paganus*, "living in a country district"; later meaning, "heathen." A name introduced into England by the Normans and very popular as a first name for centuries. As a last name it was given fame through John Howard Payne (1791-1852), actor and playwright, author of *Home, Sweet Home*.

Pedro Spanish form; see PETER.

Percival French, "pierce the valley," with implication of "perceive the veil (of religious mystery".) PERCEVAL. A name invented by Chrétien de Troyes, a twelfth-century poet who wrote about the quest of the Holy Grail by a hero Percevale. Opera: *Parsifal* by Richard Wag-

ner. Literature: Malory's *Morte d'Arthur* and Tennyson's *Idylls of the King;* Percival C. Wren, author of *Beau Geste* (1924), a story of the Foreign Legion, based on his own experience.

*From noiseful arms, and acts of
    prowess done
In tournament or tilt, Sir Perce-
    vale,
Whom Arthur and his knight-
    hood call'd the Pure,
Had pass'd into the silent life of
    prayer.*

ALFRED, LORD TENNYSON,
The Holy Grail

Percy French place name, village near St. Lô. PERCIE. The family name of William de Perci, who came to England with William the Conqueror, was not used as a first name until the eighteenth century. The poet Percy Bysshe Shelley was distantly related to the Percy family. Like PERCIVAL, of which *Percy* is sometimes regarded as a diminutive, the name *Percy* was borne and popularized by warriors.

*I never heard the old song of
Percy and Douglas, that I found
not my heart moved more than
with a trumpet.*

SIR PHILIP SIDNEY,
Defence of Poesy

Music: Percy Grainger, pianist-composer (*Molly on the Shore, Shepherd's Hey, Country Gardens*).

Perry French, "pear tree"; or Welsh, "son of Harry." A popular last name, made notable by Oliver Hazard Perry (see under OLIVER); and even more familiar in later times through TV by attorney Perry Mason, Erle Stanley Gardner's famous creation, and by singer Perry Como.

Peter Greek via Latin, "stone, rock." PETE, PIERS, PIERCE, PIERRE, Fem. PETA, PETRA. Biblical: Simon called Peter, one of the Twelve Disciples; his change of name was made by Christ in the words which established Papal authority.

And I say unto thee, That thou are Peter, and upon this rock I will build my church.
MATTHEW 16:18

Literature: George du Maurier's novel *Peter Ibbetson* (1891), which has been turned into a play and opera. Theater: *Peer Gynt*, a poetic drama by Henrik Ibsen; *Peter Pan* by James Barrie, a favorite of old and young; Peter Ustinov, actor and dramatist.

History: Peter the Great of Russia (1672-1725); Peter Minuit, purchaser of Manhattan from the Indians for the famous price of $24; Peter Stuyvesant, doughty governor of New Amsterdam from 1647 to 1664. Music: The composer Peter Ilyich Tchaikovsky (1840-1893); his first name is actually *Piotr*, or *Pëtr*, the Russian forms.

Screen: Peter Sellers (*The Pink Panther*).

Philemon (fi LEE' mon) Greek "loving." Mythology: Baucis (BAW' sis) and Philemon, corresponding to Noah and his wife, saved from destruction by Zeus and Hermes during a flood. Biblical: A Greek to whom Paul wrote an Epistle.

Philip Greek, "lover of horses." PHIL. Spanish, *Felipe;* Italian, *Filippo.* Fem., PHILIPPA. Biblical: One of the Apostles. History: Father of Alexander the Great; speeches of Demosthenes delivered against him gave rise to the word *philippic*, "a denunciation." Literature: Philip Freneau (1752-1832), "Poet of the American Revolution"; Philip Carey, hero of Somerset Maugham's masterpiece *Of Human Bondage* (1916); Philip Van Doren Stern, novelist, essayist, authority on Lincoln and the Civil War. TV: Phil Donahue, host of unique discussion show.

Look at me with thy large brown eyes, Philip, my king!
Round whom the enshadowing purple lies
Of babyhood's royal dignities.
DINAH M. M. CRAIK,
Philip, My King

Philo (FYE' loe) Greek, "friendly." Philosophy and Literature: Philo Judaeus of Alexandria (30 B.C.-45 A.D.), whose mission to Rome protesting the worship of the Emperor Caligula is so cleverly described in *Philo's Little Trip* by E. M. Forster; Philo Vance, the learned detective created by S. S. Van Dine.

Phineas (FINN' ee us) Hebrew, "oracle" or "face of pity." Phineas T. Barnum, America's great showman (1810-1891).

Pierce Surname formed from PETER.

Pierre (pee AIR') French form; see PETER. Fem., PERRINE. Literature: Pierre Corneille, writer of classic tragedy in the Golden Age of Louis XIV (*Le Cid,* etc.).

Pliny Latin, *Plinius,* a *gens* name. Two famous Roman authors bore this name.

Powell Welsh, *ap-Howell,* "son of Howell (lofty)."

Prescott Place name, "priest's cottage."

Preston Place name "priest-town." Theater: Preston Sturges, American playwright.

Price Welsh, *ap-Rice,* "son of Rice." See RHYS. BRICE, BRYCE.

Q QUINTILIAN, *renowned trainer of wayward youth,*
QUINTILIAN, *glory of the Roman toga.*

MARTIAL, *Epigrams,* II, 90

Quartus Latin, "fourth." Biblical: Mentioned by Paul in ROMANS 16:23.

Quentin Latin "fifth." QUINTIN, QUINTON, QUINTUS. Quintus was a popular Roman first name, believed to have been given at first to a fifth son. St. Quentin was a Roman fifth-century martyr, after whom the town in France was named. Journalism: Quentin Reynolds. Literature: *Quentin Durward,* a novel by Sir Walter Scott.

QUENTIN: *Thou know'st I am by nature born a friend*
To glee and merriment; can make wild verses:
The jest or laugh has never stopp'd with me,
When once 'twas set a rolling
SIR WALTER SCOTT,
Auchindrome

Quincy Latin, name of a *gens.* See also QUENTIN. John Quincy Adams was the sixth President of the United States. Quincy Howe, commentator, won the newsanalyst award for 1961.

Quinn Celtic, "wise." Also

possible short form; see QUENTIN.

Quintilian A Roman surname formed from *Quintilius,* the name of a *gens.* See QUENTIN and QUINTUS. Literature and Education: Marcus Fabius Quintilianus (first century A.D.), author of *Principles of Oratory (De Institutione Oratoria),* a great work on rhetoric, oratory, and education, many of whose principles are applicable today.

Quintus Latin, "fifth." Fem., QUINTA. *Sextus,* "sixth," and *Decimus,* "tenth," were the only other number words used as first names. Although the meaning of such names is generally given as a number, it is highly possible that originally these names had to do with the name of a family or clan (*gens*). Used as family or *gens* names were a few other words coming from numbers or resembling number words. Of this group, these are occasionally used as first names today: *Tertius,* "third," QUARTUS, *Septimus* and *Septimius,* "seventh," and OCTAVUS, "eighth."

R

It was the time when lilies blow,
And clouds are highest up in air,
Lord RONALD brought a lily-white doe
To give his cousin, Lady Clare.

ALFRED, LORD TENNYSON, *Lady Clare*

Ralph Anglo-Saxon, "wolf-counsel." RAOUL, ROLF. Music: Ralph Rackstraw, the "audacious tar," who loves the Captain's daughter. The English pronunciation of *Ralph* is indicated by the rhyme in the following verses:

In time each little waif
Forsook his foster-mother,
The well-born babe was Ralph—
Your captain was the other!!!
WILLIAM S. GILBERT,
H.M.S. Pinafore

Nobel Peace Prize: Ralph J. Bunche, in 1950. Literature: Ralph Waldo Emerson (1803-1882), philosopher, poet, and essayist. Stage: Sir Ralph Richardson, Ralph Bellamy.

Ramon (RAY' mon), **Ramón** (ra MUN') Spanish variation; see RAYMOND. Screen: Ramon Navarro, of the silent era, still remembered for his playing of the role of Ben Hur.

Ramsey, Ramsay Place name, "wooded or strong island." History: Ramsay MacDonald (1866-1937), Great Britain's first Labo(u)r Prime Minister.

Randal(l) Anglo-Saxon, "shield-wolf"; or place name, "fair valley." RANDOLPH. Literature: Randall Jarrell, American critic, editor, novelist, and poet.

O where hae ye been, Lord Randal, my son?
O where hae ye been, my handsome young man?
OLD BALLAD, Lord Randal

Randolph Variant form; see RANDALL.

Raphael (RAY' fee el *or* RA' fee el) Hebrew, "God cures," or "God has healed." RAY, RAFE, RAFAEL. Art: Raffaello Sanzio (1483-1520), painter of beautiful Madonnas, better known as Raphael or Rafael. Biblical: An archangel.

Say, goddess, what ensued when Raphael,
The affable Archangel, had forewarned Adam. . . .
JOHN MILTON, *Paradise Lost*

Ray Short form; see RAYMOND and also RAPHAEL. Hollywood: Ray Milland, winner of 1945 Oscar (*Lost Weekend*). Stage and Screen; Ray Bolger, dancer and actor. Literature: Ray Bradbury, author of science fiction having social implications (*Fahrenheit 451*).

Raymond Germanic, "counsel-protection." RAE, RAY, RAMÓN. RAYMOND was the name borne by the Counts of Toulouse, one of whom, Raymond IV, was a noted crusader.

It is he that saith not "Kismet";
it is he that knows not Fate;
It is Richard, it is Raymond, it
is Godfrey in the Gate!
CHESTERTON, *Lepanto*

Screen, Stage, and TV: Raymond Massey, especially noted for his interpretations of Abraham Lincoln.

Reed, Reid, Read(e) Anglo-Saxon, "red."

Reginald Germanic, "power-might." REGGIE, REYNOLD. Like ALGERNON, PERCIVAL, and PERCY, this is a favorite warrior's name, a name of virile antecedents. Literature: The lovable Reggie, the detective in the *Reggie Fortune* stories by H. C. Bailey. Music: Reginald de Koven (1859-1920), composer of *Robin Hood*, which contains the song *O Promise Me*.

Reginald bold in the tourney, the
first and the last in the field:
Reginald, mighty of arm and the
cleaver of helmet and shield:
Reginald, last of the line of the
crest blazoned never to yield!
CLINTON SCOLLARD,
The Banquet of Sir Reginald

Reinhold Germanic, "powerful." See also REGINALD, REYNOLD, and RONALD. Philosophy: Reinhold Niebuhr.

René (ruh NAY') French, from Latin *renatus*, "reborn." RENE. Fem., RENATA, RENÉ(E). Philosophy: René Descartes (1595-1650), who exercised a great influence on modern philosophy ("I think, therefore I am"). Films: Director René Clair (*Sous les Toits de Paris, A Nous la Liberté*).

Reuben Hebrew, "Behold a son." REUVEN, RUBE, RUBEN, RUBIN. Biblical: Eldest son of Jacob; name of one of the tribes. Literature: *Reuben, Reuben* by Peter de Vries.

Rex Latin, "king." REGIS. Fem., REGINA. Literature: Rex Beach, novelist of "he-man" school; Rex Stout, creator of the Epicurean detective Nero Wolfe. Stage and Screen: Rex Harrison, Oscar 1964 (*My Fair Lady*).

Reynold (RENN' uld) Variant form; see REGINALD. In medieval romances *Reynold* appears in the forms *Renault* and *Rinaldo*. Rinaldo was one of the great paladins of Charlemagne and the cousin of Orlando (see under ROLAND).

Rhys (REES) Celtic, "hero,"; Welsh, "ardor, rush." REES, RICE.

Richard Germanic, "strong ruler" or "powerful-strong." DICK, RICK, RICKY, RICHIE, RITCHIE. Fem., RICA, RICCA. Long one of the most popular names for boys, as seen from the proverbial expression, "Every Tom, DICK, and Harry." Three English kings were named Richard; the adventures of Richard I, *Coeur de Lion* ("The Lion-Hearted"), did much to establish the popularity of the name. Benjamin Franklin used the pen name Richard Saunders when he wrote *Poor Richard's Almanack.* Literature: Richard Lovelace (1618-1658), Cavalier poet (see under ALTHEA and LUCASTA); Richard Brinsley Sheridan (1751-1816), dramatist, author of *The Rivals* and *School for Scandal;* Richard Burton (1821-1890), translator of *The Arabian Nights.* Music: Richard Wagner (1813-1883), composer, author of the books of his operas; Richard Strauss (1864-1949), composer of *Der Rosenkavalier, Don Juan,* etc. Theater: Richard Rodgers, composer of some of the outstanding musicals of our time (*Oklahoma!, South Pacific,* winner of a Pulitzer Prize in 1950). Stage and Screen: Richard Burton.

Rip Pet name or short form of ROBERT or RUPERT, often used as a nickname without reference to these names. As used today it probably has no connection with the *Rip Van Winkle* of Washington Irving. Robert P. Hansen, writer of mysteries (*Walk a Wicked Mile,* etc.), signs himself "Rip." Hollywood: Rip Torn (Elmore Torn). His name seems ready-made for Hollywood, but actually it was not made up for Hollywood. Rip Torn's uncle and father are called Rip also. "With our last name, Rip is a pretty obvious nickname," he is quoted as saying by Thomas McDonald in the *New York Times* of September 24, 1961.

As a Dutch name, *Rip* means "ripe, full-grown."

Roald Teutonic, "fame-might." See also Reginald, ROLF, RONALD; compare with RAOUL. Two well-known bearers of this name: Roald Amundsen (1872-1928), who flew across the North Pole in 1926; Roald Dahl, brilliant short story writer of the macabre.

Robert Anglo-Saxon, "bright fame." BOB, BOBBY, ROB, RAB, ROBIN. Fem., ROBERTA. See also ROGER, ROLF, RUPERT. Literature: Five outstanding Roberts in English letters: Herrick, Burton (author of *The Anatomy of Melancholy*), Burns, Browning, and Stevenson (RLS). In the U.S.A.: Robert E. Sherwood, the playwright, winner of the Pulitzer Prize three times, for *Idiot's Delight* in 1936, *Abe Lincoln in Illinois* in 1939, and *There Shall Be No Night* in 1941: Robert Frost, official poet laureate of Vermont, unofficial poet laureate of the United States, winner of the Pulitzer Poetry Prize four times!

*How do I love thee? Let me
  count the ways. . . .
I love thee to the level of every-
  day's
Most quiet need, by sun and
  candlelight,
I love thee freely, as men strive
  for Right;
I love thee purely, as they turn
  from Praise.*
ELIZABETH BARRETT BROWNING,
  Sonnets from the Portuguese,
  XLIII

(Written to her husband, Robert)

Music: Robert Schumann,
composer of symphonies, *Dich-
terliebe*, etc.; Robert Casadesus,
French pianist. History: Robert
Fulton of steamboat fame; General Robert E. Lee, the gallant
commander of the Southern
armies. Screen: Robert Redford; Robert De Niro, Oscar
1980 (*Raging Bull*).

Robin Dim. form; see ROBERT.
Fem., ROBINA, ROBENA, ROBIN.
At one time Robin was used
more frequently as a name than
Robert. In France *Robin et
Marion* correspond to *Jack and
Jill*. Robin figures greatly in
song and story.

  *Come to my heart again,
    Robin Adair;
  Never to part again
    Robin Adair*
CAROLINE KEPPEL, *Robin Adair*

Robin Goodfellow is the fun-
loving sprite sometimes called
Puck. And also:

*In Sherwood lived stout Robin
  Hood,
An archer great, none greater.
His bows and shafts were sure
  and good.*
ELIZABETHAN SONG

Robinson Patronymic, "son of
Robert." See ROBERT and ROBIN.
Literature: Robinson Jeffers
(1887-1962), American poet and
dramatist; and, of course, *Robinson Crusoe*.

Rockwell Place name, "spring
by the rock." Art: Rockwell
Kent.

Rocky Nickname denoting
pride in strength; now becoming
a given name. Also used as substitute for Italian *Rocco* (Rocky
Graziano, boxer and author of
Somebody up There Likes Me).
Hollywood: Rock Hudson (for
the story behind this name, see
under "Hollywood" in chapter
"Where Our Names Come
From.")

Roderick Germanic, "famous
ruler." ROD, RODDY. As *Rodrigo,
Roderigo,* and *Ruy* (dim. form),
this name became popular in
Spain. Literature: *Ruy Blas*
(1838), a play by Victor Hugo;
Le Cid (1636) by Pierre Corneille, a drama about Roderigo
de Bivar, the eleventh-century
Spanish hero better known as
the Cid; *Roderick Random*
(1748), a novel by Tobias Smol-
let; *Roderick Hudson* (1876), a
novel by Henry James. Stage

and Screen: Roddy McDowall (Roderick Andrew McDowall).

*These are Clan-Alpine's warriors
true
And, Saxon,—I am Roderick
Dhu!*

SIR WALTER SCOTT,
The Lady of the Lake

Rodman Occupational n a m e, Anglo-Saxon, "man who *rod(e)* with a knight, a knight's helper."

Rodney English place name and surname. Anglo-Saxon, "island clearing." ROD, RODDY. History: Lord Rodney (1719–1792), noted for victories over the French and Spaniards. The ride of Caesar Rodney on the night of July 1–2, 1776, though less spectacular than Paul Revere's Ride, was equally important. Riding eighty miles in one night, as a delegate to the Continental Congress, he arrived in time to break the tie vote of Delaware in favor of declaring independence:

*The Congress is met; the debate's
begun,
And Liberty lags for the vote of
one—
When into the hall, not a
moment late,
Walks Caesar Rodney, the
delegate.*

ELBRIDGE S. BROOKS,
Rodney's Ride

Stage and Screen: Rod Steiger (Rodney Steven Steiger).

Roger Germanic, "fame-spear." RODGER, ROGERS. A famous man with this first name was Roger Williams (1603–1683), advocate of democracy and religious tolerance, founder of Rhode Island. In World War II, "Roger" was used to mean, "OK, I understand." as an arbitrary signal for "[Message] RECEIVED [and Understood]." Rogers Hornsby, batter extraordinary, only modern player to hit above .400 three times, member of baseball's Hall of Fame; Roger Maris, as a Yankee outfielder the first player to hit 61 home runs in a single season (1961).

Roland (ROE' land) Germanic, "famous land." ROLLAND, ROLLIE, ROLLY, ROWLAND, ORLANDO. See also OLIVER. The mighty deeds of Roland, greatest of Charlemagne's champions, are celebrated in Ariosto's *Orlando Furioso* and in the medieval *Song of Roland.*

*In front of the foremost footman
he spurs with a clarion cry,
And raises the song of Roland to
the apse of the glowing sky.*

CLINTON SCOLLARD,
Taillefer the Trouvère

Stage, Screen, TV: The ever likable Roland Young. Ballet and Screen: Roland Petit.

Rolf Germanic, "fame-wolf." ROLFE, ROLPH, ROLLO, ROLLIN. See also ROBERT, ROGER, RUDOLPH. The Normans, whose first duke was the Viking Rollo, introduced this name into England. Literature: *Rollo* books by Jacob Abbott, juvenile favorites of the last century; Rolfe Humphries, poet, translator of Vergil's *Aeneid*. Ovid's *Art of Love,* and Federico García Lorca's *Gypsy Ballads.* Fem., ROLLA.

Romain French form; see RO-MAN. Literature: Romain Rolland (1866-1944), author of *Jean Christophe;* Romain Gary, contemporary writer, author of *Roots of Heaven* and *Promise at Dawn.*

Roman Latin, "of Rome." Fem., ROMAINE, ROMA.

Romeo The origin of this name is not clear. It may be Germanic, "strength," or Latin via Italian, from *Romulus,* the name of the legendary founder of Rome, which was turned into *Romolo,* or from *Romanus, Romano,* "Roman." There was a fourteenth century St. Romeo, or *Romaeus.* Whatever the origin, the name lives, of course, because Shakespeare used it in *Romeo and Juliet:*

> *O, be some other name!*
> *What's in a name? that which we call a rose*
> *By any other name would smell as sweet.*
> *So Romeo would, were he not Romeo called,*
> *Retain that dear perfection which he owes*
> *Without that title.*

Ronald Scottish variation; see REGINALD and REYNOLD. RON, RONNIE. Fem., RONA, RONALDA. Screen: Ronald Colman, winner of 1947 Oscar (*A Double Life*). Politics: Ronald Reagan, 40th president of the U.S.

> *My bosom throbb'd when Ronald's name*
> *Came gracing Fame's heroic tale,*
> *Like perfume on the summer gale.*
> SIR WALTER SCOTT,
> *The Lord of the Isles*

Rory Irish, "red." Often used as translation of ROY, ROGER, and RODERICK. History and Poetry: Rory O'More, name of three Irish chieftains celebrated in songs and ballads.

> *"That's eight times today that you've kissed me before."*
> *"Then here goes another," says he, "to make sure.*
> *For there's luck in odd numbers," says Rory O'More.*
> SAMUEL LOVER, *Rory O'More*

Hollywood: Rory Calhoun (Francis Durgin).

Roscoe Place name, "deer forest"; or Anglo-Saxon, "swift horse." Law: Roscoe Pound, eminent American writer on the law.

Ross Scottish place name, Gaelic, "headland" or Norman-French, "red." Also Anglo-Saxon, "horse"; originally masculine name corresponding to ROSE. Theater: Terence Rattigan's play *Ross* about Lawrence of Arabia, who at one time had assumed this name. (See under THOMAS.)

Roy Celtic, "red-haired"; French, "king." ROI. Literature: Scott's novel *Rob Roy*, about Robert M'Gregor, a Scottish chieftain, nicknamed Rob Roy because of his red hair. Screen and Radio: Roy Rogers, singing cowboy.

Royal French, "kingly"; or derived from ROLLO. See also LE-ROY. Fem., ROYALENE.

Rudolph Germanic, "famous wolf." RUDOLF, RUDY, DOLPH, DOLF. See also ROLF. A favorite name of former Austrian nobility. Opera: Rodolfo, hero of Puccini's *La Boheme;* Rudolf Friml, composer of *The Firefly* and *Rose Marie;* Rudolf Serkin, renowned pianist. Literature: Rudolf Rassendyll, glamorous hero of *The Prisoner of Zenda* by Anthony Hope. Screen: Rudolph Valentino (1895-1926), romantic idol of the silent movies (*The Sheik*). Radio, Stage, Screen, and TV: The ever popular Rudy Vallee (first name actually Hubert).

Rufus (ROOF' us) Latin, "red-haired." RUFE. William II of England (1087-1100) was called William Rufus because of his florid complexion.

Rupert Germanic, "bright fame." RUPPRECHT. See also ROB-ERT. History: Prince Rupert of Bavaria (1619-1682), grandson of James I, military commander for Charles I against Cromwell. Literature: *Rupert of Hentzau* by Anthony Hope, sequel to the famous *Prisoner of Zenda;* Rupert Brooke (1887-1915), a hero of World War I, author of famous sonnets entitled *1914.*

Russel(l) French, "red." RUSS. Theater: Russel Crouse, co-author of *Life with Father* and *State of the Union,* which won a Pulitzer Prize in 1946.

Rutherford Scottish place name, "red crossing"; Anglo-Saxon, "cattle crossing." Rutherford B. Hayes, nineteenth President, winner over Samuel J. Tilden in the disputed 1876 election.

S

SOCRATES . . .
Whom, well inspired, the oracle pronounced
Wisest of men; from whose mouth issued forth
Mellifluous streams, that watered all the schools
Of Academics old and new.

JOHN MILTON, *Paradise Regained*

Salvatore Italian, "savior." Often Americanized as SAL. Spanish, SALVADOR. Art: Salvador Dali, ultramodernist, surrealist painter.

Sam Short form; see SAMUEL. Politics: "Mr. Sam," the name by which Sam Rayburn (1882-1961), long-time Speaker of the House of Representatives, was known. Literature: Sam Weller in Dickens' *Pickwick Papers*. Stage and Screen: Sam Levene. However, the best known Sam is naturally *Uncle Sam*, a nickname said to have come from the name of Samuel Wilson (1766-1854), an army contractor of Troy, N.Y.

Samson Hebrew, "like the sun." SAMPSON. Samson is that hero of the Old Testament whose strength depended on his unshorn hair, and who was betrayed to the Philistines by Delilah. His story has been retold in opera, drama, poetry, and in super-colossal movie epics.

Can this be he
That heroic, that renowned,
Irresistible Samson? whom, unarmed,
No strength of man, of fiercest
wild beast, could withstand;
Who tore the lion as the lion
tears the kid.

JOHN MILTON, *Samson Agonistes*

Music: Samson François, modern French pianist. Theater: Samson Raphaelson, author of *The Skylark*.

Samuel Hebrew, "heard of God" or "name of God." SAM, SAMMY. Biblical: The prophet who anointed Saul as the first king of Israel.

Oh! give me Samuel's ear,
The open ear, O Lord,
Alive and quiet to hear
Each whisper of thy word.

JAMES D. BURNS, *Speak, Lord,*
for Thy Servant Listeneth

History: Samuel Adams of Revolutionary f a m e. Science: Samuel Finley Breese Morse (1791-1872), artist, inventor of the Morse telegraphic code (the first message being "What hath God wrought?").

Famous authors named Samuel: Butler (1612-1680), poet known for the satirical *Hudibras;* Butler (1835-1902), author of the novel *The Way of All Flesh;* Samuel Taylor Coleridge (*The Rime of the Ancient Mariner*); Dr. Samuel Johnson, the lexicographer, novelist, poet, essayist (known as "The Great Cham"); Pepys of the *Diary.*

Sander See ALEXANDER. SANDOR, SANDY. Fem., SANDRA, SONDRA.

Sanford English place name, "by the sandy crossing." SANDY.

Saul Hebrew, "asked for." Biblical: King of Israel and father of Jonathan. St. Paul is also referred to as Saul of Tarsus (ACTS 13 : 9).

Saul and Jonathan were lovely and pleasant in their lives, and in their death they were not divided: they were swifter than eagles, they were stronger than lions.

II SAMUEL 1 : 23

Literature: Saul Bellow, novelist (*The Adventures of Augie March, Henderson, The Rain King*).

Schuyler (SKY' ler) Dutch, "scholar."

Scott English, "native of Scotland." Fem., SCOTTIE. Aeronautics: (Malcom) Scott Carpenter.

Sean (SHAWN) Irish form of JOHN. SHAUN, SHAWN. Literature: Sean O'Casey, modern Irish playwright (*Juno and the Paycock, The Plough and the Stars*); Sean O'Faolain, short-story writer.

Sebastian Greek, "venerated" or "majestic." BASTIAN, BASTIEN. St. Sebastian, a Roman soldier, who suffered martyrdom by being shot with arrows. His martyrdom was a favorite subject of medieval art. History: Sebastian Cabot (1476-1557), explorer, son of John Cabot. Literature: In Shakespeare's *Twelfth Night,* the twin brother of Viola, for whom she is mistaken. Screen: Sebastian Cabot, actor.

Sedg(e)wick Place name, "victory town."

Selby Place name, "village by the mansion." SHELBY.

Selden, Seldon Place name, "shops."

Selig (SEE' lig) Germanic, "blessed." ZELIG. See also BARUCH and FELIX.

Selwyn Anglo-Saxon, "palace-friend"; Welsh, "zeal-fear."

Serge Latin via French, *Sergius, gens* name. Russian, SERGEI (sur GAY'). The original is known to Latin students through Cicero's orations against Lucius

Sergius Catiline. Music: Sergei Rachmaninoff; Sergei Prokofiev; Serge Koussevitsky. Films: Sergei Eisenstein, one of the truly great creators in this medium (*Ten Days That Shook the World, Potemkin, Alexander Nevsky,* etc.).

Seth Hebrew, "substitute" or "compensation" or "appointed." Seth Low (1830-1916) was president of Columbia University (1890-1901) and Mayor of New York (1901-1903). Biblical: Son of Adam and Eve.

> . . . and she bare a son, and called his name Seth: For God, said she, hath appointed me another seed instead of Abel, whom Cain slew.
>
> GENESIS 4 : 25

Seamus (SHAY' mus) Irish form of JAMES. SHAMUS.

Seward, Siward Anglo-Saxon "victorious defender."

Seymour French place name, *St. Maur.* See MAURICE. This last name of English nobility may also be derived from the English word *seamer,* "tailor."

Shawn Irish, variant spelling of SEAN.

Sheldon English place name, Anglo-Saxon, "hut on the hill" or "ledge farm" or "shield town." SHELTON, SHELL(E)Y. Lyricist: Sheldon Harnick (*Fiorello!, Fiddler on the Roof, Carmen*).

> Ah, did you once see Shelley plain?
> And did he stop and speak to you?
> And did you speak to him again?
> How strange it seems and new!
>
> ROBERT BROWNING, *Memorabilia*

Shep(p)ard, Shepherd Anglo-Saxon occupational name. SHEPPERD. Stage, Screen, and TV: Actor Sheppard Strudwick.

Sherlock Anglo-Saxon, "shear hair" or "fair-haired" or "shining hair." The fame of the detective Sherlock Holmes has made this name as renowned as any in or out of books. It is not used as often as one would expect but the Baker Street Irregulars, a society devoted to the adoration of Sherlock Holmes, have found a number of men who bear not only the first name Sherlock but also the last name Holmes with it! The following is an oft-quoted principle of Sherlock Holmes' reasoning:

> It is an old maxim of mine that when you have excluded the impossible, whatever remains, however improbable, must be the truth.
>
> ARTHUR CONAN DOYLE, *The Adventure of the Beryl Coronet*

Sherman English occupational name, Anglo-Saxon, "cloth-cutter." SHERM, SHERMIE. The original form of this surname was *Shearman.* Two Americans who gave prominence to *Sherman* as a last name were Roger Sherman (1721-1793), a signer of the Declaration of Independence, and General William Tecumseh Sherman (1820-1891).

Sherwin Anglo-Saxon, "shining friend" or "shear-wind."

Sherwood Anglo-Saxon, place name (Sherwood Forest), meaning "shear-wood" or "shining wood." Literature: Sherwood Anderson (1876-1941), author of *Winesburg, Ohio*, etc.

Merry, merry England is waking as of old,
With eyes of blither hazel and hair of brighter gold
For Robin Hood is here again beneath the bursting spray
In Sherwood, in Sherwood, about the break of day.
ALFRED NOYES,
A Song of Sherwood

Sidney English run-together form of French, *Saint Denis.* See DENIS. SID, SYD, SYDNEY. Fem., SYDNEY, SIDONIA, SYDELLE. *Sidney* probably became popular as a first name in admiration of the romantic and heroic poet and courtier, Sir Philip Sidney (1554-1586), author of *Arcadia* and *Astrophel and Stella.* According to the story, Sidney, fatally wounded at the battle of Zutphen, gave up his cup of water to a wounded soldier with these immortal words, "Thy necessity is yet greater than mine."

Battles nor songs can from oblivion save,
But Fame upon a white deed loves to build;
From out that cup of water Sidney gave,
Not one drop has been spilled.
LIZETTE W. REESE, *Immortality*

Literature: Sidney Lanier (1842-1881), American musician and poet, noted for musical effects (*Song of the Chattahoochee*); Sydney Carton, hero of Dickens' *Tale of Two Cities* ("It is a far, far better thing I do than I have ever done; it is a far, far better rest I go to than I have ever known"). Theater: Sidney Kingsley, author of *Men in White*, Pulitzer Prize play (1934). Stage and Screen: Sidney Poitier. TV: Sid Caesar.

Siegfried Germanic, "victory-peace." Teutonic Mythology: Handsome and powerful hero of *The Nibelungenlied* and of Wagner's operas *The Ring* based on it. Literature: Siegfried Sassoon, satirist of British upper classes, poet of World War I.

Sigmund, Sigismund Germanic, "victorious protection." Medicine: Sigmund Freud (1856-1939), founder of the science of psychoanalysis. Music: Sigmund Romberg, composer (*Blossom Time*, etc.).

Silas (SIGH' liss) Latin, *Silvanus,* name of the woodland god. SI. Biblical: Companion of Paul on his missionary journey. Literature: *Silas Marner* (1861) by George Eliot; *The Rise of Silas Lapham* (1885), a novel by William Dean Howells.

Simeon (SIMM' ee un) Hebrew, "hearing." SI, SIMON. Biblical: Simeon carried the infant Jesus into the temple at Jerusalem, saying in part, "Lord, now lettest thou thy servant depart in peace, according to thy word" (LUKE, 2 : 29), which is called the *Nunc Dimittis,* from the Latin translation of the opening words. St. Simeon Stylites was an early ascetic who is said to have spent sixty-eight years on top of various columns.

I, Simeon of the pillar by surname,
Stylites among men—I, Simeon,
The watcher on the column till the end.

ALFRED, LORD TENNYSON,
St. Simeon Stylites

Simon This form of SIMEON appears in the New Testament; it may be related to the Greek personal name *Simon,* "snubnosed," which is found in *Simonides,* "son of Simon." SI. Fem., SIMONE. St. Simon Zelotes ("Zealot") is one of the Twelve Disciples. The expression "Simon called Peter" refers to the fact that St. Peter was also called Simon, probably his surname (JOHN 1 : 42); see under PETER.

"What is thy name, thou fine fellow?
I pray thee heartily tell to me";
"In mine own country where I was borne,
Men called me Simon over the Lee."

OLD BALLAD,
The Noble Fisherman

History: Simon Bolívar (1783-1830), after whom Bolivia was named, known as the George Washington of South America and *El Libertador* ("Liberator") for his part in freeing South American countries from Spanish rule.

Sinclair Latin via French, "saint" and "famous." Literature: Two distinguished novelists with this name: Upton Sinclair, and (Harry) Sinclair Lewis.

Solomon Hebrew, "peaceful." SALOMON, SALMON, SHALOM. Fem., SALOME. *Shalom* (sha LOME'), the Hebrew greeting, "Peace" is used as a salutation in Israel, corresponding to our "Hello" and "Goodbye."

And Solomon's wisdom excelled the wisdom of all the children of the east country. . . .
For he was wiser than all men. . . .
And he spake three thousand proverbs: and his songs were a thousand and five.

I KINGS 4 : 30, 31, 32

Literature: Sholom Aleichem (1859-1916), beloved story teller; Sholem Asch, modern novelist.

Solon Greek name. *Solon,* the name of the lawgiver of ancient Athens, one of the Seven Wise Men, has become a synonym for a wise man or a legislator.

Solon compared the people unto the sea, and orators to the winds; for that the sea would be calm and quiet, if the winds did not trouble it.
FRANCIS BACON, *Apothegms*

Spencer English occupational name, "house-steward." SPENCE, SPENSER. This was formerly a last name through the poet Edmund Spenser and the philosopher and social scientist Herbert Spencer, but today it has been tinged with Hollywood glamour as a first name through Spencer Tracy, winner of an Oscar in 1937 (*Captains Courageous*) and in 1938 (*Boys Town*).

Stanford Place name, "at the stony crossing."

Stanisla(u)s (STANN' iss laws) Polish, "camp glory"; Americanized as STANLEY. STANISLAW.

Stanley English place name, "stone field." STAN. The name *Stanley* received world-wide fame from the incident involving the explorer Sir Henry Morton Stanley (1840-1904), who went to Africa in search of the lost missionary, David Livingstone. Finding him, Stanley greeted him with that epitome of *sang-froid* and casualness, "Dr. Livingstone, I presume."

Baseball: Stan "the Man" Musial, one of the really great players of modern baseball.

Stanton Place name, "stony town."

Stephen (STEEV' en) Greek, "crown." STEVE, STEVEN, STEFAN, STEFFEN, ÉTIENNE (French), ESTEBAN (Spanish). Fem., STEPHANIE, STEFFA. The crown of St. Stephen, first king of Hungary (1000-1038), is the symbol of that country. Another St. Stephen was the first martyr (commemorated December 26).

Good King Wenceslas look'd out
On the feast of Stephen;
When the snow lay round about,
Deep and crisp and even.
JOHN M. NEALE,
Good King Wenceslas

Music: Stephen C. Foster (1826-1864), writer and composer of some of America's most cherished folk songs (*My Old Kentucky Home, Oh! Susanna, Nelly Was a Lady,* etc.). History: Stephen Decatur, American naval hero, War of 1812; Stephen A. Douglas, "The Little Giant," Lincoln's opponent in the famous debates. Literature: Stephen Crane (1871-1900), author of *The Red Badge of Courage;*

Stephen Vincent Benét (1898-1943), author of the poem *John Brown's Body* (Pulitzer Prize, 1929), the short story *The Devil and Daniel Webster*, which has been made into a movie and opera, also of the poem *Western Star*, posthumously awarded a Pulitzer Prize in 1944; Stefan Zweig (1881-1942), novelist (*The Case of Sergeant Grischa*); Stephen Dedalus, hero of James Joyce's *Portrait of the Artist as a Young Man* and an important character in *Ulysses*.

Sterling English, "standard, of excellent quality." Early English money was called *sterling*. Here are three explanations for the use of this term, each plausible, none proved beyond doubt. (1) *Sterling* is a shortening of *Easterling*, "from the east." The early English coins were minted in the eastern part of Europe. (2) *Sterling* comes from the Anglo-Saxon, "star"; early Norman coins had stars on them. (3) *Sterling* is *starling;* some Anglo-Saxon coins had four birds on them. In addition, *Sterling* is spelled *Stirling*, being identified with the famous castle of Stirling in Scotland. Whatever the origin, *Sterling* came to mean "excellent," because of the solidity and purity of English coinage.

Strephon Probably from Greek, "one who turns." A name from literature, used by Sir Philip Sidney in his pastoral romance *Arcadia* (1590) for the lovesick shepherd. Hence, the name came to be used later to denote a rustic gallant or even any lover. See also CORYDON and ROBIN. *Strephon* is being used again, either because of its literary association or the perennial desire for the unusual. Music: Strephon, hero of the operetta *Iolanthe* by Gilbert and Sullivan.

Strephon kissed me in the spring,
Robin in the fall,
But Colin only looked at me
And never kissed at all.
SARA TEASDALE, *The Look*

Stuart Anglo-Saxon, "caretaker." STEWART, STEWARD, STU. The descendants of Walter Fitz-Alan, whom David I of Scotland appointed as Lord High Steward or Keeper of the Mansion in the twelfth century, adopted the title as their last name. The royal line of Stuarts descended from him, among them Mary, Queen of Scots, and James I of England.

Literature: *Stuart Little*, popular children's book by E. B. White.

Stuyvesant Dutch family name made famous by Peter Stuyvesant, last Dutch governor of New Amsterdam.

Sumner Occupational name, "summoner, a court attendant."

Sylvan Latin, "of the forest." SYLVANUS, SILVANUS. Fem., SYLVIA. Mythology Roman god of the woodlands. Colonel Sylvanus Thayer, superintendent of the U. S. Military Academy, West Point, from 1817 to 1833, is called "The Father of the Military Academy." The Thayer Hotel, familiar to visitors to the Point, was named for him.

Sylvester Latin, "of the woods." SILVESTER. Literature: *Le Crime de Sylvestre Bonnard* by Anatole France. Screen: Sylvester Stallone (*Rocky*).

T

But THOMAS *and* William, *and such pretty names,*
Should be cleanly and harmless as doves or as
lambs,
Those lovely and innocent creatures.

ISAAC WATTS, *Innocent Play*

Tab Short form of surnames such as Taber, Tabor, Talbot, e t c. Tabor, an occupational name, "drummer" (French, *tambour*), and Taber, from *tabard*, "cloak, jacket," were confused. TABB. See also TALBOT. Hollywood: Tab Hunter (Art Gelien; see under "Hollywood" in chapter "Where Our Names Come From.")

Tad Short form: see THADDEUS and THEODORE.

Talbot (TAWL′ butt *or* TAL′ butt). This name of a famous English family is said to be derived via French from the Germanic *Talabert,* "valley-bright," which was contracted into TALBOT and *Talbert.* See also ADALBERT and DALE. Lord Talbert and his son appear prominently in Shakespeare's *I Henry VI;* the family name is mentioned in *Richard III* and *Henry V:*

Then shall our names,
Familiar in his mouth as household words,
Harry the King, Bedford and Exeter,
Warwick and Talbot, Salisbury and Gloucester,—

Be in their flowing cups freshly remembered.

WILLIAM SHAKESPEARE, *Henry V*

Tam Short form of Scottish TAMMIE and TAMMAS; see THOMAS. Fem., TAMMI(E), TAMMY. Literature: *Tam o' Shanter* by Robert Burns:

Kings may be blest, but Tam was glorious,
O'er a' the ills of life victorious.

Taylor Occupational name; French, *tailleur,* "tailor" or "cutter," English, "tailor."

Ted Short form; see THEODORE and EDWARD. Baseball: Ted Williams, one of the greatest hitters of all time.

Terence Latin, name of a *gens.* TERRY. Literature: Terence (Publius Terentius Afer), Latin writer of comedies; Terence Mulvaney in Kipling's stories *Soldiers Three.* Theater: Terence Rattigan, author of *The Winslow Boy, The Browning Version, Separate Tables,* and *Ross.*

Thaddeus (THADD' ee us) Greek and Latin form of JUDAH and JUDE. THAD. Literature: *Thaddeus of Warsaw* (1803), historical novel by Jane Porter. History: Thaddeus Stevens (1792-1838), remembered for his impeachment proceedings against President Johnson.

Thayer Origin undertermined, possibly "son of Theodoric," or English place name, "pasture land."

Theobald (THEE' o bald) Germanic, "people's prince" or "bold for the people." See TYBALT.

Theodore Greek, "God's gift." TAD, TED, TEDDY, THEO. Fem., THEODORA, DOROTHEA, DOROTHY, DORA. The name *Tudor* is believed to be derived from this name. In this country, our twenty-sixth President, Theodore Roosevelt, brought fame to the names *Teddy* and *Theodore*.

> ... *Theodore the brave, above the rest,*
> *With gifts of fortune and of nature blessed,*
> *The foremost place for wealth and honor held,*
> *And all in feats of chivalry excelled.*
>
> JOHN DRYDEN,
> *Theodore and Honoria*

Literature: Theodore Dreiser (1871-1945), realistic novelist, author of *An American Tragedy*. Stage and TV: Theodore Bikel, actor, singer of folk songs of many nations.

See also FEODOR.

Theodoric (thee ODD' o rick) Germanic, "powerful people" or "rule of the people." Often used instead of unrelated THEODORE, because of similar spelling. History: Theodoric the Great (455-526,) one of the most enlightened rulers of ancient times.

Thomas Aramaic via Hebrew, "twin." TOM, TOMMY. Fem., THOMASIN(E). Biblical: One of the Twelve Apostles, referred to as the Doubting Thomas because at first he refused to believe in Christ. The martydrom of St. Thomas à Becket of Canterbury in 1170 established *Thomas* as one of the most popular of English names. St. Thomas Aquinas, thirteenth-century philosopher, author of *Summa Theologiae*, is called the Prince of Scholastics and the Angelic Doctor. St. Thomas à Kempis (fourteenth century) wrote *The Imitation of Christ*. Thomas Henry Huxley (1825-1895), grandfather of Julian and Aldous Huxley, was a noted biologist who was called "Darwin's Bulldog" because of his defense of the theory of evolution.

The full name of T. E. Lawrence, better known as Lawrence of Arabia, was Thomas Edward Lawrence, which he changed legally to T. E. Shaw.

Actually there have been two Presidents with the first name

Thomas: Jefferson and Wilson, but the latter dropped the *Thomas* early in life, preferring to be known as Woodrow Wilson.

Literature: In alphabetical order here is a list of noted authors bearing the first name Thomas: Carlyle, De Quincey, Eliot, Gray, Hardy, Hood, Macaulay, Mann, Moore, More, Paine, and Wolfe. Many other luminaries in other fields have given honor to this name, but additional luster was given to it by the brilliant achievements of Thomas Alva Edison (1847-1931). He is credited with the saying, "Genius is 99% perspiration and 1% inspiration."

True Thomas lay on Huntlie
* bank;*
A ferlie [marvel] he spied wi'
* his e'e;*
And there he saw a ladye bright
* Come riding down by the Eil-*
* don Tree.*

> OLD BALLAD,
> *Thomas the Rhymer*

Thor Old Norwegian, "thunder." TOR, TOR(R)E. Thor the Thunderer was after Odin the most important god in Norse mythology. He is often confused with Tyr, the god of battle. See TYRUS and TYRA. Fem., THORA. *Thursday* is derived from THOR.

I am the God Thor,
I am the War God,
I am the Thunderer!

Here in my Northland,
My fastness and fortress,
Reign I forever!

> HENRY WADSWORTH
>   LONGFELLOW,
> *The Challenge of Thor*

Literature: Thor Heyerdahl, author of *Kon-Tiki*, story of crossing the Pacific on a balsawood raft.

Thornton Place name, "thorntown." Literature: Thornton Wilder, author of the novel *The Bridge of San Luis Rey*, Pulitzer Prize, 1928, and the plays *Our Town* and *The Skin of Our Teeth*, Pulitzer Prize winners, 1938 and 1943, respectively.

Thurman "Thor's protection." THURMOND. See THOR.

Thurston Scandinavian, "Thor's stone"; see THOR. THORSTEIN. Economics: Thorstein Veblen (1857-1929), author of the classic study *The Theory of The Leisure Class*.

Tiffany Greek, *Theophane(s)*, "appearance of God," similar to Epiphany, "appearance." Literature: Tiffany Thayer, writer of fiction.

Timothy Greek, "Honor God." TIM. Biblical: Companion of St. Paul, who addressed two Epistles to him. The story of Tiny Tim is a perennial Christmas favorite.

*"God bless us every one," said
Tiny Tim, the last of all.*
> CHARLES DICKENS,
> *A Christmas Carol*

Titus (TY′ tus) Latin, probably "safe." Name of an early Roman emperor. TITO.

Tobias (toe BYE′ as) Hebrew, "God is good." TOBE, TOBIAH, TOBIT, TOBY. Biblical: Book of Tobit, a romance in the Apocrypha. Literature: Uncle Toby in Laurence Sterne's *Tristram Shandy; Toby Tyler, or Ten Weeks with a Circus* by James Otis, a juvenile favorite since its appearance in 1881; Tobias Smollett (1721-1771), author of the novels *Roderick Random* and *Peregrine Pickle*.

Todd Scottish, "fox." TOD.

Tom Dim. form; see THOMAS. Literature: *Tom Jones,* one of the greatest of English novels, by Henry Fielding; *Uncle Tom's Cabin* by Harriet Beecher Stowe; *Tom Brown's Schooldays* and *Tom Brown at Oxford* by Thomas Hughes; *The Adventures of Tom Sawyer* by Mark Twain.

*I hold he loves me best that calls
me Tom.*
> THOMAS HEYWOOD,
> *Hierarchie of the Blessed Angells*

Tommy Pet form; see THOMAS. Literature: *Sentimental Tommy* by James M. Barrie, a charming novel of youth. English soldiers received the nickname "Tommies," because the hypothetical name "Thomas Atkins" was put on samples of forms the soldiers had to fill out.

*For it's Tommy this, an' Tommy
that, an "Chuck 'im out, the
brute!"
But it's "Saviour of 'is country"
when the guns begin to shoot.*
> RUDYARD KIPLING, *Tommy*

Tony Short and pet form; see ANTONY. Fem., TONI(E). Hollywood: Tony Curtis, Tony Perkins, Tony Randall.

Torin (TAW′ rin) Irish family name, "chief" or Gaelic, *torr,* "round hill" or *tor,* "tower." TORIN may also be derived from such names as *Thorfinn* and THORSTEIN; see THOR. In a letter to us, Torin Thatcher, noted character actor, writes that both his father and his grandfather had this first name; he himself associates it with THOR and THORA.

Trac(e)y French place name, village near Caën. Also dim. form; see THERESA.

Travis, Travers Place name, French origin, "at the *traverse,* or crossway."

Trevor (TREV′ or) Cornish "house-great." *Tre* is a common Cornish name-syllable, as seen in the old rhyme handed down by Camden:

By Tre, Ros, Pol, Lan, Car, *and*
Pen,
*Ye shall know the most Cornish-
men.*

As a Welsh name TREVOR appears as *Trefor;* it is used also as
a place name. Trefor Randall
Davies is an authority on Welsh
names. Screen: British actor
Trevor Howard.

Tristram Celtic, "bold"; but
also associated with French,
"sad." TRIS, TRISTAN. The tragic
story of the loves of Tristan and
Iseult (Tristram and Isolde) has
been related in romance, poetry,
music, and drama. Malory, Matthew Arnold, Swinburne, and
Edward Arlington Robinson are
some of the authors who have
retold the story taken from the
old French romances; Wagner
wrote both the words and the
music of *Tristan und Isolde.*

In *The Romance of Tristan
and Iseult* by Joseph Bédier,
Blanchefleur, the mother of
Tristan, tells why she gave him
this name:

"In sadness came I hither, in
sadness did I bring forth, and in
sadness has your first feast-day
gone. And as by sadness you
came into the world, your name
shall be called Tristan; that is,
the child of sadness."

*Tristram, the loud accredited
strong warrior,
Tristram, the loved of women,
the harp-player,*

*Tristram, the learned Nimrod
among hunters.*
EDWIN ARLINGTON ROBINSON,
Tristram

Literature: *Tristram Shandy,*
the delightful novel by Laurence
Sterne; (Robert Peter) Tristram
Coffin, winner of the Pulitzer
Poetry Prize (1936). Baseball:
Tris (Tristram E.) Speaker, su-
perb outfielder of the Boston
Red Sox some decades ago,
member of the National Base-
ball Hall of Fame.

Tru(e)man Anglo-Saxon, "faithful man." Literature: Truman
Capote, author of *The Grass
Harp, Breakfast at Tiffany's*
etc.).

Tully Latin, *Tullius,* name of
a *gens.* Best known to us because
of Marcus Tullius Cicero (106-
63 B.C.), great Roman orator,
essayist, and letter writer. He is
sometimes called Tully instead
of Cicero, especially in poetry.

*The arm of Hector, and the
might
Of Tully, to maintain the right
In truth's just cause.*
HENRY WADSWORTH
LONGFELLOW,
Coplas de Manrique ("Couplets
of Manrique," translation from
the Spanish of an ode by Don
Jorge Manrique)

Tybalt (TIBB' alt) Variant
form; see THEOBALD. Literature:
Tybalt, the impetuous cousin of
Juliet in *Romeo and Juliet.*

*O Tybalt, love, Tybalt, awake
me not yet,
Around my soft pillow while
softer dreams flit;
For what are the joys that in
waking we prove
Compared with these visions, O
Tybalt! my love?*

SIR WALTER SCOTT, *Ivanhoe*

Tyler Occupational name, "tiler."

Tyrone Irish, "land of Owen." Screen: Tyrone Power. Theater: Tyrone Guthrie, outstanding director and writer on the theater.

Tyrus Latin name of Tyre in Phoenicia; or a Latinization of *Tyr;* see under THOR. TY. Fem., TYRA. Baseball: The peerless Ty (Tyrus Raymond) Cobb, "the Georgia Peach," first player elected to the National Baseball Hall of Fame (1936).

U

Come worthy Greek, ULYSSES *come*
Possess these shores with me:
The winds and seas are troublesome,
And here we may be free.

SAMUEL DANIEL, *Ulysses and the Siren*

Ulric(h), Ulrick Germanic "wolf-rule." Fem., ULRICA.

Ulysses From *Ulixes,* the Latin equivalent of the Greek *Odysseus,* "wounded in the thigh." The name is also believed to mean "wrathful." ULICK. Ulysses is the proverbial wise man and wanderer whose adventures form the subject of Homer's *Odyssey.* James Joyce called his masterpiece *Ulysses* because it parallels parts of the *Odyssey* with modern themes, techniques, and treatment.

> *I am become a name:*
> *For always roaming with a hungry heart*
> *Much have I seen and known; cities of men,*
> *And manners, climates, councils, governments,*
> *Myself not least, but honor'd of them all;*
> *And drunk delight of battle with my peers;*
> *Far on the ringing plains of windy Troy.*
> ALFRED, LORD TENNYSON,
> *Ulysses*

President Ulysses Simpson Grant was originally named Hiram Ulysses Grant.

Upton Place name, "from the hill town." Literature: Upton Sinclair, prolific novelist, Pulitzer Prize winner in 1943 (*The Dragon's Teeth*).

Urban Latin, "town dweller" or "courteous." Eight Popes have borne the name URBAN. Fem., URBANA.

Uriah (you RYE' a) Hebrew, "Jehovah is my light." Biblical: Captain in King David's army and the husband of Bathsheba. Literature: Uriah Heep in Dickens' *David Copperfield.*

Uriel (YOU' ree 'l) Hebrew, "flame of God" or "angel of light." Related to URIAH. URI, URY. Uriel was an angel whom Milton described as the "Regent of the Sun."

> *The Archangel Uriel, one of the seven*
> *Who in God's presence, nearest to his throne,*
> *Stands ready at command, and are his eyes*
> *That run through all the Heavens, or down to the Earth.*
> JOHN MILTON, *Paradise Lost*

V

For aye VALERIUS *loathed the wrong,*
And aye upheld the right.

THOMAS BABINGTON MACAULAY,
The Battle of Lake Regillus

Vachel (VAY' chel) Occupational name from French, "cowkeeper." Literature: (Nicholas) Vachel Lindsay (1879-1931), author of *The Congo, General William Booth Enters into Heaven,* and *Abraham Lincoln Walks at Midnight.*

Valentine Latin, "healthy" or "strong." VAL. Fem., VALENTINA. February 14, the day on which St. Valentine became a martyr, practically coincided with the observance of the festival of Juno on which lots were drawn for lovers, and with the legendary date on which birds are supposed to choose their mates.

Tomorrow is St. Valentine's Day,
All in the morning betime,
And I a maid at your window,
    To be your Valentine.
WILLIAM SHAKESPEARE, *Hamlet*

Valerian (va LEER' e an) Latin, name of renowned gens. VALERIUS.

Van Dutch preposition showing place of origin, like French and Spanish *de,* Italian *da, de,* and *di,* German *von.* Used also as an abbrev. of names like Vanderbilt. Hollywood: Van Johnson,

Van Heflin. Music: Van Cliburn (full name Harry Lavan Cliburn), the young pianist who won his way to fame and a sensational career with a victory in an international contest held in Moscow.

Vance Dutch, "son of Van"; or English occupational name, "thresher." A *van* or fan is a threshing instrument. Literature: Vance Packard, author of *The Status Seekers* and *Hidden Persuaders.*

Van Wyck Dutch, place name, "from the refuge." Literature: Van Wyck Brooks, American literary critic (*The Flowering of New England,* etc.).

Vaughan Welsh, "small." Music: Ralph Vaughan Williams (here *Vaughan* is part of the last name), greatest modern English composer; bandleader Vaughn Monroe.

Vergil Classical scholars now hold that this is the correct spelling instead of the long established Virgil. See VIRGIL.

Vernon French, "spring-like." VERN, VERNE, LAVERNE. Fem.,

171

VERNA. Literature: Vernon L. Parrington (1871-1929), influential literary critic, author of *Main Currents in American Thought*.

Victor Latin, "conqueror." VIC. Fem., VICTORIA, VICKI. Three Popes, about thirty-five saints, and a number of Italian kings have had this name. (Italian, VITTORIO.) The American composer Victor Herbert and the French novelist and poet Victor Hugo have added to its glory.

> *Victor in Drama, Victor in Romance,*
> *Cloud-weaver of phantasmal hopes and fears,*
> *French of the French, and Lord of human tears.*
> ALFRED, LORD TENNYSON,
> *To Victor Hugo*

Stage and TV: Victor Borge, pianist-comedian. Hollywood: Victor Mature. Screen: Vittorio de Sica, actor and director (*Bicycle Thief*, etc.).

Vincent Latin, "conquering." VIN, VINNIE, VINCE. St. Vincent Ferrer was a famous fifteenth-century Dominican; St. Vincent de Paul founded the Vincentian Order of the Sisters of Charity in the seventeenth century. Art: Vincent van Gogh (1835-1890). Music: Vincent Youmans (1899-1946), composer (*No, No, Nanette, Hit the Deck, Tea for Two*, etc.). Stage: Vincent Price.

> *What I shall leave thee none can tell,*
> *But all shall say I wish you well:*
> *I wish thee, Vin, before all wealth,*
> *Both bodily and ghostly [spiritual] health.*
> RICHARD CORBET,
> *To His Son, Vincent*

Vinton Place name, "winetown" or "friendly town or hill." Theater: Vinton Freedley, producer.

Virgil Latin, "flourishing" or pertaining to a wand." VERGIL. Fem., VIRGILIA. Music and Journalism: Virgil Thomson, composer, music reviewer. Literature: Virgil (70 B.C.-19 B.C.), greatest of Roman poets, author of the *Aeneid, Georgics*, and *Eclogues*.

> *Roman Virgil, thou that singest Ilion's lofty temples robed in fire,*
> *Ilion falling, Rome arising, wars, and filial faith, and Dido's pyre.*
> ALFRED, LORD TENNYSON,
> *To Virgil*

Aeronautics: Virgil Ivan Grissom.

Virginius Name of a Roman *gens*. This name may be related to VIRGIL. Roman History: Lucius Virginius, who killed his own daughter Virginia, to keep her from being enslaved, and thereby began a successful revolt against the decemvirs, a governing body of ten headed by the cruel Appius Claudius. This legend is the subject of Macaulay's poem *Virginia*. See also VIRGINIA.

Vivian When used as a boys' name in England, it is derived from a surname. VYVYAN. See also VIVIAN (f).

Vladimir (VLA' di mir) Russian, "prince of the world" or "glory of the prince." Music: Vladimir Horowitz, virtuoso pianist famed for pyrotechnics. Literature: Vladimir Nabokov, author of the *Pnin* stories and *Lolita* (novel and film version).

W

TOUCHSTONE: *Is thy name* WILLIAM?
WILLIAM: WILLIAM, *sir.*
TOUCHSTONE: *A fair name.*

SHAKESPEARE, *As You Like It*

Wade Place name, "river crossing."

Waldemar (WAHL' de mar) Germanic, "strong and famous."

Waldo Germanic, "strong." Literature: Waldo Frank, American journalist, critic, and novelist; and of course Ralph Waldo Emerson.

Wallace Anglo-Saxon, "foreigner" or "stranger" or "Welshman"; originally a Scottish surname. WALLIE, WALLY, WALLAS. Fem., WALLIS. William Wallace (1272-1305) takes his place with Robert Bruce as a national hero of Scotland. Literature: *The Scottish Chiefs* by Jane Porter (1810), a romantic novel about both these heroes.

Scots, wha hae wi' Wallace bled,
Scots, wham Bruce has aften led;
Welcome to your gory bed,
  Or to victorie!
            ROBERT BURNS,
            Battle of Bannockburn

Screen: Wallace Reid, a matinee idol of the silent-film era. Literature: Wallace Stegner, short-story writer and novelist (*A Shooting Star*, etc.).

Walter Germanic, "powerful warrior" or "ruling the people." WALT, WAT, WALTHER. From *Walter* come the last names Watson, Watts, Watkins, Waters, and Gautier (French). Sir Walter Raleigh, the renowned courtier, author of the Elizabethan Age, gave great prominence to this name. In Scott's novel *Kenilworth* the story is told that he put down his cloak on a muddy spot for the Queen to step on. She then ordered him to wear the "muddy cloak till her pleasure be further known." James Thurber's short story *The Secret Life of Walter Mitty* has made "Walter Mitty" a symbolic expression denoting the dreams and frustrations of everyday human beings. Among the real-life Walters in literature there are Sir Walter Scott, novelist and poet; Walter Savage Landor, essayist and poet; Walter Pater, novelist and critic; Walter de la Mare, poet; and Walt Whitman, "The Good Gray Poet."

Who has held the heights more
    sure than thou,
O Walt!
HART CRANE, *To Walt Whitman*

Music: In *The Mastersingers of Nuremberg* by Richard Wag-

174

ner, Walter, successful suitor of Eva, wins the song contest with his famous "Prize Song."

Many other Walters have distinguished themselves in various fields. Sports: Walter Camp, who began the practice of making All-America selections in football; Walter Johnson, the fastball king; Walter Hagen, the matchless golfer. Medicine: Walter Reed, one of the team that discovered the causes of yellow fever ("yellow jack"). Journalism: Few would recognize in the name Walter Wellesley Smith, whom his colleague Stanley Woodward has called the only man to have been named after two women's colleges, the name of the columnist who writes pungently with style and distinction —the peerless Red Smith.

Three other Walters of our time reach millions through radio, movies, TV, and the press: Walt Disney, Walter Winchell, and Walter Lippmann.

Ward Germanic, "guard."

Warner Germanic, "protecting army." WERNER. May also be related to WARREN.

Warren Germanic, "protecting friend"; or English place name, "living near an enclosure." President with this name: Warren G. Harding (see under GAMALIEL). Baseball: Warren Spahn, one of the all-time great pitchers. Hollywood: Warren Beatty.

Wayne Anglo-Saxon, short form of *Wainwright*, "maker of wagons." The fame of Anthony Wayne, a hero of the Revolutionary War, helped to popularize the use of this surname as a first name.

Webster Anglo-Saxon occupational name, "female weaver."

Wendell Germanic, "wanderer"; or Anglo-Saxon, "dweller by the passage." Famous men: Wendell Phillips (1811-1884), Abolitionist, supporter of William Lloyd Garrison; Oliver Wendell Holmes, the poet, and his son Oliver Wendell Holmes, Chief Justice of the Supreme Court from 1902 to 1932; Wendell Willkie (1892-1944), Presidential candidate in 1940, author of *One World*.

Wesley (WESS' lee *or* WEZZ' lee) English place name, Anglo-Saxon, "west field" or "well field." WES. A last name used as a first name in honor of the Wesley brothers, John Wesley (1703-1791), founder of Methodism, and Charles Wesley (1707-1788), writer of hymns. The Duke of Wellington (1769-1852), conqueror of Napoleon at Waterloo, was born Arthur Wesley but he changed his last name to Wellesley.

Whitney English place name, Anglo-Saxon, "white island" or "fair water." WHIT. A last name best known through Eli Whitney, inventor of the cotton gin.

Wilbert See GILBERT. WIL-BUR(T).

Wilbur See GILBERT. Aviation: Wilbur Wright (1867-1912); see under ORVILLE.

Wiley, Wylie English place name, possibly "water meadow" or "Will's meadow." Aviation: Wiley Post (1900-1935), pioneer flyer, killed with Will Rogers in crash.

Wilford Place name, "at Will's or Wilfred's crossing."

Wilfred Anglo-Saxon, "will-peace." WILFRID. Fem., WILFRE-DA. St. Wilfrid (634-709) was a famous bishop of York. Literature: Name of hero in *Ivanhoe* and *Rokeby*, both by Sir Walter Scott.

Wilfrid, docile, soft, and mild.
   SIR WALTER SCOTT, *Rokeby*

Wilhelm German form; see WILLIAM. F e m., WILHELMINA, WILMA, HELMA. Literature: *Wilhelm Meister*, a two-part novel by Goethe; *Wilhelm Tell*, play by Schiller. Science: Wilhelm Konrad Roentgen (1845-1923), discoverer of X-rays (also called Roentgen rays in Germany), winner of the Nobel Prize for Physics (1901).

Will . Short form; see WILLIAM. Fem., WILLA.

Make but my name thy love, and
   love that still,
And then thou lovest me, for my
   name is 'Will.'
   WILLIAM SHAKESPEARE,
      Sonnet 136

Known also as Will was that lovable, popular, wry and witty humorist and actor who used to swing a lasso while making penetrating comments on politics and other aspects of living—Will Rogers ("No, folks, all I know is what I read in the papers").

Willard Germanic, "of resolute will." Literature: Willard Huntington Wright (1888-1939), art critic who, under the pseudonym S. S. Van Dine, created the detective Philo Vance (see under PHILO).

William Germanic, "will-helmet." BILL, WILL, WILLIE, BILLY, WILLIS. French, GUILLAUME; German, WILHELM; Dutch, WIL-LEM; Italian, GUGLIELMO; Spanish, GUILLERMO. Fem., WILHEL-MINA. *William* is second only to JOHN as the most widely used boy's name in the United States and England. Three of our presidents were named William: William Henry Harrison, William McKinley, and William Howard Taft. In England, the fact that it was the name of William the Conqueror (1066) gave it a vogue which it has never lost.

*Oh! Where shall I my true
love find!
Tell me, jovial sailors, tell me
true,
If my sweet William sails among
the crew?*
JOHN GAY, *William and Susan*

Of the many authors named
William, Shakespeare of course
stands alone:

*He was not of an age, but for
all time!*

BEN JONSON,
To the Memory of Shakespeare

An alphabetical list of some
other authors named William:
Blake, Bryant, Congreve, Gilbert, Hazlitt, Thackeray, Wordsworth, and Yeats. In our time
William Faulkner was honored
with a Nobel Prize in 1949, and
a Pulitzer Prize for the novel *A
Fable* in 1955. Finally, William
is the first name of W. Somerset
Maugham, novelist, essayist,
dramatist, and the grand master
of modern short-story writers.

History: William Penn (1644-1718), member of the Society of
Friends (Quakers), founder of
Pennsylvania. Legend and History: William (Wilhelm) Tell,
Swiss national hero, whose
shooting of an apple off his son's
head is the subject of poetry,
drama, and opera. (See under
WILHELM.) Art: William Hogarth (1697-1764), painter and
engraver, master of pictorial satire (*The Rake's Progress, Marriage à la Mode*, etc.). Science:
William Harvey (1578-1657),
discoverer of the circulation of
the blood. (See also under
GUGLIELMO.)

Willy See WILLIAM. WILLIE.

*Willy's rare and Willy's fair
And Willy's wondrous bonny.*
OLD BALLAD, *Rare Willy*

Science, Willy Ley, who writes
in a popular way on such topics
as the Space Age. Baseball: Willie Mays, scintillating and spectacular.

Wilmer Germanic, "will-fame"
or "warrior." Fem., WILMA.

Wilson Patronymic; son of
WILL.

Wilton English place name
"Will's hill or town." WILT. Basketball: Wilt "the Stilt" Chamberlain, record-breaking scorer.

Winfield Place name, "friendly
field." History: General Winfield
Scott (1786-1866), U. S. commander in the war with Mexico.

Winston Anglo-Saxon, place
name, "friend" and "stone" or
"friendly town." WIN, WINNIE.
Naturally, the name *Winston* is
known in our time through Winston ("Winnie") Churchill, English leader of World War II.
Winston has been used in the
Churchill family since the days
of Sir Winston Churchill, born
in 1620, son of Sarah Winston
and father of the first Duke of
Marlborough.

Winthrop Place name, "wine-village" or "friendly village." Theater: Winthrop Ames, producer.

Wolcott Place name, "cottage in the woods" or "cottage where wool is kept." Theater: Wolcott Gibbs, critic and playwright.

Woodrow Place name, "passage in the woods." Thomas Woodrow Wilson was the full name of our twenty-eighth President.

Wright Occupational name, "worker" or "artisan."

Wystan (wiss' t'n) Anglo-Saxon, "battle-stone." Literature: Wystan Hugh Auden, modern English poet.

X
Why wish we warfare? Wherefore welcome were
XERXES, XIMENES, XANTHUS, XAVIER?

ALARIC ALEXANDER WATTS, *The Siege of Belgrade*

Xanthus (ZAN′ thus) Latin-Greek, "golden-haired." See XANTHE (f).

Xavier (ZAY′ vi er) Arabic, "splendid"; also Spanish place name. JAVIER. XAVIER was adopted by the Spaniards during the Moorish occupation. The Arabic original, *Giaffar* or *Jaffar*, was the name of the Grand Vizier of Haroun-al-Raschid in *The Arabian Nights' Entertainments*. St. Francis (of) Xavier (1506-1552), "The Apostle to the Indies," helped Ignatius of Loyola establish the Society of Jesus (Jesuits). Music and TV: Xavier Cugat, band leader.

The most modern interpretation of *Xavier* is that it is from Jaberri, the Spanish place name from Basque, *etcheberri*, or *etchaberri*, "new house."

Xerxes (ZERKS′ eez) Persian via Greek, the name of a number of Persian emperors. One of them invaded Greece and was defeated at Salamis (480 B.C.), as he watched from a throne on the heights above the bay:

Xerxes, the Persian king, yet I
*   saw there,*
With his huge host, that drank
*   the rivers dry.*

THOMAS SACKVILLE,
The Induction

Lord Byron alludes to Xerxes in *Don Juan:*

A king sate on the rocky brow
*   Which looks o'er sea-born*
*   Salamis;*
And ships, by thousands, lay
*   below,*
*   And men in nations—all were*
*   his!*
He counted them at break of
*   day—*
*   And when the sun set where*
*   were they?*

In the Old Testament the original Persian form of Xerxes (*Khshayarasha*) is transliterated into the Hebrew *Ahasuerus.*

Now it came to pass in the days of Ahasuerus, (this is A-hăs-ū-ē-rŭs which reigned, from India even unto Ethiopia, over an hundred and seven and twenty provinces).   ESTHER 1 : 1

Ximenes (English, zye MEEN′ eez *or* ZYE′ muh NESS′; Spanish, (*hee* MAY′ ness), XIMENEZ (Spanish, hee MAY′ neth). Spanish patronymic, possibly from SIM-(E)ON; see SIMEON and SIMON. Ximenia (zie MEE′ ni a), a genus of tropical herbs and trees, received its name from a Spanish missionary named Ximenes. Fem., XIMENA. *Ximenia* could be used as a fem. flower name if a new name beginning with X is needed.

Y

Alas, poor YORICK! *I knew him, Horatio: a fellow of infinite jest, of most excellent fancy.*

WILLIAM SHAKESPEARE, *Hamlet*

Yale Welsh place name; old English family name.

Yancey French, "Englishman"; or variant of "Yankee"; Southern place name. YANCY. Literature: Yancey Cravat, an interesting character in Edna Ferber's *Cimarron.*

Yardley Place name, "enclosed meadow."

Yates Place name, Anglo-Saxon, "at the gate." The surname of the renowned Irish poet William Butler Yeats is a variant of this name.

York Place name, Celtic, "yew tree." The name *York* is an honored one in English history. Edmund, son of Edward III, founded the House of York, which took part in the War of the Roses, and which later ruled England. The second son of the King is often called the Duke of York. New York City was named in honor of a Duke of York.

Now is the winter of our discontent
Made glorious summer by this sun of York.

WILLIAM SHAKESPEARE, *Richard III*

Yul In a letter to us the noted actor Yul Brynner, winner of an Oscar in 1956 (*The King and I*), declares that his first name has nothing to do with JULIUS or YULE, but that it is an adaptation of a Mongolian name meaning "beyond the horizon." "Actually," Mr. Brynner writes, "*Yul* is an adaptation of the Mongolian sound which more properly pronounced would be *Yaugh.*" (Yul Brynner's mother is Swiss-Mongolian.)

Yule Anglo-Saxon name f o r December or January; Scottish name for Christmas.

Love's old songs shall never die
Yet the new shall suffer proof:
Love's old drink of Yule brew I,
Wassail for new love's behoof.

THEODORE WATTS-DUNTON, *Christmas at the Mermaid Tavern*

Yvan Variant form; see IVAN.

Yves (EEV) See IVOR. Stage, Screen, and TV: Yves Montand, *chanteur* and actor. Fashions: Yves Saint-Laurent.

Z

ZACCHEUS, *he*
Did climb the tree
His Lord to see.

NEW ENGLAND PRIMER

Zaccheus (zak EE' us), **Zacchaeus** Hebrew, "innocent, pure." Biblical: A rich publican of Jericho, who, being short, climbed a "sycomore" tree to see Jesus (LUKE 19 : 4).

Zacharias (zak a RYE' as) Greek form; see ZECHARIAH. ZACHARIAH, ZACHARY, ZACH, ZACK. Biblical: Father of John the Baptist.

Zachary (ZAK' a ree). See ZACHARIAS. ZACH, ZACK, ZACHRY. General Zachary Taylor ("Old Rough and Ready") was our twelfth President. Hollywood: Zachary Scott.

Zander Terminal abbreviation; see ALEXANDER.

Zane One of the many forms of JOHN, from Latin, *Joannes*, via Italian and French. Literature: Zane Grey (1875-1925), New York dentist, prolific writer of best-selling Western adventure novels (*Riders of the Purple Sage*, etc.).

Zebulon (ZEBB' you lun) Hebrew, "dwelling-place." History: General Zebulon M. Pike (1779-1813), after whom Pike's Peak was named.

Zechariah (zek a RYE' a) Hebrew, "Jehovah has remembered." ZACHARIAH. Biblical: A prophet; name of a book of the Old Testament.

And the word of the LORD came unto Zechariah, saying,

Thus speaketh the LORD of hosts, saying, Execute true judgment, and shew mercy and compassions every man to his brother. ZECHARIAH 7 : 8, 9

Law: Zechariah Chafee, eminent authority and writer on the Constitution (*Freedom of Speech and Press, The Blessings of Liberty*).

Zedekiah (zed e KYE' a) Hebrew, "God is mighty or righteous." ZED. Biblical: Last King of Judah.

Zeke Short form; see EZEKIEL.

Zelig (ZEE' lig) Variant spelling; see SELIG. ZELIX.

Zeno Greek, "shining" or "bright day" from the same root as *Zeus*. Name of several Greek philosophers, one of whom founded the Stoic school, so named because he taught in the *Stoa*, or Porch, at Athens.

Zephaniah (zef a NYE′ a) Hebrew, "protection" or "Jehovah has ordered." Biblical: Prophet who lived at the time of Jeremiah; name of a book of the Old Testament.

Zion (ZYE′ on) Hebrew, probably "fortress." At first the name was applied only to an elevated section of Jerusalem, then to the whole city. On the rocky ridge David built his palace and Solomon his temple. *Zion* is often used as a poetic name for Israel. Fem., ZIONR.

Beautiful for situation, the joy of the whole earth, is mount Zion, on the sides of the north, the city of the great King.
PSALMS, 48:2

Zvi (TSVEE) Hebrew, deer." ZEV, ZEVIE. Fem., SIVIA, SIVIE, ZIVIA, ZIVIE.

NAMES FOR GIRLS

And who of Rosamund or Rosalind
Can part the rosy-petall'd syllables?
For women's names keep murmuring like the wind
The hidden things that none for ever tells.

ERNEST RHYS, *Words*

Names for Girls

A *Don't you remember sweet ALICE, Ben Bolt,—*
Sweet Alice whose hair was so brown,
Who wept with delight when you gave her a smile,
And trembled with fear at your frown?

THOMAS DUNN ENGLISH, *Ben Bolt*

Abbe, Abb(e)y, Abbie See ABI-
GAIL.

The advice column *Dear
Abby,* which is syndicated in
more than 500 newspapers
throughout the world, is written
by Abigail Van Buren, pen name
of Mrs. Morton Phillips (born
Pauline Esther Friedman).

Abigail Hebrew, "My father is
joy." ABBE, ABBIE, ABBY, GAIL,
GALE, GAEL. Biblical: Wife of
King David.

*. . . and let thine handmaid, I
pray thee, speak in thine audi-
ence, and hear the words of thine
handmaid.* (Abigail to David)
I SAMUEL 25:24

Abigail went out of favor for
a while because *abigail* became a
slang term for a lady's maid,
from the name of the "waiting
gentlewoman" in Beaumont and
Fletcher's *Scornful Lady.* It is
now again very much in favor,
especially in one of its many abbreviated forms.

History: Abigail Adams, wife
of one President (John) and

mother of another (John
Quincy), who paid her this tribute in his *Diary:*

*There is not a virtue that can
abide in the female heart but it
was the ornament of hers. She
had been fifty-four years the delight of my father's heart, the
sweetener of all his toils, the
comforter of all his sorrows, the
sharer and heightener of all his
joys.*

Ada (AY' da) Germanic "happy." *Ada* was probably a pet
form of EDITH or ADELAIDE, but it
is an independent name now.
Some authorities think it is the
same as ADAH.

*Is thy face like thy mother's, my
fair child?*
*Adal sole daughter of my house
and heart?*
GEORGE GORDON BYRON,
Childe Harold

Adah (AY' da) Hebrew, "ornament." Adah Menken (1835-
1868), glamorous actress who
attracted to her such leading

185

literary figures as Charles Reade, Walt Whitman, Mark Twain, Bret Harte, Dickens, Swinburne, Rossetti, and the elder Dumas.

Addie, Addy See ADELAIDE.

Adela (a DELL' a) See ADELE.

Adelaide Germanic, "nobleness" ADELINE, ALINE. Literature. Adelaide Anne Procter (1825-1864), author of *The Lost Chord* ("Seated one day at the organ").

Adele Germanic via French, "noble," the equivalent of ETHEL. ADELIA, DELLY.

Adeline Lengthened form of ADELE but used independently. ADALINE. The name of *Adeline* (1903) became famous as "the flower of my heart" in a song warbled by countless males in barber-shop quartets. The name is also honored by Byron in the following lines:

Sweet Adeline, amidst the gay world's hum,
Was the Queen-Bee, the glass of all that's fair.
      GEORGE GORDON BYRON,
              Don Juan

Adina (a DEE' na) Hebrew, "gentle." Israeli name. ADENA.

Adorée French, "beloved."

Adrienne (AY' dree en) French feminine; see ADRIAN. ADRIANNE.

Agatha (AG' a tha) Greek, "good." AGGIE. Third-century saint, patron of Catania, Sicily, whose veil, according to legend, saved that city from destruction during an eruption of Mt. Etna. Literature: Agatha Christie, famous contemporary British writer of detective fiction, creator of Hercule Poirot.

Agnes Greek, "pure, chaste." Very popular in the sixteenth and seventeenth centuries, *Agnes* or one of its variants (INEZ, INES, YNES, NESSIE, NEYSA) is still in great favor. St. Agnes, martyred when she was thirteen, is commemorated on January 21. The oft-quoted opening lines of *The Eve of St. Agnes* by Keats are:

St. Agnes' Eve—Ah! bitter chill it was!
The owl, for all his feathers, was a-cold.

    Dance: Agnes de Mille, choreographer and writer.

Aida (ah EE' dah) In Verdi's famous opera of the same name, Aida is a slave girl who is in reality the daughter of Amonasro, King of Ethiopia. In the famous aria she is called *celeste* (heavenly) *Aida*.

    The librettist Piave may have taken the name from ZAIDA, ZENAIDA, ZORAIDA, or even *Iraida*.

Aileen (eye LEEN') Irish form; see HELEN, EILEEN, ILENE, ILEANE, AILENE. Music: Eileen Farrell, opera star.

Alaine, Alayne (a LAYN'). May be regarded as femine forms of ALAN or as variants of HELEN. ALAN(N)A.

Alberta See ALBERT. ALBERTINA, ELBERTA, BERTIE.

Alda Germanic, "old." ALTA, AUDA. A short form of *Aldith*, in which the added syllable means "battle" or "war." See EDITH.

Alethea Greek, "truth." ALETHEIA, ALITHIA, ALETHIA, ALETHA, ALITHEA.

Alexandra See ALEXANDER. From each half of this name we get the additional names ALEXA, ALEXIA, ALIX, SANDRA, SONDRA. In England the name *Alexandra* became popular after the marriage in 1863 of Prince Edward, later King of England as Edward VII, to the Danish princess Alexandra Caroline Marie Charlotte Louise Julia.

The sea-king's daughter as happy
as fair,
Blissful bride of a blissful heir
. . . Alexandra!
    ALFRED, LORD TENNYSON,
    A Welcome to Alexandra

Alexis See ALEXANDRA. St. Alexis was the patron saint of hermits, but *Alexis* is now almost exclusively a girl's name, one that will probably become more popular than the longer and statelier ALEXANDRA, with which it is associated. Hollywood: Alexis Smith.

Alfreda (al FREE' da) See ALFRED.

Alice Greek, "truth"; or Germanic via French "noble." ALYCE, ALYS, ALICIA (a LISH' ee a *or* a LISH' a) ALEECE, ALISON, ALISSA, ALIX. A popular name in literature, boasting such famous representatives as Lewis Carroll's *Alice in Wonderland*, J. M. Barrie's *Alice-Sit-By-the-Fire*, Booth Tarkington's 1922 Pulitzer Prize novel *Alice Adams*, William de Morgan's *Alice for Short*, and Maurice Thompson's *Alice of Old Vincennes*, best seller of 1900. Alice appears in the phrase "Alice-blue gown," from the color preferred by Alice Roosevelt Longworth, daughter of President Theodore Roosevelt.

Of deepest blue of summer skies
Is wrought the heaven of her
eyes.
Of that fine gold the autumns
wear
Is wrought the glory of her hair.
Of rose leaves fashioned in the
south
Is shaped the marvel of her
mouth.
    HERBERT BASHFORD, *Alice*

Ballet: Alicia Alonso, Alicia Markova.

Alida (a LYE' da) Perhaps from the name of a city in Asia Minor. LIDA.

Aline (a LEEN' *or* AL'een). See ADELINE. ALEEN, ALENE, ALLENE.

Stage and Screen: Aline Mac-Mahon.

Alison, Alyson See ALICE. An old but increasingly popular variant of ALICE. In Chaucer's *Miller's Tale*, Alison was "more pleasant to look on than a flowering pear tree." Robert Louis Stevenson dedicated *A Child's Garden of Verses* to his nurse, Alison Cunningham.

Alissa, Elissa Variants; see ALICE. Also used for the Israeli name ALISA (ah LEEZ' a), "joy."

Alla Russian dim. of ALEXANDRA. Theater: Alla Nazimova, best known for her performances in plays by Ibsen.

Allegra Italian, "lively, joyful, merry." Ballet: Allegra Kent of the New York City Center Ballet Company is aptly named.

From my study I see in the lamplight,
  Descending the broad hall stair,
Grave Alice, and laughing Allegra,
  And Edith with golden hair.
    HENRY WADSWORTH LONGFELLOW, *The Children's Hour*

Allie Possible dim. of such names as ALICE, ALINE, etc.

Alma Latin, "loving, kind, bountiful." Alma is the name of a river near Sevastopol in the Crimea, where the British,

French, and Turkish troops defeated the Russians in 1854. Many children of that period owed their name to this event. In more recent times, however, the association has certainly been with the *alma* of *alma mater,* "nourishing mother." Music: Alma Gluck, former opera star.

Almira (al MY' ra) Variously given as a Spanish place name, Arabic, "the exalted," and a feminine form of ELMER. ELMIRA. The poetic name ALMERIA may be another variant, as in:

ALMERIA: *Music has charms to soothe a savage breast,*
To soften rocks, or bend a knotted oak.
    WILLIAM CONGREVE,
    The Mourning Bride

Alouise (a loo EEZ')See ALOYSIUS.

Alta Latin, "high"; Germanic, "old."

Althea (AL' thee a *or* al THEE' a) Greek, "wholesome, healing." A name with a pleasing sound, a meaning of good omen, and a literary past, two of our most famous lines coming from Richard Lovelace's *To Althea from Prison:*

Stone walls do not a prison make — Nor iron bars a cage.

Alvina See ALVIN.

Alvira Variant of ELVIRA.

Alyce, Alys Variant spellings; see ALICE.

Amanda Latin, "beloved." A name popular in Restoration plays, perhaps made up by Vanbrugh to describe the fair heroine of *The Relapse* (1697).

All other blessings I resign,
Make but the dear Amanda
mine.
   JAMES THOMPSON, *To Fortune*

Amelia A derivative of EMILY. See EMIL. Literature: Model of a devoted wife, heroine of Joseph Fielding's *Amelia;* Amelia Sedley, gentle and affectionate, one of the heroines of Thackeray's *Vanity Fair.* Aeronautics: Amelia Earhart, American aviatrix, first woman to fly across the Atlantic; lost on Pacific flight (1937). Politics: Amelia Bloomer (1818-1894), American pioneer in the fight for social reform and woman's suffrage from whose advocacy of "full trousers" for women comes the word *bloomers.*

Whene'er mine eyes do my
*   Amelia greet,*
*   It is with such emotion*
As when, in childhood turning
*   a dim street,*
*   I first beheld the ocean.*
   COVENTRY PATMORE, *Amelia*

Aminta Greek, "protect." MINDY, AMYNTA.

Alas! 'tis too late at thy fate to
repine;

Poor shepherd, Amynta can
*   never be thine:*
Thy tears are all fruitless, thy
*   wishes are vain,*
The moments neglected return
*   not again.*
   GILBERT ELLIOT, *Amynta*

Amity Latin via French, "friendship." A quality name; see under CHARITY.

Amy Latin via French, "the beloved." AMI, AMIE, AIMEE (AY MAY'). The most famous American to bear this lovely name was the poet Amy Lawrence Lowell (1874-1925), Pulitzer Prize for poetry, 1926.

Her fingers shame the ivory
*   keys,*
They dance so light along,
The bloom upon her parted lips
Is sweeter than the song.
   JOHN GREENLEAF WHITTIER,
      Amy Wentworth

Anastasia Greek, "resurrection." Screen: Nastassia Kinski (*Tess*).

Andrea (AN' dree a) See ANDREW.

Angela (AN' jell a) Greek, "messenger." ANGIE. See ANGELINA. TV: Angie Dickinson. Screen and Stage: Angela Lansbury.

Angelica (an JELL' i ka) Latin, "angelic."

The fairest of her sex, Angelica.
   JOHN MILTON,
      Paradise Regained

Angelina (an jell EE′ na). Dim. of ANGELA. ANGELENE, ANGELINE. Heroine of Gilbert and Sullivan's *Trial by Jury*, of whom the susceptible judge sings:

*Oh, never, never, never, since I joined the human race,
Saw I so exquisitely fair a face.*

Anita Spanish dim. form; see ANN. Hollywood: Anita Louise; Anita Ekberg, spectacular actress.

Anitra From literature; now used as a variant of ANITA. In Ibsen's play *Peer Gynt* Anitra is the Arabic girl with whom Peer Gynt falls in love. Music: *Anitra's Dance* by Edvard Grieg.

Ann, Anne Variant of ANNA. ANA, AN, ANNI, ANI, ANNIE, ANNIS, ANNETTE, ANITA, ANITRA, NAN, NANCY, NANETTE, NANICE, NINA, NINON, NINETTE. St. Anne (in apocryphal gospel) was the mother of the Virgin Mary. *Anne* has been a popular name in Russia and England; sometimes it was used as a masc. name: there was a Lord Anne Hamilton named after Queen Anne.

Education: Anne Sullivan, famed teacher of Helen Keller. Literature: *Anne of Green Gables* (1909) by Lucy Maud Montgomery, which Mark Twain called "the sweetest creation of child life yet published"; the famous *Diary of Anne Frank*, by a victim of the Nazis who has become a symbol of the invincibility of the human spirit; Anne Morrow Lindbergh, author of such sensitive books as *Gift from the Sea* and *Dearly Beloved* (1962).

Two other Ann(e)'s appear in literature: Ann Rutledge, early love of Abraham Lincoln, subject of novels, poems, and plays; Anne Hathaway, wife of William Shakespeare:

*How often in the summer-tide,
His summer business set aside,
Has stripling Will the thoughtful-eyed
Stepped blithesomely with lover's pride
Across the fields to Anne.*
    RICHARD FRANCIS BURTON,
    Across the Fields to Anne

Anna Greek-Latin form of Hebrew Hannah, "grace." ANA, ANIA, ANYA. See ANN. HANNAH. Literature: *Anna Karénina* by Leo Tolstoy, one of the world's greatest novels; *Anna Christie*, play for which Eugene O'Neill was awarded the Pulitzer Prize in 1922; *Anna and the King of Siam* by Margaret Dorothea Landon, on which the musical and movie *The King and I* were based. Art: Grandma Moses (1860-1961), born Anna Mary Robertson, the grand "Old Master" of American primitive painting. Theater: An almost legendary beauty of another day, once wife of Florenz Ziegfeld, the incomparable Anna Held. Ballet:

The fabulous Anna Pavlova (1885-1931). Hollywood: Anna Magnani, winner of an Oscar in 1955 (*The Rose Tattoo*).

Awa, thou flaunting God of Day!
   Awa, thou pale Diana!
Ilk star, gae hide thy twinkling
      ray,
   When I'm to meet my Anna!
            ROBERT BURNS, *Anna*

Annabel(la) See MABEL. ANNA-BELLE.

For the moon never beams, with-
      out bringing me dreams
   Of the beautiful Annabel Lee,
And the stars never rise, but I
      feel the bright eyes
   Of the beautiful Annabel Lee,
      EDGAR ALAN POE, *Annabel Lee*

Annette French dim. form; see ANN.

Annie Pet form; see ANN. Because Annie Oakley could shoot holes into tossed-up playing cards, free tickets, which generally have holes punched in them, are called *Annie Oakleys*. The musical *Annie Get Your Gun* by Irving Berlin was based on her story, (incidentally, her true name was Phoebe Anne Oakley Mozee.) Another Annie, famous in song, was the eldest daughter of Sir Robert Laurie, of Maxwelton.

And for bonnie Annie Laurie,
   I'd lay me doun and dee.
            WILLIAM DOUGLAS,
               Annie Laurie

Anthea (AN' thee a *or* an THEE' a) Greek, "flowery." The Greek equivalent of Latin FLORA, French FLEUR, and the Germanic BLUMA. An *anthology* is literally a collection of flowers.

Fairest Anthea! thou whose
      grace
   Leads me enchantedly along
Till the sweet windings that we
      trace
   Seem like the image of a song!
         GEORGE DARLEY, *Nepenthe*

Antonia (an TOE' nia *or* an to NEE' a) See ANTHONY. ANTOIN-ETTE, ANTONETTA, ANTONIE, NETTY, TONI, TONY. Literature: *My Antonia* (1918), a novel by Willa Cather, dealing with Bohemian immigrants in the frontier farmlands of Nebraska. Theater: Antoinette Perry (1888-1946), actress, director, producer, leader in American Theater Wing. The Tony Awards, given each year to best actors and actresses in Broadway plays, were named in her honor.

April A month name from a Latin word meaning "to open up," as nature does during that delightful month. AVRIL.

Thou art thy mother's glass, and
   she in thee
Calls back the lovely April of
   her prime.
            WILLIAM SHAKESPEARE,
               Sonnets, 3

*Now that the April of your youth
    adorns
    The garden of your face.*
    EDWARD HERBERT (1583-1648),
        Ditty: Now That April

Arabella Possibly from ANNA-BEL but it may be from Latin *orabilis,* "capable of being moved by entreaty." Music: *Arabella,* opera by Richard Strauss.

Ardelia See ARDIS. ARDELLE.

Arden Place name, Anglo-Saxon, "eagle-valley" or "dwelling house." Also used as masc. name. ARDENIA. There was a tract of land by that name in Warwickshire, not far from Shakespeare's home. The name occurs in *The Ballad of Dowsabel* by Michael Drayton, contemporary of Shakespeare, which opens with "Far in the country of Arden." However, Arden became famous after Shakespeare introduced it in *As You Like It* as a romantic place of refuge. Here the older Duke declared that "sweet are the uses of adversity," for in Arden:

*This our life exempt from public
    haunt
Finds tongue in trees, books in
    the running brooks,
Sermons in stone and good in
    everything.*

Ardis This name, apparently of modern origin, is growing in popularity. The derivation is not definitely established. The first element seems to be related either to the French surname *Ardent,* "burning," or to *Ardin,* "bold, hardy." The ending looks like the feminine ending found in such names as CHLORIS, DORIS, etc. ARDYS, ARDYCE, ARDELLA, ARDELLE.

Ardith This seems to be a variant of ARDIS. However, it also resembles a once popular Old English name *Aldith,* "old-battle.." (See ALDA.) The ending is therefore like that of EDITH or a fem. ending as in JUDITH. ARDYTH.

Ariadne (a ree AD' nee) Greek mythology, "the holy one." ARIANE, ARIANNA. Ariadne, daughter of King Minos of Crete, falling in love with Theseus, helped him thread his way out of the Labyrinth after he had slain the Minotaur. Opera: *Ariadne auf Naxos* by Richard Strauss.

Ariel See ARIEL (m). ARIELLE, AERIELLE.

*Of these am I, who thy protec-
    tion claim,
A watchful sprite, and Ariel is
    my name.*

        ALEXANDER POPE,
        The Rape of the Lock

Arlene ARLINE, ARLEEN, ARLEN, ARLIENE, ARLYNE, ARLEYNE. A very popular name these days, with an interesting assortment of spellings to choose from. The only thing authorities agree upon about this name is that they don't know what the origin is and that it is probably Gaelic—because of the *een* ending (as in AILEEN, KATHLEEN, MAUREEN). Our guess is that it's just another variant of ALINE or AILEEN. Music: Arline, heroine of Balfe's opera *The Bohemian Girl*. Stage, TV, and Radio: Arlene Francis, hostess of "At Sardi's."

Armina (arm EEN′ a) Fem. form; see HERMAN.

Artemis Greek goddess of the hunt; her Roman equivalent is Diana. Also called Cynthia.

Or shall we run with Artemis
Or yield the breast to Aphrodite?
Both are mighty;
Both give bliss.
> GEORGE MEREDITH,
> *The Vital Choice*

Astrid Norse, "divine strength."

Atalanta Greek, "unswaying." Mythology: A maiden, fleet of foot and fond of hunting, who refused to marry unless the suitor overcame her in a race.

Arcadian Atalanta, snowy-
souled,
Fair as the snow and footed as
the wind.
> ALGERNON C. SWINBURNE,
> *Atalanta in Calydon*

Audrey (AW′ dree) From old English name ETHELDREDA,

"noble strength." AUDRA, AUDRE, AUDRY. A popular English saint, Etheldreda,—later called Audrey —was commemorated on October 17, in a huge fair, which was particularly noted for its fine silk necklaces or neckties worn by the girls of the period. At first, these were called St. Audrey's laces, but soon the clipped speech of the people turned *St. Audrey* into *tawdry*. Actually, the word *tawdry* once meant something attractive and desirable.

Hollywood: Audrey Hepburn winner of an Oscar in 1953 (*Roman Holiday*).

Augusta Fem. of AUGUST. GUS, GUSSIE. Literature and theater: Lady Augusta Gregory, Irish playwright, co-founder of the Irish National Theater Society, director of the Abbey Theatre, Dublin (1904).

A girl with a presence superb as
her name,
And charmingly fitted for love—
in a palace.
> JOHN G. SAXE, *Augusta*

Aurelia Latin, "golden." AURA.

Aura Lee! Aura Lee!
Maid of golden hair!
Sunshine comes along with thee
And swallows in the air.
> OLD SONG

Aurora Latin, "dawn."

Like to rosy-born Aurora,
Glowing freshly into view.
> GEORGE MEREDITH, *Daphne*

Ava (AY′ va) German pronunciation of EVA. Also old Germanic-Norman form of HEDWIG. See also EVELYN. AVIS (AY′ vis). Hollywood: Ava Gardner.

Avis A once popular name, probably of Germanic origin, which the Normans brought with them to England and which is again becoming popular. It is derived from Teutonic *Avice*, probably "fight."

Aviva (a VEE′ va) Hebrew, "spring."

B

Babette See BARBARA. BABE, BABS.

Barbara Greek, "strange, foreign." BABS, BABETTE, BOBBIE, BONNIE. A third-century virgin martyr and saint. Story-book Barbaras were called Babs, but modern Barbaras prefer the pet names Bobbie or Bonnie. Theater: Barbara Bel Geddes; Shaw's *Major Barbara.* Hollywood: Barbra Streisand (*Yentl*).

Bathsheba Hebrew, "daughter of the oath." BATSHEVA, SHEBA. Biblical: Mother of Solomon, the woman referred to in these lines:

. . . and the woman was very beautiful to look upon.
And David sent and enquired after the woman.

II SAMUEL 11 : 2, 3

Open, I say, and, as you open,
sing:
Welcome fair Bethsabe, King
David's darling.

GEORGE PEELE, *The Love of King David and Fair Bethsabe*

Beatrice Latin, "bringer of joy." BEATRIX, BEA, BEBE, TRIXIE. Important literary associations have maintained the popularity of this name. The most famous of all Beatrices is Dante's Beatrice Portinari, who acts as his guide through Paradise in *The Divine Comedy.* Another Beatrice is the witty, high-spirited heroine of Shakespeare's *Much Ado About Nothing.* Beatrix Castlewood is the coquettish heroine of Thackeray's *Henry Esmond.* Stage: Beatrice Lillie *comédienne extraordinaire.*

Because mine eyes can never
have their fill
Of looking at my lady's lovely
face,
I will so fix my gaze
That I may become blessed,
beholding her.

DANTE,
He Will Gaze Upon Beatrice
(Dante Gabriel Rossetti's
translation)

Becky See REBECCA.

Belinda From literature. Pope used this name for the heroine of *The Rape of the Lock,* a poem based on an actual family feud that resulted when Lord Petre cut a lock of hair from the head

195

of Miss Arabella ("Belinda")
Fermor.

This lock the Muse shall conse-
crate to fame,
And 'midst the stars inscribe
Belinda's name.
ALEXANDER POPE

Bella See ISABELLA. BELLE.
Some think that Bella comes
from Latin *bella,* "beautiful."
There's no harm in thinking so.

Benay (ben AY′) Fem. variant;
see BEN.

Benedicta See BENEDICT.

Benetta See BENEDICT.

Benita (be NEE′ ta) Spanish
variant; see BENEDICT.

Berenice, Bernice (burn EES′
or BURN′ ees.) Greek, "bringer
of victory." BERNELLE, BARRIE,
VERNICE, BUNNY. Literature:
Both Corneille and Racine in a
literary prize contest (1670)
wrote a play about the Judaean
princess Berenice, the promised
wife of the Roman prince Titus.
Racine won; to him *Berenice*
was literally "a bringer of victory."

Berna Feminine derivative of
BERNARD or short form of BER-
NADETTE.

Bernadette (burn a DET′)
French fem. dim. form; see BER-
NARD. BERNADETTE became pop-

ular because of the maid of
Lourdes, Bernadette Soubirous,
(1844-1879). She was fourteen
years old when she reported seeing the vision of the Virgin
Mary, who revealed to her the
healing powers of the waters at
Lourdes. The popularity of the
name was revived by Franz
Werfel's novel *Song of Berna-*
dette (1942), Hollywood's pic-
turization of it, and a French
film (1962) on her life.

Bernardine See BERNARD. BER-
NARDA.

Bernette See BERNARD.

Bertha Germanic, "bright."
BERTA, BERTIE, BERTINA, BIRDIE.
The name *Bertha* is actually the
feminine of the element meaning
"bright" in such compound masculine names as *Bert*ram, Her-
bert, and Al*bert*. BIRDIE is used
as pet form.

Beryl Greek name of a pre-
cious stone.

Bess Pet form; see ELIZABETH.
BESSIE, BETSIE, BETSY, BETTA,
BETTE (BET′ ee), BETTY, BETTI-
NA, BETH. All of the above and,
by this time, several additional
spellings are variations on the
last syllable of ELIZABETH.

Dear Bess with her elegant figure
and face,
Looks quite a Diana, the queen
of the place.
THOMAS HAYNES BAYLY,
The Archery Meeting

Bessie See ELIZABETH.

*And every brave gallant that
once did her see,
Was straitway enamour'd of
pretty Bessie.*
OLD BALLAD

Beth See ELIZABETH. May also
be from the Hebrew, "house."

Bethany (BETH' a nee) Aramaic, "house of poverty." Place
name, village near Jerusalem.

Bethel Hebrew, "house of
God."

Betsy See ELIZABETH. Betsy
Ross (1752-1836) is generally
credited with having made the
first American flag, which was
adopted as the official emblem
of the Continental Congress on
June 4, 1777.

*Did you ever hear tell of
sweet Betsy from Pike?*
OLD BALLAD

Bette (BET' ee), **Betty** See
ELIZABETH. Hollywood: Bette
Davis, winner of Oscar in 1935
(*Dangerous*) and 1938 (*Jezebel*);
Bette Midler (*The Rose*).

*Dear Betty, come, give my sweet
kisses,
For sweeter no girl ever gave.*
SIR CHARLES HANSBURY
WILLIAMS, *Ballad
in Imitation of Martial*

Bettina (beh TEEN' a) See BESS.

Beulah Hebrew, "married."
The land of Beulah is mentioned
in the Bible as a name for Israel.

*Thy land [shall be called]
Beulah: for the Lord delighteth
in thee and thy land shall be
married.*
ISAIAH 62 : 4

In *The Pilgrim's Progress*
Beulah is the land of heavenly
joy where the pilgrims rest until
they are summoned to enter the
Celestial City.

Beverl(e)y Anglo-Saxon, "bea-
ver meadow." A popular name,
from a family name, which
comes from Beverley, a town in
Yorkshire, England. In England
also used as a masculine name.
Screen: Beverly Bayne, an early
silent-movie star. BEVERLEE.

Bianca (BYAHNG' kah *or* BYAN'
ka) Italian, "white." BIANCHA,
BLANCA. The Italian counterpart
of BLANCHE. Bianca is Kate's
sister in *The Taming of the
Shrew* and a Cole Porter song-
title in *Kiss Me, Kate.*

*Biancha, let
Me pay the debt
I owe thee for a kiss
Thou lent'st to me,
And I to thee
Will render ten for this.*
ROBERT HERRICK, *Kissing Usury*

Billie See BILL. Also used as a
pet name for BELLA. Theater:
Billie Burke, former popular
stage and screen star.

Blair See BLAIR (m).

Blanche French, "white." BLANCH. Hollywood: Blanche Sweet of the silent era.

If lusty love should go in search of beauty,
Where should he find it fairer than in Blanch?
If zealous love should go in search of virtue
Where should he find it purer than in Blanch?
    WILLIAM SHAKESPEARE,
        King John

Blossom A flower name; from Anglo-Saxon, "flower."

Bluma Germanic, "flower."

Blythe Anglo-Saxon, "joyous, blithe."

Bobette Fem. of BOB, sometimes used as a nickname for BARBARA, but also used as an independent name.

Bonita (bo NEE' ta) Spanish, "pretty."

Bonnie Latin, "good." The Scottish word *bonnie* is generally used in the sense of "beautiful," the goodness being taken for granted.

As fair thou art, my bonnie lass,
So deep in luve am I;
And I will luve thee still, my dear,
Till a' the seas gang dry.
ROBERT BURNS, *A Red, Red Rose*

Brenda Germanic, "a sword-blade" or "a flame." About this name Helena Swan, back in 1905, wrote that it "has, in the modern craving for unhackneyed names, steadily gained ground with the English public." In an age when unhackneyed names are even more earnestly craved, it is still holding its own. See BRENDAN. Music: Brenda Lewis of the Metropolitan Opera.

Bretta See BRET(T).

Bridget, Brigid Irish, "strength." BRIGIDA (Italian), BRIGITTE (German), BRIDE (Scottish), BIDDY (Irish), BERET, BIRGIT(TA) (Scandinavian). A patron saint of Ireland, who shares with St. Patrick the place of honor in the hearts of the Irish people. Literature: Beret, heroine of *Giants in the Earth*, Rölvaag's fine novel of Norwegian pioneers in America. Bridget is the name Charles Lamb gives his sister Mary in his famous *Essays of Elia*. Opera: Birgit Nilsson, great soprano of the Metropolitan Opera. Screen: Brigitte Bardot.

Sweet Bridget blush'd, and therewithal
Fresh blossoms from her cheeks did fall.
    ROBERT HERRICK,
    To Bridget Herrick

Brier (BRY' er) A plant name like FERN and HEATHER; from French, "heather."

Brina, Bryna Slavic, "protector," from Polish, *Bronislava.*

Bruna, Brunetta See BRUNO.

Brunhild(a) Germanic, possibly "breast-battle." One of the Valkyries. BRUNHILDE, BRYNHILD(A). Opera: Brunhild plays a leading role in three of the four operas of Wagner's *Nibelungen Ring.*

C

My songs they be of CYNTHIA's *praise,*
I wear her ring on holy-days,
In every tree I write her name,
And every day I read the same.

FULKE GRENVILLE, LORD BROOKE,
Cynthia

Callista Greek, "most beautiful." CALYSTA, CALESTA, CALLIE, KALLISTA.

Camilla (ka MILL' a) Latin, "a noble maiden of unblemished character." CAMILLA, MILLY. See CAMILLUS.

. . . but a light step of freest grace,
Light as Camilla's o'er the unbent corn.
WILLIAM CULLEN BRYANT,
Spring in Town

Camille (ka MEEL') French form; see CAMILLA. Literature: In the American adaptation of the younger Dumas' famous *Lady of the Camellias,* the heroine's name is Camille. But in the original novel and play, her name is Marguerite. And in *La Traviata,* Verdi's opera based on the same story, her name is Violetta!

Candace (KAN' da see *or* kan DAY' see *or popularly* KAN' diss) Greek and Latin, title and name of the Queens of ancient Ethiopia, one of whom is mentioned in ACTS 8:27. CANDIS, CANDICE,

CANDY. Literature: Candace Stevenson, winner of 1949 Poetry Society of America Award.

Candida (KAN' did a) Latin, "dazzling white." CANDY. Literature: George Bernard Shaw called one of his loveliest and most sympathetic heroines Candida.

Cara Celtic, "friend," but as used today, more probably Latin via Italian, "dear." TV: Cara Williams. CARINA.

Caren See KAREN.

Carla, Carley See CHARLES. CARLYS, KARLA.

Carlotta Italian form; see CHARLOTTE.

Carmel Hebrew, "God's vineyard." CARMELA (kar MELL' a). Place name, Mt. Carmel in Israel, near Haifa, looking down almost 2000 feet upon the beautiful Mediterranean. On this mountain the order of mendicant friars known as Carmelites was founded in the twelfth century.

*Carmela dear, even as the
golden ball
That Venus got, such
are thy goodly eyes.*
ROBERT GREENE,
Doron and Carmela

Carmen Latin, "song"; from
Spanish, *Santa Maria del Car-
men,* "Mary of Mt. Carmel
(Carmelite Order)." See also
DOLORES. Literature: Prosper
Merimée's novelette on which
the libretto for Bizet's opera was
based.

Carol, Carole See CAROLINE.
CARYL, CAROLA, CAROLEE, CAR-
ROLL, KAREL. Three Hollywood
stars, three different spellings:
Carole Lombard, Carol Law-
rence, Carroll Baker.

Caroline, Carolyn See CHARLES.

*A fairer form than cherub loves
And let the name be—Caroline.*
THOMAS CAMPBELL, *Caroline: 1*

Carrie, Car(r)y See CAROLINE.
Politics: Carrie Chapman Catt,
American woman-suffrage lead-
er, educator, and lecturer.

Caryl See CAROL, CARROL.

Cassandra Greek, "entangling
men." CASS, CASSIE, SANDRA.
Mythology and Drama: Name of
the Trojan King Priam's daughter, with whom Apollo fell in
love. Apollo bestowed the gift
of prophecy upon Cassandra, but
when she failed to carry out her

promise to love him, he decreed
that nobody should believe her,
although she invariably spoke
the truth.

*A prophet that, Cassandra-like,
Tells truth without belief.*
ANON., *Elizabethan Poem*

Today the name is applied to
anyone who utters warning of
trouble to come whether the
prophecy is believed or not.

*Cassandra is my flame,
Or call her name Marie;
The letters of her name
Are food and drink to me.*
PIERRE RONSARD, *To Cassandra*

(Written to Cassandre Salvi-
ati, a Florentine banker's daughter)

The novelist Jane Austen had
a sister Cassandra, to whom she
wrote charming and cheerful
letters. Jane wrote about her:

*I always loved Cassandra for
her dark eyes and sweet temper.*

Catherine See KATHERINE.
CATHARINE, CATHY, CAREN. Liter-
ature: Catherine Barkley, hero-
ine of Hemingway's novel *A
Farewell to Arms;* Catherine
Earnshaw, the beautiful but
headstrong heroine of Emily
Brontë's great novel *Wuthering
Heights;* Catherine Drinker Bo-
wen, biographer (*Yankee from
Olympus*).

Cathleen See KATHLEEN. Literature: *Cathleen ni Houlihan*
(poetic name for Ireland), a

prose play by William Butler Yeats.

Cecile (se SEEL' *or* SESS' il). See CECILIA. CEIL.

Cecilia (se SEE' lya *or* se SILL' ya). Fem. of CECIL. CECELIA. St. Cecilia is regarded by poets as the patroness of music, Pope and Dryden making her the subject of long poems.

But bright Cecilia rais'd t h e
wonder higher:
When to her organ vocal breath
was given,
 An angel heard, and straight
 appear'd
 Mistaking Earth for Heaven.
   JOHN DRYDEN,
   Song for St. Cecilia's Day

Cecily (SESS' i ly) Variant of CECILIA. CICELY (SISS' i ly), CICILY.

"We two," she said, "will seek
 the groves
Where the lady Mary is,
With her five handmaidens,
 whose names
Are five sweet symphonies,
Cecily, Gertrude, Magdalen,
 Margaret and Rosalys."
  DANTE GABRIEL ROSSETTI,
   The Blessed Damozel

Celeste (se LEST') Latin, "heavenly." Theater and Hollywood: Celeste Holm, winner of an Oscar (supporting role) in 1947 (*Gentlemen's Agreement*).

Celia Latin, "heavenly," from *Caelius,* the name of a *gens.* CELINE, CELINDA.

 My goddess Celia
 Heav'nly fair,
 As lilies sweet,
 So soft as air.
 ANON., 18th Century Song.

It was to Celia that Ben Jonson penned his lovely lines:

Drink to me only with thine eyes,
 And I will pledge with mine;
Or leave a kiss within the cup
 And I'll not look for wine.

Charity From Latin via French, in the sense of "brotherly love," not "almsgiving." CHERRY. A quality or virtue name. See under "Puritan Names" in chapter "Where Our Names Come From."

And now abideth faith, hope,
charity, these three; but t h e
greatest of these is charity (I CORINTHIANS 13:13. In the Revised Version "love" is substituted for "charity."

Literature: The nickname CHERRY is found in *The Beaux' Stratagem* by George Farquhar and in *Nicholas Nickleby*.

Charleen, Charlene See CHARLES.

Charlotte See CHARLES. CARLOTTA. Literature: Charlotte Brontë, author of *Jane Eyre*, one of the world's great novels.

Ilka lovely British lass,
Frae ladies Charlotte, Anne, and
Jean,
Down to ilka bonny singing Bess
Wha dances barefoot on the
green.

ALLAN RAMSAY, *Song*

Charmaine (SHAHR MAIN') Possibly Latin via French, "song." See CARMEN. Literature: The girl in *What Price Glory?* (1924) by Maxwell Anderson and Laurence Stallings.

Charmian (CHAR' me an *or* KAR' me an) Greek, "a little joy." Literature: Cleopatra's faithful attendant in Shakespeare's *Antony and Cleopatra.*

Cherie (SHERR' ee) French, "cherished one, sweetheart." CHERE.

Cheryl (CHERR' il) May be variant of CARYL *or* dim. of CHERIE. Theater: Cheryl Crawford, producer. SHERRELL.

Chloe, Cloe (KLO' ee) Greek, "young grass." A favorite name used by eighteenth-century poets.

What I speak, my fair Cloe, and
what I write shows
The difference there is betwixt
Nature and Art;
I court others in verse, but I love
thee in prose;
And they have my whimsies, but
thou hast my heart.

MATTHEW PRIOR,
A Better Answer

Chloris, Cloris (KLAW' riss) Greek, "pale." Greek Mythology: According to one version of the Niobe story, the name of the youngest and the only one of Niobe's seven daughters who escaped the jealous and vengeful arrows of Apollo and Diana. Because of her terrifying experience, Chloris became completely white; hence, her name. Also the name of a Greek goddess whose Roman counterpart was Flora. Along with CELIA and PHYLLIS, *Chloris* was a favorite name among seventeenth-century poets.

I saw fair Cloris walk alone,
Whilst feather'd rain came
swiftly down.

WILLIAM STRODE,
On a Gentlewoman
Walking in the Snow

Christabel CHRIST+BELLE. CHRISTABELLE.

The lovely lady, Christabel,
Whom her father loves so well.
SAMUEL TAYLOR COLERIDGE,
Christabel

Christina (krist TEE' na) Fem. dim. of Christ. CHRISTINE, KRISTINE, TINA. Literature: Most famous woman bearing this name, the English poet Christina Rossetti, sister of Dante Gabriel Rossetti; most famous novel, *Kristin Lavransdatter* (1922) by Sigrid Undset.

*The beauty of the northern
dawns,
Their pure, pale light is thine;
Yet all the dreams of tropic
nights
Within thy blue eyes shine.*
JOHN HAY, *Christine*

C(h)rystal A jewel name of
Greek origin.

Cicely See CECILIA. CICILY.

Cindy See CYNTHIA and LUCIN-
DA. CINDA.

*You oughta see my Cindy.
She lives a way down South.
She's so sweet the honey bees
All swarm around her mouth.*
FOLK SONG

Cissie, Cissy Pet form of CECI-
LIA. Theater: Cissie Loftus, famous Scottish actress of stage
and early movies.

Clara, Clare Latin, "clear,
bright." CLAIRE, CLARICE, CLARIS-
SA, CLARINDA. Hollywood: Clara
Bow, the "IT" girl. History:
Clara H. Barton, full name Clar-
issa Harlowe Barton, founder of
American Red Cross. Screen:
Claire Bloom.

*In Clara's eyes the light'nings
view;
Her lips with all the rose's hue
Have all its sweets combin'd.*
WILLIAM SHENSTONE, *Ode*

Claribel CLARA+BELLE.

Clarice French derivative; see
CLARA.

Clarinda See CLARA.

Clarissa (kla RISS' a) Latinized
form; see CLARICE. Literature:
Heroine of Samuel Richardson's
important novel *The History of
Clarissa Harlowe* (1749), the
story told entirely in the letters
written by Clarissa to her friend.

Claudia Fem. of CLAUDE. CLAU-
DETTE, CLAUDINE. Stage and Hollywood: Claudette Colbert, winner of Oscar in 1934 (*It
Happened One Night*).

Clelia See CLOELIA.

*Coy Clelia, veil those charming
eyes,
From whose surprise there's
none can part;
For he that gazes, surely dies
Or leaves behind a conquered
heart.*
MATTHEW COPPINGER, *To Clelia*

Clemence See CLEMENT. CLEM-
ENTINA, CLEMENTINE. Literature:
Clemence Dane, pseudonym of
Winifred Ashton, novelist and
playwright (*A Bill of Divorce-
ment, Will Shakespeare*, etc.).
Foods: Clementine Paddleford,
writer on dining out and on
menus 'round the world.

*In a cavern, in a canyon,
Excavating for a mine,
Dwelt a miner, forty-niner,
And his daughter, Clementine.*
PERCY MONTROSS,
My Darling Clementine

Cleo Short form; see CLEONA and CLEOPATRA.

Cleona See CLEON (m).

Cleopatra (clee o PAY' tra *or* clee o PAH' tra *or* CLEE' o pay tra) Greek via Latin, "of a famed father." Cleopatra was the renowned Egyptian Queen to whom this tribute is paid in Shakespeare's *Antony and Cleopatra:* "Age cannot wither her, nor custom stale / Her infinite variety."

> Come thou unto me
> As Cleopatra came to Antony,
> When her high carriage did at
> once present
> To the triumvir love and
> wonderment.
> ROBERT HERRICK,
> *The Welcome to Sack*

Clo(e)lia (KLEE' *li* a) Latin *Cloelius,* name of a *gens.* Cloelia was a legendary heroine who was given as a hostage to the Etruscans, but escaped by swimming the Tiber. The Romans returned her to Lars Porsena, the Etruscan chief, who then set her free in admiration of her courage.

Clotilda Germanic "famous battle maid." CLOT(H)ILD(E) (klo TEELD').

Clover Flower name from Anglo-Saxon.

Colette (ko LET') Clipped form of *Nicolette.* See COLIN and NICHOLAS. Literature: Colette is the pen name of the popular French novelist Sidonie Gabrielle Claudine Colette.

Coleen Irish, "a girl." Theater: Colleen Dewhurst.

> *Where my heart is I am going*
> *To my little Irish rose.*
> *And the moment that I meet her,*
> *With a hug and kiss I'll greet her,*
> *For there's not a colleen sweeter*
> *Where the River Shannon*
> *flows.*
> JAMES I. RUSSELL,
> *Where the River Shannon Flows*

Constance Latin, "constancy." CONSTANTIA, CONNIE. Literature: Constance Garnett, whose translations introduced English readers to the great Russian novelists. Singer: Connie Francis.

> *I have no life, Constantia, now,*
> *but thee,*
> *Whilst, like the world-*
> *surrounding air, thy song*
> *Flows on, and fills all things*
> *with melody.*
> PERCY BYSSHE SHELLEY,
> *To Constantia, Singing*

Consuelo (kon soo AY' lo *or* kon SWAY' lo) Spanish, "consolation." See also DOLORES. Literature: Consuelo, the beautiful Venetian singer in George Sand's famous novel of the same name.

Cora Greek, "maiden." Cora Munroe is the heroine of James

Fenimore Cooper's *Last of the Mohicans.*

Coral A jewel name; from Greek via Latin.

Coralie French form of CORAL.

Cordelia Celtic, meaning unknown. King Lear's faithful daughter. CORDULA, DELIA, DELLA.

Cordelia, Cordelia! . . .
*   Her voice was ever soft,*
Gentle and low, an excellent
*   thing in woman.*
        WILLIAM SHAKESPEARE,
        King Lear

Corinna (kaw RINN' a), **Corinne** (kaw RINN' or kaw REEN') Greek, "a maiden." See CORA. Corinna, a Greek lyric poet of the fifth century B.C. and one of the most beautiful women of her age, competed, according to legend, with the great Pindar and won the poetry prize on five different occasions at public games. Hollywood: Corinne Calvet.

When to her lute Corinna sings,
Her voice revives the leaden
*   strings.*
        THOMAS CAMPION,
When to Her Lute Corinna Sings

Cornelia See CORNELIUS. NEILA, NELIA, CONNIE. History: Cornelia, a Roman matron, considered the paragon of Roman womanly virtues, mother of two famous sons, Tiberius and Caius

Gracchus. It is told of her that when several other women were boasting of their finery, she turned to her two boys and said simply, *"These* are my jewels."

Cosima (CO SEEM' a) See COSMO.

Crystal See CHRYSTAL.

Cynara Greek, "artichoke." CINARA. The island of Cinara (now called Zinara) in the Aegean was famous for its artichokes. Literature: A lady who appears in poems by the Roman poet Horace, from one of which Dowson got his inspiration for:

I have forgot much, Cynara! gone with the wind,
Flung roses, roses riotously with the throng,
Dancing, to put thy pale, lost lilies out of mind;
But I was desolate and sick of an old passion,
*   Yea, all the time, because the dance was long:*
I have been faithful to thee, Cynara! in my fashion.
        ERNEST DOWSON,
    Non Sum Qualis Eram Bonae
        sub Regno Cynarae

Cynthia Greek Mythology. CINDY. One of the titles of Artemis, Greek goddess of the moon, corresponding to the Roman Diana. Literature: A name given to Queen Elizabeth I by Ben Johnson, Walter Raleigh, and Edmund Spenser.

There hath none pleased mine eye but Cynthia, none delighted mine ears but Cynthia, none possessed my heart but Cynthia. I have forsaken all other fortunes to follow Cynthia, and here I stand ready to die, if it please Cynthia.

　　　JOHN LYLY, *Endymion*

Cyra Fem. of CYRUS. Greek, "lord, rule"; used in saints' names for *Dominica,* "of the Lord." CIRA.

Cyrene (sye REE' nee *or* pronounced like *serene*) Greek Mythology: A nymph carried by Apollo to Libya. CYRENA.

Cyrilla (sirr ILL' a) See CYRIL. (Masc.)

D

Oft do I marvel, whether DELIA's eyes
Are eyes, or else two radiant stars that shine
For how could Nature ever thus devise
Of earth, on earth, a substance so divine?

SAMUEL DANIEL, from *Sonnets to Delia*

Dagmar Danish, "clearness + famous" or "glory of the day."

Daisy Anglo-Saxon, flower name, "the day's eye." Literature: Heroine of Henry James' novelette *Daisy Miller*

Daisy, Daisy, give me your answer, do!
I'm half crazy, all for the love of you!
HARRY DACRE, *Daisy Bell*

Dale See DALE (m). DAIL, DAILE.

Damaris (DAM' a riss) Biblical: Acts, 17:34. Greek, "wife." Associated with *Damalis*, Greek, "heifer." DAMARA.

Dana See DANA (m).

Daphne Greek, "bay tree or laurel." Greek Mythology: The lovely nymph, who loved and pursued by the god Apollo; was at her own request changed into a laurel, from that time on the favorite tree of this god of music and poetry.

Musing on the fate of Daphne
Many feelings urged my breast
For the God so keen desiring

And the Nymph so deep distrest.
GEORGE MEREDITH, *Daphne*

In England a poet who figuratively has a crown of laurels bestowed on him becomes the Poet Laureate. Literature: Daphne du Maurier, author of *Rebecca*.

My Daphne's voice tunes all the
spheres,
My Daphne's music charms all
ears.
Fond am I thus to sing her
praise;
These glories now are turned to
bays.
JOHN LYLY, *Apollo's Song*

Daria See DARIUS.

Darleen, Darlene Anglo-Saxon, "darling," a word that is a dim. of *dear* (dear + ling). DARLA.

Davida (da VEE' da). See DAVID. DAVITA, VIDA, VEDA, VETA, VITA.

Davina (de VEE' na) Scottish fem. form; see DAVID.

Dawn Anglo-Saxon, "to become day." Literature: Homer's "rosy-fingered dawn."

Deanna (dee AN' a) Variant; see DIANA, a name which in ancient Latin was also written as DEANA. Hollywood: Deanna Durbin.

Deborah Hebrew, "a bee." DEVORAH, DEBERA, DEBRA, DEBBY, DEB(s). Biblical: Deborah was a prophetess and judge in Israel, who predicted the defeat of the Canaanites and celebrated the victory in a famous song of triumph (JUDGES 5 : 31). Hollywood: Deborah Kerr, Debby Reynolds.

Of Deborah who mustered
Her brethren, long oppressed,
And routed the heathen army,
And gave her people rest.
        WILLIAM CULLEN BRYANT,
                A Lifetime

Debra An increasingly popular respelling; see DEBORAH.

Dee Pet form, often used independently, of such names as DEANNA, DELIA, DEIRDRE, DIANA. DEDE.

Deirdre (DEER' dree) Irish legend; also Gaelic for DORCAS. DEERDRE, DEDEE, DEE. A legendary Irish heroine with a beauty like Helen's. Literature: Two plays, *Deirdre* (1907) by William Butler Yeats, and *Deirdre of the Sorrows* (1909) by John Millington Synge; and a novel, *Deirdre*, (1923) by James Stephens.

But there has been again no
*   woman born*
Who was so beautiful, not one
*   so beautiful*
Of all the women born.
        JAMES STEPHENS, *Deirdre*

Delia Greek, "of Delos," birthplace of Artemis (Diana). DELINDA.

Ask'st thou how long my love
*   shall stay,*
*   When all that's new is past?*
How long? Ah! Delia, can I say,
*   How long my life shall last?*
        RICHARD BRINSLEY SHERIDAN,
                Dry Be That Tear

Delicia Latin via Italian, "delight."

Delight Latin via French, "delight."

She was a phantom of delight
When first she gleamed upon my
*   sight;*
A lovely apparition, sent
To be a moment's ornament.
        WILLIAM WORDSWORTH,
        She Was a Phantom of Delight

Della Abbrev. of ADELA. See ADELE. DELLY.

Delphine (del FEEN') Greek, "a dolphin" or "of Delphi," a town in ancient Greece noted for its mystic oracle. DELFINE.

Demetria (de MEE' tri a) Fem. form; see DEMETRIUS. DEMETRIS, DEMETRA.

Dena Hebrew "vindicated." A form of DINAH; see also DEAN (m).

Denise (den EEZ'). See DENIS.

Desirée (day zee RAY') French, "longed for."

Diana Latin, "divine." DIANE, DIAN, DIAHANN, DEE, DEDE. Diana was the Roman goddess known also as Cynthia. As goddess of the moon and of the chase, she corresponded to Phoebe and Artemis of Greek mythology.

Diana . . . charms the sight
When in the dance the graceful
*   goddess leads*
The choir of nymphs, and over-
*   tops their heads.*
Knokn by her quiver, and her
*   lofty mien,*
She walks majestic, and she
*   looks their queen.*
        VERGIL, *Aeneid* (translated
            by John Dryden)

The Temple of Diana at Ephesus was one of the Seven Wonders of the ancient world.
Great is Diana of the Ephesians.
        ACTS 19 : 28

Literature: George Meredith's famous novel *Diana of the Crossways* (1875) popularized the later use of the name. Screen: Diahann Carroll, singer and actress, receiver of *Cue's* first Entertainer of the Year Award, for 1961; Diane Keaton, Oscar 1979 (*Annie Hall*).

Dianthe (dye AN' thee) Greek, "divine flower." DIANTHA.

Dina(h) (DYE' na *or* DEE' na) Hebrew, "vindicated." Biblical: Daughter of Leah and Jacob and reputed to be very beautiful. Literature: Dinah Maria Muloch Craik, author of the famous best-seller *John Halifax, Gentleman* (1856). TV: Dinah Shore.

Dione (dye o' *nee*) Greek, "divine queen." Mythology: Female Titan, mother of Aphrodite.

So young Dione, nursed beneath
*   the waves,*
And rocked by Nereids in their
*   coral caves. . .*
Lisped her sweet tones, and tried
*   her tender smiles.*
            ERASMUS DARWIN,
            Economy of Vegetation

Like CHLOE, CHLORIS, etc., *Dione* was a name used by earlier poets to denote a lady-love:

Ah! who that hears Dione's
*   tuneful tongue,*
Shall doubt that music may with
*   sense agree?*
    WILLIAM SHENSTONE, *Elegy VI*

Dionne (dye ON') See DION (m).

Dirce From Greek mythology. Greek, probably "double"; also associated with the ancient Greek word for "pine."

Stand close around, ye Stygian
*   set,*
With Dirce in one boat con-
*   veyed,*
Or Charon, seeing may forget
That he is old and she a shade.
        WALTER SAVAGE LANDOR,
                Dirce

Dixie From name for the South, used independently and as a nickname.

Dody Probably a duplicative pet form; see DORA. DODE.

Doe Anglo-Saxon, "deer."

Dolly See DOROTHY. Doll(e)y Madison, a most popular First Lady, lent dignity and charm to the name.

When Dolly took the air,
Each lad that happened near,
Forgetting all save she was fair,
Turned English cavalier.
LIZETTE WOODWORTH REESE,
On a Colonial Picture

Dolores Latin via Spanish, "(Mary of) the Sorrows." DO-LORIS, LOLA. Since the name of the Virgin Mary was for a long time held to be too sacred for ordinary use, in Spain girls were often given names connected with Her life or attributes, such names as CARMEN, CONSUELO, DOLORES, MERCEDES. Hollywood: Dolores Costello, Dolores Del Rio.

. . . . Dolores,
Tawny flower of Spain,
Wild rose of Granada.
THOMAS BAILEY ALDRICH,
Amontillado

Dominica (do MINN' i ka) Fem. form: see DOMINIC. DOMINIQUE; see also CYRA.

Donna Italian, "lady." Hollywood: Donna Reed.

Dora See DOROTHY. DORELLE, DORETTA, DORITA, DORENE, DORO. DORA is a shortened form of DOR-OTHY, but has long been used as an independent name. Literature: David's pretty child-wife in *David Copperfield*.

Dora's eyes of heavenly blue
Pass all painting's reach;
Ringdoves' notes are discords to
The music of her speech.
THOMAS CAMPBELL,
Margaret and Dora

Dorcas The Greek name *Dor-cas*, as well as the Aramaic *Tabitha*, both meaning "gazelle," is found in ACTS 9 : 36. See TABITHA.

Doreen Irish, "sullen"; French, "golden." See also DORA.

Dorinda A sixteenth century literary name with the elements *Dora* and *Inda* as in BELINDA.

Dorinda's sparkling wit and eyes
United, cast too fierce a light.
CHARLES SACKVILLE, EARL OF
DORSET, *Dorinda*

Doris Greek, "bountiful." See DORIAN. Mythology: Doris was the "gray-eyed" wife of Nereus and mother of the Nereids, fifty sea nymphs! Now generally taken as a variant for the more usual DORA.

Hollywood: Glamorous Doris Day.

Choose thou whatever suits the
line;
Call me Sappho, call me Chloris,
Call me Lalage or Doris
Only, only call me thine.
SAMUEL T. COLERIDGE, *Names*

Dorothy Greek, "gift of God." DOROTHEA, DORA, DOLLY, DOTTIE, DOT, DEDE. To Lady Dorothea Sidney, Edmund Waller dedicated (in 1645) his famous poem beginning:

Go, lovely rose!
Tell her that wastes her time
and me,
That now she knows
When I resemble her to thee,
How sweet and fair she seems
to be.

Hollywood: Dorothy Gish. Literature: Dorothy Parker, poet, wit, short-story writer; Dorothy Sayers, scholar and much admired writer of detective fiction, creator of Lord Peter Wimsey.

Dove Bird name, Germanic, "dark."

Drusilla From *Drusus*, a Roman family name. DRUSIE, DRUCIE.

Dulcie Latin, "sweet." DULCY, DULCE. For his lady love, whose name was Aldonza, Don Quixote chose the name *Dulcinea* as being more "harmonious, uncommon, and significant."

Dymphna Irish, "poetess."

E

ELIZABETH, *Betsy, Betty, and Bess*
Went out one day to find a bird's nest.
They found a nest with five eggs in it,
They each took one and left four in it.

OLD RIDDLE RHYME
(For answer to this riddle, see ELIZABETH.)

Eda Shortened form; see EDITH, but also used as an independent name. EDIE. Stage, Hollywood, TV: Edie Adams.

Eden Possibly Hebrew, "delight" or from Babylonian, "a plain." Also used as a dim. of EDITH. EDIN. Biblical: The earthly Paradise which was the home of Adam and Eve.

He that question would anew
What fair Eden was of old,
Let him rightly study you,
And a brief of that behold.
WILLIAM BROWNE, *Welcome,*
Welcome, Do I Sing

Edith Germanic "rich-war." EDIE, EDIT(H)A. Some authorities, disdaining this martial origin, prefer "rich gift" as more appropriate to this lovely name. Whatever it may mean, Samuel Taylor Coleridge once asserted: "Edith and Rotha are my favorite names for women."

Literature: Edith Wharton, novelist (*Ethan Frome*); Edith Hamilton, *grande dame* of classical studies (*The Greek Way*). History: Edith Cavell, martyred nurse of World War I. Stage: Dame Edith Evans.

He felt the charm of Edith's
eyes,
Nor wanted hope to gain the
prize.
THOMAS PARNELL,
A Fairy Tale

Edna Hebrew, "rejuvenation." Literature: Edna Ferber, *Show Boat* and Pulitzer Prize novel *So Big* (1925); Edna St. Vincent Millay, Pulitzer Prize for poetry in 1923, who was called Vincent by her friends and family.

Edwina See EDWIN. EDWYNA.

Effie Greek, "well spoken of." EPPIE, PHEMIE. Almost all that now remains of EUPHEMIA, a once popular Scottish name, is the pet form *Effie*.

She was to her father the licht o'
his een,
He said she wad be what her
mither had been—
A fair an' sweet sample o' true
womanhood,
Sae carefu' an' clever, sae
bonnie an' guid.
JANET HAMILTON,
Effie—A Ballad

213

Eileen, Aileen Irish equivalent of HELEN. Literature: Ruth McKenney's *My Sister Eileen* delighted millions as book, play, movie, and musical (*Wonderful Town*).

Dear were her charms to me,
Dearer her laughter free,
Dearest her constancy,—
Eileen aroon! [my treasure]
GERALD GRIFFIN,
Eileen Aroon

Elaine, Elayne (e LAYN´) An old French form; see HELEN. Came into wide use with the publication of Tennyson's *Idylls of the King* (1859), one of the most popular of which told the story of Lancelot and Elaine, beginning with:

Elaine the fair, Elaine the loveable,
Elaine the lily maid of Astolat.

Elberta See ALBERT.

Elda See ALDA.

Eleanor(e) See HELEN. ELINOR, ELEANORA, LENORE, ELLA, NELL. In the year 1950 two biographies of Eleanor of Aquitaine were published and two books by a modern Eleanor, Mrs. Eleanor Roosevelt. Elinor Trent in Charles Dickens' *Old Curiosity Shop* (1840) is better known as "Little Nell." Stage: Eleonora Duse (1859-1924), one of the greatest actresses of all time.

I stand before thee, Eleanore;
I see thy beauty gradually unfold,
Daily and hourly, more and more.
ALFRED, LORD TENNYSON,
Eleanore

Electra Greek, "amber." Greek Mythology and Drama: Daughter of Clytemnestra and Agamemnon, who with her brother Orestes avenged the murder of her father. She figures in plays by all three of the great Greek writers of tragedy and in opera, ballet, and modern drama, as in the title of O'Neill's tragedy *Mourning Becomes Electra*.

I dare not ask a kiss,
I dare not beg a smile,
Lest having that or this,
I might grow proud the while.

No, No, the utmost share
Of my desire shall be
Only to kiss that air
That lately kissed thee.
ROBERT HERRICK, *To Electra*

Elfrida Anglo-Saxon, "elf-peace." ELFRIDE, ELFREDA. See also FREDA.

Elise (ay LEEZ´) French form of ELIZA. See ELIZABETH, ELYSE.

Elissa Variant of ALISSA. Also Greek-Latin, poetic name of Vergil's Queen Dido.

Eliza Short form of ELIZABETH.

Nymphs of sea and land, away,
This, Eliza's wedding day,
Help to dress our gallant bride
With the treasures that ye hide.
HENRY PEACHAM,
Nuptial Hymn

Elizabeth Hebrew, "oath of God." LIZABETH, ELIZA, LIZA, LIZ, LIZZIE, LIBBY, ELSIE, ELSA, LISE, ELISSA, LISETTE, ELSPET, ELSPETH, BESS, BESSIE, BETTE, BETTY, BETH, ISABEL, BELLE, etc. The many names into which ELIZABETH breaks down explains the *Riddle Rhyme* at the head of this section, for all four names represent one person. Biblical: Mother of John the Baptist. St. Elizabeth of Hungary, remembered for her daily care of the poor, made the name popular in medieval Europe. The most famous women to bear the name were Elizabeth Barrett of Wimpole Street and "Good Queen Bess" of England. Literature: Elizabeth, the altogether charming heroine of *Pride and Prejudice.* Hollywood: Elizabeth Taylor, winner of an Oscar in 1960, 1966.

A sweeter woman ne'er drew breath
Than my sonne's wife Elizabeth.
JEAN INGELOW, *High Tide*

Ella Probably from Germanic, "all," via French. Also abbrev. of ELEANOR.

Ellen Earlier English form of HELEN, now an independent name. ELLIN, ELLYN, ELYN, ELIN, ELENA. Famous women gracing this name: Ellen Terry, distinguished Shakespearean actress, famous for her correspondence with George Bernard Shaw; and Ellen Glasgow, American novelist, Pulitzer Prize winner in 1942 for *In This Our Life.*

Her kindness and her worth to spy,
You need but gaze on Ellen's eye.

WALTER SCOTT,
The Lady of the Lake

Eloise (ell oh EEZ') Germanic via French, "hale" and "wide." HELOISE.

But sweeter, dearer, yes, dearer far than these . . .
Is blue-eyed, bonny, bonny, Eloise.
OLD SONG

Elsa See ELIZABETH. Music: In Wagner's opera *Lohengrin,* the bride for whom the famous wedding march is played.

Elsie See ELIZABETH. Twenty-six *Elsie Dinsmore* books, written by Mrs. Martha Finley, brought copious tears to the eyes of girls of an earlier generation.

Elsie from Chelsea, I thought of nobody elsie
But Elsie from Chelsea! Nobody elsie for me!
HARRY DACRE, *Elsie from Chelsea* (Popular song of 1896)

Elspeth Scottish; see ELIZA-BETH.

Elva, Elvia Germanic, "elf-like." See ELVIN.

Elvira (el VEE' ra or el VYE' ra) Germanic via Spanish, "elf counsel," or "excelling." See ALFRED. Music: Character in Mozart's opera *Don Giovanni*, which popularized the name in Germany.

Emily Fem. of EMIL. The two most famous women to bear this name were Emily Brontë, author of one of the world's great novels, *Wuthering Heights* (1847), and Emily Dickinson (1830-1886), one of America's great poets. Emily Bissell designed the first Christmas seal in 1909. Emily Post is America's authority on etiquette.

> . . . *Emilie, that fayrer was to sene*
> *Than is the lilie upon his stalke grene,*
> *And fresher than the May with floures newe.*
>
> GEOFFREY CHAUCER,
> *The Knightes Tale*

Emma Germanic, "universal" or "nurse." Literature: Heroine of one of the world's great novels, Flaubert's *Madame Bovary;* Jane Austen's *Emma.* The lines inscribed on the base of the Statue of Liberty are taken from *The New Colossus,* a poem written by Emma Lazarus. Education: Emma Willard (1787-

1870), member of the American Hall of Fame, pioneer in field of women's higher education, also author of poetry (*Rocked in the Cradle of the Deep*).

Emmy See EMMA and also EMILY.

> *Emmy's laughter rings in my ears, as bright*
> *Fresh and sweet as the voice of a mountain brook.*
>
> ARTHUR SYMONS, *Emmy*

The Emmy Awards, given each year by the National Academy of Arts and Sciences, have nothing to do with *Emmy* but eveything to do with Immy, a pet name given by the cameramen to the *Image Orthicon* (the pickup tube in a TV camera). When a name was needed for the awards, Immy was favored, but it wasn't a name really as *Oscar, Tony,* and *Edgar* are. So the *I* was changed to *E,* and now every year—since 1948—each of the outstanding achievements in the various fields of television is given an Emmy. (See under OSCAR, TONY, and EDGAR.)

Ena (EE' na) Gaelic, "fire."

Enid (EE' nid) Welsh, "spotless purity" or "a woodlark." In the King Arthur legends, the beautiful Enid is the personification of all that is noble and true in womanhood. With the publication and wide reading of Tennyson's *Idylls of the King, Enid* (as Tennyson predicted in his poem) became a popular name.

*But Enid, whom the ladies loved
    to call
Enid the Fair, a grateful people
    named
Enid the Good; and in their halls
    arose
The cry of children, Enids and
    Geraints
Of times to be.*
    ALFRED, LORD TENNYSON,
        Geraint and Enid

Eppie See EFFIE. See also HEP(H)ZIBAH. Literature: Famous character in George Eliot's *Silas Marner*. Silas wanted to name his adopted baby Hephzibah after his mother and sister but settled for Eppie when a neighbor thought Hephzibah too large a name for such a little thing.

Erda Germanic, "earth." See also HERT(H)A. ERTA.

Erica (ERR' i ca) Fem. of ERIC. ERIKA. Music: Erica Morini, concert violinist.

Erin (AIR' in) Gaelic, "Ireland." Name of a legendary queen. ERINA.

*Dear Erin, how sweetly
    thy green bosom rises!
An emerald set in the
    ring of the sea.*
    JOHN PHILPOT CURRAN,
        Cushla-ma-Chree
    ("Darling of My Heart")

Erma See IRMA.

Erna Dim. form; see ERNESTINE.

Ernestine See ERNEST. ERNA, TINA.

Esma, Esme (EZZ' me) Old English for AIMÉE. See AMY and ESME (m). Literature: J. D. Salinger's appealing heroine in his fine short story *For Esme with Love and Squalor.*

Esta See ESTHER.

Estelle, Estella See STELLA. Literature: Estella is the heroine of Dickens' *Great Expectations.*

Esther (ESS' ter) Persian, "star." ESTA, ESTER, HESTER, ESSIE, ISTAR. The Persian name of the Jewish captive Hadassah, whom Ahasuerus made his queen in place of Vashti. Esther saved her people from destruction at the hands of Haman. The feast of Purim commemorates this deliverance. See also MORDECAI.

*And he brought up Hadassah,
that is, Esther, his uncle's daughter: for she had neither father
nor mother, and the maiden was
fair and beautiful.*
            ESTHER 2 : 7

*Then I remembered that I once
    was young
And lived with Esther the
    world's gods among.*
    WILFRID SCAWEN BLUNT,
        Esther

Ethel Germanic, "noble." See ADELE. This name is really the shortened form of such compound names as *Ethelred* (see AUDREY), *Ethelinda*, *Ethelburga*, etc. We were about to write that *Ethel* has no variant spelling when we came across ETHYL and ETHYLE! Theater: Ethel Barrymore; Ethel Merman.

Ethelberta See ETHELBERT.

Etta A pet form of HENRIETTA, it has become an independent name. *Etta* or *ette* at end of names means "little," an affectionate diminutive.

Eudora (you DAW' ra) Greek, "pleasant gift." Literature: Eudora Welty.

Eugenia (you JEE' nia) Greek, "nobility." See EUGENE.

Eugenia, young and fair and sweet,
The glories of the plains,
In thee alone the graces meet
To conquer all the swains.
 CHARLES COTTON,
 Old Tityrus to Eugenia

Eugenie (you JEE' nee) See EUGENIA. Empress Eugénie, wife of Napoleon III, gave vogue to the name, once used to describe women's fashions.

Eula Greek, "well-spoken." EULALIE.

Eunice (YOU' niss) Greek, "happy victory." See NICHOLAS. Biblical: Mother of Timothy.

Euphemia (you FEE' me a) Greek, "well spoken of." EFFIE, PHEMIE.

Eustacia See EUSTACE. STACEY. Literature: Eustacia Vye, unforgettable heroine of Hardy's *Return of the Native*.

Eva See EVE. Theater: Eva Le Gallienne, actress, producer, important influence in the theater. Literature: As used in *Uncle Tom's Cabin*, "Little Eva" is a short form of Evangeline:

"What's little missy's name?" said Tom. . . .
"Evangeline St. Clare," said the little one, "though papa and everybody else call me Eva."
 HARRIET BEECHER STOWE

O fair and stately maid, whose eyes
Were kindled in the upper skies.
 EMERSON, *To Eva*

Evadne Probably from *Evanthe*, Greek "beautifully flowering." EUANTHE.

Evangeline Greek, "bringer of good news." A name apparently invented by Longfellow for the heroine of his poem. EVANGELIA.

*Fair was she to behold, that
maiden of seventeen summers,
Black were her eyes as the berry
that grows on the thorn by
the wayside,
Black, yet how softly they
gleamed beneath the brown
shade of her tresses.*
HENRY WADSWORTH LONG-
FELLOW, *Evangeline*

Evangeline Cory Booth, musician, poet, and orator, was a
commander of The Salvation
Army.

Eve Hebrew, "life." EVA. See
ZOE.

*And Adam called his wife's
name Eve, because she was the
mother of all living.*
GENESIS 3 : 20

*Man to God's image; Eve
to man's was made.*
JOHN DONNE, *To the
Countess Huntington*

Evelina Variant of EVELYN.
Literature: *Evelina* (1778) by
Fanny Burney, one of the earli-
est of English novels.

Evelyn Germanic, related to
names like AVA. Also dim. of
EVE.

*I loved you, Evelyn, all the
while!
My heart seemed full as it
could hold;
There was place and to spare
for the frank young smile
And the red young mouth and
the hair's young gold.*
ROBERT BROWNING,
Evelyn Hope

F

*O daughters of dreams and of stories
That life is not wearied of yet,*
FAUSTINE, FRAGOLETTA, DOLORES,
FÉLISE *and* YOLANDE *and* JULIETTE.

ALGERNON CHARLES SWINBURNE,
Dedication (1865)

Fabia Fem. form; see FABIAN.

Fabiola Dim. of FABIA. The name of the Queen of the Belgians. Literature: Novel by Cardinal Wiseman. Art: A famous portrait by Jean-Jacques Henner.

Faith See CHARITY. Literature: Faith Baldwin, popular novelist.

*Around the child bend all three
Sweet Graces—Faith, Hope,
Charity.*
WILLIAM SAVAGE LANDOR,
Around the Child

Fanchon (FAN SHON') French form of FANNY. FANCHETTE.

Fancy From "phantasy," Greek-Latin via French, "imagination." FANCIE.

*Tell me where is fancy bred,
Or in the heart or in the head?*
WILLIAM SHAKESPEARE,
The Merchant of Venice

Literature: *To Fancy* by John Keats:

*Ever let the Fancy roam
Pleasure never is at home.*

Fanny, Fannie Pet form of FRANCES. This name has a long literary history from novelists Fanny Burney (1752-1840) to Fannie Hurst, and from Fanny Brawne, Keats' love and inspiration, to Fanny Osbourne, who became Stevenson's wife. Stage: Fanny Brice, comedienne. Film and Musical: *Fanny*, one of Pagnol's famous trilogy.

*Oh, Fanny is more fair
Than flow'rets sweet and rare;
Nor in the world you'll find
A nobler heart and mind.*
WELSH SONG

Faustine Latin, "fortunate." FAUSTA, FAUSTINA.

Fawn Latin via French, "a young deer." See also DOE, DORCAS, HINDA, TABITHA, SIVIA.

Fay(e) Perhaps the word *fay* meaning "fairy" or a shortening of FAITH. Screen: Faye Dunaway, Oscar 1976 (*Network*).

*And haply the Queen-Moon is
on her throne,
Clustered around by all her
starry fays.*
JOHN KEATS,
Ode to a Nightingale

220

Fedora (fe DAW' ra) Greek via Russian, fem. of THEODORE, "gift of God." Literature: Heroine of a celebrated play by Victorien Sardou (1883) in which Sarah Bernhardt won great success.

Felice, Felicia Fem. form; see FELIX. FELICITY. Literature: Felicia Hemans (1793-1835), whose poem *Casabianca* opens with the oft-quoted line, "The boy stood on the burning deck."

Felicity Latin, "happiness." See FELICE.

Félise (fay LEEZ') French feminine form; see FELIX. "Fortunate, blessed."

And all these only like your name,
And your name full of all of these,
I say it, and it sounds the same—
Save that I say it now at ease,
Your name, Félise.
      ALGERNON CHARLES SWINBURNE, *Félise*

Fern(e) A popular plant name (like BRIER, HAZEL, HEATHER, etc.) May also be a shortening of FERNANDA.

Fernanda See FERDINAND.

Fidelia (fid EEL' ya), **Fidelity** Latin, "faithful, faithfulness." A "quality" name. When they disguised themselves as young men,

two heroines, one of music, the other of drama, assumed masc. forms of this name. Leonora called herself *Fidelio* in Beethoven's opera of the same name; Imogen took the name *Fidele* in Shakespeare's *Cymbeline:*

LUCIUS: *Thy name?*
IMOGEN: *Fidele, sir.*
LUCIUS: *Thou dost approve thyself the very same;*
      Thy name well fits thy faith, thy faith thy name.

Fifi (FEE' FEE). Pet name of JOSEPHINE via *Fifine* (like BEBE, MIMI, LULU).

Flavia (FLAY' vee a) Latin, "golden yellow."

Marry, and love thy Flavia, for she
Hath all things, whereby others beauteous be.
      JOHN DONNE, *The Anagram*

Fle(e)ta Anglo-Saxon, "clean," "beautiful." FLEDA. Used as an ending of names like *Elfleda* and *Ethelfleda.*

Fleur French, "a flower." Literature: A charming vibrant young woman in the *Forsyte* novels by John Galsworthy.

Flora From Latin *flos, floris,* "a flower." Mythology: Roman goddess of spring and flowers. See CHLORIS. FLOSSIE, FLOREEN.

*Rise and put on your foliage,
and be seen
To come forth, like the spring-
time, fresh and green,
And sweet as Flora.*

ROBERT HERRICK,
Corinna's Going a-Maying

Florence Latin, "blooming."
FLORIS, FLORENE, FLO. At the
turn of the century many girls
were named FLORENCE in honor
of Florence Nightingale, who
received her name from her
birthplace, Florence, Italy.

*Sweet Florence! could another
ever share
This wayward, loveless heart, it
would be thine.*

GEORGE GORDON BYRON,
Childe Harold

Florinda A poetic name with
the elements FLORA and INDA as
in BELINDA. The name is sometimes used as a variant of
FLORENCE.

Floris Variant form; see FLORA.

Frances Fem. form; see FRAN-
CIS. FRANCILLE, FRANCINE,
FRANKIE, FRAN, FANNY. Although
the girl's name is now spelled
only with the *e*, both the masculine and feminine names were
spelled *Francis* until the seventeenth century. Among Elizabethan aristocracy, it was always
spelled *Francis* and abbreviated
to *Frank*. Frances Xavier Cabrini, first United States citizen to
become a saint, was canonized

by Pope Pius XII, June 1946,
and declared patron saint of all
emigrants in November 1950.

Freda Germanic, "peace."
FRIEDA, FRAYDA.

Fredelle Dim. form; see FRED.
FREDELLA.

Frederica See FREDERIC. FRED-
DIE, RICA.

Freya (FRAY' a) Norse goddess
of love and beauty, from whose
name we get *Friday*. FRAYA. Literature: Freya Stark, English authority on Asia Minor, especially the archaeology of the region; *Freya of the Seven Isles*,
Joseph Conrad's moving story.

*And Freya next came nigh with
golden tears;
The loveliest Goddess she in
Heaven by all
Most honor'd after Frea, Odin's
wife . . .
Names hath she many; Vanadis
on earth
They call her, Freya is her name
in heaven.*

MATTHEW ARNOLD, *Balder Dead*

Frieda Germanic, "peace."
FREDA, FRIDA, FREDDIE. Litera-
ture: Frieda Lawrence, wife of
D. H. Lawrence, and author of
The Memoirs & Correspondence.

Fritzi Fem. form; see FRITZ.

Froma (FRO' ma) Germanic,
"pious." FROMMA, FRUME (FROO'
me), FRUMIE.

G

Maid of my love, sweet GENEVIEVE
In beauty's light you glide along:
Your eye is like the star of eve,
And sweet your voice as seraph's song.

SAMUEL TAYLOR COLERIDGE, *Genevieve*

Gabrielle See GABRIEL. GABRIEL(L)A, GABY. Literature: Gabriela Mistral, Chilean poet and teacher, resident of the United States, winner of the Nobel Prize for Literature (1945).

Gail, Gayl(e), Gael See ABIGAIL. GAYLE.

Galina Russian form; see HELEN. Ballet: Galina Ulanova, one of the great dancers. Music: Galina Visnevskaya, outstanding soprano.

Garnet A jewel name, from Latin, "grain."

Gay(e) English, "light-hearted, merry." GAE.

Gemma (JEMM′ a) Latin-Italian, "jewel."

Gene Variant spelling of JEAN; or from EUGENIA. GENIA.

Geneva Variant of GENEVIEVE or named after Geneva, Switzerland. GINEVRA.

Genevieve Celtic, "white" or "magic sighs," related in origin to GUINEVERE. St. Genevieve is the patron saint of Paris, which she saved from a threatened attack by Attila the Hun. Literature: Genevieve Taggard, American poet and critic.

Fair Genevieve, my early love,
The years but make thee dearer far.
My heart shall never, never rove
Thou art my only guiding star.
GEORGE COOPER,
Sweet Genevieve

Georgian(n)a See GEORGE. GEORGINA, GEORGIA, GEORGEANNE, GEORGINE, GEORGETTE. Art: Georgia O'Keeffe, celebrated American painter.

Geraldine See GERALD, GERRI, GERI, GERRY, JERALDINE, JERRI. Music: Geraldine Farrar, famous American dramatic soprano. Stage and Screen: Geraldine Page.

So sweet did harp and voice combine
To praise the name of Geraldine.
SIR WALTER SCOTT,
Lay of the Last Minstrel

Gerda (GUR′ da) Germanic, "spear" or "knowing." A beautiful Norse goddess.

Germaine (jur MAIN') Latin via French, "a German."

Gertrude Germanic, "spear-strength" or "spear-maiden." GERT, GERTIE, TRUDY, TRUDI. State: Gertrude Lawrence (1900-1952). Radio, TV, and Stage: Gertrude Berg, the writer and the Molly of the famous Goldberg series. Literature: Gertrude Stein (1874-1946), *grande dame* of avant-garde writers.

*And paint thy Gertrude in her
bower of yore,
Whose beauty was the love of
Pennsylvania's shore!*
THOMAS CAMPBELL,
Gertrude of Wyoming

Gilda (GILL' da *or* ZHEEL' da) Anglo-Saxon, "the golden"; or Celtic, "God's servant"; but derivation is not certain. Music: Daughter of Rigoletto in Verdi's opera. Hollywood: Gilda Gray of a past era.

Gillian (JILL' yan) English form; see JULIANA. GILL.

Gina Terminal form of *Ambrogina* or *Luigina*. See AMBROSE, LOUIS, and GINO. GINETTA. Screen: Gina Lollobrigida.

Gina is also derived from *Giovanna* and *Angelina*.

Ginger Pet form; see VIRGINIA. GINNY. Hollywood: Ginger Rogers, winner of Oscar in 1940 (*Kitty Foyle*).

Gisel(l)a (ji ZELL' a) Germanic, "a pledge." GISELLE (ji ZELL'). Ballet: *Giselle,* one of the most famous of ballets, music composed by Adolphe Charles Adam. Vaslav Nijinsky and Anna Pavlova were among famous performers in it.

Gladys From *Gwladys,* Welsh variation of CLAUDIA; Celtic, "princess." GLADYCE. Music: Gladys Swarthout, glamorous soprano.

Glenda See GLEN (m). GLENNA. Screen: Glenda Jackson, Oscar 1970 (*Women in Love*), 1973 (*A Touch of Class*).

Gloria Latin, "glory." GLORY, GLORIANA. Hollywood: Gloria Swanson.

*If for a woman I would die
It should for Glorianna be.*
ANNE FINCH, *A Song*

Glynis Welsh, "little valley." GLYNNIS. Stage and Screen: Glynis Johns.

Golda Anglo-Saxon, "gold." GOLDIE, GOLDYE, GOLDIA. Politics: Golda Meir, Israeli prime minister.

Grace Latin, "grace, thanks." GRACIE, GRAY. Hollywood: Grace Kelly, late Princess of Monaco, winner of an Oscar in 1954 (*Country Girl*).

*As is your name, so is your
comely face*

*Touch'd everywhere with such
diffused grace.*
> ROBERT HERRICK,
> *To the Handsome Mistress
> Grace Potter*

Gratia Latin, "grace, favor,
thanks." GRATIANA.

*See, with what constant motion,
Even, and glorious as the sun,
Gratiana steers that noble frame.*
> RICHARD LOVELACE, *Gratiana*

Greer Abbrev. form of Scottish, GREGOR, meaning "watchman, herdsman." See GREGORY.
Screen: Greer Garson, winner of
1942 Oscar (*Mrs. Miniver*). In
a letter to us, Greer Garson
writes:
"My first name is the family
name of my mother Nina Greer.
My grandparents lived in County
Down, Northern Ireland, and
there are many Greers in Ulster.
You are correct in assuming that
'Greer' is a contraction of the
Scottish 'Mac Gregor.' "

Greta (GRETT' a *or* GRETT' a)
GRETTA. A German terminal abbreviation of MARGARET, made
popular in our time by the incomparable Greta Garbo.

Gretchen German dim. form;
see MARGARET. GRETEL. Literature: The name by which
Goethe's heroine in his great
dramatic poem *Faust* is often
called instead of by the more
formal MARGARET.

Griselda Germanic, "gray battle maid." GRIZEL, ZELDA. The
early use of the name GRIZELDA
was due to the influence of
Chaucer, who adapted Boc-
caccio's story of the patient
Griselda in his *Canterbury
Tales.*

*Art thou poor, yet hast thou
golden slumbers?
Oh sweet content!
Art thou rich, yet is thy mind
perplexed?
Oh punishment!*
> THOMAS DEKKER (1570-1641)
> *Patient Grissell*

Guinevere Welsh, "white-
cheeked." GUENEVERE, JEN(N)I-
FER, GWEN. Literature: The wife
of King Arthur. The modern
form of the name is JEN(N)IFER.

*'Tis that fair time of year,
When stately Guinevere,
In her sea-green robe and hood,
Went a-riding through the wood.*
> THOMAS BAILEY ALDRICH,
> *The Queen's Ride*

Gussie See AUGUSTA.

Gwen Welsh, "white."
GWYN(NE), GUENN. Shortened
form of GWENDOLEN and GUINE-
VERE. See BLANCHE.

Gwendolen, Gwendolyn Welsh,
"white-browed." GWEN, WENDY.

Gwyneth Welsh, "blessed."

H

HELEN, *thy beauty is to me*
Like those Nicéan barks of yore,
That gently, o'er a perfumed sea,
The weary, wayworn wanderer bore
To his own native shore.

EDGAR ALLAN POE, *To Helen*

Hadassah (ha DAH' sa) Hebrew, "myrtle." See ESTHER.

Hagar (HAY' gar) Hebrew and Aramaic, "forsaken." Biblical: Mother of Ishmael.

Haidee (HAY' dee) Greek "respectful," "bashful." Theater: Haidee Wright.

Haila Germanic, "healthy, strong." Theater: Haila Stoddard.

Hallie Fem. of HAL, therefore dim. pet name of HARRIET or HENRIETTA, but used as an independent name.

I'm dreaming now of Hallie,
sweet Hallie, sweet Hallie
ALICE HAWTHORNE,
Listen to the Mocking Bird

Hannah Hebrew, "grace." Greek and Latin form of ANNA. Biblical: Mother of the prophet Samuel.

Harmony Latin and Greek, "harmony."

From harmony, from heavenly
harmony
This universal frame began.
JOHN DRYDEN,
A Song for St. Cecelia's Day

Harriet See HARRY. HARRIOT, HATTIE, HARRIETTE, HARRIE. Literature: Harriet Beecher Stowe, author of *Uncle Tom's Cabin*, one of the all-time best sellers since 1851. History: Harriet Tubman, an escaped slave, who helped dozens of others escape and acted as important Union scout and spy during the Civil War. Music: Harriet Wingreen, pianist, specialist in chamber music and accompaniment.

Harriet! . . . . Thou wert my
purer mind;
Thou wert the inspiration of my
song.
PERCY BYSSHE SHELLEY,
To Harriet

Harriot Variant spelling; see HARRIET.

Harriot was in truth
A tall fair beauty in the bloom
of youth.
GEORGE CRABBE, *Squire Thomas*

Hatty See HARRIET.

Hazel A plant name from Anglo-Saxon.

Heather, Heath A plant or flower name (like HAZEL, FERN, BRIER, IVY, MYRTLE). Screen: Heather Angel.

Hebe (HE′ BEE) Greek, "youth." Mythology: Cup-bearer of the gods.

Nods and becks and wreathèd smiles,
Such as hang on Hebe's cheek,
And love to live in dimple sleek.
    JOHN MILTON, *L'Allegro*

Hedda Germanic, "strife." Literature: Hedda Gabler, heroine of one of Ibsen's major plays.

Hedva Hebrew, "joy." Israeli name.

Hedwig Germanic, "strife." HEDVIG, HEDY, HEDDA. See AVA.

Hedy Pet form of HEDWIG. Hollywood: Hedy Lamarr.

Heidi (HYE′ dee) From the last syllable of German name ADALHEID (see ADELAIDE). Literature: In the children's classic *Heidi*, a novel of life in Switzerland by Johanna Spyri, occurs this bit of dialogue:

"Would you rather be called Heidi or Adelaide?" *asked Clara.*

"I am never called anything but Heidi," *was the child's prompt reply.*

"Then I shall always call you by that name," *said Clara.* "It suits you. I have never heard it before."

Art: Heidi Brandt, designer of 1956 and 1961 Christmas seal.

Helen Greek, "the bright one." HELAINE, HELAYNE, ELLEN, ELEANOR. Russian form, *Galina;* Polish form, *Halina.* The most famous of all Helens was Helen of Troy, whose face "launched a thousand ships and burnt the topless towers of Ilium." Of her, Homer said, "She moves a goddess and she looks a queen." To her, Faustus in Christopher Marlowe's play said:

Oh thou art fairer than the evening air
Clad in the beauty of a thousand stars.

And it was a modern Helen who brought Poe back

To the glory that was Greece
And the grandeur that was Rome.

Despite all this, the early popularity of the name was probably due to St. Helen, the mother of Emperor Constantine the Great. Theater and Screen: Helen Hayes, winner of Oscar in 1932 (*The Sin of Madelon Claudet*). Literature and Life: Helen Keller, one of the great women of our time.

Helena (HEL′ en a or hel EEN′ a)
Latin and German form of
Greek *Helene*. See HELEN. ELE-
NA, LENA. Literature: Heroine
of Shakespeare's *All's Well That
Ends Well;* also a young lady of
Athens in *A Midsummer Night's
Dream,* of whom Lysander says:

*Fair Helena, who more engilds
the night
Than all yon fiery oes and eyes
of light.*
WILLIAM SHAKESPEARE

Helene (hel AYN′ or hel EEN′)
Ancient Greek form of the
name; French *Hélène* (ay
LENN′). See HELEN. Music: Offenbach's *La Belle Hélène,* an
operatic satire about Helen of
Troy.

Helga Norse, "holy." See OLGA.

Helma Germanic, "helmet."
Short for WILHELMINA; see WIL-
LIAM.

Heloise (HEL O EEZ′) See ELO-
ISE. Heloise, beloved of Abelard,
was one of the most learned
women of the Middle Ages.

*Where's Héloise, the learnèd
nun?*
DANTE GABRIEL ROSSETTI'S
translation of François Villon's
famous poem.

Henrie Modern fem. form of
HENRY, or short form of HENRI-
ETTA.

Henrietta From French form
HENRIETTE; see HENRY. ETTA,
YETTA, HETTY. Humanity: Henrietta Szold (1860-1945), American Zionist leader, founder and
president (1912-1926) of the
Hadassah Organization.

Henriette French fem. of *Henri.* See HENRY and HENRIETTA.
Literature: Henriette, a character in Molière's *Les Femmes
Savantes* called by the French
"the type of a perfect woman."

Hep(h)zibah (HEF′ zib a) Hebrew, "She is my delight." Biblical: Wife of King Hezekiah.
Literature: Heroine of Hawthorne's *House of the Seven Gables.* See EPPIE.

*Thou shalt be called Hephzi-
bah . . . for the* LORD *delighteth
in thee.*
ISAIAH 62 : 4

Hermia (HUR′ mee a) See HER-
MIONE.

*Happy is Hermia whereso'er she
lies;
For she hath blessèd and attrac-
tive eyes.*
WILLIAM SHAKESPEARE,
A Midsummer Night's Dream

Hermine See HERMAN. HER-
MINA.

Hermione (hur MYE′ a nee)
Greek, from *Hermes,* name of
the messenger of the gods. In
Greek mythology, the daughter

of Helen of Troy. In Shakespeare, the Queen in *The Winter's Tale.*

> *Thou hast beauty bright and*
> *fair,*
> *Manner noble, aspect free,*
> *Eyes that are untouched by care:*
> *What then do we ask from*
> *thee?*
> *Hermione, Hermione!*
>   BRYAN WALLER PROCTER,
>   *Hermione*

Two British comediennes: Gingold and Baddeley.

Herta, Hertha Germanic, "earth" or "strong." EARTHA, ERDA, ERTA. Stage and Screen: Eartha Kitt.

Herva Used as fem. form of HARVEY.

Hester See ESTHER. HETTY. Literature: Hester Prynne, heroine of Hawthorne's *Scarlet Letter.*

> *Opening one day a book of mine,*
> *I absent, Hester found a line*
> *Praised with a pencil-mark, and*
> *this*
> *She left transfigured with a kiss.*
>   JAMES RUSSELL LOWELL,
>   *The Pregnant Comment*

Hetty See HESTER and HENRIETTA. Hetty (Henrietta) Green (1834-1916), financier, was the world's richest woman.

Hil(l)ary (HILL' a ree) See HILARY (m).

Hilda Germanic, "battle-maid." Seventh-century English saint, founder and abbess of Whitby in Yorkshire. HILDE. Literature: Hilda Doolittle (1886-1961), better known as H. D., one of the most important of the Imagist poets.

> *The bloom that lies on Hilda's*
> *cheek*
> *Is all my Latin, all my Greek.*
>   T. B. ALDRICH,
>   *An Elective Course,*
> *Lines Found Among the Papers*
> *of a Harvard Undergraduate*

Hildegarde Germanic, "battle-maid." There were several saints of this name, the most famous and best loved being the eleventh-century Abbess of Bingen. TV: Hildegarde, born Loretta Sell.

Hinda (HINN' da) Anglo-Saxon, "a female deer." HYNDA.

Holly Anglo-Saxon. A plant name with Christmas overtones.

Honey Germanic, "sweet." May also be considered the dim. of HONORA or HONORIA.

Honora (ho NO' ra) Latin, "honorable." HONOR, HONORIA, NORA.

> *This noble youth to madness*
> *loved a dame*
> *Of high degree, Honoria was her*
> *name,*
> *Fair as the fairest.*
>   JOHN DRYDEN,
>   *Theodore and Honoria*

Hope Anglo-Saxon. See CHARITY.

Hope is the thing with feathers
That perches in the soul,
And sings the tune without the
words,
And never stops at all.
  EMILY DICKINSON, *Poems*

Hope springs eternal in the
human breast:
Man never is, but always to be,
blest.
ALEXANDER POPE, *Essay on Man*

Horatia See HORACE.

Hortense Latin, "of a garden." Literature: Hortense Calisher, writer of short stories.

Hulda Name of a Hebrew prophetess, but, as used in this country, a Scandinavian variant of HILDA.

Hyacinth Greek mythology; a flower name. JACINTA.

I

From you, IANTHE, little troubles pass
Like little ripples down a sunny river;
Your pleasures spring like daisies in the grass,
Cut down, and up again as blithe as ever.

WALTER SAVAGE LANDOR, *Ianthe*

Ianthe (eye AN' thee) Greek, "purple flower."

I have since written what no tide
Shall ever wash away; what men
Unborn shall read o'er ocean wide
And find Ianthe's name again.
WALTER SAVAGE LANDOR,
Her Name

Ida Germanic, "youthful" or "labor." Literature: Heroine of Tennyson's narrative poem *The Princess* (1847), a "new woman," founder of a university for women. Gilbert and Sullivan's comic opera *Princess Ida* is a "respectful" satire on the poem. Screen: Ida Lupino, actress, director, and producer.

Ileane Respelling of EILEEN.

Ilene (EYE' leen *or* ee LENN' a). May be a variant spelling of EILEEN or a variation of French *Hélène* or German *Helena*.

Ilka From ILONA via pet form ILONKA. Literature and Theater: Ilka Chase.

Ilona (ill OH' na) Hungarian form; see HELEN. Theater: Ilona Massey.

Ilsa, Ilse German forms of ELSIE.

Imogen (IMM' o jen), **Imogene** (IMM' o jeen). Celtic. Shakespeare made this name popular centuries ago as the name (Imogen) of the faithful and lovable heroine of *Cymbeline*. TV: Imogene Coca, comedienne.

Ina (EYE' na) Fem. dim. via German *Katrina*. The ending *ina*, found in a number of girls' names, has become an independent name. Also an Irish name used as the equivalent of AGNES; and also probably related to INGA. Stage: Ina Claire, comedy star.

Ines (EE' ness), **Inez** (*also* EYE' nezz), respectively the Italian and Spanish forms of AGNES. YNES. Literature: Mother of Don Juan in Byron's poem *Don Juan.*

O saw ye not fair Ines?
She's gone into the West,
To dazzle when the sun is down,
And rob the world of rest.
THOMAS HOOD, *The Fair Ines*

231

Inesita Dim. form; see INES.

Inga, Inge(r) Scandinavian, from the root *ing*, variously taken to mean "battle" or "chief" or "youth." The modern name comes from the name of an ancient Germanic deity and hero known by the different names Inge, Ingo, Ingvaar, Ingvio, Ingwi, etc. Historically, the name appears in *Ingaevones*, the name of an ancient German tribe mentioned by the Roman historian Tacitus in his *Germania*. See also IGOR, INA, INGRID. Masc., ING(O)MAR. Stage and Hollywood: Inga Swenson, especially known for Shakespearean roles; Inger Stevens (Stensland), formerly of TV. Music: Inge Borkh, renowned dramatic soprano. *Inge* is also a masc. name.

Ingrid Scandinavian, Inge + (*f*)*rid*, "beautiful"; see INGA. Stage and screen: Ingrid Bergman, winner of Oscar in 1944 (*Gaslight*) and in 1956 (*Anastasia*).

Iolanthe (eye o LAN' thee) IOLE + *anthos*, Greek, "flower." Music: Gilbert and Sullivan operetta *Iolanthe*.

Iola Welsh, fem. of *Iolo*, dim. of *Iorwerth*, "lord" + "value."

Iole (EYE' o lee) Greek Mythology: daughter-in-law of Hercules.

Iona Irish place name of an ancient seat of learning, "island"; also from Welsh month-name, *Ionaur*, "January."

Ione (eye OH' nee) Greek, "a violet." Literature: Beautiful heroine of Sir Edward Bulwer-Lytton's novel *The Last Days of Pompeii*.

Irene Greek, "peace." RENE (REE' nee), IRINA, EIRENE. In England, the name Irene was formerly (and by many still is) pronounced in three syllables, as can be seen in Herrick's lines:

Angry if Irene be
But a minute's life with me.

The usual pronunciation is called for in the American folk song *Irene*:

Irene, good night,
Irene, good night,
Good night, Irene,
*   good night, Irene,*
I'll see you in my dreams.

Literature: To Sherlock Holmes, Irene Adler was always "*The* Woman," because she outwitted him so cleverly in *A Scandal in Bohemia*. In her honor, meetings of the Baker Street Irregulars always open with a toast to "*The* Woman." See under SHERLOCK. Science: Irène and her husband Frédéric Joliot-Curie shared the Nobel Prize for Chemistry (1933).

Iris Greek, "the rainbow." Also a flower name. Mythology: In the *Iliad* Iris is the messenger of the gods.

*In the spring a livelier iris
changes on the burnished
dove;
In the spring a young man's
fancy lightly turns to
thoughts of love.*
ALFRED, LORD TENNYSON,
Locksley Hall

Literature: Iris Murdock, contemporary British novelist (*The Bell, An Unofficial Rose,* etc.).

Irita (eye REE' ta) A made-up name: IDA or IRENE + RITA.

Irita Van Doren is one of the three famous Van Dorens (Carl, Mark).

Irma Germanic, "power." ERMA. A shortened form of the old Teutonic name *Ermintrude*. IRMY.

Isa (EEZ' a *or* EYE' za) Germanic, "iron." So say some authorities, but our guess is that, as used today, it is an abbrev. of ISABELLA as witness this excerpt (quoted in the *Oxford Book of Quotations*) from the candid and irreverent child-writer Marjorie Flaming (1803-1811), who not only kept a Journal but wrote a number of letters to her friend Isabella Keith, from one of which we quote:

My dear Isa, I now sit down on my bottom to answer all your

kind and beloved letters which you was so good as to write to me.

Isabel(l)e French form; see ELIZABETH. ISOBEL, ISABELLA, BELLE. Literature: Keats' long poem *Isabella or The Pot of Basil.*

*By Saint Mary, my lady,
Your mammy and your daddy
Brought forth a goodly baby,
My maiden Isabel. . . .*
JOHN SKELTON (1460-1529),
To Mistress Isabel Pennel

Isadora, Isidora See ISIDORE. Dance: Isadora Duncan (1878-1927), of world-wide fame, a great influence on the modern dance.

Is(h)bel Scottish for ISABEL.

Isolda (ee ZOLE' da), **Isolde** Celtic legendary character. See under TRISTRAM for story. ISOLT, ISEULT, YSEULT.

*I know her by her mildness rare,
Her snow-white hands, her golden hair.
I know her by her rich silk dress
And her fragile loveliness.*
MATTHEW ARNOLD,
Tristram and Iseult: Tristram.

Ivy Greek and Germanic, plant name. *Iva.* Literature: Ivy Compton-Burnett, contemporary British novelist.

J

From the Rhine to the Po, from the Thames to the Rhone,
JOANNA *or* JANNETON, JINNY *or* JOAN,
'Twas all one to her by what name she was known.

MATTHEW PRIOR, *Jinny the Just*

Jackie See JACQUELINE.

Jacqueline Dim. of French *Jacques.* See JACQUES. JACQUELYN, JACKLIN, JACKQUELIN, JACLIN, JACQUETTA, JAQUITH, JACLYN, JACKIE. America's First Lady, Jacqueline Bouvier Kennedy.

Jacynth See HYACINTH. JACINTA.

Jamie See JAMES. JAIME, JAMESINA.

Jane Fem. form; see JOHN, JANET, JAYNE, JOAN, JEAN, JANICE, JANIS, JANITH, JAN, JANEY, JENNY, JOANNE, JOANNA, etc. Literature: *Jane Eyre,* the great novel by Charlotte Brontë. Jane Austen (1775-1817), greatest woman novelist, wrote *Pride and Prejudice* when she was 21! Hollywood: Jane Fonda, Oscars 1971 (*Klute*), 1978 (*Coming Home*). Humanity: Jane Addams, American social settlement worker, co-founder of Hull House in Chicago (1889), author of two books on Hull House.

The keen stars were twinkling,
And the fair moon was rising among them,
Dear Jane!
The guitar was tinkling,
But the notes were not sweet till you sung them
Again.
PERCY BYSSHE SHELLEY,
To Jane: The Keen Stars Were Twinkling

Janet (JANN' et) See JANE. JANETTE (ja NETT'), JANICE, JANIS, JENNET, JAN(NA). Literature: Jan Struther, author of *Mrs. Miniver;* Jennet, "the lovely witch," in Christopher Fry's *The Lady's Not for Burning.* Hollywood: Janet Gaynor, winner of the first Oscar, 1928 (*Seventh Heaven, Sunrise*).

Your lips—but I have no words, Janette—
They were fresh as the twitter of birds—my pet.
CHARLES G. HALPINE,
Janette's Hair

Janice, Janis, Janith Variants; see JANE. Literature: *Janice Meredith* (1899), a once widely read novel by Paul Leicester Ford.

Janot Variant spelling of JANET.

Jasmine Persian flower name. JESSAMYN, JESSAMINE, YASMIN.

Jasmine is sweet and has many loves.
> THOMAS HOOD, *Flowers*

Jay Medieval Latin via French. Bird name. See also JAY (m).

Jean Scottish form; see JANE or JOAN. JEANNINE, JEANNETTE, JEANIE. TV: Jean Stapleton ("All in the Family").

There's not a bonnie flower that springs
> *By fountain, shaw [woods], or green;*
There's not a bonnie bird that sings,
> *But minds me o' my Jean.*
> ROBERT BURNS, *I Love My Jean*

Janie See JEAN.

I dream of Jeanie with the light brown hair,
Borne like a vapor on the summer air.
> STEPHEN FOSTER,
> *I Dream of Jeanie*

Jeanne French fem. of JEAN (m).

Jeannette French dim. form; see JEAN.

Jeannine (ja NEEN') Dim. of JEAN. NINA, NINON.

Jemima (ja MY' ma) Hebrew, "a dove."

Jennifer See GUINEVERE. Hollywood's *Song of Bernadette* spotlighted two names: Bernadette and Jennifer (Jones), winner of Oscar in 1943.

There were three sisters fair and bright,
> *Jennifer, Gentle, and Rosemary,*
And they three loved one valiant knight—
> *As the dow [dove] flies over the mulberry-tree.*
> OLD BALLAD,
> *The Riddling Knight*

Jenny JANE became JANEY; which in turn became JENNY and JINNY, JEN. Music: Jenny Lind (Johanna Maria Lind), the Swedish Nightingale, whom Barnum persuaded to tour America with him in a sensationally successful series of operatic concerts (1850-1852); Jennie Tourel.

Jenny kissed me when we met,
> *Jumping from the chair she sat in;*
Time, you thief, who love to get
> *Sweets into your list, put that in:*
Say I'm weary, say I'm sad,
> *Say that health and wealth have missed me,*
Say I'm growing old, but add,
> *Jenny kissed me.*
> LEIGH HUNT, *Rondeau*

The Jenny that Leigh Hunt referred to was Mrs. Jane Welsh Carlyle, who kissed him when he brought her husband good news.

Jeryl Short-form variant of JERALDINE. JERYLIN. See GERALDINE.

Jessamyn Popular variant of JASMINE.

Jessica Possibly Hebrew, "Jah is looking"; but more probably invented by Shakespeare. Radio: Jessica Dragonette, singing star of the early days of radio. Theater: Jessica Tandy, star of *A Streetcar Named Desire*. Literature: The name of Shylock's daughter, whom Lorenzo describes in these words:

For she is fair, if I can judge of her,
And fair she is, if but mine eyes be true,
And true she is, as she hath prov'd herself.
　　　　WILLIAM SHAKESPEARE,
　　　　The Merchant of Venice

Jessie Scottish pet form; see JANET. In a poem called *Jessie, the Flower o' Dumblane*, the poet Robert Tannahill expressed his love for Janet Tennant:

Sae dear to this bosom, sae artless and winning,
Is charming young Jessie, the flow'r o' Dumblane.

Jewel Latin via French, "jest, toy." A jewel name like CHRYSTAL. JEWELLE.

Why, man, she is my own,
And I as rich in having such a jewel
As twenty seas, if all their sand were pearl,
The water nectar and the rocks pure gold.
　　　　WILLIAM SHAKESPEARE,
　　　　The Two Gentlemen of Verona

Jill Pet form of GILLIAN. See JULIANA. Jill is now an independent name. JILLANA. Hollywood: Jill St. John.

Jack shall have Jill;
Nought shall go ill.
　　　　WILLIAM SHAKESPEARE,
　　　　A Midsummer Night's Dream

Jinny Scottish pet form of JANE and American pet form of VIRGINIA.

Jo A shortening of JOAN, JOANNA, or JOSEPHINE, who is the Jo of *Little Women*.

Joan See JOHN. Joan of Arc, the Maid of Orleans, a patron saint of France.

First in the ranks see Joan of Arc advance,
The scourge of England and the boast of France.
　　　　GEORGE GORDON BYRON,
　　　　English Bards

Literature: *St. Joan*, play by George Bernard Shaw; *Joan of Arc*, a biography by Mark Twain. Hollywood: Joan Crawford, winner of an Oscar in 1945

(*Mildred Pierce*). Opera: Joan Sutherland, Australian soprano, acclaimed as one of the greatest singers of our time.

Joanna See JOHN. JOHANNA, JOANN, JO-ANN, JO ANN, JOJO, JOANNE. Hollywood: Joanne Woodward, winner of an Oscar in 1957 (*The Three Faces of Eve*).

Jobina, Jobyna (jo BEE′ na) See JOB.

Jocelyn (JOSS′ a linn) See JOYCE. JOSSELYN, JOYCELIN.

Jody A variant of JUDY or pet form of JOAN.

Joelle See JOEL.

Johanna See JOHN.

Jolie (JOE′ lee) French, "pretty." JOLINE.

Josepha Feminine of JOSEPH. JOSEFA.

Josephine See JOSEPH. JO, FIFI (duplicative baby-talk form via FIFINE). Napoleon's Empress Josephine, who made the name popular, was born Marie Josèphe Rose. Literature: Josephine Tey, pen name of Elizabeth Mackintosh, master of superior style of mystery novels (*The Singing Sands, A Shilling for Candles*, etc.).

I sit alone, but not alone:
A spirit all unseen
flown—
Has to my welcome bosom
flown—
My darling Josephine.
    JOHN W. WATSON,
    My Darling Josephine

Joy Latin, "joy." May also be considered a shortening of JOYCE.

"I have no name;
I am but two days old."
What shall I call thee?
"I happy am,
Joy is my name."
Sweet joy befall thee!
    WILLIAM BLAKE, *Infant Joy*

Joyce Probably Latin, "joyous"; or Germanic, "Gothic." Also used as a masculine name (novelist Joyce Cary and poet Joyce Kilmer). An increasingly popular girl's name, expressing the same idea but having more substance than JOY.

Juanita (hwah NEE′ ta) Spanish dim. of JOAN. Music: The oft-sung *Juanita*.

Judith Hebrew, "of Judah." JUDY. Biblical: In the apocryphal Book of Judith, a woman of extraordinary beauty, who saved her native town by killing the invader Holofernes. Stage: Judith Anderson. Opera: Judith Blegen.

*Who is she, the pale-browed
    stranger
    Bending o'er that son of
        slaughter?
God be with thee in thy danger
    Israel's lone and peerless
        daughter!*
    JOHN GREENLEAF WHITTIER,
    Judith at the Tent of Holofernes

Judy An independent name;
see JUDITH. Stage and Screen:
Judy Holliday, winner of 1950
Oscar (*Born Yesterday*); the
sensational Judy Garland.

*For the Colonel's Lady an' Judy
    O'Grady
Are sisters under their skins!*
    RUDYARD KIPLING, *The Ladies*

Julia See JULIUS. JULIANA, JU-
LIANNE, JULIE. Theater: Julia
Marlowe, stage name of Sarah
Frances Frost, starred in Shake-
spearean roles. Literature: Julia
Peterkin, novelist, Pulitzer Prize
for *Scarlet Sister Mary* (1929).

*Some asked me where the rubies
    grew,
    And nothing I did say;
But with my finger pointed to
    The lips of Julia.*
    ROBERT HERRICK,
    The Lock of Rubies

Juliana See JULIA. LIANA. (lee
ANN' a *or* lee AH' na).

*Your courteous lights in vain
    you waste,
    Since Juliana here is come,*

*For she my mind hath so dis-
    placed,
    That I shall never find my
        home.*
    ANDREW MARVELL,
    The Mower to the Glow-Worms

Julie See JULIUS. Stage and
TV: Julie Harris; Julie Andrews,
the first Eliza of *My Fair Lady*.
Literature: The title of one of
August Strindberg's most important plays has been variously
translated as *Miss Julie, Countess Julia,* and *Lady Julia*.

Juliet Dim. form; see JULIA.
Shakespeare, who "made" the
name, got it from the Italian
Giulietta. JULIETTE.

*But, soft! What light through
    yonder window breaks?
It is the East, and Juliet is the
    sun!*
    WILLIAM SHAKESPEARE,
    Romeo and Juliet

June A month name; from
Juno or the *gens* name *Junius*.
JUNETTA, JUNIS.

*And what is so rare as a day in
    June?
    Then, if ever, come perfect
        days;
Then Heaven tries the earth if it
    be in tune,
    And over it softly her warm
        ear lays.*
    JAMES RUSSELL LOWELL,
    The Vision of Sir Launfal

Justine See JUSTIN. JUSTINA.
Justina, a fourth-century martyr,
is a patron saint of Padua, Italy.
Literature: *Justine*, the first
novel of the *Alexandria Quartet*
by Lawrence Durrell.

I know, Justine, you wear a smile
  As beaming as the sun;
But who supposes all the while
  It shines for only one?
          JOHN GODFREY SAXE,
          Justine, You Love Me Not

K

*Sweet KATE, who could view your bright eyes
    of deep blue,*
   *Beaming humidly through the dark lashes so
    mildly,*
  *Your fair-turned arm, heaving breast, rounded
    form,*
    *Nor feel his heart warm, and his pulses throb
    wildly?*

JOHN FRANCIS WALLER, *Kitty Neil*

Karel See CAROL.

Karen Danish form; see KATHERINE. KARIN, CAREN. Psychiatry: Karen Horney.

Kate A pet form; see KATHERINE. KATIE, KATY. Literature; Kate Hardcastle, Oliver Goldsmith's heroine who "stoops to conquer" (1773); in *The Taming of the Shrew*, the strongwilled lady of Padua courted by Petruchio, whose command, *Come on, and kiss me, Kate*, furnished the title of the musical by Cole Porter—Shakespeare—the Spewacks.

Methinks I hear the maids declare,
  The promised Mary, when seen,
Not half so fragrant, half so fair,
  As Kate of Aberdeen.
        JOHN CUNNINGHAM,
        Kate of Aberdeen

Katharine, Katherine Greek, "pure." KATHRYN, KATHE, KATE, KAY, KATHLEEN, KITTY, KAREN, KASS. There are seven saints of this name, the earliest and most famous being the marthyrized fourth-century St. Katherine of Alexandria. Hollywood: Katharine Hepburn, winner of Oscars in 1933, 1967, 1968, 1981. Theater: Katharine Cornell, great lady of the American stage. Literature: Two great writers of short stories: Katherine Anne Porter, American; Katherine Mansfield, British, born in New Zealand.

Kathe, Kathy See KATHERINE.

Kathleen Irish form; see KATHERINE. Popular Song: *I'll Take You Home Again, Kathleen* (1876).

Kathleen mavourneen! [my darling] the grey dawn is breaking.
The horn of the hunter is heard on the hill.
        JULIA CRAWFORD,
        Kathleen Mavourneen

Katie See KATHERINE.

240

But only when my Katie's voice
Makes all the listening woods re-
joice
I hear—with cheeks that flush
and pale—
The passion of the nightingale.
                HENRY TIMROD, *Katie*

Kay(e)   See KATHERINE. Literature: Kay Boyle, American novelist and short-story writer.

Kim   See KIM (m). Kim Stanley
was born Patricia Kimberly
Reed (Stanley is her mother's
family name) so that in her case
the name *Kim* is a shortening of
Kimberly. The other two famous
actresses bearing the same first
name are Kim Novak and Kim
Hunter. (See under "Hollywood"
in chapter "Where Our Names
Come From.")

Kirby   See KIRBY (m).

Kitty   See KATHERINE. Literature: *Kitty Foyle* (1939), a novel
by Christopher Morley.

Fondness prevail'd, mamma gave
way;
Kitty, at heart's desire,
Obtain'd the chariot for a day,
And set the world on fire.
                MATTHEW PRIOR,
                The Female Phaeton

Kyle   See KYLE (m). Stage and
Television: Kyle MacDonnell.

Kyra   Variant of CYRA. See CY-
RUS.

L

When LAURA *smiles*
Her sight revives
Both night and day;
The earth and heaven
Views with delight
Her wanton play.

> THOMAS CAMPION,
> *When Laura Smiles*

Lana (LANN' a *or* LAH' na)
There is a Latin word *lana*,
meaning "wool," and it's nice—
but hardly accurate—to think
that wool, out of which sweaters
are made, has something to do
with the Hollywood star who
made sweaters what they are today. Hollywood: Lana Turner.

Laraine See LORRAINE and
LAURA. Hollywood: Laraine Day.

Laura See LAURENCE. LORA,
LORETTA, LORI, LAUREL, LOR-
RAINE, LAURE(N), LAURI, LOREN,
LOLLY, LAUREY, LARAINE, LOR-
RIE. See DAPHNE. In the year
1327 in a church in Avignon,
Petrarch first saw Laure de
Noves, the sight of whom, he
later said, made him a poet. The
famous sonnets that this great
Italian scholar and poet wrote in
the ensuing years immortalized
the name of Laura, but made
Byron, in his *Don Juan,* ask the
impertinent question:

Think you, if Laura had been
* Petrarch's wife,*
He would have written sonnets
* all his life?*

Hollywood: Lauren Bacall.

Laurel Derived from LAURA or
used independently as a plant
name. The ancient Greeks
crowned victors of certain games
and holders of certain offices
with a wreath of laurel leaves.
Hence, "to gain the laurels" denotes victory or honor. In England the official court poet is
called the Poet Laureate.

The laurel, meed of mighty con-
* querors*
And poets sage.

> EDMUND SPENSER,
> *Faerie Queene*

Music: Laurel Hurley, vivacious soprano of the Metropolitan Opera.

Laurette See LAURA. LORETTA,
LAURETTA. Stage: Laurette Tay-
lor, famous for roles in *Peg o'*
My Heart (1912) and *The Glass*
Menagerie (1945).

Laverne, LaVerne See VERNON.

Lavinia Literature: Wife of
Aeneas in Vergil's *Aeneid*. VIN-
NIE.

She is a woman—therefore may
be wooed;
She is a woman—therefore may
be won;
She is Lavinia, therefore must be
loved.
WILLIAM SHAKESPEARE,
Titus Andronicus

Leah Hebrew, "weary." LEA, LEE, LEIGH. Biblical: Sister of Rachel and first wife of Jacob.

Leah was tender eyed.
GENESIS 29:17

Leane (lee AYN') Perhaps LEE + ANN; also see LIANA. LEANNE.

Leatrice Probably a telescoped name, made up of LEAH and BEATRICE.

Leda Greek, "lady." Greek mythology. Zeus appeared to her in the form of a swan. Mother of four famous children: Helen, Castor, Pollux, and Clytemnestra.

Lee, Lea Short form of many names: LEAH, LELAND, LENA. Screen: Lee Remick.

Leigh See LEIGH (m). Also used as a variant of LEAH.

Leila (LEE' la) Arabic, "dark as night." LELA, LAYLA. Used as a variant of the more familiar LILY. Literature: The beautiful slave girl in Byron's long narrative poem *The Giaour*.

Lelia Latin, from *Laelius*, a *gens* name.

Lena, Lina (LEE' na) From the ending of names like HELENA and MAGDALENA. Used as an independent name. LENETTE. Stage, Screen, and TV: Lena Horne.

Leonore Probably a form of ELEANOR. See HELEN. LEONORA. Stage: Lenore Ulric.

For the rare and radiant maiden
whom the angels name
Lenore.
EDGAR ALLAN POE, *The Raven*

Leona Fem. form of LEON. See LEO. LEONIA, LEONIE, LEONE. Music: Leontyne Price, opera and concert artist.

Leonora See LENORE. Literature: Leonora Speyer, winner of Pulitzer Prize in poetry, 1927. Music: In Beethoven's opera, the heroine who assumes the name *Fidelio*. Of the four different overtures written for this opera, three are entiled *Leonora No. 1, Leonora No. 2,* and *Leonora No. 3,* the best-known.

Leopoldine See LEOPOLD.

Leora (lee o' ra) Probably a contracted variant of LEONORA. Literature: The self-effacing and altogether admirable wife of Martin Arrowsmith in Sinclair Lewis' novel.

Lesley, Leslie LESLY(E). See LESLIE (m). Hollywood: Leslie Caron (*Gigi*).

O saw ye bonnie Lesley
  As she gaed o'er the border?
She's gone like Alexander,
  To spread her conquests far-
    ther.
To see her is to love her,
  And love but her for ever,
For Nature made her what she
  is,
And ne'er made anither.
    ROBERT BURNS, *Bonnie Lesley*

Leta (LEE′ ta) See LETITIA.

Letitia (le TISH′ a) Latin, "joy." LAETITIA, LETICIA, LETIZIA, LETISHA, LETA, LETTY. TISH. Literature: Tish, the dauntless, adventurous heroine of Mary Robert Rinehart's *Tish* series of short stories and of the longer *Adventures of Letitia Carberry.*

But when we turn'd her sweet
  unlearned eye
On our own isle, she raised a
  joyous cry—
"Ol Yes, I see it, Letty's home
  is there!"
  And while she hid all England
    with a kiss,
Bright over Europe fell her
  golden hair.
    CHARLES TENNYSON TURNER,
      Letty's Globe

Liana (lee ANN′ a) Terminal abbrev. form; see JULIANA. LIANE.

Libby See ELIZABETH. LIBBIE. Stage: Libby Holman.

Lida (LYE′ da) Slavic, "beloved of the people." See also ALIDA. LYDA.

Lila (LYE′ la) See LEILA.

Lilian Latin, "the lily." LILLIAN, LILIANE, LILY, LILLA(H), LIL, LILLI, LILLES, LILLIAS. Hollywood and Stage: Lillian Gish. Theater: Lillian Hellman, playwright (*The Little Foxes,* etc.).

Airy, fairy Lilian,
Flitting, fairy Lilian,
When I ask her if she love me,
Clasps her tiny hand above me
Laughing all she can.
    ALFRED, LORD TENNYSON,
      Lillian

Lilla(h) See LILIAN.

Lilli See LILIAN. Stage, Screen, and TV: Lilli Palmer.

Lily See LILIAN. Music: Lily Pons of the Metropolitan Opera, long a favorite star.

Linda Terminal abbrev. of names like *Melinda, Belinda, Rosalinda, Sieglinda,* etc., but now associated with the Spanish word *linda,* "pretty." LYNDA. In 1957 George Gallup reported that the most popular name for girls born during the previous ten years was LINDA, passing Mary, Elizabeth, Margaret, and Ann. Music: Linda Ronstadt.

Linden English tree name.

Lindsey (LINN' dzee) See LIND-
SAY (m).

Linnet, Lynnet A bird name or
a medieval French form of
Welsh *Eiluned*, "idol." Tennyson popularized the spelling
Lynette in *Gareth and Lynette*,
in which he describes her as:

*A damsel of high lineage; and a
brow*
*May-blossom; and a cheek of
apple-blossom;*
*Hawk-eyes; and lightly was her
slender nose,*
*Tip-tilted like the petal of a
flower.*

Lisa (LEE' za) See ELIZABETH.
LEESA.

Lisle, Lyle See LYLE (m).

Lita (LEE' ta) Fem. ending of
names like *Carmelita* and *Es-
trellita;* used as an independent
name.

*So through the season, where
you go,*
All else than Lita men forget.
EDMUND CLARENCE STEDMAN,
Witchcraft

Livia Latin, *Livius*, a *gens*
name. Also pet form of OLIVIA.
LIVVIE. History: Wife of Augustus.

Liz, Lizzie Pet form of ELIZA-
BETH. LIZETTE, LISETTE, LIZA-
BETH.

White and golden Lizzie stood
Like a lily in a flood.
CHRISTINA ROSSETTI,
Goblin Market

Liza (LYE' za) See ELIZABETH.
Screen: Liza Minnelli, Oscar
1972 (*Cabaret*).

Lois (LO' iss) Biblical: Grandmother of Timothy.

Lola See DOLORES. LOLITA, LO-
LETA, LOLETTE. The baptismal
name of Lola Montez (1818-
1861), world-famous British-
born dancer, was Marie Dolores
Eliza Rosanna Gilbert. Music:
The beautiful woman in Mas-
cagni's opera *Cavalleria Rusti-
cana* based on a famous short
story by Giovanni Verga.

Lolly See LAURA. Another example of the *r* changing to *l* in
a pet name (Mary to Molly,
Harold to Hal, Sarah to Sally).
Literature: *Lolly Willowes*
(1926) by Sylvia Townsend
Warner.

Lora A variant spelling of
LAURA. LORELLA, LORELLE.

Lorelei (LAWR' a lye) Germanic, "the alluring." LURLINE,
LORILEE. Literature: The famous
poem by Heinrich Heine; Lorelei, heroine of Anita Loos's
novel and play *Gentlemen Prefer Blondes*, whose outlook on
life is summed up in "Diamonds
are a girl's best friends."

Lorene, Lorine See LAURA. LO-
RENA, LURENA.

Loretta Dim. of LORA; see
LAURA. Hollywood: Loretta
Young, winner of Oscar in 1947
(*The Farmer's Daughter*).

Lorinda See LAURA.

Lorna From literature. Invented by Richard D. Black-
more for the name of his heroine in his best-selling novel
Lorna Doone (1869).

Lorraine French, "of Lorraine." LARAINE. Generally used
as a variant of the more usual
LORA and LAURA. Theater: Lorraine Hansberry, playwright
(*Raisin in the Sun*).

Lottie See CHARLOTTE. LOTTA,
LOTTE, LOTTY. Music: Lotte Leh-
mann, beloved opera star and re-
nowned singer of *lieder*. Stage:
Lotte Lenya (*The Threepenny
Opera*), wife of Kurt Weill.

Louella, Luella Probably a telescoping of LUCY or LOUISE and
ELLA. LOU, LU.

Louisa, Louise See LOUIS. LOU,
LU, LULU. LOUISA and LOUISE
were favorite names of the European women of royalty in the
seventeenth and eighteenth centuries, but none of them are
more famous than "the little
women" of Louisa May Alcott.
Literature: Louise de la Ramée,
better known as "Ouida," a delightful baby mispronunciation
of "Louisa"; author under that
pen name of two best sellers,
Under Two Flags (1867) and *A
Dog of Flanders* (1872).
Screen: Luise Rainer.

How shall any poet's rhyme,
  Made of liquid language, be
Blended in the silver chime
  Of a madrigal for thee,
    Beautiful Louise!
      WILLIAM HENRY VENABLE,
        Louise

Luba Slavic, "love."

Lucasta From literature: Invented (Latin *lux*, "light," +
casta, "chaste") by Richard
Lovelace (1618-1658) for Lucy
Sacheverell, to whom he wrote:

Yet this inconstancy is such,
  As you too shall adore;
I could not love thee dear, so
    much,
  Lov'd I not honor more.
        To Lucasta,
      on Going to the Wars

Lucetta See LUCY.

*But say, Lucetta, now we are
    alone,*
*Wouldst thou then counsel me
    to fall in love?*
      WILLIAM SHAKESPEARE,
    The Two Gentlemen of Verona

Lucia (LOO' she) See LUCIUS.
LUCIE, LUCINE. Opera: Donizet-

ti's *Lucia di Lammermoor,* based on the novel *Bride of Lammermoor* by Sir Walter Scott; Lucine Amara of the Met.

Lucille See LUCY. TV, Stage, and Hollywood: Lucille Ball.

Lucinda Poetic variation of LUCY. CINDY, LUCKY.

When Lucinda's blooming beauty
  Did the wondering town surprise,
With the first I paid my duty,
  Fixing there my wandering eyes.

Her kind spring each hour discloses
  Charms we nowhere else can trace;
Gayer than the blush on roses
  Are the glories on her face.
    ANON.,
    Seventeenth-Century Lyric

Lucretia Latin, name of a *gens,* probably meaning "gain." LUCRECE, LUCREZIA. Fem. of *Lucretius,* name of Roman poet whose long poem, *De Rerum Natura* ("Concerning the Nature of Things"), dealing in part with atoms, is one of the world's great books. Music: Former opera star Lucrezia Bori.

Let my hands frame your face in your hair's gold,
You beautiful Lucrezia that are mine.
    ROBERT BROWNING,
    Andrea del Sarto.

Lucy See LUCIUS. LUCIE, LUCIENNE. Literature: Lucie Manette, heroine of Dickens' *A Tale of Two Cities.*

A violet by a mossy stone
  Half-hidden from the eye!
Fair as a star, when only one
  Is shining in the sky.
    WILLIAM WORDSWORTH, *Lucy*

Ludmilla (lood MEE' la) "loved by the people."

Lulu Duplicative form of LOUISE or LUCY (like BEBE, FIFI, MIMI).

Lulu is our darling pride,
Lulu bright, Lulu gay,
Dancing lightly at our side
All the livelong day.
    OLD SONG

Lydia Latin, "a woman of Lydia," an ancient country in Asia Minor once ruled by the fabulously wealthy Croesus.

When Lydia smiles, I seem to see
The walls around me fade and flee
  And, lo, in haunts of hart and hind
  I seem with lovely Rosalind
In Arden 'neath the greenwood tree . . .
Ah, me! What were this world to me
Without her smile! — What poetry,
  What glad hesperian paths I find
  Of love, that lead my soul and mind

To happy hills of Arcady
        When Lydia smiles!
            MADISON CAWEIN,
            When Lydia Smiles

Lynn(e) See LYNN (m); but this name is probably only the ending of such names as MADE-LYN, ROSLYN, etc., adopted as an independent and very popular modern name. Stage star: Lynn Fontanne, wife of Alfred Lunt, with whom she forms one of the most famous couples in theatrical history. Stage and Screen: Lynn Redgrave (*Georgy Girl*).

Lynette See LINNET.

M

I have a passion for the name of MARY,
For once it was a magic sound to me:
And still it half calls up the realm of fairy,
Where I beheld what never was to be.

LORD BYRON, *Don Juan*

Mabel Latin, *amabilis*, "lovable." Though the full name *Amabel* is rarely seen today, its shortened form *Mabel* (not a combination of MAY and BELLE) is one of our most popular names. *Amabel* has also, according to our best authorities, dissolved into ANNABEL, which is, in spite of its appearance, not related to ANNA. Hollywood: Mabel Normand, comic of silent era.

Fairest of the fairest, rival of the
rose,
That is Mabel of the Hills, as
everybody knows. . .
Has she scores of lovers, heaps
of bleeding beaux?
That question's quite superfluous, as everybody knows.
JAMES T. FIELDS, *Mabel in*
New Hampshire

Madeline Hebrew, "woman of Magdala," an ancient town on the sea of Galilee. MADELAINE, MADELYN, MADLIN, MAGDALINE, MAGDALENE, MAGDA, MATTY, MADELEINE. Literature: Heroine of John Keats' *Eve of St. Agnes.*

My Madeline! sweet dreamer!
lovely bride!

Say, may I be for aye thy vassal
blest?
Thy beauty's shield, heart-shaped
and vermeil dyed?
Ah, silver shrine, here will I
take my rest.

Madelon French form; see MAUD(E). Also considered variant of MADELEINE. Music: The song of the *poilus* and doughboys of World War I:

She laughs; that's all the harm
she knows to do,
Madelon, Madelon, Madelon!

Madge See MARGARET.

I'm Madge of the country; I'm
Madge of the town,
And I'm Madge of the lad I
am blithest to own—
The Lady of Beever in diamonds
may shine,
But has not a heart half so
lightsome as mine.
SIR WALTER SCOTT,
Heart of Midlothian

Mae See MAY. Hollywood: Mae Murray of the silent era.

Magda See MADELINE. Literature: Leading character in plays by Hauptmann (*The Sunken Bell*) and Sudermann (*Magda*).

Maggie See MARGARET. MAGGI. Literature: Maggie Wylie, heroine of Barrie's *What Every Woman Knows;* Maggie Tulliver, heroine of George Eliot's *Mill on the Floss*. Screen: Maggie Smith, Oscar 1969 (*The Prime of Miss Jean Brodie*).

Magna See MAGNUS.

Magnolia Flower name.

Mahala, Mahalia Hebrew: "tenderness." Music: Mahalia Jackson, singer of spirituals.

Maia Greek, "nurse," or "mother." Mythology: One of the Pleiades, daughter of Atlas and Pleione, and mother of Hermes (Mercury) by Zeus (Jupiter). The month of May was named after her by the Romans.

Maida Germanic, "maiden." Also place name in Italy, scene of a British victory (1806).

Maisie Scottish dim. form; see MARGARET.

Proud Maisie is in the wood Walking so early.
SIR WALTER SCOTT, *Proud Maisie*

Malvina (mal VEE′ na) See MELVIN. MALVEEN. Arts: Malvina Hoffman, American sculptor

and author; elected to National Academy of Design in 1931.

Mamie Pet form; see MARY, MAY, or MARGARET. MAYMIE.

Boys and girls together, Me and Mamie O'Rourke, Tripped the light fantastic On the sidewalks of New York.
JAMES W. BLAKE, *The Sidewalks of New York* (1894)

Manon (MAN AWN′) French pet form of MARIANNE. See MARY. Literature: Heroine of a celebrated novel by the Abbé Prévost (1751). Opera: *Manon* by Massenet; *Manon Lescaut* by Puccini.

Ah, Manon, say, why is it we Are one and all so fain of thee?
ERNEST DOWSON, *Rondeau*

Manuela Spanish fem. form; see EMANUEL.

Manya (MONN′ ya) Slavic pet form; see MARY and MOLLY.

Mara Hebrew, "bitter." This name is actually considered to be a variant of MARY, especially as used today. However, in its appearance in the book of Ruth (1:20), *Mara* is not really a name. Moreover, *Miriam*, from which *Mary* is derived, occurs independently (see MIRIAM).

And she said unto them, Call me not Naomi, call me Mara: for the Almighty hath dealt very bitterly with me.

Marcella See MARCELLUS. MARCELLE, MARCELLINE, MARCIE, MARCY. In *Don Quixote,* Marcella, a shepherdess, is described as "the most beautiful creature ever sent into the world," with whom every eligible young man falls madly in love.

Marchette Dim. of MARCIA. MARQUITA, MARKETA. Literature: Marchette Chute, author of *Shakespeare of London and the* fascinating retelling, *Stories from Shakespeare.*

Marcia (MAR' sha) See MARCUS. MARSHA, MARTIA.

Marcy See MARCELLA. MARCIA.

Margalo (MAR' ga lo) Variant; see MARGO. Stage: Margalo Gilmore.

Margaret Latin via Greek, "a pearl." MARGARETTE, MARGUERITE, MARGUERITA, MARGHERITA, RITA, MARGERY, MARJORIE, MAGGY, MEG, PEG, PEGGY, META, MAISIE, MADGE, MARGO(T), MARGA, MARGALO, GRETTA, GRETCHEN, GRETEL. In Matthew Arnold's poem, Margaret is the lovely mortal who forsakes her merman husband and her children to return to her native town. Her children frantically call her back to the kingdom of the sea in these words:

"Mother dear, we cannot stay!
The wild white horses foam and
fret."
Margaret! Margaret!
     The Forsaken Merman

Literature: Margaret Mitchell, author of *Gone With the Wind,* one of the best sellers of all time. Won Pulitzer Prize in 1937. The moving-picture version broke all existing records. Stage and screen: Margaret Leighton, winner of a Tony in 1962 (*The Night of the Iguana*).

Margery, Marjorie See MARGARET. MADGE, MARGIE.

Of a' the maids o' fair Scotland,
The fairest was Marjorie.
     OLD BALLAD, *Young Benjie*

Margo(t) (MAR' go) See MARGARET. Stage and Screen: Margo (Maria Margarita Bolado), born in Mexico City. Ballet: Dame Margot Fonteyn, prima ballerina of the Royal Ballet Company.

Marguerite (mar ga REET') French form of MARGARET. MARGIT. Opera: Heroine of Gounod's *Faust.* The French word *marguerite* means "daisy," the meaning Charles Lamb gives to the name in the poem called *To Margaret W:*

Margaret, in happy hour
Christen'd from that humble
     flower
  Which we a daisy call!
May thy pretty namesake be
In all things a type of thee,
  And image thee in all.

Maria (ma REE' a *or* ma RYE' a) Latin form of MARY. Ballet: Maria Tallchief.

Mariamne Ancient form of MIRIAM. MARIAM. Mariamne, the Jewish princess, wife of Herod the Greek, is the subject of a number of plays, among them Voltaire's *Mariamne* (1724).

Marian See MARY and MARION (m). *Marianne* (ma ree AHN') is to the French Republic what *Uncle Sam* and *John Bull* are to the United States and England. Literature: Marianne Moore, distinguished American poet, winner of 1952 Pulitzer Prize for poetry. Folklore and Literature: Maid Marian, Queen of the May in the old May games in England; sweetheart of Robin Hood in the legends, ballads, and later poems about him:

Honor to Maid Marian,
And to all the Sherwood clan!
    JOHN KEATS, *Robin Hood*

Mariana See MARY. Literature: the charming and beautiful wife of Angelo in Shakespeare's *Measure for Measure.*

Maribel(l)e A combination of MARY and BEL(LE) (like CLARIBEL).

Maridel, Meridel A lengthened form of MARY.

Marie French form; see MARY. MARITA, MARITTA, MARIETTA, MARILEE, MARILLA, MARILISSE. Hollywood: Marie Dressler, winner of Oscar in 1931 (*Min and Bill*). Science: Born Maria Skladowska, she became famous as Marie Curie, sharing Nobel Prize (1911) with her husband, Pierre Curie, for work on radium and its compounds.

Come to me, sweet Marie, sweet
*   Marie, come to me,*
Not because your face is fair,
*   love, to see,*
But your soul, so pure and sweet,
Makes my happiness complete,
Makes me falter at your feet,
*   sweet Marie.*
    CY WARMAN, *Sweet Marie*

Marigold Flower name.

Marilyn At the moment the most popular variation of MARY. Stage: Marilyn Miller (1898-1936), beloved musical star of *Ziegfeld Follies, Sunny, Sally, Rosalie,* etc., whom John Mason Brown called "the smiling embodiment of grace." Hollywood: The incomparable Marilyn Monroe.

Marina (ma REE' na *or* MA' rinn a) Latin, "of the sea." MARNA, RENA. Royalty: Name of the Duchess of Kent, known as one of the best-dressed women in the world. Literature: Shakespearean heroine, beautiful and courageous.

My gentle babe Marina,
*   whom,*
For she was born at sea, I have
*   named so.*
    WILLIAM SHAKESPEARE,
    Pericles, Prince of Tyre

Maris Latin, "of the sea." See MARINA, MARRIS. Also a variant of MARY or shortened form of MARISA.

Maris(s)a See MARY. MARESSA, MARITZA.

Marjorie See MARGERY. Literature: *Marjorie Daw*, celebrated short story by Thomas Bailey Aldrich; Marjorie Kinnan Rawlings, winner of Pulitzer Prize (1938) for *The Yearling*.

Marlene (mar LEEN' *or* mar LAYN' a) One of the lengthened variations of MARY. MARLENA, MARLEEN. Screen star: Marlene Dietrich, who coincidentally popularized *Lili Marlene*, the soldier song of World War II, originally sung by the Germans.

Marna See MARINA. MARNI, MARNIE, MARNY, MARNETTE. Hollywood: Marni Nixon, famous "ghost" singer who does the singing for well-known actresses in equally well-known films (*The King and I, West Side Story*, etc.); her voice is heard, her name unheard! However, Miss Nixon's name is printed on recordings of songs and on theater programs; she received due credit when she sang with the New York Philharmonic, Leonard Bernstein conducting!

Down the world with Marna,
Daughter of the air!
Marna of the subtle grace,
And the vision in her face!
　　　　RICHARD HOVEY,
　　　　The Wander-Lovers

Martha Aramaic, "a lady." MARTA, MATTY, MARTY, MARTITA, Biblical: Sister of Mary Magdalen and Lazarus; patron saint of housewives. History: America's first First Lady. Music: Friedrich von Flotow's light opera *Martha*. Choreography: Martha Graham, pioneer in American modern dance. Folk Singer: Martha Schlamme.

Martina (mar TEE' na) Fem. form; see MARTIN.

Marva See MARVEL.

Marvel(a) Latin, "wonderful."

Mary New Testament form of MIRIAM. MARIA, MARIE, MARIAN, MOLLY. Biblical: Mother of Christ; also the name of a number of saints and numerous queens of England and Europe. Music: Mary Garden, one of the great dramatic sopranos. Hollywood: Mary Pickford, darling of the silent pictures.

Is thy name Mary, maiden fair?
　　Such should, methinks, its
　　　　music be;
The sweetest name that mortals
　　bear
　　Were best befitting thee;
And she to whom it once was
　　given,
　　Was half of earth and half of
　　　　heaven.
　　　　OLIVER WENDELL HOLMES,
　　　　L'Inconnue

Mat(h)ilda Germanic, "mighty battlemaid." MAUD(E), MATTY, TILLY, MATTIE, TILDA. Music: Famous Australian folk song *Waltzing Matilda*.

Maud(e) Dim. form; see MA-TILDA. Stage: Maude Adams, famous American actress, still remembered for her Peter Pan. Literature: Tennyson's long dramatic poem *Maud* (1855) with its famous line "Come into the garden, Maud" helped to popularize the use of this name, as did Whittier's *Maud Muller* (1856).

Maud Muller, on a summer's day,
Raked the meadow sweet with hay.
Beneath her torn hat glowed the wealth
Of simple beauty and rustic health.
  JOHN GREENLEAF WHITTIER, *Maud Muller*

History and Literature: Maud Gonne, the great lady of the Irish Republican movement, to whom William Butler Yeats wrote several of his plays and poems. The loveliest of the latter is *When You Are Old*.

Maureen Irish dim. form; see MARY. MAURINE, MAURA. Hollywood: Maureen O'Hara. Music: Maureen Forrester, contralto. Stage: Maureen Stapleton.

O you plant the pain in my heart with your wistful eyes,
Girl of my choice, Maureen!
Will you drive me mad for the kisses your shy sweet mouth denies, Maureen?
  JOHN TODHUNTER, *Maureen*

Mavis (MAY' viss) French, "thrush."

Maxine See MAX. Stage: Maxine Elliott, famous American actress.

May Dim. of MARY; also a month name. See MAIA.

Then came fair May, the fairest maid on the ground,
Deck'd all with dainties of her season's pride.
  EDMUND SPENSER, *The Seasons*

Meg See MARGARET. The more usual modern dim. is the rhyming Peg(gy).

Meg was meek, and Meg was mild
Sweet and harmless as a child.
  ROBERT BURNS, *Whistle O'er the Lave o't.*

Megan (MEGG' an *or* MAY' g'n) Irish and Welsh dim. form; see MARGARET. Literature: The lovely Welsh heroine of Galsworthy's tender and exquisite short story *The Apple Tree*.

Melanie (MELL' a nee) Greek, "dark." MELLONEY. The original vogue of *Melanie* is due to two saints at the time of St. Jerome. Its present use owes something to *Gone With the Wind*.

Melba Place name, from Melbourne. See NELLIE.

Melinda A seventeenth-century poetic name coined in imitation of BELINDA.

Melissa Greek, "a bee." See also DEBORAH. Ballet: Melissa Hayden. MELITTA.

Mella See CARMELA. MELA.

Melodie, Melody Greek, "song."

Melva. See MELVINA and MELBA.

Mercedes (mur SEE' deez or MUR' sid eez) Spanish, *Maria de Mercedes*, "Mary of Mercies." See under DOLORES. Literature: The sweetheart of Edmond Dantès, Count of Monte Cristo.

Mercedes in her hammock swings;
In her court a palm-tree flings
Its slender shadow on the ground,
The fountain falls with silver sound.
ELIZABETH STODDARD, *Mercedes*

Mercy See CHARITY. MERRY.

Meredith Welsh, "magnificent"; Celtic, "sea protector." MERRY.

Merit, Merritt English, "merit." MERRY.

Merle Latin via French, "a blackbird." MERLA, MYRLE. Screen star: Merle Oberon.

Merrie Anglo-Saxon, "pleasant, merry." Also pet name of MEREDITH and MERCY. MERRIELLE.

Merrill See MERRILL. (m). MERYL. MERRILEE, MERRILY.

Meryl Variant of MERLE or MURIEL. Screen: Meryl Streep, Oscar 1982 (*Sophie's Choice*).

Michaela (mick EYE' la *or* mick ah AY' la) Fem. of MICHAEL.

Michel(l)e French fem. form; see MICHAEL. MICHELINE, MIDGE, MICKIE. Screen: Michelle Morgan.

Mignon (min YUN') French, "delicate, dainty." MIGNONNE, MIGNON(N)ETTE. Literature: Mignon Eberhart, American detective-story writer. Music: Heroine of Ambroise Thomas' opera *Mignon*, based on Goethe's *Wilhelm Meister*.

Mildred Germanic, "mildpower." MILLIE.

Mil(l)icent Germanic, "workstrength." MELICENT, MILLIE.

Millie See MILDRED, MILLICENT, EMILY, and CAMILLE.

Mimi (MEE MEE') Baby-talk duplicative of MIRIAM (formed like BEBE, FIFI, etc.). MIMSIE. Music: Opera star Mimi Benzell; Mimi, heroine of Puccini's opera *La Bohème*, whose given name is something else—as she tells us:

Mi chiamano Mimi, ma il mio
nome è Lucia. . .
Mi chiamano Mimi, il perchè
non so.

("They call me Mimi, but my name is Lucia. They call me Mimi, why, I do not know.")

Mina (MINN' a) Pet form of WILHELMINA or variant of MINNIE. MYNA, MINETTE.

Mindy Probably a variant of MINNA or AMINTA. MINDA, MENDY.

Minerva Latin, from same root as *mens,* "mind." Mythology: Goddess of wisdom corresponding to the Greek Athena, or Pallas Athēnē.

She is Venus when she smiles,
But she's Juno when she walks,
And Minerva when she talks.
　　　　BEN JONSON,
　　　　Celebration of Charis

Minna Germanic, probably, "memory" or "love."

Minnie See WILHELMINA. Scottish pet form of MARY. MINETTE. Literature: Heroine of Belasco's drama *The Girl of the Golden West* and Puccini's opera of the same name. Stage: Minnie Maddern Fiske (1865-1932), famous actress who did so much to popularize Ibsen's plays in America.

Mira Latin, "wonderful." See MYRA. MIRELLE, MIREILLE (mi RAY'). Astronomy: Name of a very bright star.

Mirabel Latin, "wonderful." See MARVEL.

Miranda Latin, "admirable."

. . . . Admired Miranda!
Indeed the top of admiration!
　worth
What's dearest to the world!
　　　　WILLIAM SHAKESPEARE,
　　　　The Tempest

Miriam Original Hebrew form of MARY. There are many conjectures about the meaning of *Miriam,* none established, but the best is that it means "rebellious" or "obstinate."

And Miriam the prophetess, the sister of Aaron, took a timbrel in her hand; and all the women went out after her with timbrels and with dances.

And Miriam answered them, Sing ye to the LORD, for He hath triumphed gloriously; the horse and his rider hath He thrown into the sea.
　　　　EXODUS 15:20-21

Literature: The hero's first love in D. H. Lawrence's greatest novel, *Sons and Lovers* (1913).

Mirth Anglo-Saxon, "joy, pleasure."

And if I give thee honor due,
Mirth, admit me of thy crew,
To live with her, [Liberty], and
live with thee,
In unreproved pleasures free.
    JOHN MILTON, *L'Allegro*

Mitzi(e) Pet name; see MARY.

Moira Irish variation; see MARY. Ballet and screen: Moira Shearer, formerly of Sadler's Wells Ballet Company, star of *The Red Shoes* and *Tales of Hoffman*.

Molly Pet form; see MARY. MOLLIE. The substitution of *l* for *r* is seen in several names: Hal for Harry, Sally for Sarah, Dolly for Dorothy. History: The name of Molly Pitcher was really Mary MacCauley. The weary and wounded soldiers in affectionate gratitude for the water she carried to them on the battlefield of Monmouth (1778) renamed her Molly Pitcher.

When MOLLY *smiles beneath her cow,*
I feel my heart—I can't tell how!
When MOLLY *is on Sunday dressed,*
On Sundays I can take no rest.

What can I do? On worky days
I leave my work on her to gaze.
What shall I say? At sermons, I

Forget the text when MOLLY'S *by.*
    ANON., *When Molly Smiles*

Mona Irish, "noble"; Greek, "unique"; Welsh place name, "heath." See also MONICA. MOYNA, MOINA. Many who give the name today may be influenced by the famous painting of Mona Lisa, mistakenly thinking that Mona is the first name of the lady with the enigmatic smile. *Mona* is, of course, merely a title, being a contracted form of Italian *ma donna*, "my lady."

And down drops the anchor, the brown sails are flying,
And out on the shingle [beach] we leap in our glee.
But for all the bright eyes and the laughter and calling,
The girl of my heart is all that I see.
   Mona, my own love, Mona, my true love.

    OLD SONG

Monica (MONN' i ka) Possibly Latin, "adviser." MONIQUE (moh NEEK'). The name of the mother of St. Augustine.

Morna Gaelic, "beloved."

Moselle, Mozelle Feminine names formed from MOSES.

Muriel Irish, "sea-bright." Literature: A much-loved character in the popular novel by Dinah M. M. Craik, *John Halifax, Gentleman* (1856), responsible for revival of the name, especially when aunts named the baby. Literature: Muriel Sparks, distinguished British novelist (*Memento Mori*, *The Prime of Miss Jean Brodie*).

Musa Latin, "a muse." MUSETTE, MUSETTA. Mythology: One of the nine goddesses presiding over all the arts. Their names are Calliope, Clio, Erato, Euterpe, Terpsichore, Thalia, Melpomene, Polyhymnia, and Urania.

Musette French, "bag-pipe." From *Muse;* see MUSA. Italian, MUSETTA. Opera: The coquette in Puccini's *La Bohème*.

Your memory has not had time
  to pass;
    My youth has days of its life-
    time yet;
If you only knocked at the door,
  alas,
    My heart would open the
    door, Musette.
    HENRY MURGER, *Musette*
    (translated by Andrew Lang)

Of man's first disobedience and
  the fruit
Of that forbidden tree . . .
Sing, Heavenly Muse.
    JOHN MILTON, *Paradise Lost*

Myra From literature. See also MIRA. Invented as a name for the recipient of his love by Lord Brooke, an early English poet:
Was it for this that I might Myra
  see
    Washing the water with her
    beauties white?

Yet would she never write her
  love to me;
    Thinks wit of change while
    thoughts are in delight?
    FULKE GREVILLE, LORD
    BROOKE, *Myra*

Literature: Myra Kelly, teacher and author of short stories of children on the East Side of New York, *Little Citizens* (1904), *Little Aliens* (1910). Music: Dame Myra Hess, renowned pianist.

Myrna Probably Gaelic in origin. MERNA. Screen star: Myrna Loy.

Myrtilla See MYRTLE.

Myrtilla, to-night,
  Wears Jacqueminot roses.
She's the loveliest sight—
Myrtilla to-night!
    CHARLES HENRY LÜDERS,
    A Corsage Bouquet

Myrtle From Greek via Latin. A plant name like FERN, HAZEL, HEATHER, etc. MYRTILLA.

So Miss Myrtle is going to
  marry?
    What a number of hearts she
    will break!
There's Lord George, and Tom
  Brown, and Sir Harry,
    Who are dying of love for her
    sake!
    HELEN SELINA, LADY DUFFERIN,
    The Charming Woman

N

Amelia and Volatile NELL
I hope you're uncommonly well:
You two pretty girls—you extremely nice girls—
Amelia and Volatile NELL!

WILLIAM SCHWENCK GILBERT,
Sir Barnaby Bampton

Nada (NAY' da) See NADINE; also used as artificial fem. of NATHAN.

Nadia (NAD' ya) Slavic, "hope." See NADINE. Music: Nadia Boulanger, renowned composer, conductor, and teacher of many famous pupils.

Nadine (na DEEN' *or* nay DEEN') Russian via French, "hope." NADIA. Literature: Nadine Gordimer, a native Johannesburger, gifted short-story writer and award-winning novelist in 1961 (*Friday's Footprint*).

Nan See ANN. NANA, NANCY, NANETTE, NANINE, NANICE, NANCE.

My Nan shall be the queen of all the fairies,
Finely attired in a robe of white.

WILLIAM SHAKESPEARE,
The Merry Wives of Windsor

Nancy See NAN.

I'll ne'er blame my partial fancy
Naething could resist my Nancy.
But to see her was to love her;

Love but her, and love for ever.

ROBERT BURNS,
Ae Fond Kiss, And Then We Sever

Nanette, Nanine See NAN. TV: Nanette Fabray.

Naomi (nay OH' mi *or* NAY' o mi) Hebrew, "pleasant." NOMI. Biblical: Mother-in-law of Ruth, to whom Ruth said:

Intreat me not to leave thee, or to return from following after thee: for whither thou goest, I will go; and where thou lodgest, I will lodge: thy people shall be my people, and thy God my God.

RUTH 1:16

Literature: Naomi Mitchison, English short-story writer and novelist, especially known for her stories of the ancient world (*When the Bough Breaks*, etc.).

Natalie (NATT' a lee), **Nathalia** (na THAYL' ya *or* na THAL' ya) See NOEL. The Russian dim. NATASHA is sometimes used. Literature: Nathalia Crane, American poet, famous in the 20's as a child poet; her first book, *The Janitor's Boy*, was published when she was eleven. Hollywood: Natalie Wood.

Natasha See NATALIE.

Nedda Fem. form; see EDWARD.

Nedra From fiction. Name taken from the novel *Nedra* by George Barr McCutcheon, popular at the beginning of this century. It may also be *Arden* spelled backward. (Several of the Bolshoi ballerinas were named Ninel, which is Lenin spelled backward!) Literature: Nedra Newkirk Lamar, author of *How to Speak the Written Word.*

Neeta See NITA.

Nelia See CORNELIA.

Nell Pet form; see ELLEN.

O once I lov'd a bonnie lass,
Ay, and I love her still;
And whilst that virtue warms my
    breast,
I'll love my handsome Nell.
    ROBERT BURNS, *Handsome Nell*

Stage: Nell Gwyn, famous British actress of seventeenth century, was born Eleanor. She is referred to in Samuel Pepys' *Diary* as "Pretty witty Nell."

Nellie, Nelly Pet form; see ELLEN, ELEANOR, and HELEN. Music: Nellie Melba, stage name of Helen Porter Mitchell (1861-

1931), famous Australian operatic soprano, who took her last name from Melbourne, the city of her birth. Songs: *Nelly Bly* and *Nelly Was a Lady*, both by Stephen Foster.

On my arm a soft hand rested,
    Rested light as ocean foam;
And 'twas from Aunt Dinah's
    quilting party,
    I was seeing Nelly home.
    OLD SONG, *The Quilting Party*

Nerissa (ne RISS' a) In Shakespeare's *Merchant of Venice*, the spirited, witty confidante of Portia.

Nessie See AGNES. NESTA.

Netta, Nettie, Netty See JEANNETTE or ANTOINETTE.

Neva (NEE' va) Spanish, "snow."

Neysa Variant; see AGNES.

Nicole, Nicolette See NICHOLAS and COLETTE. NICOLETTA. Literature: The charming heroine of one of the most popular medieval romances, *Aucassin and Nicolette.*

Nika Greek NIKE "victory." Cookbook: Nika Stander Hazelton's *Continental Flavor.*

Nila (NYE' la) Artificial Latin fem. of *Nilus,* "the river Nile." Radio: Nila Mack, creator and producer of *Let's Pretend,* a once favorite children's program.

Nina (NYE' na *or* NEE' na) See ANN. NINON.

Ninette (ninn ET') French dim. form; see ANN.

Nita (NEE' ta) Spanish terminal abbrev. of Juanita. See JOAN. NEETA.

Noel, Noël See NOEL (m.) and NATALIE. NOELLE.

For every lip—a glass!
For every lad—a lass!
And, ere the ardors cool,
Cry "Noel," cry "Noel," down
all the halls of Yule!
CLINTON SCOLLARD,
Twelfth Night Song

Nola Italian place name; also a dim. of OLIVIA.

Nona Latin, "ninth." NONIE, NONETTE. Formerly given as a name to a ninth child. See OCTAVIA.

Nonie Pet form of NONA or NORA.

Nora(h) Shortened Irish form; see HONORA or LEONORA. Literature: Nora Helmer, heroine of Ibsen's *A Doll's House* (1879), whose slamming of the door when she left her husband echoed round the world.

Beauty lies
In many eyes
But love in yours, my Nora
creina [dear].
THOMAS MOORE,
Lesbia Hath a Beaming Eye

Noreen Irish dim. form; see NORA. NORINE.

Norma See NORMAN. Music: Bellini's opera *Norma* (1831) made name popular. Hollywood: Norma Talmadge; Norma Shearer, winner of Oscar in 1930 (*The Divorcee*).

OLIVIA: *Why, what would you?*
VIOLA: *Holla your name to the reverberate hills*
And make the babbling gossip of the air
Cry out, "OLIVIA!"

WILLIAM SHAKESPEARE, *Twelfth Night*

Octavia Latin, "eighth." See AUGUSTUS, OCTAVIUS, QUINTA, and NONA.

Odette French form; see OTTILIE.

Olga Norse via Russian, "holy" or "wholesome."

Olive Latin, "olive" or fem. of OLIVER. OLIVIA. Since ancient times the olive tree has been a symbol of peace. It was with an olive leaf in its mouth that the dove sent out by Noah returned to the ark. Today we speak of "holding out the olive branch," and of "the dove of peace."

More bright than moon or sun,
All the heavens of heaven in one
Little child.

ALGERNON CHARLES
SWINBURNE,
Olive

Olivia See OLIVE. Literature: Name of the rich and beautiful countess in Shakespeare's *Twelfth Night.* Stage and Screen: The lovely Olivia de Havilland, winner of the 1946 Oscar (*To Each His Own*) and the 1949 Oscar (*The Heiress*).

Say thou, whereon I carved her name,
If ever maid or spouse

As fair as my Olivia came
To rest beneath thy boughs.

ALFRED, LORD TENNYSON,
The Talking Oak

Olympia Greek, "of Olympus," mountain home of the Greek gods. Music: Olympia, one of the heroines in Offenbach's opera *Tales of Hoffman* (1881).

Ona, Oona See UNA.

Opal Jewel name.

Ophelia Probably Greek, "help."

Soft you now!
The fair Ophelia! Nymph in thy orisons
Be all my sins remember'd.
WILLIAM SHAKESPEARE, *Hamlet*

Ora Latin, *Aurea,* "golden." ORLENE. A longer form of this name is ORIANA, the name of the heroine of the medieval romance *Amadis of Gaul.* "She is represented as the fairest, gentlest and most faithful of womankind" (William Rose Benét). Two Queens, Elizabeth I and Anne, were called Oriana by poets. The wife of Brooks Atkinson is a modern bearer of this name.

Or, robed in raiment of romantic lore,
Like Oriana, dark of eye and hair,

*Riding through realms of legend
evermore
And ever young and fair.*
MADISON CAWEIN, *Romance*

Orna Irish, "olive-colored";
Latin "decorate."

Ottillie (OTT' ill ee) Germanic,
"fatherland." OTTILLIA, UTA,
ODILLE, ODETTE.

Ouida (WEE' da) Baby mispronunciation of LOUISA. See
LOUISE.

P

If with a frown
I am cast down,
PHYLLIS *smiling*
And beguiling,
Makes me happier than before.

SIR CHARLES SEDLEY, *Phyllis*

Page Occupational name when knighthood was in flower.

Pamela (PAM′ e la) From literature. PAM. This name was first used by Sir Philip Sidney for a character in his *Arcadia,* but it was Samuel Richardson's famous and very popular novel *Pamela, or Virtue Rewarded* (1740) that called attention to the name. It is now again very much in vogue. Stage and Screen: Pamela Brown. Hollywood: Pamela Tiffin. Three modern British novelists: Pamela Frankau, Pamela Hansford Johnson, Pamela Moore.

The fair Pamela came to town,
  To London town, in early
    summer;
And up and down and round
    about
  The beaux discussed the
    bright newcomer,
With "Gadzooks, sir," and
  "Ma'am, my duty,"
  And "Odds my life, but 'tis a
    Beauty!"
      ELLEN M. H. CORTISSOZ
        Pamela in Town

Pansy Flower name. French, "thought."

CORNELIA: I pray, what flowers are these?

GAZETTA: The pansy this.

CORNELIA: Oh, that's for lovers' thoughts.
  GEORGE CHAPMAN, *All Fools*

Parthenia Greek, "maidenly." An appellation of Athena; hence, Parthenon as the name of the temple of Athena.

Pat See PATRICIA. PATTY. Stage and Screen: the youthful star Patty Duke.

Patience See CHARITY. Sir Thomas Carew, Speaker of the House of Commons in the seventeenth century and evidently a believer in "quality" names, had four daughters, whom he named Patience, Temperance, Silence, and Prudence. Music: Heroine of Gilbert and Sullivan's comic opera *Patience.*

Patricia See PATRICK. PATRICE, PAT, TRICIA, TRISH. Music: Patrice Munsel, Metropolitan Opera singer.

Paula See PAUL. PAULINE, PAULETTE. Literature: Paula, heroine of Pinero's most famous play, *The Second Mrs. Tanqueray* (1893). Hollywood: Paulette Goddard.

Paulina, Pauline See PAUL. PAULENE.

Love me—love me, Pauline . . .
  Be still to me
A key to music's mystery when
  mind fails,
A reason, a solution and a clue!
  ROBERT BROWNING, *Pauline*

Pearl Latin via French. A jewel name. PERLIE. Literature: Pearl Buck, Pulitzer Prize in 1932 for *The Good Earth*; Nobel Prize in 1938. Dance: Pearl Primus.

Peg Pet name; see MARGARET. Peg is a rhyming form of MEG, dim., of MARGARET. PEGGY.

O, the month of May, the merry
  month of May,
So frolic, so gay, and so green,
  so green, so green;
And then did I unto my true
  love say,
Sweet Peg, thou shalt be my
  Summer's Queen.
        THOMAS DEKKER,
        The Shoemaker's Holiday

Pegeen (peg EEN') Irish dim. of PEG(GY). PEGENE.

Peggy Pet form; see MEG. The Hon. Lady Miss Margaret Cavendish-Hollis-Harley was addressed as "My noble, lovely, little Peggy" by the poet Matthew Prior.

My Peggy is a young thing,
  Just entered in her teens,
Fair as the day, and sweet as
  May,
Fair as the day and always gay.
    ALLAN RAMSAY, *Peggy*

Pelagie Greek, "pertaining to the sea." PELAGIA. Name of a fifth-century saint.

Penelope (pen ELL' o pee) Greek, "weaver" or "with her face covered by a web." PENNY. Literature: In Homer's *Odyssey* the faithful wife who waited twenty years for the return of Odysseus (Ulysses) and who devised a subterfuge to put off her importunate suitors.

Penny Pet form; see PENELOPE. In the widely syndicated comic strip by Harry Haenigsen, Penny is the vivacious young lady who illuminates the problems of teen-agers for parents.

Peony (PEE' a nee) Flower name from *Paion*, one of the names of Apollo as the god of healing, since the flower was thought to have medicinal value.

Perian Probably a combination of PERRY and ANN. Perian

Conerly, wife of a famous football player, writes entertainingly and knowingly on football from the woman's point of view (*Backseat Quarterback*).

Perry An increasingly popular name, usually a pet form of PEARL, following the pattern of SHERRY and TERRY.

Persis Greek, "Persian woman." Biblical: Woman mentioned by St. Paul:

Salute the beloved Persis which labored much in the Lord.

ROMANS 16:12

Literature: Wife of Silas Lapham in the novel *The Rise of Silas Lapham* by William Dean Howells.

Pet(r)a (PEET' a) Fem. form; see PETER. French pet form, PERRINE.

Phemie From EUPHEMIA. See also EFFIE.

In the class-room blue-eyed Phemie
sits, half-listening, hushed and dreamy,
To the grey-haired pinched Professor droning to his class of girls.

WILLIAM CANTON,
Through the Ages

Philippa See PHILIP. *Pippa* (dim. form) is the name of "the little silk winder of Asolo [Italy]" who is the heroine of Robert Browning's dramatic poem *Pippa Passes*. As Pippa passes through the town on New Year's Day she sings, and her songs affect the lives of the leading characters at critical moments. One of her songs contains the well-known lines:

The year's at the spring,
 And day's at the morn;
  Morning's at seven . . .
God's in his heaven—
  All's right with the world!

Philomena (fill oh MEE' na) Greek, "friend-power," FILOMENA. Name of several saints.

Phoebe Greek, "the shining one." PHEBE. One of the names of the goddess of the moon. See ARTEMIS, CYNTHIA, and DIANA.

Two summers since, I saw at Lammas fair
The sweetest flower that ever blossomed there,
When Phoebe Dawson gaily cross'd the green,
In haste to see, and happy to be seen.

GEORGE CRABBE,
Parish Register

Phyllida (FILL' a da) Related to *Phyllis* with the added idea of blossoming. PHYLLADA PHILLIDA.

The ladies of St. James's!
They're painted to the eyes,
Their white it stays for ever,

Their red it never dies:
But Phyllida, my Phyllida!
Her colour comes and goes;
It trembles to a lily,—
It wavers to a rose.

> HENRY AUSTIN DOBSON,
> *The Ladies of St. James's*

Phyllis Greek, "a green bough" or "leaf." PHILLIS, PHILIS. A name much used in pastoral poetry. Literature: Phyllis Mc-Ginley, author of humorous poems that show a delightful insight into problems of people of all ages (*Three Times Three* etc.).

Phyllis, why should we delay
Pleasures shorter than the day?

> EDMUND WALLER,
> *17th Century Song*

Pia (PEE′ a) Italian, "pious."

Polly Pet name; see MARY. Derived as follows: Mary to Mally to Molly to Polly. Stage, Hollywood, and TV: Polly Bergen.

> *Polly put the kettle on, we'll all have tea.*

> CHARLES DICKENS,
> *Barnaby Rudge*

Still shall my voice's tender lays
Of love remain unbroken;
And still my charming Polly praise,
Sweet smiling and sweet spoken.

> JOHN QUINCY ADAMS
> (Sixth President of the U. S.)
> *To Polly*

Portia Latin, from *Porcius,* a Roman *gens* name. History: Wife of "the noble" Brutus, both of whom appear in Shakespeare's *Julius Caesar*. Literature: Heroine of Shakespeare's *Merchant of Venice,* famous for her "mercy" speech:

The quality of mercy is not strain'd,
It droppeth as the gentle rain from heaven
Upon the place beneath: it is twice bless'd;
It blesseth him that gives and him that takes.

Priscilla Latin, "of ancient birth." The name appears in the New Testament as both Priscilla and Prisca. Literature: The charming heroine of Longfellow's poem, who put the question to John Alden:

Archly the maiden smiled, and, with eyes overrunning with laughter,
Said in a tremulous voice: Why don't you speak for yourself, John?

> HENRY WADSWORTH
> LONGFELLOW,
> *The Courtship of Miles Standish*

Prudence Latin, "wise." PRUE. See CHARITY and PATIENCE.

Psyche (SYE′ kee) Greek, "the soul." Mythology: The mortal loved by Cupid. Literature: Story in Latin by Apuleius, retold by William Morris in *The*

Earthly Paradise and by Walter Pater in *Marius the Epicurean.*

Surely I dreamt today, or did I see

The winged Psyche with awakened eyes?

JOHN KEATS, *To Psyche*

Q

*Tomorrow 'ill be of all the years the maddest
merriest day,
For I'm to be* QUEEN *o' the May, mother,
I'm to be* QUEEN *o' the May.*

TENNYSON, *The May Queen*

Queenie, Queena Dim. of "queen." See REGINA.

Querida (kay REE' da) Spanish, "loved one." See CHERIE and DÉSIRÉE.

Quinta Fem. form; see QUENTIN. QUINTILLA. Once given to a fifth daughter.

Quartilla See QUARTUS. A saint's name.

R

JAQUES: ROSALIND *is your love's name?*
ORLANDO: *Yes, just.*
JAQUES: *I do not like her name.*
ORLANDO: *There was no thought of pleasing you when she was christened.*

WILLIAM SHAKESPEARE, *As You Like It*

Rachel (RAY' chel) Hebrew, "little lamb." RAHEL, RAY; French, RACHELLE (ra SHELL'); SHELLIE, SHELLEY; Spanish, RAQUEL (ra KELL'). Again becoming popular with spelling and pronunciation of RACHELLE and pet-name SHELLEY. Biblical: Wife of Jacob, younger sister of Leah.

Rachel was beautiful and well-favoured.

GENESIS 29:17

Literature: Rachel Field, author of *Hitty* (1929), the story of a doll, and *All This, and Heaven Too* (1938). Theater: Rachel (ra SHELL'), stage name of Élisa Félix (1820-1858), an actress generally ranked with Duse, Bernhardt, and Sarah Siddons.

O Rachel is fair as the dew
    pearls o'morning,
And Rachel is sweet as the buds
    of sweet brere [brier],
Her dark jetty curls o'er her
    eyelashes dawning,
The moss of the rose is nothing
    so dear.

JOHN CLARE, *Rachel Cooks*

270

Rae, Ray See RACHEL.

Ramona (ra MOAN' a) Fem. of Spanish RAMON; see RAYMOND. Literature: Heroine of Helen Hunt Jackson's popular romance (1884), dealing with Spanish and Indian life in California.

Raya (RYE' a) Variant of RAY.

Reba, Reeba (REE' ba) See REBECCA.

Rebecca Hebrew, "yoke." REBEKAH, REBA, RIVA, BECKY. Biblical: Wife of Isaac and mother of Jacob and Esau.

Behold Rebekah came forth with her pitcher on her shoulder; and she went down unto the well, and drew water.

GENESIS 24:45

Literature: Rebecca, one of the two heroines of Scott's *Ivanhoe;* Rebecca Sharp, better known as Becky, chief character in Thackeray's *Vanity Fair;* Kate Douglas Wiggin's *Rebecca of Sunnybrook Farm* (1903), a perennial children's favorite.

Rebecca West, pen name of Cecily Isabel Fairfield, was taken from a character in Ibsen's *Rosmersholm*.

Regina (ra JEE' na *or* ra JYE' na) Latin, "queen." REGINE. Spanish, REINA (RAY' na). Literature: Leading character of Lillian Hellman's *Little Foxes* and the name of Marc Blitzstein's fine opera based on the play.

Rena (REE' na) Hebrew, "song."

Renata (re NAH' ta) Latin, "reborn." Music: Renata Tebaldi, favorite of opera-goers.

Rene (REE' nee and REEN) From IRENE (eye REE' nee, as pronounced in England, or eye REEN', as pronounced in the United States) RENIE.

Renée (ruh NAY') *French,* "born again."

Re(e)va See RIVA.

Rhea Greek, "earth," figurative meaning from root meaning "flow," since rivers, etc. *flow* from the earth. Greek Mythology: Rhea, mother of Zeus. Roman Mythology: Rhea (old Italian name) Silvia, mother of Romulus and Remus, legendary founders of Rome.

Rhoda Greek, "roses," or "a person from Rhodes (the island of roses)." RODA, RODINA.

Rhonda Place name of southern Wales; possible meaning, "grand." RONDA. Not so long ago some parents named daughters Rhonda because of the film star Rhonda Fleming.

Rica (RICK' a) Dim. of FREDERICA or probably artificial fem. of RICHARD. RICCA, RYCCA.

Rietta, Riette Terminal forms of names like HENRIETTA.

Rima (REE' ma) From literature: The natural and yet almost supernatural heroine of W. H. Hudson's beautiful novel *Green Mansions* (1904). In the novel, *Rima* is a shortening of the place name Riolama.

"When I was a child and the priest baptised me, he named me Riolama—the place where my mother was found. But it was long to say, and they called me Rima."

There is a statue of Rima by Jacob Epstein in Kensington Garden, London, erected as a memorial to her literary creator.

Rita A shortened form of Italian *Margherita,* now used as an independent name. See MARGARET. Hollywood: Rita Hayworth.

Riva (REE' va) From REBECCA, closer in sound to the original Hebrew, RIVY, RIVI, REE, REEVA, RIVALEE.

Roanna, Roanne Probably a telescoping of ROSE and ANN. ROS(E)ANNE.

Roberta See ROBERT. Music: That perennial favorite *Smoke Gets in Your Eyes* was one of the song hits of Jerome Kern's light opera *Roberta*. Music: Roberta Peters of the Metropolitan.

Robin See ROBIN (m). ROBYN, ROBINA, ROBENA, ROBENIA, ROBBIN, ROBINETT.

Rochelle (ro SHELL') French, "little rock." Probably used as a variant of RACHELLE, also yielding the very attractive abbreviated form SHELLEY.

Rolla See ROLF.

Roma Latin, name of the Eternal City. ROMAINE, ROMINA, ROMILDA, ROMELLE. See ROMAN.

Rona Probably abbrev. of *Ronalda;* see RONALD. RHONA. Possibly a place name; Rona is one of the Hebrides islands, Scotland.

Ronalda See RONALD. RONNY, RENNIE.

Ronnie, Ronni Attractive pet name for ROANNE, ROWENA, or VERONICA. Often used as an independent name. See RONALD.

Rosalie See ROSE. ROSALEEN. Irish; often used in Irish poetry, as in the famous poem quoted here, to represent Ireland:

'Tis you shall have the golden
  throne,
'Tis you shall reign, and reign
  alone,
My dark Rosaleen!
  JAMES CLARENCE MANGAN,
    Dark Rosaleen

Rosalind Probably coined by the poet Spenser but now generally associated with Spanish *rosa linda,* "pretty rose." ROZ, ROSLYN, ROSELIN, ROSALINE. Shakespeare popularized the name by giving it to one of his most charming heroines in *As You Like It.* Stage and Screen: Rosalind Russell, the ever popular.

JAQUES (Inquiring about Rosalind). *What stature is she of?*

ORLANDO: *Just as high as my heart.*

Rosaline Variant of ROSALIND.

Her cheeks are like the blushing
  cloud
  That beautifies Aurora's face,
Or like the silver crimson
  shroud
  That Phoebus' smiling looks
  doth grace:
Heigh-ho, fair Rosaline!
  THOMAS LODGE, *Rosaline*

Rosamond Germanic, "horse-protection"; Latin, "pure rose."

My Rosamonde, my only Rose,
That pleased best mine eye;
The fairest flower in all the
worlde
To feed my fantasye.

OLD BALLAD,
Fair Rosamonde

Rosanne See ROANNA. ROSIAN.

Why didn't you say you was
promised, Rose-Ann?
Why didn't you name it to
me,
Ere ever you tempted me hither,
Rose-Ann,
So often so wearifully?

THOMAS HARDY, *Rose-Ann*

Rose, Rosa Latin, "rose." ROS-
ELLE, ROZELLE. Various other
derivations are given by authorities, but we'd like to agree with
Gertrude Stein that "Rose is a
rose is a rose is a rose." (See
ROSAMOND.)

Rose kissed me to-day.
Will she kiss me to-morrow?
Let it be as it may,
Rose kissed me to-day.
But the pleasure gives way
To a feeling of sorrow;
Rose kissed me to-day,—
Will she kiss me to-morrow?

HENRY AUSTIN DOBSON,
Rose-Leaves: A Kiss

Rosemary, Rosemarie A plant
name or a combined name:
ROSE + MARY; or Latin, "sea
dew." Music: *Rose Marie*, a
still popular light opera by
Rudolf Friml.

There's rosemary, that's for re-
membrance: pray you, love, re-
member. (Ophelia in *Hamlet*)

Rosette Dim. form; see ROSE.
ROSETTA.

Rosina, Rosine, Rosita See
ROSE. Music: Rosina Lhevinne,
concert pianist and teacher of
many famous pianists.

Rowena Anglo-Saxon, "fame-
friend"; or Welsh, "long, white
hair." A stately name made
popular in *Ivanhoe*.

Roxane Probably from a Persian place name meaning "the
dawn." History: The name of
the Persian wife of Alexander
the Great. Literature: In Rostand's immortal romantic play,
the beautiful heroine who loved
but one man in her life and
"lost him twice."

Your name is like a golden bell
Hung in my heart; and when I
think of you,
I tremble, and the bell swings
and rings— "Roxane!"
"Roxane!" . . . along my veins,
"Roxane!" . . .

EDMOND ROSTAND,
Cyrano de Bergerac
(translated by Brian Hooker)

Roxanne, Roxanna Popular respelling of ROXANE.

Ruby Latin, "red." A jewel
name.

Ruth Hebrew, probably "beauty" or "companion." Biblical: The idyllic story of Ruth and Naomi is one of the loveliest and most moving in the Old Testament.

And Ruth the Moabitess said unto Naomi, Let me now go to the field, and glean ears of corn.
RUTH 2:2

Literature: Some of the loveliest lines written by John Keats make reference to that same story:

> *Perhaps the self-same song that found a path*
> *Through the sad heart of Ruth, when sick for home,*
> *She stood in tears amid the alien corn;*
> *The same that oft-times hath*
> *Charm'd magic casements, opening on the foam*
> *Of perilous seas, in faery lands forlorn.*
>
> JOHN KEATS,
> *Ode to a Nightingale*

S

SYLVIA'S *hair is like the night*
Touched with glancing starry beams;
Such a face as drifts through dreams—
This is SYLVIA *to the sight.*

CLINTON SCOLLARD, *Sylvia*

Sabina (sa BEE′ na *or* sa BYE′ na) Latin, "a Sabine woman." MASC., SABIN.

See! see, she wakes! Sabina wakes!
And now the sun begins to rise!
Less glorious is the morn that breaks
From his bright beams than her fair eyes.

WILLIAM CONGREVE,
Sabina Wakes

Sabrina Legendary goddess of the River Severn, England, for which the Latin form is *Sabrina.*

Sabrina fair,
Listen where thou art sitting
Under the glassy cool, translucent wave,
In twisted braids of lilies knitting
The loose train of thy amber-dropping hair.

JOHN MILTON, *Comus*

Sadie Pet form; see SARAH. SADA, SAIDEE, SADYE.

Sally Pet name; see SARAH (like Hal for Harry, Molly for Mary, Dolly for Dorothy). SALLIE, SALINA.

Of all the girls that are so smart,
There's none like pretty Sally,
She is the darling of my heart,
And she lives in our alley.

HENRY CAREY,
Sally in Our Alley

Salome (sal oh MAY′) See SOLOMON. In the New Testament, Salome is the daughter of Herodias and Herod Philip. Her story has been told many times. Literature: Play by Oscar Wilde, which he wrote in both English and French. Music: Opera by Richard Strauss based on Wilde's play.

Samantha Hebrew, "listener." Screen: Samantha Eggar.

Sandra See ALEXANDRA.

Sapphira Hebrew, "gem," or Aramaic, "beautiful." Biblical: Wife of Ananias (ACTS 5:1).

Sappho Greek lyric poetess known as "The Tenth Muse" for her great talent. SAPHO. Literature: *Sapho*, novel by Daudet.

*The isles of Greece, the isles
   of Greece!
Where burning Sappho loved
   and sung.*
            GEORGE GORDON BYRON,
                        Don Juan

Sara(h) Hebrew, "princess."
SADIE, SARETTE, SARI, SAR(E)Y,
SERITA, SARITA, SERYL, SYRIL, SO-
RALE, SORALIE, SORELLA. Bibli-
cal: Wife of Abraham, mother
of Isaac.

*And God said unto Abraham,
as for Sarai thy wife, thou
shalt not call her name Sarai,
but Sarah shall her name be.*
                        GENESIS 17:15

Literature: Many famous
women have borne this name,
among them Sarah Kemble Sid-
dons, English tragic actress
(portrait by Reynolds, "The
Tragic Muse"); Sarah Bernhardt
("The Divine Sarah"); and Sara
Teasdale, lyric poet, Pulitzer
Prize winner in 1918 (*Love
Songs*).

Seema Hebrew, "treasure" or
"joy." SIMAH, CYMA, SEENA.

Selda See ZELDA.

Selena (se LEE' na) Greek,
"moon." SELENE (sell EE' nee).

Selma See ANSELM (m). Literature: Selma Lagerlöf, Swedish novelist, author of the children's classic, *The Wonderful
Adventures of Nils*, winner of
Nobel Prize (1909).

Seraphina, Serafina (se ra FEE'
na) Hebrew, "an angel." SERA-
PHINE.

Serena (se REE' na) Latin,
"calm, serene." Used as variant
of SARA.

Shari Hungarian form of SARA.

Sharon Hebrew, possibly, "level plain." Biblical: A plain in
western Palestine, famed for its
fertility.

*I am the rose of Sharon,
   And the lily of the valleys.*
      THE SONG OF SOLOMON 2:1

Sheba Place name. Biblical: A
region in the southwestern part
of Arabia n o w known as
Yemen. SABA. The name is famous because of the visit of the
Queen of Sheba to Solomon:

*And when the Queen of Sheba
heard of the fame of Solomon,
she came to prove Solomon
with hard questions.*
               II CHRONICLES 9:1

*I loved a lass, a fair one,
As fair as e'er was seen;
She was indeed a rare one,
Another Sheba queen.*
      GEORGE WITHERS, *I Loved a
            Lass, A Fair One.*

Sheera Hebrew, "song." Israeli
name.

Sheila Irish form; see CELIA.
SHE(E)LAGH, SHEILAH, SHEELAH.
Literature. Shelagh D e l a n y,
playwright, wrote *A Taste of
Honey* when she was nineteen.

*On the green banks of Shannon,
when Sheelah was nigh,
No blithe Irish lad was so
happy as I.*
THOMAS CAMPBELL,
The Harper

Shelah (SHEE' la) Hebrew, "request, petition."

Shelley English place name, "shell island." Name given, however, consciously or unconsciously in honor of the great poet Percy Bysshe Shelley (1792-1822). Coming into popularity as a variation of SHIRLEY and SHEILA and as a pet form from the last syllable of RACHELLE and ROCHELLE. Stage and Hollywood: Shelley Winters.

Sherry, Sheri, Sherrie The wine gets its name from the Spanish town of Xeres, which was named after Caesar. However, its use as a girl's name is probably merely a respelling of the French CHERIE, "cherished one," or a pet name or variant of SHIRLEY or SARAH. SHEREE, SHERYE. Stage and Hollywood: Sheree North.

Shirley Place name, "district meadow." SHERLEY, SHERYL, SHYRLE. First used by Charlotte Brontë as the name of the heroine of her novel *Shirley* (1849), a name which already existed as a surname. The fame of Shirley Temple gave the name a great impetus. Stage, Screen,

and TV: Shirley Booth, winner of an Oscar in 1952 (*Come Back, Little Sheba*) and of an Emmy in 1962 (*Hazel*).

Shoshannah (show SHANN' ah) Hebrew, "rose." See SUSAN.

Shulamith (shoo LAM' ith) Hebrew, "peace" or Biblical place name. SULAMITH, SULA.

*Return, return, O Shulamite;
return, return, that we may
look upon thee.*
THE SONG OF SOLOMON 6:13

Sibyl, Sybil Greek, "prophetess." SYBILA, SYBILLA, SYBILLE, SIBELLA. The sibyls were the women stationed at the oracles, who, while in a trance, relayed the messages of the gods. Literature: *Sybil* (1845), a novel by Benjamin Disraeli, Prime Minister of England. Stage: Dame Sybil Thorndike, British actress.

Sidney, Sydney See SIDNEY (m).

Sidonia Latin, from the name of the city of Sidon in Phoenicia. Vergil called Dido of Carthage *Sidonia Dido* because she came from Phoenicia. However, the name may also come from the Greek word *sindon*, meaning *linen*, and the name was supposedly given to girls born at the time of the Feast of the Winding Sheet, or the Sacred Sendon. SIDONIE, SADONIA. Whatever may be the origin, the name is used today most probably as an alternate for SADIE and similar names or as a feminine form of SIDNEY (m).

Silvia Variant spelling; see SYLVIA.

Then to Silvia let us sing,
That Silvia is excelling;
She excels each mortal thing
Upon the dull earth dwelling.
WILLIAM SHAKESPEARE,
The Two Gentlemen of Verona

Simone (see MOAN') See SIMON. SIMONNE. Literature: Simone de Beauvoir, French Existentialist novelist. Films: Simone Signoret, winner of an Oscar in 1959 (*Room at the Top*).

Sivia, Sivie Hebrew, "doe" (see DORCAS and TABITHA) or "beautiful woman." See also ZEV (m).

Sondra Terminal abbrev. See ALEXANDRA. SANDRA, SANDY.

Sonia, Sonya Russian dim. form; see SOPHIA. SONJA, SUNNY. Literature: Sonya, the loyal and faithful heroine of Dostoyevsky's great psychological novel *Crime and Punishment*.

Sophia (so FYE' a *or* SO' fee a) Greek, "wisdom." SOPHY, SOPHIE. Literature: Heroine of Fielding's novel *Tom Jones*. Theater: The irrepressible Sophie Tucker. Screen: Sophia Loren, winner of the 1961 New York Film Critics Award (*Two Women*),

the first time a performer was honored for work in a foreign-made film. Also Oscar winner in 1962 (*Two Women*).

Stacy See ANASTASIA and EUSTACIA.

Star, Starr English, "star."

Stella Latin, "a star." Literature: *Astrophel and Stella* (Greek, "star-lover," and Latin, "star"), a famous and popular sequence of 108 sonnets by Sir Philip Sidney. Stella was the name given by Jonathan Swift to Esther Johnson by converting Esther to Greek *aster* ("star") then translating *aster* to Latin *stella*. Swift's *Journal to Stella* was addressed to Esther Johnson. (Esther means "star"; see ESTHER.)

Gone is the winter of my misery!
My spring appears, O, see what here doth grow:
For Stella hath, with words where faith doth shine,
Of her high heart giv'n me the monarchy;
I, I, or I, may say that she is mine.
PHILIP SIDNEY,
Astrophel and Stella

Theater: Stella Adler, actress and teacher of acting.

Stephanie See STEPHEN. STEFFA.

Susan, Susannah Hebrew, "lily"; modern usage in Israel, "rose." SUE, SUS(I)E, SUKEY, SUZY, SUZELLE, SUSANNE, S U Z A N N E, SUZETTE. Biblical: Story of Susannah and the Elders in the *Apocrypha*. Falsely accused of infidelity, the chaste and beautiful Susannah was saved by the wisdom of Daniel, who, using modern detective techniques, cross-examined her accusers separately and proved by their contradictory evidence that they had lied. Literature: Susan Glaspell, one of the founders of the Provincetown Playhouse, winner of the Pulitzer Prize (1931) for her play *Alison's House;* Susannah Centlivre, whose *Bold Stroke for a Wife* was the first play ever produced on Broadway (Jan. 8, 1751). History: Susan B. Anthony, fighter for women's rights. The Nineteenth Amendment to the Constitution, giving nation-wide suffrage to women, is often called the Susan B. Anthony amendment in her honor. Hollywood: Susan Hayward, winner of an Oscar in 1958 (*I Want to Live*).

> O Susan, Susan, lovely dear,
>   My vows shall ever true
>   remain;
> Let me kiss off that falling
>   tear,
>   We only part to meet
>   again.
> Change, as ye list, ye winds;
>   my heart shall be
> The faithful compass that still
>   points to thee.
>   JOHN GAY, *Sweet
>   William's Farewell*

Sydel(le) (sid ELL') Probably a variant of SADIE or SYDNEY.

Sylvia, Silvia Latin, "a girl of the forest."

> With silent step and graceful air,
>   See gentle Sylvia move:
> Whilst heedless gazers, unaware
>   Resign their soul to love.
> WILLIAM SHENSTONE, *On Miss
>   M—s' Dancing*

T

There sleeps TITANIA *some time of the night,*
Lull'd in these flowers wtth dances and delight.

WILLIAM SHAKESPEARE,
A Midsummer Night's Dream

Tabitha (TAB' ith a) Aramaic, "a gazelle." Equivalent of DORCAS. See DORCAS.

Tabitha, which by interpretation is called Dorcas. This woman was full of good works and almsdeeds which she did. ACTS 9:36.

Tabitha, sweet Tabitha, I never can forget,
Nor how the music sounded, nor how our glances met,
When underneath the swinging lamps we danced the minuet.
ARTHUR COLTON, *Concerning Tabitha's Dancing of the Minuet*

Tallula(h) American Indian place name. Stage, Screen, and Radio: Who else but Tallulah Bankhead?

Tama(h) (TAY' ma) Hebrew, "astonishment."

Tamar(a) Hebrew, "palm tree." Several women named Tamar appear in the Old Testament.

Tammy See THOMAS. A letter from the young and vivacious star Tammy Grimes, tells us:

"My correct name is Tammy Grimes. This is a Scottish name that my great, great grandmoth-er and my grandmother also bore. I hope this will not confuse you even more."

It certainly doesn't confuse us; it confirms our belief that it is the feminine form of TAM, a Scottish form of TOM.

Tania, Tanya Abbrev. of the Russian name *Tatiana* (origin unknown) or of TITANIA, name of the fairy queen in Shakespeare's *A Midsummer Night's Dream.*

Tecla Greek, "divine fame." TEKLA, THECLA, TELCA, TELKA. St. Thecla, first woman martyr, a convert and disciple of St. Paul.

Telka, she was passing fair;
And the glory of her hair
Was such glory as the sun
With his blessing casts upon
Yonder lonely mountain height.
EUGENE FIELD, *Telka*

Tedra Telescoped f o r m of THEODORA.

Teena, Tina Dim. fem. ending; see CHRISTINA, ERNESTINA, etc.

Teresa, Theresa (te REE' sa *or* te RAY' za) Perhaps Greek, "to reap." A sixteenth-century Spanish nun and saint, founder of thirty-two convents and famed for her mystical visions. Although this name is not as much used as formerly, two of its pet forms, TERRY and TRACY, are steadily increasing in popularity. Hollywood: Teresa Wright.

Terry Pet form; see TERESA.

Tess, Tessie Dim. form; see TERESA. TESSA. Literature: *Tess of the D'Urbervilles* (1891), famous novel by Thomas Hardy.

Thalia (thal EYE' a *or* THAL' ya) Greek "blooming." Muse of comedy. See MUSA.

Thea Greek, "goddess." See DOROTHEA.

Theda See THEODOSIA. Screen: Theda Bara, star of the silent movies.

Thelma Greek, "nursling." Literature: *Thelma* (1887), novel by the once very popular Marie Corelli. Hollywood, Stage, and TV: Thelma Ritter, comedienne.

Themis Greek, "order, custom, justice." T(H)EMA. In Homer, Themis personifies the order of things established by equity, custom, and law. She visits not only the assemblies of men but also calls together the gathering of the gods. Her dwelling place is Olympus.

Theodora See THEODORE. TEDDIE, TEDI. History: a beautiful actress who as the Empress, wife of Justinian, became a power behind the throne. See JUSTINIAN.

Theodosia (thee a DOE' sha) Greek, "divinely given." THEDA.

Theone (thee OH' nee) Greek, "godly."

Thérèse (tay REZZ') French form; see TERESA. Literature: Novel *Thérèse Raquin* (1867) by Émile Zola.

Thirza, Tirza Hebrew, "linden tree" or "pleasantness." THYRZA, TIRTZAH.

Thou art beautiful, O my love, as Tirzah, comely as Jerusalem.

THE SONG OF SOLOMON 6:4

Literature: George Gissing's *Thyrza* (1887), a beautiful and tender story of an idealized type of girlhood, a novel called the author's own "Song of Joy."

Thisbe Greek place name, "region of doves." Mythology: The Babylonian lovers, Pyramus and Thisbe, whose story is an ancient version of *Romeo and Juliet*. Literature: *Pyramus and Thisbe*, the play within a play in Shakespeare's *Midsummer Night's Dream*.

Today, fair Thisbe, winsome girl!

*Strays o'er the meads where
   daisies blow,
Or, ling'ring where the brooklets
   purl,
   Laves in the cool, refreshing
   flow.*
                  EUGENE FIELD,
                  Chicago Weather

Thomasin(e) (TOM' a seen) See.
THOMAS. TAMZIN. Literature:
Thomasin, the kind and gentle
country girl, in *The Return of
the Native* by Thomas Hardy.

Thora   Fem. form; see THOR(m).

*At the ring in her finger
Gazed Thora, the fairest of
   women.*
                  LONGFELLOW,
                  Thora of Rimol

Tilda   See MATILDA.

Tilly   See MATILDA. TILDA.

Timothea   See TIMOTHY.

Tina   See TEENA.

Tish   See LETITIA.

Tobey   Germanic, "a dove"; or
Hebrew "good." See TOBIAS (m).
TOBI, TOBYE, TYBIE, TOBE, TOVA,
TOVE.

Toni   See ANTOINETTE, TONIE,
TONY.

Tova   See TOBEY.

Tracy   See TERESA.

Trina   (TREE' na) Terminal
dim. of KATRINA. See KATHER-
INE. TRENNA.

Trixie   See BEATRICE.

Troth   Anglo-Saxon, "truth" or
"pledge."

Truda   See GERTRUDE, TRUDE,
TRUDY.

True   English, "true."
   *This above all; to thine own
self be true.*
WILLIAM SHAKESPEARE, *Hamlet*

Tyra   Fem. form of THOR or
TYRUS or even of TYRONE. See
THORA. In Norse mythology Tyr
was the god of battle.

U

Edgar Allan Poe
Walking in the moonlight,
In the woods of Albemarle,
'Neath the trees of Richmond,
Pondering names of women,
>*Annabel—Annie*
>*Lenore—ULALUME.*

MARY JOHNSTON, *Virginiana*

Ula Variant spelling of EULA. ULLA.

Ulalume (OO' la LOOM *or* YOU' la LOOM) Poetic name invented by Poe, suggested perhaps by a Latin word meaning "wailing."

Ulrica (ULL' ric a) Fem. form; see ULRIC (m).

Una (YOU' na *or* OO' na) Gaelic; also English, from Latin, "one." ONA, OONA. Used in Ireland in its three forms, as an equivalent of AGNES and as a diminutive of WINIFRED. Screen: Una O'Connor; Oona O'Neill Chaplin. Literature: Heroine of first book of Spenser's *Faërie Queene*, symbolizing Truth. Stage and TV: Una Merkel.

The gentle Una I have loved,
The snowy maiden pure and wild,
Since ever by her side I roved
Through ventures strange, a wondering child.
>JAMES RUSSELL LOWELL
>*Dedication* of book
>*A Year's Life* (1841)

Undine (un DEEN' *or* UN' deen) Latin and French, "wave." ONDINE. Literature: Heroine of celebrated romance by Baron de La Motte-Fouqué. Music: a ballet (*Ondine*) and two operas (*Undine*).

Urania (you RAY' nee a) Greek, "heavenly." Mythology: Muse of astronomy.

About thee sports sweet Liberty;
And rapt Urania sings to thee.
>JAMES THOMSON,
>*Hymn on Solitude*

Urbana (ur BAN' a) Latin, "courteous." See URBAN.

Ursula (URR' syou la) Latin, "little she-bear." A fifth-century saint of Cornish birth. Screen: Ursula Jeans.

I see her in the festal warmth to-night,
Her rest all grace, her motion all delight.
Endowed with all the woman's arts that please,
In her soft gown she seems a thing of ease,

*Whom sorrow may not reach or
evil blight.*
ROBERT UNDERWOOD JOHNSON,
Ursula

Uta (oo' ta) Dim. of OTTILIE.
Theater: Uta Hagen was named
after the historical Countess of
Naumburg. In mythology Queen
Ute of Burgundy was the mother
of Gunther and Kriemhild, the
heroine of Richard Wagner's
Nibelungen Ring.

V

There goes the Lady VI: *How well,*
How well I know the spectacle
  The earth presents
  And its events
  To her sweet sight
  Each day and night.

THOMAS HARDY, *Lady Vi*

Valentina (val en TEE′ na) See
VALENTINE. VALLI, VALLY.

Valerie (VALL′ e ree), **Valeria**
(va LEE′ ri a) Latin, "strong."
VALERA, VALLY, VAL, VALE. TV:
Valerie Harper ("Rhoda" series).

Vanessa (va NESS′ a) From literature. Invented by Dean Swift
for Esther Vanhomrigh. He took
the *Van* of her surname and
added *Essa*, an abbrev. of
ESTHER, to get this lovely name.
Theater: Vanessa Redgrave,
British stage star.

The Queen of Love was pleas'd
  and proud
To see Vanessa thus endow'd:
She doubted not but such a dame
Through every breast would dart
  a flame,
That ev'ry rich and lordly swain
With pride would drag about her
  chain;
That scholars would forsake
  their books
To study bright Vanessa's looks.
    DEAN JONATHAN SWIFT,
      Cadenus and Vanessa

(*Cadenus* is a pun on *catena*,
Latin word for *chain*, and an
anagram of the Latin word *decanus*, from which we get our
word *dean*. See DEAN.)

Hollywood: Vanessa Brown.
Music: *Vanessa*, an American
opera given at the Metropolitan
Opera House, composed by
Samuel Barber, who, it is re-
ported, got his title by consult-
ing a book of babies' names!
The opera won the Pulitzer
Music Prize in 1958.

Velma See WILHELMINA. VILMA.
Screen: Vilma Banky, star of
silent films, leading lady in Valentino films.

Vanetia Either from a place
name, the Latin and poetic name
of Venice (Italian, *Venezia*), or
supposedly a Latinization of
Welsh GWYNETH.

Vera (VEE′ ra) Russian, "faith";
Latin, "true"; also short form
of VERONICA. Ballet and Theater: Vera Zorina.

Verity Latin, "truth." VERITA.
See under CHARITY.

Verna See VERNON. VERNICE.

Veronica (ve RONN′ ic a) Latin-Greek, "true image." RONNIE. The "true image" refers to the cloth or handkerchief which, according to legend, a pious woman of Jerusalem named Veronica gave to Jesus. After He had wiped His face with the cloth, His image was miraculously imprinted on it. Screen: Veronica Lake.

Vesta Sanskrit-Latin, "burn" or "day." Similar to Greek *Hestia*, "hearth." Vesta was the Roman goddess of the hearth in whose temple there was no statue but a fire kept eternally alive by the Vestal Virgins, the most sacred object in Roman religion.

A glorious city thou [Romulus]
  shalt build,
And name it by thy name:
And there unquenched through
  ages,
  Like Vesta's sacred fire,
Shall live the spirit of thy nurse,
  The spirit of thy sire.
        THOMAS B. MACAULAY,
          The Prophecy of Capys

Victoria Latin "victory." VICKI. Queen Victoria, who reigned in England for sixty-four years (1837-1901), gave her name to a period in history. Music: Victoria de los Angeles, operatic soprano.

Vida (VEE′ da) From DAVIDA.

Vinnie Pet form used as fem. of VINCENT. VINITA, VINETTA, VINETTE, VINNY, VINCENTA. *Vinita, Vinette* may be from *Viña,* Spanish, "vineyard," or Germanic root meaning "waker."

Viola (vye OH′ la, VYE′ o la, *or* VEE′ o la) Latin, "violet." VI. Literature: Heroine of Shakespeare's *Twelfth Night.*

Violet See VIOLA. VIOLETTA, VIOLETTE. VI. Flower name. The poet Ernest Dowson thought that *v* was the most beautiful of all the letters, and therefore considered this the ideal line in English poetry:

The viol, the violet and the vine.
        EDGAR ALLAN POE,
          The City in the Sea

  Ballet: Violette Verdy of the New York City Center.

Virgilia See VIRGIL. VERGILIA. Literature: Virgilia Peterson, literary critic and author of autobiography *A Matter of Life and Death.*

Virginia Place name. GINNIE, JINNY, VIRGY, GINGER. In America, from the colony of Virginia, named in honor of Elizabeth, the Virgin Queen of England. The first white child born in America was named Virginia Dare. See VIRGINIUS(m) for another origin of the name.

  This name is perpetuated at Christmas time with the reprinting of the famous editorial *Is There a Santa Claus?* written by

Francis Pharcellus Church (September 21, 1897) in the *New York Sun* answering a query of Virginia O'Hanlon, then aged eight. The answer, "Yes, Virginia, there is a Santa Claus," has become almost proverbial. Literature: *Paul and Virginia*, (1788), famous French romantic novel by Bernardin St. Pierre; Virginia Woolf (1882-1941), critic and one of the most important novelists of this century (*Orlando, The Waves,* etc.).

Vita (VEE' ta) Latin, "life" or variant of VIDA.

Vivian, Vivien Latin, "full of life." VIVIENNE. VYVYAN. Vivien Leigh, winner of Oscar in 1939 for her portrayal of Scarlett O'Hara in *Gone with the Wind,* and in 1951 for that of Blanche Du Bois in *A Streetcar Named Desire.* Literature: *Merlin and Vivien* in Tennyson's *Idylls of the King.*

W

Fair Nokomis bore a daughter
And she called her name WENONAH
As the first-born of her daughters.

HENRY WADSWORTH LONGFELLOW,
Hiawatha

Wallis See WALLACE. WALLY.

Wanda Germanic, of uncertain origin, possibly related to "wand" or "wanderer." VANDA. Music: Wanda Landowska, greatest interpreter of harpsichord music.

Wanita Sometimes used as a variant of JUANITA.

Weda A respelling of OUIDA.

Wendy Pet name; see GWENDOLEN. WENDI, WENDA. Used as independent name. Literature: The "love interest" in *Peter Pan* (1904), which Barrie based on his own earlier novel *Peter and Wendy*. Actresses Wendy Barrie and Wendy Hiller have helped to popularize the name and give it independent status.

Wenonah American Indian, "first-born." WINONA. Literature: Mother of Hiawatha.

Wilfreda See WILFRED.

Wilhelmina Fem. of German WILHELM. See WILLIAM. WILMA, VILMA, VELMA, MINA, MINNIE.

Willa See WILL. Literature: Willa Cather, American novelist, Pulitzer Prize winner in 1922 (*One of Ours*).

Wilma See WILHELMINA and WILMER (m). Sports: Wilma Rudolph Ward, winner of three gold medals in 1960 Olympics, voted woman athlete of the year in 1960 and 1961.

Winifred Welsh, "white wave," probably a variant of GUINEVERE. WINFRIED, WINNIE, FREDDIE. Legendary seventh-century Welsh saint. Theater: Winifred Lenihan, first actress to play the role of St. Joan in the United States.

And when with envy time trans-
   ported,
   Shall think to rob us of our
      joys,
You'll in your girls again be
   courted,
   And I'll go a-wooing in my
      boys.

ANON, *Winefreda*

Winnie See WINIFRED. Literature: *Winnie-the-Pooh*, delightful volume of children's stories by A. A. Milne, recently translated into Latin as *Winnie Ille Pu.*

Minnie and Winnie slept in a shell.

Sleep, little ladies! And they slept well.

ALFRED LORD TENNYSON,
Minnie and Winnie

Winona See WENONAH.

X

*Nearer came the storm and nearer, rolling fast
        and frightful on!
Speak, XIMENA, speak and tell us, who has lost
        and who has won?
"Alas! alas! I know not; friend and foe together
        fall,
O'er the dying rush the living: pray, my sisters,
        for them all!"*

WHITTIER, *The Angels of Buena Vista*

Xanthe (ZAN′ thee) Greek, "golden yellow." XANTHA. Masc., XANTHUS.

Xant(h)ippe (zan TIPP′ e) Greek, "yellow (or auburn) horse." The long-suffering wife of the philosopher Socrates who has achieved a reputation as a scold:

*He had by heart the whole detail
        of woe
Xantippe made her good man
        undergo.*

ALEXANDER POPE,
The Wife of Bath: Prologue

However, it appears that Xantippe has been much maligned. Wise as he was, Socrates would have been a trial to any woman as he wandered about the marketplace, unkempt, often barefooted, neglecting his family and livelihood.

Xena (ZEE′ na) Greek, "guest." XENIA. See also ZENA.

Ximena (him AY′ na or zim EE′ na) Spanish; see XIMENES. French, *Chimène*, heroine of Corneille's *Le Cid* who marries the Cid. See under RODERICK.

Y

But when the silver dove descends
I find the little flower of friends
Whose very name that sweetly ends
I say when I have said YASMIN.

JAMES ELROY FLECKER, *Yasmin*

Yasmin See JASMINE. YASMINE.

Yetta See HENRIETTA.

Ynez See INEZ.

Yolanda From old French form *Violante;* see VIOLA. YOLANDE, YOLANE.

I know not how, but I must find
Fair Yoland with the yellow
hair.
OWEN MEREDITH, *Fair Yoland*

Yseult Variant form; see ISOLDA.

Yseult, Irish Yseult, Yseult the
Fair.
RICHARD HOVEY,
The Birth of Galahad

Yvette (ee VET') See YVONNE. Screen: Yvette Mimieux (*The Black Hole*).

Yvonne (ee VUNN' *or* ee VONN') French fem. of YVON. See IVOR. YVETTE. Theater: Yvonne Printemps, French actress. Hollywood: Yvonne De Carlo.

In your mother's apple orchard,
When the world was left be-
hind:
You were shy, so shy, Yvonne
But your eyes were calm and
kind.
ERNEST DOWSON,
Yvonne of Brittany

Z

Ah, fair ZENOCRATE, divine ZENOCRATE,
Fair is too foul an epithet for thee.

CHRISTOPHER MARLOWE,
Tamerlaine the Great

Zaida (ZAY′ da) Arabic, probably "good fortune," or "growth"; also possibly "huntress." Name used occasionally today in honor of a Moorish girl of noble birth who lived in Alzira, near Valencia, Spain. Together with her sister Zoraida, she was converted and later was sanctified as St. Mary of Alzira. ZADA.

Zelda Terminal dim. of GRISELDA. SELDA, ZELDE. See GRISELDA.

Zena, Zeena Either variant of XENIA, or more probably dim. of ZENOBIA. ZENIA, ZINA, ZENECIA, ZENIJA.

Zenobia Zenobia Septimia was the beautiful and intelligent queen of Palmyra in the third century who conquered parts of the Near East but was subdued by the Roman emperor Aurelian. In Aramaic her name was *Bat Zabbai*, "daughter of Zabbai,"; the transliteration to Latin via Greek may mean "Zeus gives life."

Zillah Hebrew, "shade," figurative for "protection." Biblical: Mother of Tubal-cain, the smith.

Zippora(h) (zipp o′ rah) Hebrew "bird." Biblical: Wife of Moses.

Zita (ZEE′ ta) Probably terminal fem. dim. seen in such names as *Rosita, Teresita, Carmencita,* etc. ZITELLA, which is also Italian, "girl."

Gentle Zitella, whither away?
Love's ritornella, list while I play.

JAMES ROBINSON PLANCHE,
Love's Ritornella

Zoë, Zoe (ZOE′ ee) Greek, "life." ZOA. A name first used in Alexandria to translate the Biblical EVE. Literature: Zoë Akins, winner of a Pulitzer Prize (1935) for her play *The Old Maid* adapted from the short novel by Edith Wharton.

Maid of Athens, ere we part,
Give, oh, give me back my heart,
Or, since that has left my breast,
Keep it now, and take the rest!
Hear my vow before I go,
Zoë mou, sas agapo.
    ["Life of mine, I love you."]
GEORGE GORDON BYRON,
Maid of Athens

Zola Italian, "ball of earth." Used symbolically in honor of

292

the famous French novelist and fighter for justice. See under EMILE.

Zona Greek via Latin, "girdle, belt." Literature: Zona Gale, winner of Pulitzer Prize (1921) for her play *Miss Lulu Bett*, based on her best-selling novel.

Zora Slavic, "dawn." Also possibly from Hebrew place name, "scourge" or "hornet." ZORAH, ZOHRA, ZARYA. Screen: Zorah Lampert (also TV series, "The Nurses").

Zoraida (zo RAY' da *or* zo RYE' da) Arabic, possibly "captive." See ZAIDA. Zoraida became St. Gratia, or Gracia, of Alzira.

Zuleika (zoo LAYE' ka *or* zoo LEE' ka) Arabic, "the fair one." Biblical: Name ascribed to Potiphar's wife. Literature: *Zuleika Dobson* (1911), a novel by Max Beerbohm which made the name *Zuleika* the toast of the Oxford students. In *The Bride of Abydos* by Byron, Zuleika is the pure and noble heroine.

Zuleika is fled away,
Though your bolts and your
*   bars are strong;*
A minstrel came today
And stole her away with a song.
                    ARTHUR O'SHAUGHNESSY,
                                    Zuleika

A GALAXY OF THE UNUSUAL

Names for Boys

Bright with names that men remember,
Loud with names that men forget.

ALGERNON CHARLES SWINBURNE,
Eton: An Ode

Achilles (a KILL′ eez) Greek, "lipless." French, ACHILLE (A SHEEL′); Italian, ACHILLE (a KEEL′ lay). The peerless hero of the Greeks in the Trojan War.

For who can match Achilles? He who can,
Must yet be more than hero, more than man.

HOMER, *Iliad*
(translated by Alexander Pope)

Alaric (AL′ a rik) Germanic, "all-rich" or "all-rule." History: Gothic king who sacked Rome in 410 A.D. There was also a St. Alaric.

Alph(a)eus (AL′ fee us *or* al FEE′ us) Greek-Latin, possibly from Aramaic; meaning not known. Biblical: Father of James the Less.

Antenor (an TEN′ or) Greek, "for a man." Mythology: Wise old Trojan counselor.

Athelstan Old English, "noble" + "stone." History: A king of Wessex. Literature: Character in Scott's *Ivanhoe*.

Avon (AY′ von) Celtic, "river." Literature: River on which Stratford, birthplace of Shakespeare, is located. Ben Jonson called Shakespeare "Sweet Swan of Avon."

Booth Germanic and Celtic, "dwelling." Literature: Booth Tarkington (1869-1946), novelist, winner of a Pulitzer Prize in 1919 (*The Magnificent Ambersons*) and in 1922 (*Alice Adams*).

Boyd Gaelic, "yellow-haired."

Byam Anglo-Saxon place name, possibly "at the manor." Art: Byam Shaw, known especially for book illustrations. Theater: Glen Byam Shaw, director.

Charlemagne See CHARLES.

Clovis See LOUIS.

Compton Old English, "town in a valley" or "valley of the fields."

Damian, Damien From same root as DAMON; see DAMON. Name of third-century saint who is named in the Canon of the Mass. Father Damien (1840-1889) was a missionary famed for his work among lepers in the Hawaiian Islands; he is the subject of *Father Damien* by Robert Louis Stevenson.

Danton French, "of Anthony." Surname of Georges Jacques Danton (1759-1794), a leader of the French Revolution.

Deems Anglo-Saxon, "judge." Music: Deems Taylor, composer (*The King's Henchman*, etc.).

Delos (DEE' los) Greek, "visible" or possibly "arising suddenly." Name of the island-birthplace of Artemis and Phoebus Apollo.

Where grew the arts of war and peace,
  Where Delos rose, and Phoebus sprung!
    GEORGE GORDON BYRON,
      Don Juan

Diomedes (dye o MEE' deez), **Diomede** (DYE' o meed), **Diomed** (DYE' o med) Greek, "divine cunning." Mighty Greek warrior in Homer's *Iliad*, second only to Achilles.

Doron Greek, "gift." Name used in poetry like CORYDON and STREPHON.

I thank you, Doron, and will think on you;
I love you, Doron, and will wink on you.
    ROBERT GREENE,
      Doron and Carmela

Durward Old English, "door" + "ward" (keeper). Literature: Sir Walter Scott's *Quentin Durward*.

Edsel Anglo-Saxon, "rich" or "happy," possibly a dim. of EDWARD; also possibly Old English, "son of Eda, or Edith." Edsel Ford was the son of Henry Ford; another Edsel Ford is a poet.

Elbridge Anglo-Saxon place name, "old bridge." History. Elbridge Gerry, signer of the Declaration of Independence; from his last name comes the word *gerrymander*.

Elgin Place name.

Elric Variant of ELDRIDGE; see also ALARIC and OLDRIC.

Euclid Greek, "son of glory." Science: Famous mathematician of Alexandria (about 300 B.C.) whose work on geometry was long a school text. Euclid is credited with saying to his pupil Ptolemy that there was no royal road to geometry.

Euclid alone has looked on beauty bare.
    EDNA ST. VINCENT MILLAY,
      The Harp-Weaver

Finis Latin, "the end."

Flavius Latin *gens* name; see FLAVIA. History: From Vespasian on, many Roman emperors bore this name as part of their full name.

Fortune Latin, "good luck."

There is a tide in the affairs of men,
Which, taken at the flood, leads on to fortune.
WILLIAM SHAKESPEARE, *Julius Caesar*

Franchot Thought by some to be a dim. of FRANCOIS, but this form is not found in French lexicons. As used by the actor Franchot Tone, it was originally a surname, his mother's maiden name.

Fulbert Germanic, "very bright." FILBERT, FILIBERT, PHILIBERT. St. Philibert founded the Abbey of Jumièges, France, in the seventh century.

Garland Germanic via French, "wreath."

Where Past and Present, wound in one,
Do make a garland for the heart.
ALFRED, LORD TENNYSON, *The Miller's Daughter*

Haskell Norse and Germanic, "divine inhabitant of Asgard (the Norse Olympus)."

Hereward Anglo-Saxon, "army-protection." History: Hereward the Wake, Saxon leader against the Norman invaders. Literature: Charles Kingsley's novel *Hereward the Wake* (1866).

Herschel(l) German, "little stag." Originally a surname. HERSHEL, HERSH(E)Y. Astronomy: Sir William Herschel (1738-1822), discoverer of the p l a n e t Uranus. Aeronautics: *Herschel* is the middle name of astronaut John H. Glenn Jr. Music: Hershy Kay, composer and orchestrator.

Hilton English place name, "hill town." Originally a surname.

Idris Welsh, "lord" + "impulsive."

Idwal Welsh, "lord" + "rampart." Literature: Idwal Jones, contemporary novelist, critic, and essayist.

Ing(e)mar Scandinavian, *Inge* + "fame." See INGA and INGRID. Screen: (Ernst) Ingmar Bergman, talented producer and director (*Wild Strawberries, The Seventh Seal, The Virgin Spring,* etc.).

Innis Gaelic, "island." Also related to *Angus* and *John*. ENNIS.

Ion Greek, "moon man." Mythology: Son of Apollo. Literature: Tragedy by Euripides; dialogue by Plato.

Jubal Hebrew, "stream (of music)." JUBE. Biblical: Called the "father of all such as handle the harp and organ" (GENESIS 4:21); also considered the legendary inventor of the lyre and flute.

The name may also refer to the ram's horn used as a musical instrument.

Kip Germanic, "to swell," hence, figuratively "rotund." Also possible a place name, "edge" or "brink." In Dutch the name means "a chicken."

Lyall, Lyell Old English pet form of LIONEL or LEON (once pronounced *Lyon*); p o s s i b l y also a variant of LYLE.

Manley Anglo-Saxon place name, "common wood" or possibly "man or servant" + "meadow."

Manning Germanic, "helper's son" or related to "people."

Newman Germanic, "newcomer" or "new servant." NIEMAN.

Nicanor Greek, "victorious." Biblical: General defeated by the Maccabees; also name of deacon of the early Christian Church. Music: Nicanor Zabaleta, virtuoso harpist.

Ninian Name of an early British saint. This name is still occasionally used in Scotland.

Odin Germanic, "fury." Mythology: Chief god in Norse myths.

Odin, thou whirlwind, what a threat is this! . . .

For of all powers the mightiest far art thou,
Lord over men on earth, and Gods in Heaven.
> MATTHEW ARNOLD,
> *Balder Dead*

Oldric Germanic, "rich or old ruler." See ALDRICH.

Orion (oh RYE' 'n) Greek "moon man of the mountain." Mythology: Handsome giant and mighty hunter placed in the heavens as a constellation still followed by his faithful dog which was transformed into Sirius, the Dog Star, brightest in the sky.

Many a night from yonder ivied casement, ere I went to rest,
Did I look on great Orion sloping gently to the west.
> ALFRED, LORD TENNYSON,
> *Locksley Hall*

Orvin Possibly a variant of IRWIN.

Osmer Germanic, "divine fame." HOSMER.

Othniel (OTH' ni el) Hebrew, possibly "God is might." Biblical: A man of Judah who captured a city (JOSHUA 15: 17).

Philetus (fi LEE' tus) Greek, "worthy of love." Biblical: Mentioned in II TIMOTHY 2:17-18 as being in error concerning resurrection.

Rhawn Welsh, possibly "lance."

Romney Old English place name, possibly "spacious river" or "marshy island." More often found as a surname. Art: George Romney (1734-1802), English portrait painter. Theater: Romney Brent.

Tancred Germanic, "thought" + "counsel." History: Heroic Crusader. Music: Opera by Rossini. Literature: *Tancred, or the New Crusade* (1847), novel by Benjamin Disraeli.

Theophane Greek, "God + appearance." Related to *Epiphany*. Fem., EPIFANIA. *Theophane* is a saint's name; a *theophany* is the manifestation of God to an individual, as to Moses, Gideon, etc.

Theron Greek, "hunter."

Theseus (THEES' yus) Greek, "he who puts down." Mythology: Mighty hero whose exploits resemble those of Hercules, famous slayer of the Minotaur, legendary king of Athens. See also under ARIADNE. Literature: Two remarkable novels about Theseus by Mary Renault, *The King Must Die* and *The Bull from the Sea.*

> *Behind him there came*
> *The winner of a great and dreadful name,*
> *Theseus, the slayer of the fearful beast.*
>
> WILLIAM MORRIS,
> *Life and Death of Jason*

Varian Latin, possibly from the family name *Varus,* "bent," hence, "knock-kneed," nickname used as a surname.

Wyman Anglo-Saxon, "warrior" or "road protector"; also place name, possibly related to "dairy." WIMOND, WYMUND.

Names for Girls

Ailsa Gaelic, probably "glory."

Almeda Origin uncertain but the name may be a variant of Welsh *Almedha,* which in turn is related to *Eiluned,* "idol." The latter name is the LYNETTE of the King Arthur stories. See ALODIA.

Alodia Name of a Spanish saint. However, *Alodia* is supposedly connected with the Welsh *Eiluned;* see ALMEDA, above. ELODIA.

Alpha First letter of the Greek alphabet, from Phoenician and Hebrew, "ox."

I am Alpha and Omega, the beginning and the ending, saith the Lord.

REVELATION 1:7

Alynn Probably a newly-coined variant of ALAN.

Asenath Ancient Egyptian, "favorite of or belonging to the goddess Neith." ASENETH. Biblical: Egyptian wife of Joseph (GENESIS 41:45).

Beata (bay AH′ ta) Latin, "blessed." The Beatitudes are a group of sayings by Jesus (MATTHEW 5:3-12; LUKE 6:20-23) which, in the Vulgate, begin with the word *Beati,* "blessed."

Blessed are the peacemakers: for they shall see God.

Bijou French, "jewel."

Binnie Probably pet name for BESS or BONNIE or BRIDGET.

Bronwen, Bronwyn Welsh, "breast + white or beautiful." See under BRAM. *Bronwen* is sometimes confused with *Branwen,* or *Brangwain,* "dark + beautiful," name of the attendant of Isolde.

Buena Spanish, "good." See also BONITA.

Cadence Latin, "rhythm."

How soft the music of those village bells
Falling at intervals upon the ear
In cadence sweet!
WILLIAM COWPER, *The Task*

Cavada Derivation uncertain; possibly from Spanish place

302

name *Cavada*, "hollow" or "pit."
The actress Cavada Humphrey
wrote to us that it goes far back
in her family as a surname.

Cheerful Literally, "full of face
(spirit)," from Latin *cara*,
"face."

*A merry heart maketh a cheerful
countenance.*

APOCRYPHA,
Ecclesiasticus 13:25

Cleora Combination of elements of names like CLEON,
CLEOPATRA, and HONORA.

Colombe French, "dove," from
Latin *Columba*. COLOMBA. Literature: Robert Browning's
poem *Colombe's Birthday;*
Prosper Merimée's famous short
novel *Colomba*. The Italian form
Columbina, "dovelike," was
used as the name of a stock
character in old comedy, sweetheart of Harlequin or Pierrot.
Columbine is also a flower
name; the columbine receiving
its name from a fancied resem-
blance to a group of five pigeons.

*If you were a white rose Colum-
bine*
And I were a Harlequin,
*I'd leap and sway on my span-
gled hips,*
*And blow you a kiss with my
finger tips,*
*And woo a smile to your petal
lips*
With every glittering spin.

CROSBIE GARSTIN,
A Fantasy

Dare Anglo-Saxon, "to be
bold."

Delila(h) Semitic, probably
"coquette." DALILA(H). Biblical:
Philistine woman who betrayed
Samson. See under SAMSON.
Music: *Samson et Dalila* (1877),
opera by Camille Saint-Saëns.

Delta Fourth letter of the
Greek alphabet, from Phoenician and Hebrew, "door."

Diosa Spanish, "goddess."
DIOSE. See DIONE.

Eloda, Elodia, Elodie Possibly
variants of ALODIA.

Epifania See THEOPHANE. Literature: Character in Shaw's
Millionairess.

Ethelinda Combination of
ETHEL and LINDA. See also BE-
LINDA, DORINDA.

Eudice Greek, "Pleasant justice."

Eurydice (you RID' i see) Greek,
"wide-justice." Mythology: Wife
of Orpheus, who by the power of
his music almost succeeded in
bringing her back from the lower
world. Music: Gluck's opera
Orpheus and Eurydice (*Orfeo et
Euridice*).

*. . . and hear
Such strains as would have won
the ear
Of Pluto to have quite set free
His half-regained Eurydice.*

JOHN MILTON, *L'Allegro*

Fama Latin, "fame."

*Fame is the spur that the clear
    spirit doth raise.*
          JOHN MILTON, *Lycidas*

Feena Irish, "deer."

Fiona Irish, *Fionnghuala,
Fionnuala,* "of the white shoul-
ders." The long form has been
changed to FENELLA, which, in
Ireland, is often used for
PENELOPE. The short form is
more usual; sometimes it re-
places FLORA. In addition, the
ending, NUALA, is sometimes
used as an independent name.
Mythology and Literature: Fionnuala, daughter of Lir, an Irish
deity; Fenella, a character in Sir
Walter Scott's *Peveril of the
Peak.*

Fira Probably coined from
"fire."

Flaminia Latin *gens* name, related to "flame."

G(h)ita Possibly pet form of
GERTRUDE and GUSSIE; also tele-
scoped terminal form of MAR-
GHERITA or of a form of BRIDGET.

Gia (JEE′ a) Italian; short
forms of names like GIACOMA,
GIANNETTA, and GIOVANNA, or
ending of LUIGIA. See GIACOMO,
JACQUELINE, JANE, and JANET.

Hannalynn Combination of
HANNAH and LYNN.

Heritage Latin via French, "in-
heritance." Quality name; see
under CHARITY.

*The lines are fallen unto me in
pleasant places; yea, I have a
goodly heritage.*
          PSALMS 16:6

Hesper Greek via Latin *Hesperus,* "vesper," or "evening,"
name of the Evening Star.

*Hesperus with the host of heaven
    came,
And lo! Creation widened in
    man's view.*
          JOSEPH BLANCO WHITE,
                 To Night

Hypatia (hye PAY′ sha) Greek,
"of high rank." History: A
woman of Alexandria (fifth
century A.D.) famous for her
learning and wisdom; her lec-
tures on philosophy, astronomy,
and mechanics attracted thousands from all parts of the Greek
world. Literature: Charles Kingsley's historical novel *Hypatia*
(1853) about her life; name of
a leading character in Shaw's
Misalliance.

Ila Probably short form of
ILENE.

Inglis Anglo-Saxon, "English."
Literature: Inglis Fletcher, author of the "Carolina" novels;
her *Wicked Lady* (1962) is about
the American Revolution.

Isis (EYE′ sis) Greek and
Latin form of ancient Egyptian

Aset, probably "(heavenly) seat, or throne," represented by a chair in hieroglyphics. Name of the chief goddess, wife of Osiris.

Lalage (LAL' a jee) Greek via Latin, "prattling." Literature: The "sweet-smiling, sweet-chattering Lalage" of Horace's *Odes.*

Lalla Hindustani, "tulip." Name sometimes given because of Thomas Moore's long work in prose and poetry, *Lalla Rookh* ("Tulip-Cheek"). The author wrote about Lalla Rookh, daughter of the Emperor of Delhi, India:

"A Princess described by the poets of her time as more beautiful than Leila, Shirine, Dewildé, or any of those heroines whose names and loves embellish the songs of Persia and Hindostan."

Lani Hawaiian, "heavenly" or "royal" or "of noble birth." *Lani* is used as an ending of many Hawaiian names, as in that of Lydia Kamehaha Liliuokalani (1838-1917), once Queen of the Hawaiian Islands.

Lannie See LANNY.

Laryssa Used as a fem. of LARRY. See LAURENCE.

Leueen Celtic, fem. of LEWIS or LLEWELLYN. See LAURENCE. LEULLA. Stage: Leueen Mac-Grath.

Lys French, "lily."

Madine Probably combination of element of MADELINE and fem. ending *ine.*

Mattiwilda Combination of first part of MATILDA and WILDA. Music: Mattiwilda Dobbs of the Metropolitan Opera.

Medora Literary name from Byron's poem *The Corsair,* of which Medora is the lovely heroine.

Mia Terminal form of names like EUPHEMIA or telescoped short form of MARIA. Ballet: Mia Slavenska.

Moneta Latin, "adviser." This name was used by Latin authors to translate the *Greek Mnemosyne,* "memory," name of the mother of the Muses. *Moneta* was also a surname of Juno; from it come the English words *mint* and *money,* because money was coined in the temple of Juno Moneta at Rome.

Muna Arabic, "wish."

Narcissa Modern fem. form of *Narcissus,* name of the handsome youth of the Greek myths who was loved by the Nymph Echo and who was turned into the flower bearing his name (meaning "benumbing, narcotic"). History: Narcissa Whitman, "the ideal American pioneer," first white woman to cross the Rockies. She and her husband, Dr. Marcus Whitman, are considered the founders of Oregon.

Navarre French place name thought of as "low country" by the Basques of that region.

Nelda, Nerine Greek via Latin *Nerinus*, belonging to Nereus ("damp"). Nereus was a marine divinity, the "Old Man of the Sea," ruling over the Mediterranean. The fifty daughters of Nereus and Doris, the Nereids, or Nereides, were the Nymphs of the same sea. The most celebrated of the Nereids was Thetis, mother of Achilles.

Ninon (NEE NAWN') French pet form of names like *Jeannin;* see ANN, JEAN, JANE, and JOAN. Also derived from *nina*, used in southern France to mean "little girl." NINET. Ninon (Anne) de Lenclos (1620-1705), famous for her wit and beauty, attracted to her salon the notables of her day, including Cardinal Richelieu.

Norlene Combination of NORA and ending of names like ARLENE.

Nova Latin, "new."

Ola Fem. of Norwegian *Ole*, "protector." Also possible fem. of OLIN. OLINE, which is also terminal form of CAROLINE, NICOLINE, etc.

Omega Greek, "large *o*," last letter of the Greek alphabet. See under ALPHA.

Oriel On the surface this appears to be a bird name, a variant of *oriole*, similar to the French surnames *Lauriol* and *Loriol*. However, it may be derived from the Germanic *Aurildis*, or *Orieldis*, "fire + strife." In England the use of the name may be related to Oriel College, Oxford, which, for unknown reasons, was called *La Oriole* at one time. Here, *Oriel* may be related to the word meaning a bay window.

Orinda Poetic name formed from ORA and the ending *inda*, as in BELINDA. See ORA, LINDA, BELINDA, and MELINDA.

Orinda on the Female courts of Fame
Ingrosses all the Goods of a Poetique Name.
ABRAHAM COWLEY, from *Verses on Several Occasions*

Orletta Combination of first element of names like ORMOND, ORSON, ORLANDO, etc., and fem. dim. ending.

Orpah Biblical: Sister-in-law of Ruth. The name may mean "freshness" or "stubbornness."

Orpha Origin unknown, possibly variant of ORPAH, but there is always the possibility that the giver of this name may be thinking of it as coined fem. of *Orpheus*.

Ottora Possibly from OTTO.

Perdita Latin, "lost one." Literature: Delightful heroine of Shakespeare's *Winter's Tale*, so named for a particular reason:

> . . . *and, for the babe*
> *Is counted lost for ever, Perdita,*
> *I prithee, call't.*

But, Perdita, when "grown in grace equal with wondering," was found again. As in the cases of other names whose meaning may not be pleasant, the name is used, however, because of flattering associations, all thought of the original meaning forgotten.

Peregrine Latin, "wanderer, pilgrim." Originally used only as a masc. name but now returning to use as a fem. name. Peregrine White(m), born to a Pilgrim couple on the *Mayflower*, was the first English child born in the New World.

Pleasance (PLEZ' ans) French, "pleasure"; a "quality" name.

Ralee, Raley (RAY' lee) Combination of RAE and LEE. RAELA.

Ravelle Either a variant of RACHEL, or name formed in honor of the composer Maurice Ravel; see under ZOLA.

Rolinda Combination of ROSE and LINDA.

Scottie Fem. of SCOTT. The daughter of F. Scott Fitzgerald is Scottie Fitzgerald Lanahan.

Serilda Combination of parts of SARA or SERENA and names like MATILDA.

Siobhan, Siubhan (sh' VAWN') Gaelic name used as equivalent of JUDITH. Stage: Actress Siobhan McKenna.

Sophonisba Latinized form of a Phoenician name containing the element *Baal*, "master, lord," chief god of the Canaanites. History: Sophoni(s)ba, Carthaginian lady who became Queen of Numidia but suffered a tragic fate which is the theme of many tragedies.

Talma Origin unknown; possibilities are (1) whimsical variation of THELMA (2) French place name or family name (3) fem. for family name like *Talmadge*, from French nickname, "knapsack."

Thais, Thaïs (French, TA EES' English, THAY' is) Greek, probably "blooming" or "giving joy." Literature: Anatole France's novel *Thaïs* (1890); Music: Massenet's opera (1894) based on the novel. History: Athenian lady who accompanied Alexander on his march of conquest:

> *The lovely Thais by his side*
> *Sat like a blooming Eastern*
> *bride*

In flower of youth and beauty's
pride.

> JOHN DRYDEN,
> *Alexander's Feast*

Treva Origin unknown, possibly a formation from TREVOR or a similar family name.

Tryph(a)ena Greek, "delicate." Biblical: Lady mentioned in the New Testament by Paul:

> *Salute Tryphena and Tryphosa, who labour in the Lord.*
> ROMANS 16:12

Tryphosa Greek, "delicate." See TRYPHENA.

Vale Sometimes used as a short form of VALERIE but entered here as an independent name, poetic form of *valley,* which is from Latin via French.

Far from the madding crowd's
ignoble strife
   Their sober wishes never
   learned to stray;
Along the cool sequestered vale
of life
   They kept the noiseless tenor
   of their way.

> THOMAS GRAY,
> *Elegy Written*
> *in a Country Churchyard*

Vanita Latin, "vanity."

Vanity of vanities, saith the
Preacher, vanity of vanities; all
is vanity.

> ECCLESIASTES 1:2

Verbenia Flower name from Latin *verbena.*

Verlinda Combination of VERA and LINDA.

Vieva Terminal short form of GENEVIEVE or from Latin *viva,* "alive." See also VIVIAN.

Viveca Swedish, from German-Danish *Vibeke,* dim. of *Viborg,* Danish place name, "brilliant in battle" or "fortress." In ancient Scandinavia *Vi* meant a holy place. *Borg* may also mean "harvest." TV, Stage, and Hollywood: Viveca Lindfors.

Wandra Possibly variant of WANDA.

Wilda Germanic, "wild."

Wren Anglo-Saxon bird name.

Zama(h) Hebrew, "plant" or "growth."

Zara Probably Arabic, "flowery." French, ZAIRE. Literature: Tragedy by Voltaire. However, as used today, the name may represent nothing more than a desire to vary the more usual SARA.

Zelia This may be a variant of ZILLAH or even of CELIA; see remarks under ZARA above.

Zella See ZELIA, above; also possible short terminal form of ROSELLE, which some spell ROZELLE.

Zilpha Possibly variant of ZIL-PHA, derivation unknown, "dignity" suggested. Biblical: Zilpah, who bore Gad and Asher to Jacob (GENESIS 30:9-13).

Zenaida, Zinaida Greek, "daughter of Zeno." See ZENO. Zenais was a saint of the first century; the name may also be derived from this name or from Zenas, name of "the lawyer" mentioned by Paul in TITUS 3:13. Joseph Bonaparte, older brother of Napoleon, had a daughter named Zénaïde.

Farewells are meant for going,
And greetings bid return:
But names are made for knowing
All things that hearts can learn.

When one name is a treasure,
Another is a troth:
Ring out a lyric measure
To the melody of both!

Names are romance, I swear it!
Hear, when the heart exclaims
That lovers must inherit
The talisman of names.

CARL JOHN BOSTELMANN,
The Talisman of Names

Names in Other Lands

> Lo, Soul! seest thou not God's purpose
> from the first?
> The earth to be spann'd, connected by
> net-work,
> The people to become brothers and sisters,
> The races, neighbors, to marry and to be
> given in marriage,
> The oceans to be cross'd, the distant
> brought near,
> The lands to be welded together.
>
> WALT WHITMAN, *Passage to India*

All of our people—except full-blooded Indians—are immigrants, or descendants of immigrants, including even those who came here on the Mayflower.

FRANKLIN D. ROOSEVELT,
Campaign Speech,
Boston, November 4, 1944

With "the immigrants" came their names sometimes kept in the original form, sometimes adapted to the speech-ways of their new home.

We have included here lists of names widely used in continental Europe because we thought you might be interested in them for any or all of the following reasons:

1. These lists may contain names used by people you know.

2. They may give you an idea of what your name or your child's name sounds like in another language. In foreign-language classes, young Stephen is thrilled with his French name *Étienne,* and little Mary is equally delighted with her Spanish pet name *Mariquita.*

3. With international news crowding the pages of our newspapers and with U.N. proceedings being telecast, these lists may help you to satisfy your curiosity about the first names of the other members of the United Nations. Does the Polish name *Jerzy* mean "George" or "Jerry"? Was the Yugoslavian speaker *Milan* named after a city? After all, one of the hopes of the U.N. is that some day the people of all nations will want to know each other by their first names.

4. Many first names now unfamiliar to you may, through a foreign artist's sensational suc-

cess, suddenly become household words and develop a vogue. One of your children or grandchildren—who knows?—may be named that way. It has happened. *Ingrid, Hedy, Marlene,* and *Ilona* were once unfamiliar names in America.

5. Finally, if you are interested in probing a little more deeply into etymology and the relationship of names and words, you will surely be impressed by discovering that names in unrelated languages may be cousins or brothers and sisters under the skin. For example, *Bohuslav* (Czechoslovakian) and *Timothy* (formed from Greek) both refer to honor paid to God, the former meaning "praise of God" and the latter "respect for God."

We have compiled these lists with the help of the Embassies, Consulates, Information Offices, and the United Nations Delegates of most European countries. We have added a few names of interest or popularity taken from reference works, the daily press, and foreign-language newspapers.

The names are entered in the following ways:

1. Where the foreign name is the same as or easily identifiable with an English name, or has been taken over into English, we have entered only the foreign name. Examples: French, Henri; Portuguese, Ana; Swedish, Einar.

The meaning of names of this kind is not given here, since you can find it under the corresponding English names in "Names for Boys" and "Names for Girls." There you will also find some other names of foreign origin.

2. Where the foreign name does not so readily reveal its English equivalent, we have entered the English equivalent in parentheses. Examples: Polish, Jerzi (George); Swedish, Lars (Laurence).

3. Where the foreign name has no corresponding English equivalent, we have, first of all, put in parentheses and quotation marks the meaning of the name or information about it, or both, as far as can be ascertained. If the meaning is unknown, we have made an entry to that effect.

We have then divided the names for which information can be given, into three categories:

A. We have given only the meaning. Example: Finnish, Sirka ("making music like a cricket").

B. We have given an English name that bearers of the foreign-language name often adopt as an Americanization. This adopted name is without related meaning or etymological correspondence, and its sound may only slightly resemble the sound of the foreign-language name. Examples: Greek, Eleutherios ("free man," changed to "Al"); Polish, Stanislas, Stanislaw ("camp-glory," changed to "Stan," or "Stanley").

C. We have sometimes given an English name that has the same meaning as the foreign-language name (see No. 5 in this section, above). However, this English name does not have the same derivation. Examples: Finnish, Voitto ("winner," equivalent to "Victor"); Norwegian, Laila ("great woods," equivalent to "Lelia" and "Leila" or parallel to "Sylvia").

FROM THE ROMANCE LANGUAGES

(Derived from Latin)

All the Latin I construe is "amo," I love!
ROBERT BROWNING,
Fra Lippo Lippi

Latin America, Our Spanish West and Southwest, and Spain

BOYS: Alfonso, Ángel, Antonio, Francisco, Luis, Manuel, Martín, Ramón, Victor; Andrés (Andrew), Carlos (Charles), Diego (James), Domingo (Dominic), Enrique (Henry), Esteban (Stephen), Federico (Frederic), Felipe (Philip), Fernando or Hernando (Ferdinand), Ignacio (Ignatius), Jaime (James), Jesús (often changed to José in this country), Joaquín (Joachim), José (Joseph), Juan (John), Miguel (Michael), Pablo (Paul), Pancho (dim. of Francisco, "Frank"), Pedro (Peter), Pepe (dim. of José,

"Joey"), Rodrigo (Roderick), Vicente (Vincent).

GIRLS: Adela, Adelina, Adelita, Ana, Anita, Beatriz, Carlota, Carmen, Consuelo, Dolores, Francisca, Inés, Luisa, María, Marta, Mercedes, Ofelia, Rosa, Teresa; Catalina (Catherine), Isabel (Elizabeth), Juana, Juanita (Joan), Manuela (Emma); Amparo (from María del Amparo, "Mary of the Refuge or Shelter"), Concepción (from "Immaculate Conception"), Conchita (dim. of Concepción), Lupe, Lupita (from Mexican shrine of Mary of Guadalupe), Luz (from "Mary of Light," "Lucy"), Nieves (from shrine, "Mary of the Snows," "Neva"), Pilar (from María del Pilar, "Mary of the Column"), Rosario (from "Mary of the Rosary").

Brazil

BOYS: Antonio, Joao (John), Joaquim, José, Manuel.
GIRLS: Ana, Emilia, Joana, Maria, Teresa.

Portugal

BOYS: Antonio, Eduardo, Eugenio, Francisco, Henrique, Raimundo, Ricardo; Carlos (Charles), Jorge (George), Jaime (James), Joao (John), José (Joseph), Lourenço (Lawrence), Luiz (Louis), Miguel (Michael), Pedro (Peter), Reinaldo (Reynold, Ronald).

GIRLS: Ana, Carlota, Emilia, Francisca, Joana, Margarida, Maria; Inês (Agnes), Leonor

(Eleanor), Isabel (Elizabeth). Graça (Grace), Manuela (Emma).

Italy

BOYS: Alfredo, Angelo, Antonio, Arturo, Francesco, Giorgio, Marco, Roberto; Carlo (Charles), Domenico (Dominic), Enrico (Henry), Ercole (Hercules), Giovanni (John), Giulio (Julius), Giuseppe (Joseph), Guglielmo (William), Lorenzo (Laurence), Luigi (Louis), Mario (Marius, but also considered masc. of Mary), Niccolò (Nicholas, "Nick"), Pietro or Piero (Peter), Vincenzo (Vincent), Vittorio (Victor); Carmine (masc. of Carmela, from "Mary of Mt. Carmel"), Dino (from dim. of names like Bernardo-Bernardino), Ezio (from Aetius, name of Roman general who defeated Attila the Hun), Gennaro (from "St. Januarius"), Gino (from dim. of names like Luigi-Luigino), Italo ("Italian"), Pasquale ("Easter," often changed to "Pat" and "Patsy'), Rocco (saint's name, changed to "Rocky"), Salvatore ("Saviour," changed to "Sal"), Gaetano.

GIRLS: Amelia, Angela, Caterina, Francesca, Ida, Lucia, Louisa, Margherita, Maria, Rosa, Silvia, Teresa; Bianca (Blanche), Elena (Helen), Giulietta (Juliet); Assunta (from "The Assumption," often changed to "Nancy"), Concetta (from "The Immaculate Conception," often changed to "Tina" from dim. Concettina), Pier (Piera, fem. of Piero), Pina (dim. of Giuseppina).

France

BOYS: André, Antoine, Armand, Charles, Claude, François, Georges, Gilbert, Henri, Jules, Louis, Lucien, Philippe; Étienne (Stephen), Jacques (James), Jean (John), Pierre (Peter), Michel (Michael), Raoul (Ralph); René ("born again").

GIRLS: Françoise, Genevieve, Georgette, Henriette, Jacqueline, Jeanne, Louise, Luçienne, Madeleine, Marcelle, Marie, Michèle, Odette, Simone, Solange ("solemn," from the name of St. Solemnia), Suzanne, Yvonne.

Rumania

BOYS: Alexándru, Andréiu, Antón, Marcú, Nicolae, Petrú, Stefan; Ioán (John), Mihaí (Michael).

GIRLS: Ána, Eléna, Ilená, Ileana, Lína (dim. of Magdalína), Magdalína or Mina, María, Sofía.

And learning other tongues, you'll learn
   All times are one; all men, one race;
Hear Homer speak, as Greek to Greek;
   See Dante, face to face.
           RUPERT HUGHES,
           With a First Reader

FROM THE GREEK LANGUAGE

Athens, the eye of Greece,
mother of arts
And eloquence.
  MILTON, *Paradise Regained*

BOYS: Alexandros, Andreas, Basileos (see Vasilos), Georgios, Gregori(o)s, Nikolaos, Petros (Peter), Stephanos; Joannes (John), Pavlos (Paul), Socratis (Socrates), Sophocles, Vasilos (Basil, changed to "William"), Yiannis (John); Athanasios (immortal," changed to "Tom" and "Thomas"), Chrístos ("Chris"), Constantinos (changed to "Dean"), Costa, or Kosta (dim. of Constantinos, changed to "Gus"), Eleutherios ("a free man," changed to "Al"), Panayiotos ("all holy," changed to "Peter"), Stávros ("cross," changed to "Steve").

GIRLS: Anna, Athena or Athina, or Atena, Georgia, Irene, Katina, Katerini, Maria, Marina, Marika, Olympia(s), Penelope, Sophia, Thalia; Eleni, or Elena (Helen), Calliope, or Kalliope ("beautiful face," changed to "Poppy"), Chrysanthemis ("gold" + "right," shortened to "Memi"); Filia (last part of the next name, changed to "Peggy"), Triantafil(l)ia ("Rose"); Hariclea (translated by "Harriet"), Hrisoula ("little golden one," parallel to "Goldie").

In addition, other names taken from ancient Greek history, literature, and mythology are often used today.

BOYS: Agamemnon ("resolute," leader of the Greeks in the Trojan War); Aristides ("son of the best," statesman known as "the Just"); Aristotle ("best" + "accomplish," philosopher); Demosthenes ("people" + "might," greatest ancient orator); Kimon (Cimon, Athenian admiral and statesman, see SIMON and SIMEON); Perikles (Pericles, "far-famed," Athenian statesman); Platon (Plato, "broad-shouldered," Philosopher); Sophokles (Sophocles, "wise" + "famed," writer of tragedies); T(h)emistokles (Themistocles, "law and right" + "famed," Athenian statesman).

GIRLS: Aphrodite ("foam-born," goddess of love); Aspasia ("welcome," companion of Pericles); Euterpe, or Efterpi ("well" + "delight," Muse of music); Persephone ("destroyer," Queen of Hades, Latin Proserpina, English Proserpine).

(*C* often appears as k; *ph* as *f*; *th* as *t*, *u* as *f*.)

FROM THE GERMANIC LANGUAGES

Saxon and Norman and Dane
are we.
  ALFRED, LORD TENNYSON,
  A Welcome to Alexandra

Germany and Austria

BOYS: Adolf, August, Emil, Erich, Ernst, Ferdinand, Georg,

Gustav or Gustave, Hermann, Josef, Karl, Konrad, Maximilian, Otto, Rudolf, Siegfried, Stefan, Ulrich, Walt(h)er; Albrecht (Albert), Bernhard (Bernard), Dieter ("strong people"), or equivalent to Dietrich (Theodore, Theodoric), Franz (Francis), Friedrich (Frederic), Fritz (dim. of Friedrich), Gerhard (Gerard), Gottfried (Godfrey), Hans (dim. of Johann), Heinrich (Henry), Heinz (dim. of Heinrich), Horst ("thicket," like For[r]est, or possibly "highborn"), Johann (John), Kurt (dim. of Konrad), Ludwig (Louis), Werner (Warner), Wilhelm (William), Wolfgang ("wolf" + "way").

GIRLS: Berta, Dorothea, Elisabeth, Elsa, Emilie, Ernestina, Frida, Gertrud, Helena, Hildegard, Johanna, Katharina, Lilli, Lisa, Luise, Margarete, Maria, Marlene, Marta, Ursula, Wilhelmina; Amalie (Amelia), Gretchen (dim. of Margarete), Gretel (dim. of Margarete), Kathe (dim. of Katharina), Magda (Madeleine).

The Netherlands (Holland)

BOYS: Bernhard or Ben, Daniel or Daan, Hendrik or Hen, Herman, Willem or Wim; Dirk or Dik (Derek), Frans (Francis, Frank), Hans or Jan or Johannes (John), Koenraad or Koen (Conrad), Pieter or Piet (Peter).

GIRLS: Anna, Annie, Elisabeth or Els, Emilie or Emmie, Geertruïda or Gerda, Henriette or Jet, Johanna or Hannie, Maria or Marietje, Margaretha or Greet, Martha, Wilhelmina.

Denmark

BOYS: Christian, Edvard, Einar, Erik, Frederick, Georg, Henrik, Johannes or Johan, Karl, Peter; Anders (Andrew), Jans or Jens (James), Knud (Knut, Canute), Lars (Lawrence), Ludwig (Louis), Poul (Paul); Aage ("respected by the people," changed to "Eugene" or "Owen"); Axel ("mighty defender"), Vang ("cultivator" or place name, "field, slope"), Viggo ("warrior").

GIRLS: Anna, Dorthea, Elisabeth, Ellen, Ellinor, Emilia, Gerda, Greta, Helene, Hilda, Johanne, Julie, Karen, Marie, Martha, Olga, Ruth; Jytte (Judith, Yvette), Margethe (Margaret).

Norway

BOYS: Einar, Fredrik, Harald, Kristian; Per (Peter), Nils (dim. of Nicholas, "Niles," "Neil," "Nelson"), Rolf (Ralph, Rolfe); Aage (see entry under Denmark), Arne ("eagle," "Arnold"), Bjorn ("bear" or "warrior," similar to names like "Bernard"), Erling ("elf-son"), Finn ("wise as a Finn"), Haakon ("noble kin"), Kaare (from mythology, "god of the winds," or "sword-bearer"), Leif, Leiv ("love"), Odd (probably "edge"), Ole ("squire, protector"), Sigurd ("victory-counsel"), S v e i n ("young man," like English word "swain"), Trygve ("dedicated to protection"), Thorstein ("Thor's stone").

GIRLS: Astrid, Karen or Kari, Ingrid or Inger; Berit (Bridget), Marit (dim. of Margaret); Aase ("like a goddess" or "powerful"), Bjorg ("help" or "salvation"), Laila ("great woods," or equivalent of "Lelia" and "Leila"), Ragnhild ("counsel-war" or "like a goddess"), Randi ("warlike"), Reidun ("fond of riding to war"), Solveig ("gleaming like sunlight" or "lively, gay").

Sweden

BOYS: Adolf, Einar, Fredrick, Gustav, Harald, Knut, Niles, Olaf, Oscar; Alf (Alfred), Anders (Andrew), Arne ("Arnold"), Axel ("mighty defender"), Dag, ("clearness, brightness, day") Gunnar (Gunther), Hans (John), Ivar (Ivor), Lars (Lawrence), Lennart (Leonard), Per (Peter), Reinhold (Reynold), Folke ("people" or "well-behaved, honest," like English "Fulke"), Gösta (Gustave), Holger ("faithful warrior"), Inge ("youth," name of an ancient hero), Ingvar ("youth" and "protector"), Sten ("stone"), Sven, Sveinn, Swen (see under Norway), Hellmut ("strong" or "helmet" and "courage," similar to "William").

GIRLS: Anna, Elsa, Eva, Gerda, Hedvig, Hildegard, Hulda, Ingrid, Karin, Kristina (variants Kristin, Kirsten), Lovisa or Louisa, Märta, Selma; Barbro (Barbara), Birgitta (Bridget); Gudrun ("war" and "rune," meaning "early writings"), Inga (fem. of Inge), Ragnhild (see under Norway), Signe ("sign," "interpreting magic"), Sigrid ("counsel-rule"), Maj, Mai (May).

FROM THE SLAVIC LANGUAGES

Slav, Teuton, Kelt, I count them all
My friend and brother souls,
With all the peoples, great and small,
That wheel between the poles.
    TENNYSON, *Epilogue to the Charge of the Light Brigade*

Russia (USSR)

BOYS: Alexei, Alexandre, Anatoli, Andrei, Anton, Boris, Dmitri, Georgei, Gregor, Igor, Mikhail, Nikolai, Vladimir; Evgeni, (Eugene), Feodor (Theodore), Grischa (dim. of Gregor), Ilya (Elias, Elijah), Ivan (John), Jascha (dim. of James or Jacob), Leonid (Leonidas), Lev (Leo), Mischa (dim. of Mikhail), Pavel (Paul), Piotr (Peter), Sascha (dim. of Alexandre and fem. Alexandra, used both as m. and f. name), Sergei (Serge), Vanya (dim. of Ivan), Vas(s)ili (Basil), Yuri (George); Aram (popular Armenian name, as in the title of the book by William Saroyan *My Name Is Aram;* name included here for geographical reasons only, for Armenian is not a Slavic language; this Aram is very probably the Biblical Aram, meaning "height" in Hebrew, the name of one of Noah's grandsons).

GIRLS: Anastasia, Anna, Elena, Katerina, Katinka and Katya (dim. of Katerina), Ludmilla, Maria, Nadia, Natasha, Olga, Sofia, Sonia, Tamara, Tania, Tatiana, Vera; Feodóra (Theodora), Irina (Irene), Luba ("love"), Nina (dim. of Anna), Varvara (Barbara); Galina (Helen), Vassilia (fem. of Basil), Zara (Sara).

Poland

BOYS: Antoni, Casimir, Michal, Stefan, Tadeusz, Zygmunt; Andrzej (Andrew), Jan (John), Jerzy (George), Stanislaw, or Stanislas ("camp-glory," changed to "Stanley"), Wladyslaw ("power-glory," changed to "Walter"), Wojciech ("battle" and "soldier," name of a saint coming from Prague, who changed his name to "Adalbert"); Boguslaw (from *Bog,* "God," and *Slaw,* "famous" or "glory," parallel to "Osbert"), Boleslaw ("suffering" and "glory"), Mieczyslaw ("sword-famous," parallel to "Egbert").

GIRLS: Barbara, Hanna, Irena, Magdalena, Maria, Marya, Mira, Stefania, Wanda (a legendary Polish name); Aniela (Angela), Ewa (Eve), Halina (Helen), Katarzyna (Katherine), Romana (Romaine), Zofia (Sophia); Danuta (origin unknown,

may be Lithuanian, "young deer" or "given").

Czechoslovakia

BOYS: Jan, Peter, Vladimír; Ivan (John), Jiří (George), Karel (Charles), Pavel (Paul); Milan ("beloved," translated as "Michael"), Stanislav (see under Poland); Bohuslav ("God" and "praise," practically parallel to "Timothy"), Miroslav ("peace-glory," parallel to "Frederic"), Jaroslav ("praise of spring," often translated as "Gerald" although closer to "Vernon"), Miloslav ("crowned with glory"), Václav ("crowned with a wreath," equivalent to Wenceslas, and similar in meaning to "Stephen").

GIRLS: Alena or Helena, Běla ("Blanche"), Cecilie, Jitka (Judith), Libuša ("beloved," "Luba"), Lida, Olga, Pavla (Paula), Ruzena (Rose), Sárka (Sara); Jarmila (probably "spring" and "love" or "crowned"), Vlasta ("fatherland").

Yugoslavia

BOYS: Anton, Boris, Nikola; Djuro (George), Frane (Frank), Ivan (John), Josip (Joseph); Milan (see under Czechoslovakia); Bozidar, Bozo ("gift of God," parallel to "Theodore"), Vlado ("rule").

GIRLS: Ana, Mariya, Donje, Vera; Darinka (Dorothy), Ivanka (Joan), Liljana (Lillian), Ruza (Rose); Ljubica (pronounced LOO' bitza, "lovely as a flower," like "Violet"), Vesna ("spring," "Verna.").

FROM THE FINNO-UGRIC LANGUAGES

Sinun Nimesi On Runo ("Your Name Is a Poem")
FINNISH SAYING

Finland

BOYS: Anti (Anthony), Errki (Eric), Halle (Carl), Hannu (John), Heikki (Henry), Jussi (John), Matti (Matthew), Paavali, Paavo (Paul), Pekka (Peter), Tauno ("Donald"), Tuomas, Tuomo (Thomas), Ville, Viljo (William), Yrjö (George); Esko ("chief" or "divine protection"), Veikko ("brother," a name sometimes given to a second son); Voitto ("winner," equivalent to "Victor").

GIRLS: Dorotea, Leena; Aino (Anne), Kaisa (Kate), Katri (Katherine), Kerttu (Gertrude), Kirsti (Christine), Laila (see under Norway, also "light, gentle, airy," or "Leila" and "Lelia"), Liisa (Elizabeth), Lilja (Lily), Mija (Mary), Riita ("plenty," "Rita"), Ruusu (Rose), Siiri (Sara); Eila, Elli (m e a n i n g unknown), Irja ("smiling"), Sirkka ("making music like the cricket").

A child that is loved has many names
HUNGARIAN PROVERB

Hungary

BOYS: Ferenc (Francis), György (George), István (Stephen), János (John), József (Joseph), Károly (Charles), Lajos (Louis), Mátyás (Matthew), Mihály (Michael), Miklós (Nicholas), Sándor (Alexander); Béla (a popular hero-name, "Adalbert," possibly connected with Biblical name of the son of Benjamin, or of the King of Edom), László ("power-glory," like "Ladislaus," but often changed to "Lester"); Árpád (name of founder of Kingdom of Hungary, possibly from Biblical place name, Hebrew, "lost, wandering"), Géza (possibly related to Hebrew "Asa"), Tibor (presumably from the Latin Tiberius, the name of the second Roman emperor, meaning "of the Tiber").

GIRLS: Agnes, Eva, Julia, Klára, Mária; Erzsebét (Elizabeth), Ilona (Helen), Katalin (Katherine), Zsuzsa (Susan); Prioska ("blushing" or "pink").

NAMES IN A NEW NATION

At that time will I bring you again, even in the time that I gather you: for I will make you a name and a praise among all people of the earth.
ZEPHANIAH 3 : 20

Israel

Because of the interest of many people in the new state of Israel we have included a special section on Israeli names.

Among the tendencies in naming Israeli children these two are prominent:

1. In addition to the well-known Biblical names such as Isaac, Jacob, Naomi, Ruth, etc., names of less prominent figures of the Old Testament are being revived in the eternal quest of the "new"—names such as Amon, Gad, and Nimrod, "the mighty hunter before the Lord."

2. The traditional English spelling of many names (usually based on the King James Bible) is being revised to represent more closely the Hebrew pronunciation. So, Avner is written for Abner, Avrohom for Abraham, Eliyahu for Elijah, Moshe for Moses, Shaul for Saul, Shelomo for Solomon, Shmuel for Samuel, Yaakov for Jacob, Yehoshua for Joshua, Avigail for Abigail, Dlilah for Delilah, Sharonah for Sharon, etc.

One new Israeli boys' name, *Dror*, meaning "liberty," occurs in the original of the famous passage: *"Proclaim liberty throughout all the land and unto all the inhabitants thereof"* (Leviticus 25:10). These are the words engraved on our Liberty Bell!

(We compiled this list with the aid of the Israeli Consular Information Office in New York City. Many other names of Hebrew origin, both new and old, are included in "Names for Boys" and "Names for Girls.")

BOYS: Alon ("oak tree"), Amatzia or Amaziah ("strength of God"), Amirov ("My people are great"), Amnon ("faithful"), Amon ("trustworthy" or "master workman"), Abijah ("Jehovah is my father"), Asaph ("gatherer"), Avir ("strong, noble"), Boaz ("In him there is strength"), Chaim, Haym, Hayyim ("life"), Doron ("dweller"), Ehud ("praise"), Gad ("fortune" or "assembly"), Gil ("joy"), Gilad (place name, "Gilead"), Gurion ("dwelling place of God"; Ben-Gurion, "son of Gurion"), Ittamar ("island of palms"), Lael ("belonging to the Lord"), Lior ("I have light"), Marnin ("bringing song"), Menachin, Menahem ("comforter"), Naphtali ("wrestling with God"), Nimrod ("valiant"), Noam ("pleasantness"), Ran ("exalted" or "song"), Shai ("gift"), Uri ("light"), Uzi ("my strength"), Yael ("strength of God"), Yigal ("He redeems"), Yoav or Joab ("God is my father"), Yoram or Joram ("God is exalted"), Yuval or Jubal ("a stream of music"), Zev, Zevie, Zvi ("deer").

GIRLS: Ahuda ("praise" or "sympathetic"), Anat ("charming"), Atalia or Athalie ("God is exalted"), Avishag ("father's delight"), Avital ("God protects"), Beruria ("chosen by God"), Carmelit (place name, "Carmel"), Chava, or Hava, or Haya (for Eve, "life"), Ditzah ("joy"), Elana ("oak tree"), Galilah (place name, "Galilee"), Gilah ("joy"), Kinnereth (place name, "Sea of Galilee"),

Liorah ("I have light"), Michal ("brook" or "God is perfect"), Na'amah ("pleasant"), Nehama ("comfort"), Nili ("blue" or "like the Nile"), Nirah ("light"), Ofrah ("young hind" or "lively maiden"), Osnat ("favorite of the deity"), Peninah ("pearl"), Rinah ("song" or "joy"), Tikvah ("hope"), Zephirah ("dawn"), Ziona or Zionah (fem. of ZION), Zofeyah ("God sees").

CHOOSING A SAINT'S NAME

How to Use the Calendar

> But this she knows, in joys and woes,
> That SAINTS will aid if men will call;
> For the blue sky bends over all!
>
> SAMUEL TAYLOR COLERIDGE,
> *Christabel*

For the benefit of those parents who wish to select the name of a Saint for their child we have prepared this Calendar of Feast Days of the Saints based on official, authoritative sources. A Saint's Feast Day is a day of festival commemorating an event in the life of a Saint, usually the day of his death, which is called his "birthday."

"Blessed," here designated by Bl., indicates that the one bearing this title has been beatified but not yet canonized as a Saint. For the purpose of choosing a name no distinction is made between the name of a Saint and the name of one called "Blessed." For the sake of brevity any reference to the term "Saint" in this introduction applies equally to those called "Blessed."

According to Canon 761 of the Code of Canon Law, "Pastors should see to it that a Christian name be given to the one being baptized, and if they cannot effect this, they should add the name of some Saint to the name given by the parents, and they should enter both names in the Record of Baptisms."

"CHRISTIAN" NAMES

"Christian" names include Abraham, Isaac, Jacob, Moses, Eve, Esther, Ruth, and the names of other figures of the Old Testament who were not Christians, certain virtues like Faith, Hope, Charity, and Patience common to all mankind, and a few names like Alfred and Arthur which are not found among the Saints.

The Saint whose name is given to a child serves as a protector, patron, and guardian of that child and as an ideal model to be imitated.

NAME DAYS

The child's Name Day is the Feast Day of the Saint whose name is chosen. Parents may select the name of a Saint whose Feast Day is not the same as the date of the child's birth. In that case the Feast Day of the Saint after whom the child is named is kept as the child's Name Day.

323

MODERN NAMES

Modern adaptations of names no longer current may be used, as Juliet for Julitta, Denis or Sidney for Dionysius, etc. In choosing a name for a girl, parents may use the feminine derivative of a masculine names, as Alfreda derived from Alfred, Antonia from Antony, Felicia from Felix, etc. In this Calendar we have listed for the most part only names that are used frequently in modern times, or names that can be modernized.

We have placed in parentheses either modern forms of old names or modern names suggested by the old names, as for example: Etheldreda (Audrey); Mechtilidis (Mathilda); Alberic (Aubrey); Odo (Otto); etc. We have given also the simplest and most popular form of an English name related to variations of Latin names, as Honorata (Honora); and Paulinus (Paul). When the Latin form obviously suggests the English equivalent, as Celesta-Celeste, Albinus-Albin, we have usually left it to the readers to do their own modernizing.

The names are arranged in alphabetical order for each day—male first, then *female names in italics*. Wherever information was available, we have identified the Saints by a descriptive phrase or a reference. This information may be a title, an appellation, a date, a place associated with the Saint, a relationship to another Saint, or a Biblical allusion.

VARYING FEAST DAYS

Some of the Saints have more than one Feast Day assigned to them. In addition, the Feast Days of certain Saints vary according to locality, being celebrated on different days in different parts of the world. Finally, the dates of early Saints are often a matter of approximation so that even official authorities do not agree. We have combined and even repeated conflicting conclusions but wherever possible we have followed the Missal for the dates of universal and varying festivals.

FACTS ABOUT THE NAMES

Almost all the names in the Calendar are entered in the sections devoted to "Names for Boys" and "Names for Girls." There you will find the origin of the names, their meanings, pet forms, variations, female equivalents of male names, male equivalents of female names, and occasional biographical, historical, and literary notes.

Even if you do not consult the Calendar for the purpose of choosing a name, you will find it profitable to look through it for the rewarding information it reveals about names. Among other interesting facts, you will learn that names like Florence and Hedda now considered exclusively feminine were once used as masculine names; you will see how many modern names developed from ancient names; and you will discover that some names like Alena and Alvin which seem to be modern inventions were in use centuries ago. Finally, the names of the places associated with the Saints recall history and geography, the splendor and romance of the Old World.

A CALENDAR OF SAINTS

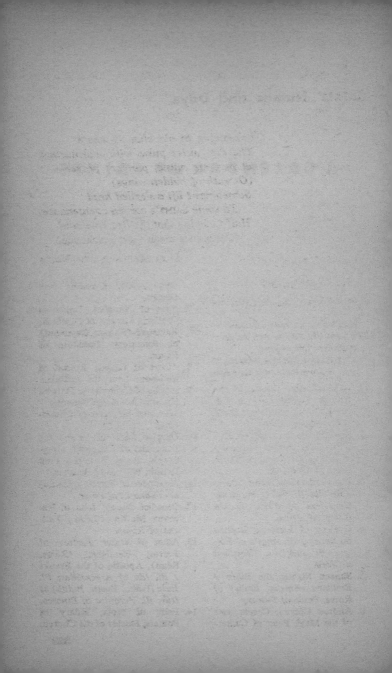

Saints' Names and Days

Or dreaming in old chapels where
The dim aisles pulse with murmurings
That part are music, part are prayer—
(Or rush of hidden wings)
Sometimes I lift a startled head
To some SAINT's carven countenance,
Half fancying that the lips have said,
"All names mean God perchance."

DON MARQUIS, *The Name*

JANUARY

Even while we sing, he smiles his last,
And leaves our sphere behind.
The good Old Year is with the past,
O be the New as kind!
WILLIAM CULLEN BRYANT,
A Song for New Year's Eve

1. Basil of Aix, Doctor of the Church; Felix of Bourges; Justin of Chieti; William of Dijon / *Martina of Rome.*

2. Stephen, Protomartyr, or First Martyr; Vincentian (Vincent) of Tulle / *Bl. Stephana (Stephanie) of Quinzani.*

3. Daniel of Padua; Peter Absolo / *Bertilia (Bertha) of Marolles; Genevieve of Paris; Lucida (Lucy) of Africa.*

4. Gregory of Langres; Stephen du Bourg / *Bl. Angela of Foligno; Bl. Christiana (Christine) a Croce.*

5. Simeon Stylites the Elder / *Emiliana (Amelia, Emily) of Rome; Paula of Tuscany.*

6. Andrew Corsini; Caspar, one of the Magi; Peter of Canter-

bury / *Bl. Gertrude van Oosten.*

7. Felix of Heraclea; Julian of Cagliari; Lucian of Antioch; Raymond (Ramon, Raymond) of Pennafort; Theodore of Egypt.

8. Albert of Cashel; Erhard of Ratisbon; Laurence Justinian.

9. Adrian of Canterbury; Peter of Sebaste; Bl. Philip Berruyer / *Marciana (Marcia) of Mauretania.*

10. Dermot (used in Ireland for Jeremiah) of Longford; Gregory X, Pope; Paul the First Hermit; William of Bourges.

11. Alexander of Fermo / *Honorata (Honora) of Pavia.*

12. Benedict Biscop; John of Ravenna; Martin of León / *Tatiana of Rome.*

13. Allan of Wales; Andrew of Trèves; Remigius (Rémy, Rémi), Apostle of the Franks / *Bl. Ida of Argensolles; Bl. Jutta (Ivetta, Yvette, Judith) of Huy; Bl. Veronica of Binasco.*

14. Felix of Nola; Hilary of Poitiers; Doctor of the Church;

Malachi (Malachy) the Prophet.

15. Alexander Akimetes; Maurus (Maurice) of Glanfeuil; Micheas (Michael) the Prophet; Paul the First Hermit / *Ita (Ida) of Limerick.*

16. James of Tarentaise; Marcellus (Mark, Marcel) I, Pope / *Bl. Jane of Bagno; Priscilla of Rome.*

17. Anthony the Great; Julian Sabas the Elder / *Leonilla (Leona, Leonie) of Langres; Bl. Roseline of Villeneuve.*

18. Paul the Apostle; Peter the Apostle, Chair at Rome / *Bl. Beatrice II of Este; Bl. Christine Ciccarelli; Faustina of Como; Priscilla of Rome; Susanna of Nola.*

19. Canute (Knud) IV, King of Denmark; Julian of Africa; Marius (Mario) of Persia; Paul of Africa / *Martha of Persia; Pia of Africa.*

20. Fabian, Pope; Sebastian of Rome.

21. Bl. Edward Stransham; Bl. Thomas Reynolds / *Agnes of Rome; Brigid of Kilbride; Inés of Beniganim.*

22. Dominic of Sora; Enoch the Patriarch; Vincent the Deacon of Saragossa; Bl. Walter of Himmerode / *Inés (Agnes) of Beniganim.*

23. Barnard of Vienne; Clement of Ancyra; Raymund (Ramon, Raymond) of Pennafort / *Gladys of Monmouthshire; Bl. Margaret of Ravenna.*

24. Bernard of St. Quentin; Timothy of Ephesus / *Vera of Clermont.*

25. Joel of Pulsano; Paul the Apostle; Peter the Apostle.

26. Alberic (Aubrey) of Cîteaux; Alphonsus of Astorga; Conan of Iona / *Margaret of Hungary; Paula of Rome.*

27. John Chrysostom, "The Golden-Mouthed," Doctor of the Church; Julian of Sora / *Angelo Merici; Candida (Blanche) of Banoles.*

28. James the Hermit; Julian of Cuenca; Leonidas of Egypt; Valerius (Valerian) of Saragossa / *Agnes of Rome; Constance, daughter of Constantine the Great; Bl. Mary of Pisa.*

29. Constant of Perugia; Francis of Sales, Doctor of the Church; Gildas the Wise; Valerius (Valerian) of Trèves.

30. Alexander (third century, during reign of Decius); Matthias (Matthew) of Jerusalem / *Hyacintha Mariscotti; Martina of Rome.*

31. John Bosco; Mark the Evangelist; Martin Manuel; Peter Nolasco / *Marcella of Rome; Bl. Mary Christina, Queen of the Two Sicilies.*

FEBRUARY

Muse, bid the Morn awake!
Sad Winter now declines.
Each bird doth choose a mate;
This day's Saint Valentine's.
   MICHAEL DRAYTON,
      To His Valentine

1. Ignatius of Antioch; Paul of Trois-Châteaux / *Brigid of Kildare,* "The Mary of Ireland."

2. Cornelius the Centurion; Laurence of Canterbury / *Catherine dei Ricci; Mary, the Purification (Spanish, Pura, Purificación).*

3. Bl. John Theophane Venard; Laurence the Illuminator; Oliver of Portonuovo; Oscar of Hamburg and Bremen; Philip of Vienne / *Ia (Ives, Yvette), after whom St. Ives in Cornwall was named; Margaret of England.*

4. Andrew Corsini; Gilbert of Sempringham; Joseph of Leonissa; Vincent of Troyes / *Bl. Jane of Valois.*

5. Abraham of Arbela; Philip of Jesus / *Adelaide of Willich; Agatha of Catania.*

6. Luke of Emesa; Mel of Armagh; Titus of Crete; Warren of Palestrina / *Dorothy of Caesarea.*

7. Laurence of Siponto; Luke the Younger; Richard, King of England (eighth century); Theodore of Heraclea; Thomas Sherwood / *Juliana of Bologna.*

8. Jerome Aemilian; John of Matha; Paul of Verdun; Stephen, founder of the Order of Grandmont / *Ethelfleda (Ethel and Fleta) of Whitby.*

9. Alexander of Rome, and of Seli; Cyril of Alexandria, Doctor of the Church.

10. Andrew of Bethlehem; Irenaeus of Rome; William of Maleval / *Bl. Clare Agolanti of Rimini.*

11. Adolph of Osnabruck; Benedict of Aniane; Gregory VII, Pope; Lucius of Adrianople / *Mary, Our Lady of Lourdes; Theodora the Empress.*

12. Antony Cauleas; Julian the Hospitaller / *Eulalia of Barcelona.*

13. Bl. John Theophane Venard; Julian of Lyons; Stephen of Rieti / *Bl. Beatrix d'Ornacieux; Catherine dei Ricci.*

14. Antoninus (Antony) of Sor-rento; Bl. Thomas Plumtree; Valentine of Rome, and of Terni; Bl. Vincent of Siena.

15. Bl. Claude de la Colombière; Bl. Jordan of Saxony; Joseph of Antioch; Sigfrid (Siegfried) of Wexlow / *Georgia of Clermont; Bl. Julia of Certaldo.*

16. Gilbert of Sempringham; Jeremias (Jeremiah) of Egypt and Caesarea; Julian of Egypt / *Juliana of Nicomedia; Bl. Philippa Mereri.*

17. Alexis Falconieri; Benedict of Cagliari; Bl. John Francis Clet; Julian of Caesarea.

18. Claude of Castellamare; Colman of Lindisfarne; Leo of Lycia; Simeon of Jerusalem / *Bl. Agatha Lin; Bl. Agnes De; Mary Bernard of Lourdes (see April 16).*

19. Conrad of Piacenza; George of Lodève / *Belina of Troyes; Bl. Lucy of China.*

20. Leo of Catania; Ulric of Haselborough; Valerius (Valerian) of Conserans / *Amata (Amy) of Assisi; Mildred of Thanet.*

21. Felix of Metz; George of Amastris; Peter the Scribe; Valerius (Valerian) of Astorga.

22. Elwin of Cornwall; Maximian (Max) of Ravenna; Paul the Apostle; Peter the Apostle, Chair at Antioch / *Margaret of Cortona.*

23. Felix of Brescia; Milo of Benevento; Peter Damian, Doctor of the Church / *Martha of Astorga.*

24. Ethelbert, King of Kent; Matthias the Apostle / *Adela, daughter of William the Conqueror; Bl. Ida of Hohenfels.*

25. Bl. James Carvalho; Victor of St. Gall / *Adeltrude (Ethel and Truda) of Maubège.*

26. Alexander of Alexandria; Andrew of Florence; Victor of Arcis-sur-Aube / *Bl. Isabelle of France; Mechtildis (Matilda) of Hackeborn.*

27. Gabriel of the Sorrowful Mother; John of Gorze; Leander of Seville / *Bl. Anne Line; Honorina (Honora) of Gaul.*

28. Hilary, Pope; Oswald of Worcester; Romanus (Roman) of Condat; Silvan of Bangor / *Bl. Antonia of Florence; Bl. Hedwig of Lithuania.*

29. In Leap Year the Feast of St. Matthias is kept on February 25 instead of on February 24, and all succeeding feasts in February are postponed one day.

MARCH

He [Benedict] founded here his Convent and his Rule
Of prayer and work, and counted work as prayer;
Then pen became a clarion, and his school
Flamed like a beacon in the midnight air.

LONGFELLOW, *Monte Cassino*

1. Albinus of Angers; Dewi (Dewey, David) of Wales; Leo of Rouen / *Antonina (Antonia), variously attributed to Nicomedia, Cea, Portugal, Byzantium on March 4, May 1 and 4, June 12; Bl. Jane Mary Bonomo.*

2. Chad of Mercia; Bl. Charles the Good; Bl. Henry Suso; Paul of Porto / *Bl. Agnes of Bohemia.*

3. Anselm of Nonantola; Owen of Lichfield / *Camilla of Auxerre.*

4. Casimir of Poland; Felix of Rhuis; Lucius I, Pope; Peter Pappacarbone / *Antonina (see March 1).*

5. Clement of Syracuse; Colman of Armagh; John-Joseph of the Cross; Virgil of Arles.

6. Basil of Bologna; Cyril of Constantinople; Bl. Jordan of Pisa / *Colette of Corbie; Felicitas (Felicity) of Carthage; Bl. Helen of Poland; Rose of Viterbo.*

7. Paul of Pelusium; Thomas Aquinas, "The Angelic Doctor," author of "Summa Theologica" / *Felicitas (Felicity) of Carthage.*

8. Felix of Dunwich; Humphrey of Prum; John of God; Julian of Toledo; Stephen of Obazine; Vincent Kadlubeck.

9. Anthony of Froidemont; Gregory of Nyssa / *Catherine of Bologna; Frances of Rome.*

10. Emilian (Emil) of Lagny; Bl. John of Vallumbrosa; Bl. Peter de Geremia / *Anastasia Patricia.*

11. Aengus (Angus) the Culdee; Constantine of Carthage; Peter the Spaniard / *Alberta of Agen; Bl. Teresa Margaret Redi.*

12. Bernard of Carinola; Gregory I, the Great, Pope, one of the Four Great Doctors of the West; Peter of Nicomedia / *Bl. Justina Bezzoli; Seraphina (Fina) of San Gimignano.*

13. Gerald of Mayo; Roderick of Spain / *Christina of Persia; Patricia of Nicomedia.*

14. Bl. Arnold of Padua; Leo of Rome / *Eve (thirteenth century); Mathilda the Queen, wife of Henry the Fowler; Paulina of Zell.*

15. Clement Mary Hofbauer; Raymond of Fitero; Zachary, Pope

/ Louise de Marillac; Leocritia (Lucretia) of Córdova.

16. Charles Garnier and other North American Martyrs (see September 26); Gregory Makar; Heribert (Herbert) of Cologne; Julian of Anazarbus.

17. Harold of Gloucester; Joseph of Arimathea, associated in legends with the Holy Grail or Chalice used at the Last Supper; Patrick, Patron of Ireland; Paul of Cyprus / Gertrude of Nivelles.

18. Anselm of Lucca; Cyril of Jerusalem, Doctor of the Church; Edward the Martyr; Egbert of Ripon; Salvator (Salvatore) of Horta / Bl. Sibyllina Biscossi.

19. Adrian of Maestricht; John the Syrian; Joseph, spouse of Mary / Quartilla of Sorrento; Quintilla of Sorrento; Bl. Sibyllina Biscossi.

20. Joachim, father of Mary; Martin of Braga; William of Peñacorada / Alexandria, Claudia, Euphemia, Juliana, all of Amisus.

21. Benedict of Subiaco and Monte Cassino, founder of the Benedictine Order, whose ancient motto is Laborare est orare, "To work is to pray." / Bl. Clementia (Clemence) of Oehren.

22. Basil of Ancyra; Paul of Narbonne / Catherine of Genoa; Lea of Rome.

23. Benedict of Campania; Felix of Monte Cassino; Victorian (Victor) of Adrumentum / Romula (Romola, Roma) of Rome; Bl. Sibyllina Biscossi.

24. Gabriel the Archangel, Patron of TV, Radio, Telecommunications; Simeon of Trent; William of Norwich / Bl. Bertha of Carriglia; Catherine of Sweden.

25. Harold of Gloucester; Humbert of Marolles; Irenaeus of Sirmio; Robert of Bury St. Edwards / Kennocha (Kyle and Enoch) of Fife; Lucy Filippini; Mary, the Annunciation (Italian, Annunciata, becoming Ann and Nancy; Spanish, Anunciación).

26. Basil the Younger; Felix of Trèves; Bl. Peter Marginet / Felicitas (Felicity, Felicia) of Padua.

27. John Damascene, Doctor of the Church; Matthew of Beauvais; Robert Bellarmine, Doctor of the Church; Rupert of Salzburg / Augusta of Treviso; Lydia of Illyria.

28. John Capistran (see October 23) / Gwendoline of Niedermünster.

29. Eustace of Luxeuil; Firminus (Firmin) of Viviers; Mark of Arethusa / Gladys of Wales; Bl. Jeanne Marie de Maillé.

30. Fergus of Downpatrick; John Climacus; Peter Regalado.

31. Aldo of Hasnon; Amos the Prophet; Benjamin the Deacon; Daniel of Murano; Guy of Pomposa / Cornelia of Africa; Bl. Jane of Toulouse.

APRIL

Romulus and Remus were those that Rome did build,
But St. George, St. George, the dragon he hath killed.
THOMAS D'URFEY,
Pills to Purge Melancholy

1. Bl. Gerard of Sassoferrato; Gilbert of Caithness; Hugh of Grenoble; Bl. Nicholas of Neti / Catherine Tomás; Theodora of Rome.

2. Francis of Paula; Urban of Langres / *Mary of Egypt; Theodosia of Tyre.*

3. Bl. John of Penna; Richard of Chichester / *Irene of Salonika; Rosamund of Vernon-sur-Seine.*

4. Ambrose, Bishop of Milan, noted hymn-writer and Doctor of the Church; Benedict the Moor; Isidore of Seville, Doctor of the Church; Peter of Poitiers.

5. Albert of Montecorvine; Gerald of Sauve-Majeure; Vincent Ferrer / *Bl. Juliana (Gillian) of Cornillon; Irene of Salonika.*

6. Celestine I, Pope; Timothy of Philippi; William of Eskilsoë / *Bl. Catherine of Pallanza; Marcia of Alexandria.*

7. George the Younger; Bl. Herman Joseph; John Baptist de la Salle; Llewellyn of Bardsey / *Bl. Ursulina (Ursula) of Bologna.*

8. Dionysius (Dion, Denis, Sidney) of Corinth; Walter of Pontoise / *Bl. Julia Billiart.*

9. Hugh of Rouen; Bl. Thomas of Tolentino / *Casilda of Toledo; Mary Cleophas; Monica of Carthage, mother of St. Augustine.*

10. Ezekiel the Prophet; Fulbert of Chartres; Michael of the Saints; Terence of Carthage.

11. Alger of Tours; Leo I, the Great, Pope, Doctor of the Church; Philip of Crete / *Gemma Galgani.*

12. Constantine of Gap; Julius I, Pope; Victor of Braga; Philip of Crete / *Gemma Galgani.*

13. Bl. James of Certaldo; Bl. John Lockwood; Maximus (Max) of Silistria / *Bl. Ida of Lou*vain; *Bl. Margaret of Città de Castello.*

14. Bénézet (dim. of Benedict), builder of the celebrated "Pont d'Avignon"; Bernard of Thiron; Justin Martyr the Philosopher; Lambert of Lyons; Peter Gonzales; Valerian of Rome / *Marcia of Umbria.*

15. Godwin, disciple of St. Bernard of Clairvaux; Silvester of Réome; Theodore of Byzantium / *Anastasia of Rome; Basilissa of Rome; Octavia of Antioch.*

16. Benedict-Joseph Labre; Lambert of Saragossa; Magnus of the Orkneys / *Bernadette Soubirous of Lourdes (see February 18); Celesta of Rome; Christina of Corinth.*

17. Elias Paul; Robert of Chaise-Dieu; Stephen Harding / *Bl. Clare Gambacorta.*

18. Bl. Andrew Hilbernón / *Bl. Mary of the Incarnation.*

19. St. George of Antioch; Leo IX, Pope; Vincent of Collioure / *Emma of Werden.*

20. Hugh of Anzy-le-Duc; Theodore Trichinas / *Agnes of Montepulciano; Bl. Margaret of Amelia.*

21. Anselm of Canterbury, Doctor of the Church; Conrad of Parzham; Bl. Walter of Mondsee.

22. Leo of Sens; Rufus of Glendalough; Theodore of Sikion.

23. Adalbert of Prague, Apostle of the Prussians and Slavs; George the Great, Patron of England; Ivor of Meath / *Bl. Helen Valentini.*

24. Egbert of Rathelmigisi; Fidelis (Fr. form, *Fidèle*) of Sigmaringen; Gregory of Elvira; Wil

liam Firmatus / *Musa of Rome.*

25. Mark the Evangelist; Robert of Syracuse; Stephen of Antioch / *Callista of Syracuse.*

26. Clarence of Vienne; Cletus I, Pope; Marcellinus (Mark, Marcel), Pope; Peter of *Braga* / *Alda (also known as Aude, Blanca, Bruna) of Siena; Mary, Our Lady of Good Counsel (Spanish, Consuelo).*

27. John of Constantinople; Peter Canisius, Doctor of the Church; Theodore of Tabenna / *Felicia of Nicomedia; Zita of Lucca.*

28. Gerard the Pilgrim; Mark of Galilee; Paul of the Cross / *Theodora of Alexandria; Valeria of Milan.*

29. Aemilian (Emil) of Africa; Daniel of Gerona; Hugh the Great of Cluny; Peter of Verona; Vitalis (Vitale) of Ravenna; Wilfrid the Younger / *Ava of Dinant.*

30. Joseph Benedict of Cottolongo; Laurence of Novara; Louis von Bruck; Marianus (Marius, Mario) of Numidia; Bl. Miles Gerard / *Catherine of Siena; Rosamund of Vernon-sur-Seine; Sophia of Fermo.*

MAY

No longer on Saint Denis will we cry,
But Joan la Pucelle shall be France's saint.
> SHAKESPEARE, *I Henry VI*

1. James the Apostle; Jeremias (Jeremiah) the Prophet; Philip the Apostle; Sigismund; King of Burgundy / *Antonina (see March 1); Bertha of Avenay;* *Isidora of Egypt; Patience of Loret.*

2. Felix of Seville; Noah the Patriarch; Valentine of Genoa / *Mafalda, Queen of Portugal; Zoë of Asia Minor.*

3. Alexander I, Pope; Philip of Zell / *Antonia of Constantinople; Viola of Verona.*

4. Florian of Austria; Silvan of Gaza; Bl. Richard Reynolds / *Ada (also called Edith), seventh-century Benedictine; Antonia (see March 1); Monica of Carthage, mother of St. Augustine.*

5. Hilary of Arles; Pius V, Pope; Silvanus of Rome; Theodore of Bologna / *Jutta (Judith, Yvette) of Kulmsee.*

6. John the Apostle, apparition before the Latin Gate; Lucius of Cyrene / *Benedicta of Rome; Bl. Prudentia (Prudence) Castori.*

7. John of Beverley; Michael Ulumbijski; Peter of Pavia; Stanislaus of Cracow / *Flavia Domitilla, niece of Emperors Domitian and Titus.*

8. Benedict II, Pope; Michael the Archangel, Apparition; Peter of Tarentaise; Victor the Moor / *Ida of Nivelles.*

9. Gregory Nazianzen the Theologian, Doctor of the Church; John of Chalons; Luke the Evangelist; Vincent of Montes.

10. Antoninus (Antony) of Florence; Job the Patriarch; Quartus of Capua; Quintus of Capua / *Blessed Beatrix I of Este.*

11. Francis de Geronimo; Walter of L'Esterp.

12. Dionysius (Dion, Denis, Sidney) of Asia; Philip of Arirone

/ *Flavia Domitilla, granddaughter of Emperor Vespasian (see Flavia, May 7); Bl. Gemma of Goriano; Bl. Jane of Portugal.*

13. Andrew Fournet; Robert Bellarmine, Doctor of the Church / *Agnes of Poitiers; Bl. Juliana of Norwich.*

14. Bl. Giles of Santarem; Bl. Michael Garicoïts; Paschal (Pasquale) I, Pope / *Justina of Sardinia.*

15. Bl. Andrew Abellon; Isidore the Husbandman, Patron of Madrid; John Baptist de la Salle; Nicholas the Mystic; Rupert of Bingen / *Bertha of Bingen; Dymp(h)na of Gheel, daughter of the King of Ireland.*

16. Adam of Fermo; Brendan the Voyager; John Nepomucene; Simon Stock / *Mary Anne of Jesus.*

17. Bruno of Würzburg; Paschal (Pasquale) Babylon; Paul of Noyon; Victor of Alexandria / *Basilla of Alexandria.*

18. Eric, King of Sweden; Felix of Cantalicio, called "Brother Deo Gratias" / *Alexandra, Claudia, Julitta (Juliet), all of Ancyra.*

19. Dunstan of Canterbury; Gervase (Jarvis) of Milan; Ivo (Ivor) Hélory; Peter Celestine, later Celestine V, Pope / *Bl. Joaquina (fem. of Joaquin) Vedruna de Mas; Urbana of Rome.*

20. Bernardinus (Bernard) of Siena; Ethelbert of East Anglia; Hilary of Toulouse; Theodore of Pavia / *Alfreda of Mercia.*

21. Theobald of Vienne; Timothy of Mauretania / *Bl. Catherine of Cardona.*

22. John of Parma; Marcian (Mark) of Ravenna; Peter Parenzi; Romanus (Roman) of Subiaco / *Helen of Auxerre; Julia of Corsica; Rita of Cascia.*

23. Andrew Bobola; Desiderius (French, Désiré, Didier) of Langres; Ivo (Ives, Ivor) of Chartres; John Baptist dei Rossi; Michael of Synnada; William of Rochester.

24. Edgar the Peaceful, King of the Anglo-Saxons; Gerard of Lunel; Patrick of Bayeux; Vincent of Porto / *Joanna of Galilee (see LUKE, 8); Mary, Our Lady Help of Christians, Our Lady of the Way.*

25. Gregory VII, Pope; Leo of Troyes; Urban I, Pope; Zachary of Vienne / *Madeleine Sophie Barat.*

26. Augustine (Austin) of Canterbury, Apostle of England; Eleutherius, Pope; Lambert Pélogue; Philip Neri; Zachary of Vienne / *Bl. Eva of Liége; Bl. Marianne de Flores.*

27. John I, Pope; Frederick of Liége.

28. Augustine of Canterbury (see May 26); Bernard of Menthon; Germanus (Jarman) of Paris; Justus (Justin) of Urgell / *Bl. Margaret Pole of Salisbury.*

29. Gerald of Macon; John of Atarés; Bl. Richard Thirkill / *Mary Magdalen dei Pazzi; Theodosia of Caesarea Philippi.*

30. Felix I, Pope; Ferdinand III, King of Castile and León; Bl. Thomas Cottam / *Joan of Arc, The Maid of Orleans.*

31. Bl. James Salomone; Bl. Nicholas of Vaucelles; Vitalis (Vitale) of Monte Subasio / *Angela Merici; Bl. Camilla Varani; Petronilla (fem. dim. of Peter) of Rome; Mechtildis (Mathilda) of Diessen.*

JUNE

*Saint Anthony of Padua, whom I
   bear
In effigy about me, hear my prayer:
Kind saint who findest what is lost,
   I pray
Bring back her heart: I lost it
   yesterday.*

    ARTHUR SYMONS,
      *A Prayer to Saint Anthony
      of Padua*

1. Clarus (Clare, Claire) of Aquitaine; Conrad of Trèves; Hervieu (Harvey, Hervey) of Brittany; Simon of Trèves / *Bl. Gratia (Grace), Patron of Alcira, Spain (see August 21).*

2. Erasmus (Elmo) of Formiae; Eugene I, Pope; Marcellinus (Mark, Marcel) of Rome; Nicholas Peregrinus; Peter of Rome (fourth century); Stephen of Corvey.

3. Albert of Como; Hilary of Carcassonne; Kevin of Glandalough / *Clotilde, Queen of France; Olive of Anagni; Paula of Nicomedia.*

4. Alexander of Verona; Cornelius McConchailleach; Francis Caracciolo; Walter of Fontenelle / *Bl. Margaret of Vau-le-Duc.*

5. Felix of Fritzlar; Julian of Perugia / *Marcia and Valeria, early martyrs contemporary with Christ.*

6. Bertrand of Aquileia; Claude of Besançon; Norbert of Magdeburg; Philip the Deacon / *Candida (Blanche) of Rome; Bl. Felicia of Montmorency; Paulina of Rome.*

7. Colman of Dromore; Jeremy of Córdova; Paul of Constantinople; Robert of Newminster / *Bl. Anne of St. Bartholomew; Bl. Baptista Varani.*

8. Robert of Frassinovo; Victorinus (Victor) of Camerino; William of York / *Calliope, an early martyr; Melania the Elder.*

9. Columba (Colin, Malcolm) of Donegal; Felician (Felix) of Rome; Julian of Edessa; Vincent of Agen / *Bl. Amata (Amy) of Bologna; Bl. Anne Mary Taigi; Bl. Caecilia of Bologna; Bl. Diana de Andelo of Bologna.*

10. Maximus (Max, Maxim, Maximilian) of Naples; Timothy of Prusa; Zachary of Nicomedia / *Amata, Caecilia, Diana (see June 9); Margaret, Queen of Scotland; Oliva of Palermo.*

11. Barnabas (Barnaby) the Apostle; Gregory Nazianzen the Theologian, Doctor of the Church; Bl. Hugh of Marchiennes / *Bl. Flora of Beaulieu; Bl. Paula Frassinetti.*

12. Christian of Clogher; Onupharius (called Humphrey) of Egypt; John of San Facundo; Leo III, Pope; Bl. Louis of Aisen / *Antonina of Bithynia (see March 1).*

13. Anthony of Padua; Lucian of Africa / *Felicula (Felicia) of Rome.*

14. Basil the Great, Doctor of the Church; Joseph the Hymnographer; Mark of Lucera; Valerius (Valerian) of Soissons.

15. Constantine of Beauvais; Bl. Thomas Green; Vitus (Guy, Vito) of Sicily / *Adelaide of La Cambre; Germana (Germaine) Cousin.*

16. Benno (also called Benedict) of Messines; Colman McRoi; John Francis Regis; Roland,

the Paladin of Charlemagne / *Justina of Mainz.*

17. Bl. Paul Burali d'Arezzo; Bl. Peter Gambacorta; Solomon, King of Israel / *Emma of Gurk; Bl. Euphemia of Andechs; Teresa of Portugal.*

18. Ephrem the Syrian, Doctor of the Church; Guy of Baume; Mark of Rome (under Diocletian) / *Alena (Aline, Helen) of Brabant; Constance, a companion of St. Ursula; Elisabeth of Schonau; Marina of Alexandria; Paula of Malaga.*

19. Gervase (Jarvis) of Milan; Bl. Thomas Woodhouse / *Juliana (Gillian) Falconieri.*

20. Adalbert of Magdeburg; Deodatus (Datus, Theodore; French, Dieudonné) of Nevers; Paul of Tomi / *Florentina (Florence) of Cartagena; Bl. Michelina (Michaela, Michele) of Pesaro.*

21. Alban of Mainz; Aloysius Gonzaga; Cormac of Iona; Martin of Tongres; Ralph of Bourges; Terence of Iconium / *Demetria of Rome.*

22. Alban of Britain; Everard of Salzburg; John IV of Naples; Paulinus (Paul) of Nola.

23. Felix of Sutri; James of Toul; John Fisher; Josias (Josiah), King of Judah; Peter of Juilly / *Etheldreda (Audrey) of Ely; Bl. Mary of Oignies.*

24. Bartholomew of Durham; Henry of Auxerre; Ivan of Bohemia; John the Baptist, Nativity / *Alena (see June 18).*

25. Adalbert of Holland; Solomon of Brittany; William of Monte Vergine / *Lucy of Rome.*

26. David of Thessalonica; John of the Goths; Paul of the Goths / *Bl. Frances Lanel; Bl. Jane*

Gerard; Bl. Mary Magdalena Fontaine; Bl. Teresa Fantou.

27. Deodatus (Datus, Theodore; French Dieudonné) of Nola; Ferdinand of Aragón; John of Chinon; Ladislas, King of Hungary.

28. Irenaeus of Lyons; Bl. John Southworth; Paul I, Pope / *Marcella of Alexandria.*

29. Paul the Apostle; Peter the Apostle / *Bl. Angelina of Spoleto; Benedicta of Sens; Gemma (also called Emma; see June 17); Judith of Oberaltaich; Mary, mother of John surnamed Mark* (see Acts 12:12); *Salome of Oberaltaich.*

30. Bertrand of Le Mans; Marcian of Pampeluna; Paul the Apostle; Bl. Philip Powel; Theobald of Salanigo / *Emiliana (Emily, Amelia) of Rome; Lucina (Lucy) of Rome.*

JULY

St. Swithin's day, if thou dost rain,
For forty days it will remain,
St. Swithin's day, if thou be fair,
For forty days 'twill rain no more.
ANON., *Old Adage*

(According to what is only a legend, Bishop Swithin [Swithun] of Winchester wanted to be buried in the church-yard, where "the sweet rain of heaven might fall upon his grave." The monks resolved to honor him by burying him inside the church. On the day fixed for the "translation" [moving] of his relics, it began to rain and continued for forty days. The monks took that as a sign that they should respect Swithin's wish.)

John Gay has expressed the weather forecast more poetically in *Trivia:*

*Now if on Swithin's feast the wel-
kin lours,
And every penthouse streams with
hasty showers,
Twice twenty days shall clouds their
fleeces drain
And wash the pavements with in-
cessant rain.*

1. Aaron the High Priest; Julius of Britain; Simeon Salus; Theodoric of Mont d'Or.
2. Martinian of the Mamertine Prison; Otto of Bamberg; Bl. Reginald of Baume; Swithin of Winchester (also July 15) / *Mary, the Visitation (Spanish, Visitación).*
3. Anatole of Constantinople; Bertram of Le Mans; Leo II, Pope; Thomas the Apostle.
4. Albert Quadrelli; Andrew of Crete; Martin of Tours; Odo (Otto) of Canterbury; Ulric of Augsburg / *Bertha of France.*
5. Antony Mary Zaccaria; Stephen of Reggio / *Blanch (also called Gwen) of Britain; Cyrilla of Cyrene; Edana (Edna) of Ireland; Grace of Cornwall; Zoë of Rome.*
6. Dion of Rome; Isaiah the Prophet; Thomas More / *Dominica of Campania; Bl. Mary Rose of Caderousse.*
7. Bl. Benedict XI, Pope; Cyril, the Apostle of the Slavs; Felix of Nantes; Hedda (male) of Winchester; Lawrence of Brindisi; Peter Fourier / *Claudia (also called Priscilla, Rufina, and Sabinella; see II TIMOTHY 4:21, and August 7.*
8. Adrian III, Pope; Arnold of Julich; Edgar the Peaceful; Eugene III, Pope / *Isabel (Elizabeth), Queen of Portugal;*

Priscilla of Corinth (see ACTS 18:2, ROMANS 16:3.
9. Andrew of Zabor Abbey; Benedict of Zabor Abbey (also July 8); John Fisher; Thomas More / *Anatolia of Thora; Bl. Jane Scopelli (or Sospelli); Veronica (also called Berenice) Giuliani.*
10. Daniel of Nicopolis; Maurice of Nicopolis; Peter of Perugia; Vitalis (Vitale) of Rome / *Amalburga (Amelia, Emily) of Maubège.*
11. John of Bergamo; Leontius (Leo) the Younger; Bl. Oliver Plunkett; Pius I, Pope / *Amabel of Rouen; Olga of Russia.*
12. Jason (see ACTS, 17 and ROMANS, 16); John Gualbert; Felix of Milan; Leo I of Cava / *Veronica of the True Image.*
13. Eugene of Carthage and Albi; Silas, companion of St. Paul / *Brigid and Maura of Scotland; Mildred of Mercia.*
14. Camillus de Lellis; Francis Solano; William of Breteuil.
15. Baldwin of Rieti; Donald of Ogilvy; Henry the Good of Bavaria, Emperor of the Holy Roman Empire; Swithin (see July 2); Vladimir of Russia / *Bl. Angelina of Marsciano; Edith of Polesworth; Rosalia of Palermo.*
16. Eustace of Antioch; Bl. Milo of Selincourt; Valentine of Trèves / *Mary Magdalen Postel; Mary, Blessed Lady of Mt. Carmel (Italian, masc., Carmine, Carmelo, fem., Carmela; Spanish, Carmel, Carmela, Carmelita, Carmen).*
17. Alexius (Alexis) of Rome; Andrew and Benedict (see July 9); Kenelm of Mercia; Leo IV, Pope / *Marcellina (Marcella) of Rome; Marina of Bithynia.*

18. Arnold, Patron of Musicians; Bruno of Signo; Camillus de Lellis; Frederick of Utrecht / *Bl. Bertha of Marbais; Edith of Ailesbury; Marina of Orense.*

19. Jerome of Pavia; Martin of Trèves; Vincent de Paul / *Aurea (Ora) of Córdova; Justa (Justine) of Seville.*

20. Elias (Elijah) the Prophet; Jerome Aemilian; Paul of Córdova / *Etheldwida (Ethel) of Winchester; Margaret of Antioch.*

21. Daniel the Prophet; John of Edessa / *Bl. Angelina of Corbara; Julia of Troyes.*

22. Joseph of Palestine; Laurence of Brindisi / *Mary Magdalen the Penitent.*

23. Bernard of Alcira (see August 21); John Cassian; Valerian of Constantinople, and of Cimiez / *Anne of Constaninople; Bl. Jane of Orvieto.*

24. Bl. John Boste; Francis Solano; Romanus (also known as Boris), Apostle of Russia; Vincent of Rome / *Christina of Tuscany; Bl. Louise of Savoy.*

25. Christopher the Christ-Bearer; James the Greater, Apostle; Paul of Gaza / *Valentina of Caesarea (see December 19).*

26. Erastus of Corinth; Bl. John Ingram / *Anne, mother of the Virgin Mary.*

27. Felix II, Pope; Maurus (Maurice) of Bisceglia; Bl. Rudolph of Acquaviva; Bl. Theobald Montmorency / *Camilla of San Severino; Jucunda (Joyce) and Julia, both of Nola and Nicomedia; Bl. Lucy Bufalari; Bl. Mary Magdalen Martinengo.*

28. Bl. Anthony della Chiesa; Eustace of Galatia; Sam(p)son of Brittany; Victor I, Pope.

29. Eugene (period of Emperor Gallienus); Felix II, Pope; Olaf of Norway; William of Saint-Brieuc / *Beatrice of Rome; Lucilla of Rome; Martha, sister of Mary Magdalen; Seraphina of Civitas Mamiensis.*

30. Olav, King of Sweden; Bl. Richard Featherstone; Bl. Simon of Lipnicza; Bl. Thomas Abel / *Julitta (Juliet) of Caesarea.*

31. Fabius of Mauretania; Germanus (German, Jarman) of Auxerre; Ignatius of Loyola; Bl. Peter Qui / *Helen of Sköfde.*

AUGUST

A Lady with a Lamp shall stand
In the great history of the land,
  A noble type of good,
  Heroic womanhood.

Nor even shall be wanting here
The palm, the lily, and the spear,
  The symbols that of yore
  Saint Filomena bore.
      LONGFELLOW, *Santa Filomena*

1. Kenneth of Wales; Paul the Apostle; Peter the Apostle / *Faith, Hope, and Charity, very young daughters of St. Sophia of Rome.*

2. Alphonsus Mary de Liguori, Doctor of the Church; Peter of Osma; Stephen I, Pope / *Etheldritha (Audrey, Ethel) of England.*

3. Gamaliel, teacher of St. Paul; Peter of Anagni; Stephen the Protomartyr, or First Martyr / *Cyra (also called Dominica) of Syria; Lydia Purpuraria (meaning seller of purple dye); Marana (Mary) of Syria.*

4. Dominic of Guzman; John-

Baptist Vianney; Bl. William Horne / *Ida (Ione, Violet, Viola) of Persia.*

5. Oswald of Northumbria; Theodore of Cambrai; Thomas of Dover / *Mary of the Snows (Spanish, Nieves, suggesting Neva); Nonna, mother of St. Gregory Nazianzen.*

6. James the Hermit of Amida; Bl. Octavianus of Savona; Quartus of Rome (under the Emperor Valerian); Stephen of Cardeña.

7. Albert of Trapani; Donatus (Don, Donato) of Arezzo; Bl. Vincent of Aquila / *Claudia (see* II TIMOTHY 4:21).

8. Cyriac (Cyril) of Rome; Emilian of Cyzicus; Gideon of Besançon; Myron the Wonder-Worker / *Bl. Jane of Aza.*

9. John-Baptist Vianney; Julian of Constantinople; Bl. Peter Faber; Romanus Ostiarius, soldier converted by St. Laurence.

10. Bl. Conrad Nanturin; Bl. Hugh of Montaigu; Laurence of Rome / *Appearance in Spain Mary of Ransom (Spanish, Mercedes); Paula of Carthage.*

11. Alexander Carbonarius; Bl. Nicholas Appleine; Bl. Peter Faber / *Lelia of Limerick; Philomena (Filomena) of Mugnano (also on August 10); Susanna of Rome.*

12. Antoninus (Antony) of Rome; Bl. James Nam; Bl. Michael Mi / *Clare of Assisi, co-founder with St. Francis of Assisi of convents called Poor Clares; Hilaria (Hilary) of Augsburg.*

13. Bl. Francis of Pesaro; John Berchmans; Bl. William Freeman / *Bl. Gertrude of Altenberg.*

14. Bl. Antony Primaldi; Marcellus (Marcel, Mark) of Apamea / *Athanasia of Constantinople; Bl. Juliana Puricelli.*

15. Alfred of Hildesheim; Napoleon of Alexandria; Rupert of Ottobeuren; Stanislaus Kostka / *Mary, the Assumption (Italian, Assunta; Spanish, Asunción).*

16. Ambrose of Ferentino; Joachim, father of the Virgin Mary; Titus of Rome / *Serena of Rome, Empress.*

17. Hyacinth of Cracow; Isaac the Patriarch; James the Deacon; Myron of Cyzicus / *Benedicta of Lorraine; Caecilia of Lorraine; Clare of the Cross.*

18. Evan (Eugene, John) of Ayrshire; Firmin of Metz; Hugh of Lincoln; Leo of Myra / *Helen(a), mother of Constantine the Great; Juliana of Strobylum.*

19. Andrew the Tribune; John Eudes; Julius of Rome; Louis of Anjou / *Bl. Emily Bicchieri; Sarah, wife of Abraham.*

20. Bernard of Clairvaux, "The Mellifluous Doctor"; Herbert Hoscam; Philibert (Fulbert) of Jumièges; Ronald of Orkney; Samuel the Prophet.

21. Bernard of Alcira, brother of Grace and Mary; Bl. Gilbert of Valenciennes; Leontius (Leo) the Elder / *Cyriaca (also called Dominica); Gratia (Grace); Jane Frances de Chantal; Mary of Alcira, sister of Grace, both daughters of the Caliph of Lérida, their first names being originally Zoraida and Zaida, respectively.*

22. Andrew of Tuscany; Maurus (Maurice) of Rheims; Bl. Richard Kirkman; Timothy of An-

tioch and Rome / *Ethelgitha (Ethel) of Northumbria.*

23. Eugene of Turone; Philip Benizi; Victor of Vito; Zaccheus (Zachary) of Jerusalem.

24. Bartholomew the Apostle; George Limniotes; Owen of Lichfield; Patrick the Elder / *Bl. Alice Rich; Aurea (Ora) of Ostia; Rose of Lima.*

25. Elmer of Mohaing; Gregory of Utrecht; Louis IX, King of France; Thomas of Hereford / *Lucilla of Rome; Mary-Michaela, "La Loca del Santissimo Sacramento."*

26. Adrian of Nicomedia; Alexander of Bergamo / *Margaret of Faenza; Rose of Lima.*

27. John of Pavia; Joseph Calasanctius; Rufus of Capua / *Margaret the Barefooted.*

28. Alexander of Constantinople; Ambrose of Saintes; Augustine of Hippo, one of the Four Great Doctors of the West, author of "The City of God" and "Confessions"; Julian of Auvergne / *Bl. Adelina of Poulangy.*

29. Andrew of Lydia; John the Baptist / *Candida (Blanche) of Rome; Sabina of Rome.*

30. Felix of Rome; Peter of Trevi; Silvanus of Burgos / *Bl. Bronislava (Brina, Bryna) of Cracow; Bl. Margaret Ward; Rose of Lima.*

31. Dominic del Val; Paulinus of Trèves; Raymond Nonnatus; Bl. Richard Bere / *Isabel, Princess of France.*

SEPTEMBER

Fair-haired, azure-eyed, with delicate Saxon complexion,
Having the dew of his youth, and the beauty therof, as the captives Whom Saint Gregory saw, and exclaimed "Not Angles, but Angels."

LONGFELLOW,
The Courtship of Miles Standish

1. Constant of Aquino; Gideon the Judge; Giles of Narbonne; Joshua the Patriarch / *Bl. Agnes of Venosa; Anna the Prophetess* (see LUKE, 2); *Bl. Jane Soderini; Ruth, wife of Boaz; Verena (Vera) of Baden.*

2. Stephen, King of Hungary; Valentine of Strasbourg; William of Roeskilde / *Bl. Margaret of Louvain; Maxima of Rome.*

3. Albertinus (Albert) of Montone; Ambrose of Sens; Martin of Hinokosa; Simeon Stylites the Younger / *Dorothy of Aquileia; Euphemia of Aquileia; Phebe (Phoebe) of Cenchrea, who carred Paul's Epistle to the Romans; Thecla of Aquileia.*

4. Julian of the Orient; Moses the Prophet; Marcellus (Mark) of Chalons; Theodore of the Orient / *Candida of Naples; Hermione of Ephesus; Ida of the Court of Charlemagne; Rose of Viterbo.*

5. Albert of Butrio; Bl. Jordan of Pulsano; Laurence Justinian; Urban of Constantinople; Vitus (Vito, Guy) of Pontida.

6. Augustine of Sens; Eugene of Cappadocia; Felix, Anglo-Saxon slave ransomed by Gregory the Great (see quotation at head); Magnus of Füssen; Zachary the Prophet (sixth century B.C.) / *Beata (Beatrice) of Sens.*

7. Eustace of Flay; John of Nicomedia; Stephen of Chatillon /

Regina of Autun.

8. Hadrian (Adrian) of Nicomedia; Ina (m.), King of Wessex; Peter Claver, Apostle of the Negroes; Sergius (Serge, Sergei) I, Pope; Timothy of Antioch / *Adela of Messines; Mary, the Nativity (Spanish, Natividad).*

9. Alexander of the Sabine Country; Omer of Thérouanne; Peter Claver, Apostle of the Negroes / *Bl. Seraphina (Fina) Sforza; Wilfreda of Wilton.*

10. Lucius (Luke) of Laodicea; Nicholas of Tolentino; Peter of Mozonzo / *Candida (Blanche) the Younger.*

11. Daniel of Bangor; Emilian of Vercelli; Peter of Chavanon; Vincent of León / *Theodora of Alexandria.*

12. Guy of Laken; Silvinus (Sylvan) of Verona; Valerian of Egypt / *Aloysia (Louise, Alouise) of Japan; Mary, Most Holy Name.*

13. Bl. Francis of Calderola; Bl. Martin III of Camaldoli / *Bl. Hedwig (Ava) of Herford.*

14. Cormac of Cashel; John Chrysostom, "The Golden-Mouthed," Patron of Orators, Doctor of the Church / *Judith the Judge.*

15. Albinus of Lyons; Joseph Abibos; Valerian of Lyons / *Catherine of Genoa; Mary, the Seven Sorrows or Dolors (Spanish, Dolores).*

16. Cornelius, Pope; Stephen of Perugia; Victor III, Pope / *Edith of Wilton; Eugenia of Hohenburg; Euphemia of Chalcedon; Lucy of Rome; Ludmilla of Bohemia.*

17. Francis of Assisi, the "Stigmata"; Justin of Frisingen; Lambert of Liége; Peter Arbués / *Ariadne of Phrygia; Hildegard of Bingen; Theodora of Rome.*

18. Joseph of Cupertino; Simon of Crespy / *Irene of Egypt; Sophia of Egypt.*

19. Felix of Nocera; Bl. Hugh of Sassoferrato; Januarius (Italian, Gennaro) of Beneventum; Theodore of Canterbury / *Constantia (Constance) of Nocera; Bl. Emily de Rodat; Mary de Cervellon; Susanna of Eleutheropolis.*

20. Eustace the Roman General; Dionysius (Dion, Denis, Sidney) of Phrygia; Theodore of Perge; Vincent Madelgarus / *Candida (Blanche) of Carthage; Fausta (Faustine) of Cyzicus; Philippa of Pamphylia.*

21. Alexander of Rome; Jonas (Jonah) the Prophet; Matthew the Apostle / *Bl. Agatha Kim; Iphigenia of Ethiopia; Maura of Troyes.*

22. Felix III, Pope; Mauritius (Maurice) of the Theban Legion; Thomas of Villanova / *Drusilla of Antioch.*

23. Andrew, Antony, John, all of Syracuse; Linus, second Pope; Peter of Syracuse / *Bl. Helen Duglioli; Thecla of Iconium, Protomartyr, or First Martyr, of the East.*

24. Gerard Sagredo; Bl. Robert Flower / *Mary of Ransom (Spanish, Mercedes).*

25. Albert of Jerusalem; Christopher of Guardia; Paul of Damascus; Rufus of Damascus / *Aurelia of Asia and Capua.*

26. Antony Daniel, Charles Garnier, Gabriel Lalemant, Isaac Jogues, the first United States Saint, John de Brébeuf, John

de la Lande, Noël Chabanel, and René Goupil, the North American Martyrs, commemorated on March 16 in Canada and in Jesuit churches / *Justina of Nicomedia.*

27. Adolphus of Seville; Cosmas (Cosmo, Cosimo) of Cilicia; John Mark of Alexandria; Marcellus (Mark, Marcel) of St. Gall / *Bl. Delphina of Provence.*

28. Baruch the Prophet; Bl. Laurence of Rippafratta; Martin of Romont; Solomon of Genoa.

29. Bl. Charles of Blois; Bl. John of Ghent; Bl. Richard Lolle; Michael the Archangel. (In England, September 29, Michaelmas Day, is regarded as the beginning of the last quarter of the year, a day on which quarterly payments fall due.)

30. Francis Borgia; Gregory the Illuminator; Jerome, translator of the Vulgate, Doctor of the Church; Simon of Crespy / *Sophia of Rome, mother of Faith, Hope, and Charity.*

OCTOBER

Around Assist's convent gate
The birds, God's poor who cannot wait,
From moor and mere and darksome wood
Came flocking for their dole of food.

"O brother birds," St. Francis said,
"Ye come to me and ask for bread,
But not with bread alone to-day
Shall ye be fed and sent away."
LONGFELLOW,
The Sermon of St. Francis

1. Bl. Edward Campion; Bl. Nicholas of Forca-Palena; Bl. Ralph Crockett; Remigius (Rémi, Rémy) of Rheims; Romanus the Melodist / *Julia of Lisbon.*

2. Cyril of Antioch; Thomas of Hereford: The Guardian Angels (fem., *Angela;* masc., Angelo).

3. Alvin of León; Gerard of Brogue; Thomas Cantelupe / *Teresa Martin of Lisieux, "The Little Flower."*

4. Francis of Assisi, founder of the Friars-Minor or Franciscans; Peter of Damascus; Quintus (Quentin) of Tours / *Aurea (Ora) of Paris; Berenice (also called Veronica) of Syria.*

5. Alexander of Trèves; Bl. Raymond of Capua / *Bl. Felicia Meda.*

6. Bruno of Cologne; John Leonard; Junius Lindisfarne; Magnus of Città Nuova; Romanus of Auxerre / *Faith of Agen; Mary Frances of Naples.*

7. Augustus of Bourges; Mark, Pope; Sergius (Serge, Sergei) of Syria / *Julia of Egypt; Justina of Padua; Mary, Most Holy Rosary (Spanish and Italian, Rosario).*

8. Demetrius of Salonika; Hugh Canefro; John of Bridlington; Martin Cid; Peter of Seville / *Benedicta of Laon; Brigitta (Bridget) of Sweden; Laurentia (Laura) of Ancona; Melania the Elder; Thaïs of Alexandria, the Penitent.*

9. Abraham the Patriarch; Denis of Paris, Patron of France; Gunther of Hersfeld; John Leonardi; Lambert of Saint-Ghislain; Louis Bertrand.

10. Clarus (Clare) of Nantes; Francis Borgia; Victor of the Theban Legion.

11. Alexander Sauli; Bruno the

Great; Canice (Kenneth) of Kilkenny; Emilian of Rennes / *Ethelburga (Ethel) of Barking; Juliana of Pavilly.*

12. Edwin, King of Northumbria; Maximilian of Lorsch; Wilfrid of York.

13. Colman of Stockerau; Edward the Confessor; Gerald of Aurillac; Maurice of Carnoet / *Bl. Mary Magdalen dei Panattieri.*

14. Bernard of Arce; Callistus I, Pope; Dominic Loricatus; Justus (Justin) of Lyons.

15. Leonard of Vandoeuvre / *Aurelia of Strasbourg; Teresa of Avila, only woman Doctor of the Church; Thecla of Kitzingen; Bl. Willa of Nonnberg.*

16. Ambrose of Cahors; Baldwin of Laon; Bertrand of Comminges; Gerard Majella / *Jadwiga (Hedwig) of Silesia, Queen of Poland.*

17. Colman of Kilroot; Ethelbert of Kent; Rudolph of Gubbio; Victor of Capua / *Hedwig, Queen of Poland; Margaret Mary Alacoque.*

18. Justus (Justin) of Beauvais; Luke the Evangelist; Paul of the Cross / *Gwen (also called Blanche and Candida) of Wales.*

19. Peter of Alcántara; Bl. Philip Howard / *Cleopatra of Syria; Frideswide (Freda), Patron of Oxford University; Laura of Córdova.*

20. Andrew the Calabyte; Bernard of Bagnorea; John Cantius, Patron of Poland; Wendelin (Wendell), Patron of Shepherds / *Irene of Santarem; Martha of Cologne, associated with St. Ursula; Saula, whose name is sometimes considered the origin of Ursula.*

21. Hilarion (Hilary) of Gaza; Hugh of Ambronay / *Angelina of St. Ursula's group, venerated at Valencia; Celine (Celia, Celeste), mother of St. Rémi of Rheims; Ursula of England, legendary leader of 11,000 virgins to the Rhine River.*

22. Benedict of Maserac; Mark of Jerusalem; Philip of Fermo / *Alodia of Aragon; Cordula (Cordelia), companion of St. Ursula; Mary Salome, sister-in-law of the Virgin Mary and mother of Sts. John and James.*

23. Ignatius of Constantinople; John Capistran, whose ruined Spanish Mission, San Juan Capistrano in California, the swallows leave on this day and to which they return on St. Joseph's Day, March 19; Theodore of Antioch / *Oda (Uta, Ottilie) of Amay.*

24. Bernard Calvó; Bl. Joseph Thi; Martin of Vertou; Raphael the Archangel.

25. Crispin of Soissons (see Shakespeare's *Henry V*, Act IV, Scene 3); Hilary of Mende; John of Beverly; Lucius, Mark, Peter, all of Rome; Bl. Thaddeus McCarthy / *Daria of Rome; Dorcas (also called Tabitha) of Joppa (see* ACTS 9: 36).

26. Alanus (Alan) of Quimper; Albinus of Buraburg; Aneurin (also called Gildas) of Wales; Cuthbert of Canterbury; Humbert of Fritzlar.

27. Colman of Senboth-Fola; Vincent of Avila / *Bl. Antonia of Brescia; Sabina of Avila.*

28. Godwin of Stavelot; Jude (Thaddeus) the Apostle; Rémy of Lyons; Simon the Apostle /

Cyrilla of Rome; Eunice of Constantinople.

29. Colman of Kilmacduagh; John of Autun; Stephen of Caiazzo; Terence of Metz / *Anne of Constantinople, who lived on Mt. Olympus disguised as a monk under the name Euphemian.*

30. Artemas of Lystra; Gerard of Potenza; Hubert of Tours; Victorius (Victor) of León / *Dorothy of Montau; Zenobia of Alexandretta.*

31. Alphonsus Rodríguez; Bl. Christopher of Romagnola; Quentin of Amiens; Wolfgang Ratisbon / *Lucilla of Rome.*

NOVEMBER

At last divine Cecilia came,
Inventress of the vocal frame;
The sweet enthusiast from her sacred store
Enlarged the former narrow bounds,
And added length to solemn sounds,
With Nature's mother-wit, and arts unknown before.

JOHN DRYDEN, *Alexander's Feast, or, The Power of Music; An Ode in Honor of St. Cecilia's Day*

1. All Saints (French, Toussaint) Harold, King of Denmark; James of Persia / *Cyrenia (Cyrene) of Tarsus; Juliana of Tarsus; Mary the Slave.*

2. Ambrose of Agaune; George of Vienne; Justus (Justin) of Trieste; Marcian (Mark) of Chalcis; Bl. Thomas of Walden.

3. Hubert of Liége; Malachy O'More / *Sylvia of Rome; Winifred of Wales.*

4. Charles Borromeo; Clair of Rouen; Felix of Valois; Gerard of Bazouches; Gregory of Bartscheid; Vitalis (Vitale) of Bologna / *Bertille (Bertha) of Jonarse; Bl. Helen Enselmini (also November 6).*

5. Gerald of Beziers; Bl. Martin Porres; Zachary, father of St. John the Baptist / *Bertilla (Bertha) of Chelles; Elizabeth, wife of Zachary, mother of St. John the Baptist.*

6. Felix of Thymissa; Leonard of Reresby; Stephen of Apt / *Bl. Christina of Stommeln; Bl. Margaret of Lorraine; Bl. Helen (see November 4).*

7. Ernest of Zweifalten; Leonard of Reresby; Rufus of Metz / *Gertrude of Remiremont; Bl. Lucy of Settefonti; Urania of Egypt.*

8. Clarus (Clare, Clair) of Marmoutier; Godfrey (Geoffrey) of Amiens; Gregory of Einsiedeln; Maurus (Maurice) of Verdun.

9. Alexander of Salonika; Bl. George Napper; Orestes of Cappadocia; Theodore Tyro.

10. Andrew (born Lancelot) Avellino; Demetrius of Antioch; Florence (male) of Caesarion; Justus (Justin) of Canterbury; Leo of Melun.

11. Bartholomew of Rossano; Martin of Tours (St. Martin's Day, or Martinmas, marks the beginning of the period of mild autumn weather which we call "Indian Summer," and which the English call "St. Martin's Summer"); Theodore Studites; Valentine of Ravenna / *Bl. Agnes of Bavaria.*

12. Bl. Christopher of Portugal; Bl. John Cini "della Pace"; Martin

I, Pope; Renatus (René) of Angers; Rufus of Avignon.

13. Brice of Tours; Columba (Colin, Malcolm) of Cornwall; Eugene II of Toledo; Bl. Mark of Scala; Nicholas the Great, Pope; Stanislaus Kostka.

14. Alberic (Aubrey) of Utrecht; Erkonwald (Archibald) of East Anglia; Lawrence O'Toole; Bl. Thomas Percy.

15. Albert the Great, known as Albertus Magnus, "Doctor Universalis"; Felix of Nola; Leopold the Good / Gertrude of Hefta; Valeriana (Valeria) of Hippo Regius, Africa.

16. Edmund Rich; Mark of Africa / Agnes of Assisi; Gertrude the Great; Margaret, Queen of Scotland.

17. Denis of Alexandria; Eugene of Florence; Gregory Thaumaturgus, or Wonder-Worker; Hugh of Noara; Zaccheus of Gadara / Hilda of Whitby; Bl. Jane of Segna.

18. Fergus of Ireland; Odo (Otto) of Cluny; Paul the Apostle; Peter the Apostle, dedication of Basilica of Sts. Peter and Paul; Thomas of Antioch / Bl. Rose-Philippine Duchene.

19. James of Sassean; Maximus (Max) of Rome / Elizabeth, Queen of Hungary.

20. Edmund, King of East Anglia; Felix of Valois; Gregory Decapolites; Leo of Nonantula; Octavius of Turin; Silvester of Chalon-sur-Saône.

21. Albert of Liége; Columban (Colin, Malcolm) of Luxeuil; Fergus of Salsburg; Hilary of Volturno; Rufus of Rome / Mary, the Presentation (Spanish, Presentación).

22. Mark of Antioch; Maurus (Maurice) of Africa; Philemon of Colossae / Cecelia, Patron of Musicians; Bl. Eugenia of Matera.

23. Clement I, Pope; Gregory of Girgenti / Adela of Belgium; Felicitas (Felicity, Felicia) of Rome; Lucretia of Mérida; Bl. Margaret of Savoy.

24. Alexander of Corinth; Colman of Cloyne; John of the Cross, Doctor of the Church / Flora of Córdova; Mary of Córdova.

25. Adalbert of Casauria; Erasmus of Antioch; Moses of Rome / Catherine of Alexandria, one of the most learned women of her time (fourth century), Patron of Teachers, Intellectuals, etc.; Jucunda (Joyce) of Reggio.

26. Conrad of Constance; John Berchmans; Leonard of Port Maurice; Martin of Arades; Peter of Alexandria; Sylvester Gozzolini.

27. Albert of Louvain; James Interclusus; John Angeloptes; Virgil of Salzburg / Mary, Our Lady of the Miraculous Medal, commemorated in the Diocese of Brooklyn on this day.

28. Andrew of Constantinople; Basil of Constantinople; Gregory III, Pope; James della Marca; Peter of Constantinople.

29. Brendan of Birr; Cuthbert Mayne; Bl. Frederick of Ratisbon / Bl. Jutta (Judith, Yvette) of Heiligenthal.

30. Andrew the Apostle; Arnold of Gemblours / Bl. Blanche, Queen of France, mother of St. Louis; Justina of Constantinople.

DECEMBER

I heard the bells on Christmas Day
Their old familiar carols play,
*   And wild and sweet*
*   The words repeat*
Of peace on earth, good-will to
*   men!*
    LONGFELLOW, *Christmas Bells*

1. Bl. Edmund Campion; Bl. John of Vercelli; Bl. Richard Whiting / *Natalia of Nicomedia.*

2. Bl. John Armero; Bl. Richard of Schonthal; Silvanus of Troas / *Adria, Aurelia, Bibiana (Vivian), Mary, Paulina, all of Rome.*

3. Bl. Edward Coleman; Jason of Rome; Francis Xavier, Apostle to the Indies; Lucius, King of South Wales / *Hilaria (Hilary) of Rome.*

4. Clement of Alexandria; Osmund of Salisbury; Peter Chrysologus, "Of Golden Speech," Doctor of the Church / *Ada of Le Mans; Barbara of Nicomedia.*

5. Gerald of Braga; John the Wonder-Worker; Bl. Nicholas Tavigli / *Crispina of Africa.*

6. Abraham of Kratia; Gerard of Joigny; Nicholas of Myra, "Santa Claus"; Tertius of Africa / *Dionysia (Denise) of Carthage; Gertrude the Elder; Leontia (Leona, Leonie) of Africa.*

7. Ambrose of Milan, writer of hymns, one of the Four Great Doctors of the Church; Humbert of Igny; Martin of Saujon; Urban of Teano; Victor of Piacenza.

8. Macarius (Latin, Felix) of Alexandria / *Elfrida of Caestre; Bl. Jane of Cáceres; Lucilla of Rome; Mary, the Immaculate Conception (Italian, Immacolata, Concetta; Spanish, Concepción, Conchita).*

9. Julian of Apamea; Peter Fourier / *Delphine of Naples; Valeria of Limoges.*

10. Bl. Brian Lacey; Gregory III, Pope; Thomas of Farfa / *Eulalia of Mérida; Julia of Mérida.*

11. Daniel the Stylite; Bl. David of Himmerode; Bl. Franco (Frank, Francis) Lippi.

12. Colman of Glendalough; Cormac of Cashel; Bl. Jerome Ranuzzi; Bl. Thomas Holland / *Agatha of Wimborne; Mary, Our Lady of Guadalupe (Spanish, Lupe, Lupita).*

13. Aubert (Albert) of Cambrai and Arras; John Bosco; Eugene of Sebaste / *Elizabeth-Rose of Chelles; Jane Frances de Chantal; Lucy of Syracuse; Ottilia of Hohenburg, Patron of Alsace.*

14. Bl. Bartholomew Buonopedoni; Bl. Conrad of Offida; John of the Cross, Doctor of the Church; Theodore of Antioch.

15. Paul of Latros; Valerian of Africa / *Christiana of Africa; / Christiana of Africa; Bl. Julia of Arezzo.*

16. Nicholas Chrysoberges; Urban V, Pope; Valentine of Ravenna / *Adelaide, Empress of Germany; Albina of Gaeta; Bl. Mary of the Angels.*

17. Florian of Eleutheropolis; Ignatius of Antioch; Lazarus, who was resurrected (see JOHN 11-12.)

18. Moses of Africa; Quintus of Africa; Rufus of Philippi; Salvator (Salvatore) of Africa; Victor of Africa / *Bl. Mary of the Angels.*

19. Bernard Paleara; Darius of

Nicaea; Gregory of Auxerre; Timothy of Africa / *Fausta of Rome; Thea of Gaza (also identified with Valentina; see July 25).*

20. Dominic of Brescia; Julius of Gelduba; Bl. Peter Massalenus / *Esther the Queen.*

21. Bl. Adrian of Dalmatia; John Vincent; Thomas the Apostle.

22. Bl. Adam of Saxony; Demetrius of Ostia; Flavian of Acquapendente / *Frances Xavier Cabrini of the United States.*

23. Bl. Hermann of Scheda; Bl. John Cirita; Nicholas Factor / *Victoria of Rome.*

24. Adam, the first man; Bruno of Ottobeuren; Gregory of Spoleto; John Cantius, Patron of Poland / *Adela of Pfalzel; Eve, the first woman.*

25. Bl. Matthew of Albano; Peter the Venerable; Nativity of Christ (Noël) / *Eugenia of Rome; Nativity (Christine, Noël, Natalie).*

26. Dionysius (Dion, Denis, Sidney), Pope; Stephen the Deacon, Protomartyr, or First Martyr; Theodore the Sacristan /*Christina of Markgate; Bl. Ida of Bingen; Bl. Margaret of Bingen.*

27. Alvin of León; John the Evangelist; Theodore of St. Sabba; Theophanes (Tiffany) of St. Sabba, Jerusalem / *Fabiola of Rome.*

28. Abel, son of Adam and Eve; Anthony of Lérins; Francis of Sales, Doctor of the Church; Bl. Caspar del Bufalo.

29. Albert of Gambron; David, King of Israel; Girald (Gerald) of Fontenelle; Jesse, father of King David; Nathan the Prophet; Thomas à Becket of Canterbury.

30. Eugene of Milan; Jucundus (Joyce) of Aosta; Bl. Ralph of Vaucelles; Roger of Normandy / *Alfreda of Mercia; Bl. Margaret Colonna.*

31. Columba (Colin, Malcolm) of Sens; Fabian of Catania; John Francis Regis; Stephen of Catania; Sylvester I, Pope / *Bl. Catherine Zoë Labouré; Hilaria (Hilary), Paulina, early martyrs; Melania the Youngster.*

Ring out, wild bells to the wild sky,
The flying cloud, the frosty light:
The year is dying in the night;
Ring out, wild bells, and let him die.

Ring out the old, ring in the new,
Ring, happy bells, across the snow:
The year is going, let him go;
Ring out the false, ring in the true. . . .

Ring out false pride in place and blood,
The civic slander and the spite;
Ring in the love of truth and right;
Ring in the common love of good.

Ring out old shapes of foul disease;
Ring out the narrowing lust of gold;
Ring out the thousand wars of old,
Ring in the thousand years of peace.

ALFRED, LORD TENNYSON,
In Memoriam

ANSWERS TO THE
NAME TRIVIA GAME

Agnes Moorehead, Al Pacino, Albert Finney, Alec Guinness, Alexis Smith, Ali McGraw, Angela Lansbury, Angie Dickinson, Anouk Aimée, Anthony Quinn, Audrey Hepburn, Ava Gardner.

Barbra Streisand, Beau Bridges, Bernadette Peters, Bette Davis, Bette Midler, Brenda Vaccaro, Brigitte Bardot, Brooke Shields, Bruce Dern, Burl Ives, Burt Lancaster, Burt Reynolds.

Candice Bergen, Cary Grant, Charlton Heston, Chevy Chase, Chill Wills, Chita Rivera, Christopher Plummer, Cicely Tyson, Claudette Colbert, Claudia Cardinale, Claudia McNeil, Cleavon Little, Clint Eastwood, Colleen Dewhurst, Cyd Charisse.

Deborah Kerr, Debra Winger, Diahann Carroll, Diana Rigg, Diane Keaton, Dina Merrill, Dinah Shore, Dionne Warwick, Dolly Parton, Dom DeLuise, Dudley Moore, Dustin Hoffman, Dyan Cannon.

Eartha Kitt, Edie Adams, Efrem Zimbalist, Elaine Stritch, Elizabeth Ashley, Elizabeth Montgomery, Elizabeth Taylor, Elke Sommer, Elliott Gould, Elsa Lanchester, Esther Rolle,

Esther Williams, Eva Gabor, Eva Marie Saint, Eve Arden.

Farrah Fawcett, Fay Bainter, Faye Dunaway, Fernando Lamas, Franco Nero, Frank Sinatra.

Gary Cooper, Gena Rowlands, Gene Hackman, Gene Kelly, Glenn Campbell, Glynis Johns.

Hedy La Marr, Hermione Baddeley, Hermione Gingold, Herschel Bernardi, Hope Lange.

Imogene Coca, Ingrid Bergman, Irene Dunne.

Jacqueline Bisset, Jane Fonda, Jane Wyman, Janet Gaynor, Jason Robards, Jeanette MacDonald, Jennifer Jones, Jill St. John, Joanne Woodward, Jodie Foster, Johnny Carson, José Ferrer, Judy Garland, Julie Andrews, Julie Christie.

Karen Black, Karl Malden, Katharine Hepburn, Katharine Ross, Keir Dullea, Kevin Hooks, Kevin McCarthy, Kim Hunter, Kim Novak, Kim Stanley, Kirk Douglas, Kris Kristofferson, Kristy McNichol.

Larry Hagman, Lauren Bacall, Laurence Harvey, Laurence Olivier, Lena Horne, Leslie Caron, Leslie Howard, Lili Palmer, Lily Tomlin, Linda Carter, Linda Ronstadt, Liv

Ullmann, Loni Anderson, Loretta Swit, Lynn Redgrave.

Maggie Smith, Marcello Mastroianni, Mariel Hemingway, Mariette Hartley, Marlene Dietrich, Marlon Brando, Marsha Mason, Matt Dillon, Maurice Chevalier, Max Von Sydow, Maximilian Schell, Mel Brooks, Mel Ferrer, Melvyn Douglas, Meryl Streep, Mia Farrow, Michael Caine, Michael Landon, Milton Berle, Myrna Loy.

Nastassia Kinski, Natalie Wood, Noel Coward.

Olivia de Havilland, Olivia Newton John, Omar Sharif, Orson Bean, Orson Welles.

Pamela Read, Paul Henreid, Paul Muni, Paul Newman, Pearl Bailey, Peter Finch, Peter Lorre, Peter O'Toole, Peter Sellers, Petula Clark, Phil Donahue, Piper Laurie.

Rex Harrison, Rex Ingram, Ricardo Montalban, Richard Burton, Richard Dreyfuss, Richard Pryor, Rip Torn, Rita Moreno, Robby Benson, Robert De Niro, Robert Redford, Roberta Flack, Roberta Peters, Rock Hudson, Rod Steiger, Rod Taylor, Rory Calhoun, Ruby Dee, Ryan O'Neal.

Sal Mineo, Sally Field, Samantha Eggar, Sandy Dennis, Sean Connery, Shelley Duvall, Shelley Winters, Shirley Jones, Shirley MacLaine, Signe Hasso, Siobhan McKenna, Sissy Spacek, Slim Pickens, Sophia Loren, Spencer Tracy, Susannah York, Suzanne Pleshette, Sylvester Stallone.

Tatum O'Neal, Teri Garr, Trevor Howard, Tuesday Weld.

Uta Hagen.

Valerie Harper, Valerie Perrine, Vanessa Redgrave, Vera Miles, Vincent Gardena, Vincent Price, Viveca Lindfors, Vivien Leigh, Vladimir Sokoloff.

Warren Beatty, Wendy Hiller, Will Geer, William Hurt, Woody Allen.

Yul Brynner, Yvette Mimieux.

Zero Mostel.